BORDER CROSSINGS

The Internationalization of Canadian Public Policy

EDITED BY

G. Bruce Doern, Leslie A. Pal, and Brian W. Tomlin

OXFORD UNIVERSITY PRESS
TORONTO   NEW YORK   OXFORD
1996

Oxford University Press
70 Wynford Drive, Don Mills, Ontario M3C 1J9

Oxford New York
Athens Auckland Bangkok Bombay
Calcutta Cape Town Dar es Salaam Delhi
Florence Hong Kong Istanbul Karachi
Kuala Lumpur Madras Madrid Melbourne
Mexico City Nairobi Paris Singapore
Taipei Tokyo Toronto

and associated companies in
Berlin Ibadan

Oxford is a trademark of Oxford University Press

Canadian Cataloguing in Publication Data

Main entry under title:

Border crossings : the internationalization of Canadian
  public policy

Includes bibliographical references and index.
ISBN 0-19-541177-3

1. Political planning - Canada. 2. Policy sciences.
I. Doern, G. Bruce, 1942- . II. Pal, Leslie A.
(Leslie Alexander), 1954- . III. Tomlin, Brian W.,
1944- .

JL75B67 1996   354.7107'2   C96-931749-2

Design: Max Gabriel Izod
Typesetting: Indelible Ink

Copyright © Oxford University Press Canada 1996

1 2 3 4 — 99 98 97 96
This book is printed on permanent (acid-free) paper ∞.
Printed in Canada

Contents

Preface

This book arose from our shared interest in the blurring of the line between international and domestic public policy. Forces and actors that were once considered firmly on one side or the other are now routinely crossing borders. Our individual research was convincing us that the distinction is increasingly artificial and perhaps even damaging to a clear understanding of modern policy dynamics. Doern's work on industrial and competition policy convinced him that developments at the national level in Canada and elsewhere were incomprehensible unless placed in an international context. Like Doern, Pal's research over the years has had a 'domestic' focus, but his most recent work on social movements and human rights organizations drew him into an analysis of international regimes and the way in which domestic policy communities project their interests abroad even while acting as conduits for the application of those regimes to domestic practices. Tomlin's research on trade policy, and particularly the North American free trade agreements, drew him into an analysis of the impact of domestic forces on international negotiations.

We knew this was important, but we also knew that the existing literature either tended to work in isolation (domestic-policy analysis and international relations) or that it couched the issues in very broad and formulaic arguments about 'globalization'. We were convinced that work was needed that would carefully and neutrally put the question of the impact of internationalization on Canadian domestic policy—work that would cross the conceptual border between disciplines. A conference was held in Ottawa in May 1995, and we were fortunate in gathering leading academics and practitioners to debate the issues. The chapters in this volume flowed from that stimulating process.

As editors, we stand on the shoulders of our contributors, all of whom were unfailingly perceptive and punctual—they showed that rare combination of intellectual acumen and practical follow-through without which a book is never born. We thank them for their hard work and their pioneering research as reflected in the chapters. We were also fortunate to attract to the conference commentators and guests with a wealth of knowledge about specific policy fields and how they have changed in the light of internationalization in the past decade: Robert Babe, Ron Doering, Michael Dolan, Michael Hart, Chuck Kraddock, Nick Le Pan,

David Ross, Claire Turenne-Sjolander, John Sigler, and Emmy Verdun. Financial support for the conference came from the federal departments of Environment, Foreign Affairs and International Trade, and Industry; and Carleton University's School of Public Administration, School of International Affairs, and Dean of Graduate Studies. Martha Clark and Iris Taylor of the School of Public Administration saved us many organizational headaches, and we were happy to have the assistance and support of Sandra Bach and Fabiola Bazo in managing the conference and preparing the manuscript for publication. We thank Freya Godard for editing the manuscript to such exacting standards, and Oxford University Press for its early and unflagging enthusiasm for the project.

The Internationalization of Canadian Public Policy

G. Bruce Doern, Leslie A. Pal, and Brian W. Tomlin

It is now commonplace in Canada and elsewhere to claim that globalization is transforming the political economies of all countries. The initial analyses focused on the aggregate—and largely negative—effects of globalization on the nation state. The nation state would atrophy since most contemporary problems could be solved only by giving more power to international institutions (Simeon 1990; Elkins 1995). The nation state would be further 'hollowed out' because there would be a simultaneous transfer of power and functions downwards to regions and local jurisdictions, where the problems cluster spatially and where identities would be stronger (Cox 1987, 1994). Sovereignty, in short, would be pushed both up and down from the nation state.

A second strand of this early analysis concentrated on the tensions between economic globalization—seen largely as a pro-business phenomenon—and social globalization. The former was particularly manifest in free trade and deregulatory pro-market policies, and the latter, belatedly, was producing demands for regional and international social charters, in essence, international social policy, as a partial counterweight to business power (Echenberg *et al.* 1992).

A third focal point for initial commentary was the broad implications of globalization for the administrative state as a whole (Peters and Savoie 1995). The very nature of capitalist production was changing. It was simultaneously global in scope but organized around principles of 'flexible production' (small production runs tailored to specific market segments). This larger debate was being linked to the very structure of the administrative state (Hoggett 1991). Just as earlier centralized industrial processes had helped form large public bureaucracies, so too, not surprisingly, these restructuring dynamics were beginning to affect the nature of current public administration (Aucoin 1990). Globalization and flexible production underpin the shift in public administration to alternative service delivery, the separation of the policy and delivery functions, privatization, and quasi-markets in public services (Doern 1994a).

As important as these analytical approaches are, they have often been so general that they fail to assess more specific political effects on public policy and administration. What is needed now is an examination of the effects of globalization on policy in specific fields. We need to move beyond the generalities of 'hollowing out' to see exactly what gets hollowed out and what does not. This book does just that, in the context of the internationalization of Canadian public policy.

In addition to its tighter focus, the book tries to distinguish globalization, where possible, from internationalization. It recognizes that the state is a complex arena of policy fields, processes, and institutions linked to other states and to international agencies and agreements. A focus on the internationalization of Canadian public policy seeks to examine the capacity of various policy fields both to support globalization and to resist it, depending in part on how policy-making institutions are actually structured and how they are in fact changing.

The contributing authors examine the evolution over approximately the last two decades of nine important Canadian policy fields: foreign affairs, trade and industry, banking, investment, telecommunications, human rights and security, agriculture, environment, and social programs. This list includes policy fields that are both economic and social in content. It also includes some, such as foreign affairs, that we would always think of as being international in scope; those, such as social policy, that, perhaps, have been somewhat more insulated within domestic or national boundaries; and others somewhere in between. Our emphasis is on the policies of the federal government, but, as would be expected, many of the authors extend their analysis to provincial policy as well.

In this first chapter we proceed in three stages. The first section examines the central issues and concepts and locates them within the often isolated research traditions on public-policy making and international relations. The second section draws together the evidence from the various chapters by examining in detail how policies and the policy process have been affected. The third section comments on changes in the way the federal government sets its priorities in an ever more internationalized policy-making process.

CENTRAL CONCEPTS

Three concepts are central to this book: globalization, internationalization, and the policy-making process. For our purposes, globalization is

distinct from internationalization. Globalization is primarily a technological and economic process driven by the revolution in telecommunications and computers, massive increases in the movement of capital around
the world, greatly expanded capacities for flexible world-wide production
sourcing by firms, especially multinational corporations, and growing
ecological interdependence and environmental spillovers. These forces
dramatically affect business, investment, and society in general, and
thereby force governments to change their policies and policy processes.
But globalization also affects governments directly, as policy makers figure
out how states and bureaucracies need to be reordered and as they find
their own activities transformed by the same technologies (Rosell 1992).

Put even more broadly, globalization embraces an expanding web of
interlocking markets around the world, universal norms and standards that
form common global reference points, communications that are virtually
instantaneous, and the common social and economic practices brought
about through computerization. For example, compare the nineteenth-
century European colonizer with the present-day entrepreneur. The
former had to transport 'civilization' to places that were different in every
one of the aspects listed above. The latter, however, can check into the
Holiday Inn at Kinshasa, turn on CNN, and feel perfectly at home. American Express's injunction 'never [to] leave home without it' is really a way
of saying that with 'it', you never really do leave home. This illustrates
how 'globalization' is really about 'westernization', but it denotes none the
less a world increasingly interconnected by economics, communications,
and culture. Anything of this scope has profound social consequences,
producing both great anxiety about future jobs and identities, and great
optimism about the 'wired world' and a global village.

The internationalization of public policy is linked to globalization in
the technological and economic sense, but it is different because it both
predates globalization and follows it. In this book, internationalization
means a process by which various aspects of policy or policy making are
influenced by factors outside national territorial boundaries. Imagine a
perfect autarky where *all* policy was domestic, where every aspect of every
policy problem stopped at the nation's borders. The way the problem was
defined, the terms of discourse and debate, and all the relevant actors
would be entirely confined to the national territory. This is absurd, of
course, since virtually no state in the last 500 years has been this isolated.
None the less, if we take this as an extreme standard of what it would
mean to say that policy was 'purely domestic', several things become
clearer.

First, the internationalization of public policy is a long process that
starts when at least one aspect of domestic policy begins to depend on or

be affected by forces beyond the borders of the state. States and policy fields can be internationalized gradually as more and more relevant forces are located beyond territorial boundaries. There can be weak and strong forms of internationalization.

Second, while globalization by definition implies the internationalization of public policy, it is possible to have internationalization without globalization. Most of the chapters show that their policy field was to some extent internationalized well before the post-war period. Thus a crucial point in all the chapters is the distinction between the contemporary form of internationalization and earlier forms. As several chapters show, the main difference seems to be linked to globalization—those modern forces that make internationalization more intense, with a wider range of countries, actors, and forces at play.

A third point is that internationalization is not a one-dimensional phenomenon. It is best thought of as a continuum that runs across several dimensions, namely, the source of policy ideas, policy design, implementation, and relevant policy actors. It is clear that internationalization can be relatively modest in the sense that it affects only a few of the dimensions or that it may be more dramatic in affecting them all.

Fourth, the modes of internationalization can be quite varied. Cross-border pollution can 'internationalize' the causes of a policy problem and throw it onto the global agenda, but co-ordinated international responses may take years or never be made. Internationalization may give domestic-policy issues an important foreign-policy dimension, but domestic government agencies may lag in their capacity or desire to co-ordinate policy outputs, such as laws or regulations. Some policy sectors (such as telecommunications) may be internationalized more rapidly because of the reinforcing effects of technology and markets. Others (such as income security) may remain shielded from international forces for some time.

A fifth point is that governments and other actors can react in a variety of ways to the internationalization that affects policy. The two basic reactions are accommodation and resistance. The former seeks to change institutions and instruments to achieve domestic benefits in a way that accepts the logic or inevitability of international forces. Two examples of accommodation are free trade agreements and some aspects of telecommunications deregulation. In contrast, resistance seeks at a minimum to insulate and at a maximum to control or regulate those international forces. Across a range of policy issues we can expect governments to develop a mixture of these strategies, depending on circumstances, domestic and international coalitions, and knowledge.

Finally, the strategies that governments adopt in the face of internationalization will ultimately affect the results of policy. Free trade agreements will affect some sectors of the domestic economy. Deregulation of telecommunications will affect cultural industries as well as communications.

In this discussion of the implications of these analytical distinctions, we have already begun to discuss the third concept, the policy process. Space does not allow a full discussion of the different approaches taken by public-policy and international-relations scholars. However, it is useful to highlight some aspects of their different approaches, in part because this book involves co-authorship by members of these two traditions. The need to bridge the solitudes of these analytical realms is important and of course is itself yet another indicator of how globalization is changing relationships.

The two solitudes arise from the tendency of experts in international political economy and foreign policy to concentrate on international relations, integration, and conflict but to oversimplify domestic politics and policy institutions. Policy specialists engage in the reverse set of emphases and omissions. Thus there is a strong tendency in the international relations field to treat the state as a unified, purposeful actor (Dougherty and Pfaltzgraff 1990; Gill and Law 1988). The work on international political economy that combines public-choice and interest-group theoretical approaches, especially regarding the role of business, has relaxed some of these assumptions, but the larger tendency regarding the state is still extremely strong (Nossal 1989).

For their part, domestic-policy scholars tend to treat international conditions simply as contextual factors and to ignore the influence of international agreements, regimes, and agencies (Doern and Phidd 1992; Pal 1992). Domestic-policy specialists employ various political-economy, public-choice, and neo-institutional approaches to the policy fields they are studying. In these approaches, the state is typically disaggregated to a considerable extent in order to demonstrate that power relations are more complex and that, often, the state is not a unitary actor. Departmental players, interest groups and policy communities, and policy instruments are mapped, and policies, or lack of policies, are examined with the always necessary links made to the government's priorities.

While we cannot claim total success in bridging the gap between these analytical realms, the themes on which we focus certainly show a partial merging of interests in a way that we think is crucial for students of both the Canadian policy process and Canada's international relations. Thus, in the next section of this chapter, we examine the effects of internationalization on key features of policy and the policy process, including changes in policy (including related concerns about sovereignty and policy discourse); the nature of interest-group politics and relations among policy communities within Canada and across international boundaries; changes in policy instruments, including the greater use of international 'rules-based' approaches and strengthened international agencies and agreements; and changes in interdepartmental relations within government, especially those which shape relations between the Department of Foreign Affairs and International Trade (DFAIT) and other departments and agencies with varied mixes of foreign and domestic policy mandates, statutory capacities, and kinds of expertise.

TENDENCIES AND VARIATIONS ACROSS POLICY FIELDS

Policy Change and Discourse

The logical starting point for examining the policy fields is to examine how policy definitions themselves are changing. Policy change may be understood in terms of concrete actions, such as establishing programs or agencies, or as efforts to redefine the broad context within which those actions are undertaken. The process of redefinition involves both government and societal actors. These changes are evident in several policy fields, and in general they suggest a broadening of the very definition of policy fields.

In the human-rights field, Cooper and Pal, in Chapter 9, show that the field has broadened markedly with new links being created between traditional human rights and broader concerns about security that now embrace environmental, social, and employment rights. Moreover, the nature of policy discourse has been changed, moving from a traditional concern with 'international order' and security among nations, where the nation state is the protector, to a concern for 'justice', where action may be directed at violations of rights perpetrated by countries against their own people, including countries with quite a progressive record in traditional human rights. The human rights realm also exhibits policy 'as action' in that it is not necessarily primarily state-centred action that is sought but rather actions on and by citizens and communities. In brief, it is policy by doing rather than by only 'announcing' and enforcing through state institutions.

In their analysis of banking and securities policy in Chapter 3, Coleman and Porter show that both globalization and internationalization have widened and deepened financial-services policy and have produced what they describe as a new international-national policy consensus. First, traditional protectionist devices have had to be removed; those include exchange controls and barriers to the entry of foreign firms into domestic markets. Second, policy has supported the creation of international markets in debt and securities as an alternative to domestic markets that are slow to liberalize. Third, barriers among the four pillars of financial services (banking, securities, insurance, and trusts) are being removed, though gradually. The changes in banking and securities have also had a mixed effect on national sovereignty. Financial globalization is easily portrayed as being the essence of a nation's loss of sovereignty. However, Coleman and Porter argue that, when seen over the entirety of the last two decades, there are aspects of enhanced control by the state precisely because states are co-operating in new ways. Thus a sovereignty-oriented discourse has abated, although Coleman and Porter do caution that these changes do not affect all countries equally. Powerful states, such as the United States and Japan, are still able to act unilaterally, and in some respects they have liberalized the least rapidly.

Telecommunications and computers are part of why financial-service markets are changing. Accordingly, it is hardly surprising that Schultz and Brawley find profound changes in Canadian telecommunications policy. Their chapter does not deal with the even broader realms of the 'information highway', but it does show starkly that within the narrower confines of telephony and broadcasting, the policy of a regulated monopoly has been replaced by a competitive model. In short, it too has widened and deepened as the technologies have converged and as the examples and pressures of the immediate, more radical, American competitive model took hold before changes were made in Canada. Schultz and Brawley show that the American model was partly successfully resisted, but there is little doubt that real policies and policy discourse have changed. Policy discourse now uses terms like 'convergence' and the 'information highway', and boundaries drawn around cable policy, broadcasting policy, and the like, while still relevant to some sectoral interests, seem almost quaintly narrow to others. Policy concerns about the 'content' of telecommunications policy, as opposed to the 'medium', continue to attract attention. This is not only because of the technological onslaught, but also because 'content' itself is broadened to embrace issues such as privacy, copyright, pornography, and hate literature.

One would expect policy change to be very evident in the trade-industrial policy field. Doern and Tomlin's analysis shows that change is indeed present both in substance and discourse. Canadian trade-industrial policy has continued on its larger post–Second World War trend of liberalization, but with a much greater emphasis on regional free trade through the Canada-US Free Trade Agreement (FTA) and the North American Free Trade Agreement (NAFTA). More important, trade-industrial policy has broadened in that it has 'crossed the border', embraced services and some aspects of investment, or engaged a host of policy fields which, in the past, were more domestic in nature. Trade promotion activities, different in magnitude and kind from traditional efforts, are also now a more important part of Canadian efforts to succeed in expanding markets. Because expenditure subsidization is severely constrained, trade-industrial policy now stresses knowledge and information services to enable Canadian firms to compete in international markets. It also focuses more than in the past on framework laws for business. Such framework policies are regulatory, and hence they can be a source of new 'system frictions' among countries or trading blocs as capitalist systems and cultures duel with each other.

Toner and Conway's chapter on environmental policy demonstrates similar trends. The very concept of an environmental policy shows a broadening beyond previous frameworks such as pollution. The latest goal of this policy field—sustainable development—was developed in international forums and is now a touchstone of Canadian policy. Like the other policy fields examined in this book, sustainable development has a wider lens than previous policy perspectives. For example, it links environmental issues to economic and trade issues, stressing the importance of trade in environmental industries as something that contributes both to environmental protection and economic prosperity.

Banting's chapter traces the changing emphasis in social policy from security and protection to adaptation and flexibility. The traditional postwar bargain in which the welfare state both benefited fiscally from trade liberalization and facilitated that liberalization by protecting the population from its worst consequences is being challenged by globalization. The current round of global economic liberalization is forcing governments to reduce taxes—thereby weakening their redistributive capacity—and encouraging them to see social policy as an instrument to facilitate adjustment. There is no ideological consensus on these changes, however. Banting discerns three distinctive views of what the intellectual basis of social policy should be: globalism (policy should accept international economic integration), anti-globalism (policy should resist international economic integration), and global scepticism (policy can be considerably independent because the global transformation is less dramatic than it appears). A troubling aspect of this categorization is that, according to surveys, there is a growing chasm in opinion between the élites, who tend to be globalists, and the mass public, who tend to be anti-globalists.

The comparable liberalization in agricultural policy, effected through regional and international trade agreements, has had two opposing consequences for Canadian sovereignty. Skogstad argues in her chapter that the regionalization of agricultural policy, through bilateral trade agreements with the United States, has had the effect of limiting Canadian sovereignty by creating pressures to redesign policy along American lines. Internationalization, on the other hand, because it has proceeded through multilateral agreements, offers the prospect of strengthening Canadian sovereignty by establishing rules that will govern the behaviour of the major powers.

For investment, Smythe's chapter demonstrates how the lowering of tariff barriers and the resulting requirement for restructuring to remain competitive fundamentally altered policy discourse, strengthening the view that Canada would need new capital and technology. At the same time, doubts were raised about Canada's attractiveness as an investment location and the costs of investment screening. These doubts undermined the strategy of bargaining with investors over entry in exchange for enhanced economic benefits. In fact, globalization has meant that investment policy became linked to, and was ultimately subsumed by, trade policy.

Internationalization has also resulted in a shift in the predominant ideas surrounding Canadian foreign policy. In their chapter, Doern and Kirton identify four important changes in policy: a view that the end of the Cold War offers Canada the potential to be more influential in the world; a belief that foreign economic policy should be more assertively liberal in its orientation; a diminished concern for traditional notions of sovereignty; and a broader definition of issues of international security to include threats to the environment and a need for sustainable development.

Interest Groups, Policy Communities, and Client Politics

What have been the effects of internationalization on interest groups, broader policy communities, and client relations? Client relations is a distinct category of analysis that highlights firms and users of public services whose ability to act and influence without interest groups has changed under globalization. In general, the evidence from all the policy fields suggests that internationalization forces groups and policy communities to make broader policy trade-offs and to align themselves with an ever broader coalition of interest groups.

In their analysis of telecommunications policy, Schultz and Brawley show how, in part, changes in the structure and tactics of domestic interest groups made a crucial difference in the two phases of telecommunications-policy reform which they examine. In the first phase in the early 1980s, the interest groups, despite the influence of the American model of competitive telecommunications, essentially remained in favour of a monopoly or regulated utility. It was only in the late 1980s and early 1990s that the supporters of competition became fully politicized. Schultz and Brawley show that it was the mobilization of user groups led by the Royal Bank of Canada that changed the associational politics of the telecommunications sector. Incidentally, that is how the deregulation of Canadian transportation policy in rail and trucking occurred in the mid-1980s, when new user groups and coalitions were actively fostered by the government (Hill 1988).

A further factor in the interest-group politics of the telecommunications sector is that, simultaneously, this policy field came within the orbit of the trade negotiations for the FTA, NAFTA, and the General Agreement on Tariffs and Trade (GATT). This meant that more and more interest groups began to have some say in a policy field that was increasingly being thought of less as an industrial 'sector' and more as a 'factor of production' in everyone else's sector.

The banking and securities policy field exhibits similar patterns. Coleman and Porter, in the language of policy communities, characterize the change as a shift from 'clientelism' to 'pressure pluralism'. In essence, this means that, previously, interest-group politics was organized around the four pillars of the financial-services sector: banking, securities, insurance, and trust companies. Consumers just looked in. Coleman and Porter show how this producerist politics gradually broke down over a period that predates globalization *per se*, but the widening and deepening of markets that they trace escalated these processes markedly. The gradual evolution towards a Canadian version of universal banking, in short towards a financial-services sector, meant that banking too was no longer a vertical chunk of the economy (if it ever was) but was being seen and influenced by many classes of consumers/users now shopping (within limits) on a world-wide basis. At the same time, however, Coleman and Porter show that users still had deep concerns about prudential and therefore broadly public-interest regulatory issues regarding the honesty and probity of the financial sector. These pressures, variously expressed across the falling pillars, meant that interest politics did not totally abandon the old categories of clientelism.

The themes of widening and deepening in interest-group politics can also be discerned in the policy field of human rights and security. Cooper and Pal trace the emergence, in part due to the end of the Cold War, of ever wider interests and coalitions. These include non-governmental organizations (NGOs) that heretofore have specialized in the somewhat separate realms of human rights, development, or environment. The analysis shows, as does the Toner and Conway analysis of environment policy, both an increase in the number of these groups and new efforts to bind them into influential and stable coalitions. The coalitions are still quite precarious, in both the human rights and environmental fields, partly because many groups depend financially on the state, and partly because many groups are organizationally weak. At the same time, because their goal is to change society rather than just government policy, the associational politics of NGOs is different from mainstream economic-interest-group politics. The human rights and environment fields also show that these broader national coalitions are quite adept at reaching out to use international forums and agreements, to criticize their own governments and corporate sectors. This is a mirror-image, though usually from a weaker base of power, of what business and corporate interests do in using international alliances and agreements to 'discipline' their national social sectors.

The need to consider the presence of a newer form of client politics is also a central element of the chapter on trade-industrial policy. Doern and Tomlin argue that internationalization and globalization have helped generate a separate form of client politics in trade-industrial policy making and implementation. With the policy shift to knowledge and service delivery comes a shift in targets from sectoral associations to firms. This is because a service orientation means assisting real investment and product-development decisions, something which sectoral and other interest groups, as groups, do not do. The effects of the shift to client politics are also evident in the fields of investment and foreign policy. In their chapters, Smythe, and Doern and Kirton each point to the fact that business interest groups and firms have gained the most in access to the policy process as a result of internationalization, although Doern and Kirton point out that the migration and immigration interests and environmental NGOs have become more involved in foreign-policy issues as well. The composition and roles of policy networks have also been transformed in the field of agricultural policy. Skogstad's analysis shows that producer groups have been drawn closer into decision making about policy, while at the same time having to share their influence with non-producer interests.

The analysis of trade-industrial policy interests reveals and reinforces the tendencies found in the policy fields already discussed. First, a complex new mixture of vertical and horizontal industrial sectors is in place, making it even more difficult to practice the older arts of vertical industrial-sector politics and regional-policy politics. Second, the Doern and Tomlin analysis shows that the FTA, NAFTA, and GATT agreement negotiations provided a real discipline to traditional interest-group politics. Sectors were broken down, deadlines were real, and trade-offs were made between sectors, not just within them. But with these pressures gone, industrial sectors may revert to a more traditional and fragmented mode. They may devote their attention to other line departments and ministers, but these agencies are themselves less able to deliver anything that looks even remotely like the largesse of 1960s- or 1970s-style industrial policy. Lastly, Doern and Tomlin note how internationalization has elevated human-capital and consumer interests, neither of which have traditionally been the natural clientele of either trade or industrial policy makers.

The policy community surrounding social-policy issues has also changed dramatically, though not as a direct consequence of internationalization. As Banting's chapter argues, many of these changes predate the current round of economic liberalization. The social-policy sector includes an increasingly wide range of citizens' groups representing labour, women, retired people, the disabled, the poor, aboriginals, racial and cultural minorities, churches, and so on. With this increase in diversity have come greater demands to participate in the policy process. Most social-policy advocates, however, are what Banting terms 'anti-globalists', and so participating for them largely means opposing policy. The social-policy agenda is driven by a globalist vision, and so the paradox of participation in this field is that while more groups are consulted (i.e., through the social policy review process launched in 1994), few of them have any influence on policy change. In contrast to the environmental movement, these groups have not been able to capitalize on the international opportunities to influence domestic policy, such as the United Nations Summit on Social Development in Copenhagen.

Inside the State: Interdepartmental Relations and DFAIT

The third aspect of the policy process centres on changes in the relations between departments in the federal government, in particular between DFAIT, the lead department on foreign policy and international trade, and other departments. These changes are often both formal and subtle in that they may be accompanied by announced reorganizations or simply by gradually evolving ways of making policy, including of course new ways of involving and ignoring interests. The fact that this book deals with an internationalizing process that covers at least a decade adds to the difficulty of the analytical task.

For example, in the category of formal organizational change, recent policy processes must certainly take note of the major restructuring of federal departments in 1993 (Aucoin 1995). Launched by the short-lived Campbell Conservative government, it has been retained and intensified by the Chrétien government. The original impetus was clearly domestic, as a manoeuvre to reduce the bloated federal cabinet. But the larger logic of internationalization was present as well. We noted above that policy fields have widened and deepened, and policy makers are aware that as fields change and coalesce, so should organizational capacity in the guise of departmental structures. This was obvious in the reorganizing of Industry Canada (bringing together traditional industrial sectors, telecommunications, and business framework law), and the newly consolidated Department of Human Resources Development (dealing with social policy and adjustment programs).

In the realm of foreign policy itself, a crucial structural change was made in 1982, when the then Department of External Affairs acquired a larger part of the trade-policy function. The chapters on foreign policy and trade-industrial policy set out the mixture of domestic and international forces that led to these changes. Their conclusions need to be placed against the wider backdrop of the relationship of foreign and domestic policy-making institutions and organizations in the Canadian government.

Doern and Kirton's analysis of foreign policy shows that the essential relationships are three-fold. First, foreign affairs have always been central to the Prime Minister of the day. Second, legally, the department's governing act gives DFAIT the authority to represent Canada abroad, to approve and accredit Canadian delegations, and to set Canadian foreign policy in the light of Canada's overall political, economic, and security needs. Third, DFAIT also controls the means of diplomatic communication with other countries and possesses particular legal expertise in drafting treaties. While many other line departments add some elements of foreign policy to their otherwise domestic-policy roles, DFAIT has always argued that, to avoid policy chaos, it must have the final say on foreign policy.

For their part, other federal departments—many of whose responsibilities have had international aspects for decades—point to a complementary legal and political power base. Their international roles are derived from the content and logic of their statutes. Their power is also the power of expertise, but it is primarily technical, scientific, and substantive expertise in a particularly policy area. Equally important, however, these departments can argue strongly that their minister will get the domestic political blame for things that go wrong. Foreign policy is the product of these two intersecting planes of legal and political principles.

How then has this situation been changed by internationalization as it is revealed by the policy fields examined? Or have changes occurred that essentially skirt DFAIT's relationship with other departments? In the banking and securities field, Coleman and Porter characterize changes in terms of state capacity. Though there have been overt changes in organization, such as through the strengthening of prudential regulators, much of the change has taken place within the Department of Finance and the Bank of Canada, which jointly are the *de jure* and *de facto* financial foreign-policy makers. These institutions, along with their complementary provincial financial-service agencies, have been changed by globalization and internationalization mainly by the ever increasing ways in which international co-operation and information sharing are taking place.

In the telecommunications area, Schultz and Brawley also portray a policy field whose interdepartmental relations seemed scarcely to involve

DFAIT at all, but which was gradually swept into DFAIT's orbit as successive trade negotiations increasingly included services in general and telecommunications in particular. Though DFAIT had no mandate as such for telecommunications policy, as the trade policy agenda 'crossed the border' into domestic realms, the bureaucratic politics of telecommunications policy changed. Interdepartmental relations also shifted from a relatively narrow emphasis on the Canadian Radio-television and Telecommunications Commission (CRTC) and Department of Communications.

The Doern and Tomlin chapter on trade-industrial policy also shows that the movement of crucial parts of the telecommunications-policy sector into the jurisdiction of Industry Canada reinforced the pro-competitive paradigm in which telecommunications policy was already moving. Telecommunications-policy makers were now dealing with a department whose senior officials were unlikely to concern themselves much with the cultural content of telecommunications policy. The CRTC was also affected by the globalizing pressures in that it could scarcely keep up with the wave of change engulfing the industry.

In the field of human rights–security policy, Cooper and Pal show that DFAIT's interdepartmental relations were quite directly changed. An increasingly complex institutional mechanism has evolved. DFAIT handles the international diplomacy around rights issues, but a broader range of departments, including the Human Rights Directorate of the Department of Canadian Heritage and departments such as Justice, Health, Immigration, and Environment, are also involved in policy making. Cooper and Pal also point out that because of the role of the provinces and the NGOs' growing influence the selection and preparation of Canadian delegations at international events and negotiations is not an in-house, DFAIT-only affair.

Banting's analysis of social policy reveals institutional changes due to internationalization, but ones that are less dramatic than those described above. Traditionally the antagonism in social-policy development has been between ministers of finance and the departments responsible for various components of social policy. Now, however, the Department of Finance has become so powerful that it is the *de facto* social-policy-making agency. This has happened despite a massive reorganization that incorporated the social-policy departments into the Department of Human Resources Development. The Department of Finance, with its links to the Bank of Canada, is the main conduit of internationalization in this field, and it plays the major role in co-ordinating economic policy through agencies such as the Organisation for Economic Co-operation and Development (OECD). Human Resources officials are beginning to attend global summits as well, but this itself reflects the new orientation towards better integration of social and economic policy. DFAIT is not a relevant player in this game.

Skogstad's analysis also suggests that interdepartmental relations have not been significantly affected by internationalization. The Department of Agriculture and Agri-Food retains principal responsibility for agricultural policy, and that department still needs to work closely with DFAIT to manage international diplomatic efforts to resolve trade disputes. Intergovernmental relations, however, have been affected. Skogstad shows that over the past decade international trade agreements have served to decentralize Canadian federalism by allowing provinces to enter into what was previously an exclusive federal domain.

In contrast, Smythe demonstrates that, as investment policy has been subsumed by trade policy, DFAIT now has the lead role in all aspects of promoting investment, both inward and outward. And although responsibility for investment policy was assigned to Investment Canada, Smythe's analysis shows that the most important elements of investment policy have been established through international trade negotiations, in which DFAIT also has the lead role.

The Doern and Kirton chapter on foreign policy also shows these widening webs of *de facto* shared jurisdiction and networks of influence. They conclude, first, that the capacity of the federal government to make policy has been maintained and the professionalism of DFAIT restored and, second, that DFAIT has retained its relevance through its control of the 'sherpa', or advisory and briefing, process in international summitry (see more below). It has also kept its influence as a lead department in foreign policy by reviving an earlier concept of the department as one that serves the Prime Minister directly and that co-ordinates international activities of the government as a whole by intensifying its interdepartmental activity and altering its own internal structure. But Doern and Kirton also argue that DFAIT has had to share and lose some of its power for reasons that now go well beyond the limitations of its expertise. These include the need to acquire funding and statutory power possessed by other departments, especially as nominal 'trade' policy moves more and more into the partly domestic realms of other departments.

This conclusion is reinforced in the Doern and Tomlin chapter on trade and industrial policy. In 1982, trade functions were grafted on to External Affairs, and ever since, the trade- and foreign-policy sides of the department have been trying to blend together. Even though the Minister of Trade is the junior minister, a good deal of foreign policy seems to be based on trade considerations. Moreover, in a context of internationalization, where trade is everything, and everything seems connected to trade, DFAIT is faced with strong competition from departments like Finance.

The evidence from these and other chapters seems mixed. The Toner and Conway analysis supports the view that the number of departments involved in environmental policy has multiplied, and that DFAIT is increasingly a co-ordinator of domestic departments. Here, the lead agency is likely to be the one with substantive as opposed to diplomatic expertise. As the Cooper and Pal chapter argues, the absence of a clear pattern is due in part to the tension that internationalization creates between vertical and horizontal co-ordination. In vertical co-ordination, the notion is that interests and actors should be organized domestically and that policy is then implemented internationally by a single department. This, no doubt, is DFAIT's preference. Horizontal co-ordination assumes that substantive expertise is what counts, and so the task of a foreign-affairs department is not much more than to monitor and register a process dominated by a host of equally contributing actors. Moreover, those domestic departments should have a crucial role in representing Canadian interests abroad.

It is ironic that internationalization is in many ways a threat to DFAIT. When foreign affairs was about issues of 'high' policy, like defence and geopolitics, the department could rely on its diplomatic expertise. Now that foreign affairs is increasingly about global-warming standards, sectoral and general trade agreements, and domestic compliance with international standards, other departments can rightfully claim that theirs is the relevant expertise.

Policy Instruments: Shifts and Reconfigurations

The distinction between a policy and the instruments by which that policy is implemented is not always clear (Doern and Phidd 1992; Linder and Peters 1989). Instruments are often seen first as the 'means', or even the techniques, of policy, a kind of residual aspect. But questions of exactly how, and to what extent, various interests are persuaded, offered incentives, or regulated into changing their behaviour are also imbued with ideas and disputed values. Thus instruments involve both means and ends.

Changes in policy instruments are driven by political as well as technical considerations, but once they happen, they endure. In international affairs, the primary policy instrument is diplomacy, both in bilateral representation and in relations with, and the staffing of, international organizations (in part with functional and legal expertise). The chapter by Doern and Kirton shows that spending on foreign affairs is largely on personnel rather than on grants, and that regulatory and tax instruments are extremely limited. Nonetheless, something close to regulation can arise through international agreements that stipulate rules of conduct and the sanctions that apply when those rules are broken.

How, then, has internationalization affected policy making in the policy fields covered? In their analysis of foreign policy, including broad aspects of foreign economic policy, Doern and Kirton point to three changes. First, there has been an expansion of the functions of some international agencies, which has endowed them with new or expanded rules-based dispute-settlement capacities. This enhances the importance of regulation and quasi-regulation. A second instrument shift is the continuous pressure of deficit reduction, culminating in the 1995 federal program review. Deficit reduction has both international and national causes. The third change is that international agreements—where they do involve financial commitments—increasingly require DFAIT to obtain the funds from other departments, which in turn want a say about the policy in question. Doern and Kirton also argue that the combination of these shifts has increased Prime Ministerial leadership, largely through an emphasis on plurilateral institutions and forums centred on the G7.

As might be expected, the trade-industrial policy realm also exhibits some of these tendencies in the choice of instruments. In their chapter, Doern and Tomlin point to a shift in policy instruments from spending to the delivery of knowledge and service to firms. The decline in the use of the tariff and expenditure subsidies is apparent in the analysis. But the impetus for budget cuts is also strongly driven by the forces of global change that affected the 1993 reorganization of Industry Canada, in particular by giving it the responsibility for the large realm of business and marketplace framework laws. Trade-industrial policy thus has become more regulatory, not only because the World Trade Organization (WTO) has acquired more teeth but also because framework laws, that is, laws that set the framework of a policy field, such as NAFTA for trade, are subject to more pressures for harmonization at a regional or world level.

In her chapter on agriculture, Skogstad demonstrates how international agreements have removed fiscal and regulatory policy instruments or rendered them ineffective. The government's overall policy capacity has remained strong, however, since officials serve as important intermediaries between international and domestic arenas. Instrument change has been equally fundamental in the realm of investment policy. The chapter by Smythe reveals the shift that has occurred from broad screening of acquisitions to limited screening, and the movement toward aggressively promoting inward investment. In addition, as outward flows of foreign direct investment (FDI) have risen dramatically, policy has become more concerned with gaining access to other markets for Canadian investments and with ensuring the security of investments in those markets through international agreements.

The banking and telecommunications fields reveal different patterns of instrument change. Both fields had been characterized by segmented economic regulation, centred in the nation state. In the case of banking, that was because of concerns about various prudential issues in each of the financial pillars; in the case of telecommunications, it was because of concerns about monopolies or quasi-monopolies in telephone, cable, and broadcasting. Globalization has forced both policy fields to change, for obvious technological reasons.

There has undoubtedly been national economic deregulation among sectors in both realms, as both Coleman and Porter, and Schultz and Brawley show. This has been replaced by much greater international institution building and co-operation among regulators, especially in banking and securities. There has been less international institution building in telecommunications. Indeed, it is still quite remarkably confined to national systems of regulation, although this is likely to change in the late 1990s. But when it comes to other instrument shifts, the two fields tend to part company. For example, despite spending cutbacks in general, it is likely that in telecommunications spending, both public and private, will increase. Schultz and Brawley do not deal with this issue, but an extension of their telecommunications policy boundaries to areas such as the 'information highway' would undoubtedly show spending growth, not contraction.

Another change in instrument use is also occurring, at different paces, in both fields. There is undoubtedly pressure to increase regulation in both fields on matters that could be described as the quality or content of services. This is obvious in telecommunications, where there are concerns about privacy, pornography, and copyright, but it is also prevalent in financial services, where there are privacy issues as well as concerns about marketing practices and consumer information concerning the costs of credit and related matters. Toner and Conway demonstrate that the pressure towards deregulation is also present in environmental policy.

Cooper and Pal's analysis of instrument shifts in human rights begins with the crucial fact that the Charter of Rights and Freedoms provided a constitutional-regulatory instrument of great power that had not existed before 1982. The Charter also helped produce a larger rights-oriented discourse, which has undoubtedly changed political life and, in many areas, actual policies. In the larger combined realms of human rights–security policy, the Cooper and Pal analysis shows the more traditional reliance on persuasion, ardent advocacy, and the direct education of society. Nonetheless, their chapter, like that by Toner and Conway on the environment, demonstrates that the increasingly dense web of international agreements and agencies for overseeing them is both adding to domestic policy instruments and restricting them. Monitoring, for example, is becoming an essential function of departments like Justice and Environment. As NGOs multiply and gain better access to international organizations, there is a higher premium on consultation and participation. DFAIT, as well as other departments, is wrestling with the difficulty of trying to consult with what often amounts to hundreds of groups, as well as to gather information in areas of exclusive provincial jurisdiction.

Social policy is still being redesigned, but Banting's chapter suggests that the mixture of instruments will change radically. The reorganization of the social-policy departments in the super-agency of Human Resources Development is itself evidence of the new intention to integrate social programs into a tighter configuration of labour-market-oriented instruments. Savings from cuts to unemployment insurance, for example, are being moved to training programs. The federal government's redistributive role is changing as new federal-provincial transfer programs are developed. However, Banting cautions against the facile conclusion that social policy is converging (and bottoming out) under the pressures of internationalization. The European and North American evidence shows continuing (if somewhat diminished) government capacity to maintain distinctive social policies.

Summary

Table 1.1 summarizes the main points of this overview and demonstrates several clear patterns. First, internationalization has broadened the policy discourse. Sovereignty, for example, used to be considered an either-or proposition—either a state had clear control over domestic policy or it did not. The increased salience of international forces and forums means that domestic sovereignty (in the sense of stability and control) may be enhanced by international agreement. The best examples come from banking and agriculture. As well, discourse is broadened in the sense that the conventional boundaries of policies have widened. Security used to be defined in primarily military terms; now it encompasses environmental and human rights issues. Trade used to be distinct from culture and investment; now everything seems to have a trade dimension. Though most policy areas will continue to have their distinct centres of gravity and characteristic issues and language, in an era of internationalization the boundaries between these areas become increasing elastic and permeable. That is why those who would oppose globalism seek to defend the integrity of their policy arenas—to keep, for example, social policy about welfare and not adjustment, telecommunications policy about culture and not trade.

Second, internationalization has changed the rules of the associational game. Because policy fields have widened in scope, so have the interests

TABLE 1.1 The Internationalization of Canadian Public Policy

Policy Field	Discourse	Associational System	Institutions and DFAIT	Instruments
Human Rights/Security	Rights now linked to security Shift from concern with 'order' to justice	Broader interests and coalitions, though still weak	DFAIT engaged with a broader array of other government departments (OGDs) and interests	Shift to legal instruments (Charter) International agreements Monitoring, reporting
Banking	Shift towards liberalization with reduced emphasis on sovereignty	Shift from producers to users and consumers	Finance and Bank of Canada together continue to dominate	Domestic deregulation within a framework of international agreements
Telecommunications	Shift from regulated to competitive model Shift from Canadian content to other values and concerns	Shift to a broader and more competitive structure New user groups	Policy shift into the orbit of DFAIT and Industry Canada as telecommunications linked to trade	Continued emphasis on spending Deregulation on economic side with pressures for reregulation on social side (quality and content) International agreements

TABLE 1.1 Continued

Policy Field	Discourse	Associational System	Institutions and DFAIT	Instruments
Trade-Industrial	Emphasis on liberalization and regional free trade Broadened to include services and investment	Emphasis on clients, from associations to firms Mixture of horizontal and vertical sectors	Trade side in DFAIT ascendant Competition from Finance Competition from other departments as 'trade' encompasses more policy fields	Shift to framework regulation and provision of knowledge services International agreements
Environment	Shift from pollution to sustainable development	Broader interests and coalitions	DFAIT co-ordinates; department with expertise leads	International agreements Shift to regulation and monitoring Continued pressures to spend
Social	Reduced redistributive capacity Emphasis on adjustment rather than protection Élites favour globalism	More groups in field Most oppose globalization Little influence	Finance ascendant DFAIT not relevant to this field	Integration in new ministry Tighter configuration of labour-market and social-policy goals International agreements less salient

TABLE 1.1 Continued

Policy Field	Discourse	Associational System	Institutions and DFAIT	Instruments
Agriculture	Regional liberalization constrains sovereignty	Producer groups sharing with non-producers	AgCan and DFAIT continue to share lead role	Decline of fiscal and regulatory instruments
	International liberalization enhances sovereignty		Provinces becoming more important owing to international agreements	Policy capacity remains high through international agreements
Investment	Investment subsumed by trade	Greater role for business interests	DFAIT ascendant as investment gets subsumed under trade policy	Shift from broad to limited screening of investments
	Diminished capacity to bargain with international investors			Concern with access to other markets
				International agreements
Foreign	Broadened security concerns, reduced sovereignty concerns	Greater role for business interests	Central DFAIT role drawing on expertise of other departments	Flowing from international agreements
	Economic liberalization			Money plus regulation

that conceivably have a stake in them. When human rights and the environment were considered different things, then so were the associational systems built up around them. When the environment is thought of as a human rights issue, Greenpeace joins Amnesty International in the same system. Similarly, the convergence of financial sectors means that banks and insurance companies, along with consumers, are suddenly rubbing elbows. In addition to broadening, however, some policy areas have seen a refocusing on what constitutes the relevant level. In trade and industrial policy, associations are less important than firms, and in foreign and investment policy, the emphasis on trade has heightened the influence of business interests.

Third, the role of DFAIT *vis-à-vis* other government departments is simultaneously expanding and contracting. As more policy fields are seen to have an international dimension, there is a shift from foreign policy as a vertical process (a narrow range of departments, with DFAIT clearly on top) to a horizontal process (more departments, with DFAIT acting more as a co-ordinator). This is both good and bad news for DFAIT. The good news is that as the definition of foreign policy widens, so does DFAIT's mandate. The bad news is that in the face of other departments' operating in technical areas that require special expertise or in areas with solid domestic constituencies, the range of DFAIT's technical competence will be severely tested, and it will be constrained by the interdepartmental policy process. Overall, the evidence on prevailing tendencies is mixed. In policy areas where domestic departments lack expertise or constituencies, such as human rights and investment, DFAIT has influence and a strong leadership role. In others, such as agriculture, telecommunications, and environment, it shares authority and serves more as a partner to other departments. In areas like banking and social policy, it is irrelevant.

Finally, internationalization has altered the mixture of policy instruments. The patterns are less clear here than in the other three categories, largely because the pre-existing mixture varied quite widely across fields. Nonetheless, what does emerge very clearly is that in most policy fields there is more reliance on international agreements as the touchstone for standards and frameworks. Most fields have seen pressures to deregulate, even as rearguard actions are fought either to maintain traditional forms of regulation or to find new ones. As the borders between fields dissolve, instruments that were characteristic of one are transported to another. For example, as social policy shifts from protection to adjustment, it begins to rely on tools such as training and job creation; as environmental policy overlaps with trade, it begins to draw on techniques such as export promotion.

These changes are consistent enough across policy fields to warrant a strong conclusion that internationalization is indeed rapidly changing the way public policy is made in Canada. This raises the question, however, of how policy makers react. Is the policy agenda being set by anonymous international forces, or are domestic priority-setting processes capable of moderating and amplifying them in the public interest?

INTERNATIONALIZATION AND PRIORITY SETTING

We began the chapter by showing that academic analyses of globalization initially focused on a very macro level, and that there was a need for more mid-level analysis that would focus on a number of Canadian public-policy fields. That perspective is a central feature of this book and constitutes its main contribution. However, there is one obvious area where we must return to a more macro perspective. A final look at priority setting is important, not only because it guides all policy formation, but also because of what it tells us about broad patterns of policy. The crucial question, both academic and practical, is whether internationalization is changing the very priorities of the Canadian policy-making process.

To examine this aspect of Canadian policy, it is helpful to look first at priority setting in foreign and in domestic policy making and then to show the increasing convergence. In the normal national-policy process, priorities are expressed by three means (Doern and Phidd 1992). The first is speeches from the throne, which usually emphasize legislation, are written very generally, and are given every 18 months or so. The second is budget speeches, which are made annually in February and are the result of the crucial blending of the expenditure and tax decision processes of the government and hence of real decisions about the allocation of resources. The third is periodic events, often crises, where the Prime Minister may use his or her political power to command media attention on an issue that urgently demands national attention. By definition, the last occasions for priority setting are less frequent than the others and even unpredictable.

On the other side of the coin, foreign policy would seem at first glance to have had no equivalent occasions for setting priorities. Within DFAIT and its predecessor departments, there has been internal priority setting, but much of this is unknown to most Canadians. Periodic foreign-policy reviews and defence-policy reviews have been held every few years, and, as is shown in the chapters on foreign policy and human rights, these have indeed been influenced by the growing number of interests involved. The foreign-policy process of course, is also quietly taking its cues from the Prime Minister's priorities and the need to support the Prime Minister at important international events.

Undoubtedly it is the art, substance, and strategies of summitry that are increasingly bringing the domestic and external development and expression of priorities to bear on each other. The annual G7 summits are the centre-piece of this process. They supply an event that receives enormous media attention and at which it is increasingly hard for prime ministers to say things that are too different from what they or other ministers have said to domestic audiences.

In addition to the annual G7 summits, there have been in recent years other summits that draw attention to broad fields such as social policy, employment, womens' issues, and the environment. Every year, in fact, there are hundreds of international meetings to which Canada must send ministers or officials. But there are also three or four particular summits or summit-like events against which domestic policy positions have to be assessed. The summits themselves then produce commitments, pressures, reporting requirements, or new institutions that cause ripples of change through various agencies and policy communities. Some of this activity may be purely symbolic, but for policy makers there is a need to deal with the results in some fashion.

Analyses of the internationalization of priority setting rarely deal with a 'merged' priority-setting dynamic as such. Some analyses concentrate on macro-economic co-ordination and summitry (Devereux and Wilson 1989) but without paying much attention to real institutions. Others examine economic policy more broadly and incorporate a more realistic picture of institutions as they actually are (Dobson 1991). Still others see, in realms such as tax policy, a growing international interdependence (Tanzi 1995). While these analyses certainly show an internationalizing dynamic at work, they do not envisage, nor do they necessarily even want, a world of perfectly co-ordinated economic policy.

The internationalization of priority setting also suggests that economic-policy and business interests are strongly influencing the agenda and that social-policy interests are reacting defensively. The only caveat to this conclusion about over-arching interests is that the very nature of what policy fields mean is changing as policy is internationalized. Thus the categorizing of policy realms under such rubrics as sustainable development, adjustment and human-capital policy, human rights and security, and marketplace framework policy may produce gains and losses that we cannot yet see. These new categories may also produce a more realistic view of winners and losers that disobeys all the conventional categories of simplistically defined economic and social interests.

The chapters that follow develop the preceding analysis in greater detail. They are all pioneering efforts in the careful empirical analysis of the effect of internationalization on public policy and domestic-policy processes. Whereas at one time scholars and policy makers assumed that the 'domestic' and the 'international' were divided by firm borders, that no longer holds. The chapters show that political forces and actors now routinely cross those borders. Those who seek to understand domestic and international public policy developments will need to cross a few conceptual borders of their own.

——2——

Social Policy

Keith G. Banting

Since the dawn of the state system in Europe in the seventeenth and eighteen centuries, each state has existed at the intersection between the international system and its own domestic society.[1] In the words of Theda Skocpol, 'the state . . . is fundamentally Janus-faced, with an intrinsically dual anchorage in domestic society and the international system' (Skocpol 1979: 32). Inevitably, the state must mediate and balance the pressures from these two domains. In part, the state seeks to protect domestic interests in the wider global context, seeking to nudge international developments in directions compatible with domestic interests. But in part, the state also conveys pressures emanating from the wider global context to domestic society, adapting public policy and domestic interests to international conditions that it cannot alter.

Traditionally, social policy has not been viewed that way. During the post-war era, when western nations were completing the structure of the welfare state, social policy was thought of as part of domestic policy, far distant from the high politics of international relations. Social programs were seen as a reflection of national political economies. Analysts interested in the origins and determinants of the welfare state plumbed the internal historical development of specific countries or relied on cross-national comparisons that focused on domestic factors associated with more or less expansive systems of social policy.[2]

This view understated the importance of the global economy to the evolution of social policy, even during the post-war years, and it is certainly inadequate today. During the post-war period, the massive growth of international trade and the expansion of social programs were mutually reinforcing (Keohane 1984; Ruggie 1983). On the one hand, the expansion of trade contributed significantly to unprecedented economic growth, which swelled the public coffers and helped to finance expensive new social commitments. On the other hand, the expansion of social expenditures reduced domestic opposition to international economic liberalization: in Ruggie's words, 'governments asked their publics to embrace the change and dislocation that comes with liberalization in return for the promise of help in containing and socializing the adjustment costs' (Ruggie 1994: 4–5). Given this relatively supportive international context, differences between the social programs of western nations were due to domestic influences, particularly in larger countries that did not depend heavily on international trade. Smaller countries with comparatively open economies were inevitably more sensitive to global pressures even then, and many of them adopted more expansive social programs as part of an attempt to cushion their societies from economic shocks originating outside their borders (Cameron 1978; Katzenstein 1984, 1985). Overall, however, the scope and shape of national welfare states were determined largely by domestic interests.

Since the mid-1970s, however, this comfortable symbiosis between the global economy and the welfare state has eroded. Because of economic integration on a global and regional basis, intense competition in the international trading system, rapid technological change, and a slow-down in productivity growth, there has been a deep and painful restructuring of domestic economies. This economic transformation has in turn created powerful pressures on the welfare state: it has increased the number of people who need social support but has simultaneously made the state less able to fill those needs.

The fate of national welfare states in an era of greater economic interdependence is the subject of much controversy. There is a widespread fear that governments are under pressure to harmonize their social and labour programs with those of their trading partners to avoid putting their domestic industries at a competitive disadvantage. The traditional diversity of national social policies is thought to be disappearing, largely through an erosion of social protection in countries that established generous systems in the post-war years. Though pointing to real pressures on social programs, such interpretations do not fully capture the complexity of the relationship between globalization and social policy, and they underestimate the strength of domestic politics. The pressures generated by globalization are pervasive throughout western nations, and they have created a powerful convergence in the issues facing prime ministers, presidents, and chancellors. But global pressures do not dictate the particular ways in which different countries respond to those pressures. The welfare state is adjusting, often in painful ways, but the choices being made by individual nations are also determined by their domestic politics.

The nation state thus remains Janus-faced, a point at which domestic and global pressures collide. To understand the politics of social policy requires an appreciation of the structure of political institutions, the ideologies through which global pressures are interpreted, and the links between policy makers and both domestic and international interests. In particular, it is important to understand the ways in which the policy process itself is increasingly internationalized, as global economic pressures are transmitted to the national stage.

This chapter analyses the effect of powerful twin forces, the globalization of the economy and the internationalization of the policy process, on the social policies of Canada and other western nations, with particular reference to health care and income-security programs. The first section explores the implications of globalization for the welfare state in western nations generally. The second section examines the internationalization of the policy process, with particular attention to Canada. The third section then looks at the broad pattern of policy responses to globalization in western nations and asks whether there is in fact a strong trend towards greater convergence in social programs among western nations generally and between Canada and its primary trading partner, the United States, in particular. A final section summarizes the patterns and reflects on the future.

GLOBALIZATION AND SOCIAL POLICY

Although the term 'globalization' risks becoming a cliché, it is a useful label for the growing integration on an international basis of markets for goods, services, and finance.[3] Economic borders have been opened by the extension of the General Agreement on Tariffs and Trade (GATT) and now the World Trade Organization (WTO) to a wider range of nations, the formation of formal regional trading blocks in Europe and North America, and the emergence of an informal yen block in Asia. Advances in communications and transportation have linked global and local markets more tightly. Multinational enterprises increasingly organize production on the basis of global strategies, with the result that many corporations and their products no longer have a clear nationality. Although it is important not to overstate the declining economic importance of national borders, at least in the Canadian case (McCallum and Helliwell 1995), growing interdependence among individual nations is a clear feature of the modern world. Moreover, the modern international economy is intensely competitive, as Third World nations enjoy the advantage of dramatically lower costs for wages, social security, health, and safety. Trade competition has placed intense pressures on firms in western nations, producing large-scale economic restructuring.

The effects of globalization have been reinforced by other factors. New technologies are producing sweeping changes in the production and distribution of goods and services. Information systems, computer-assisted design and manufacturing, and telecommunications technologies are transforming production and work processes. Fewer workers are needed, and those who remain require more skills than before (Wein 1991). A major slowdown in productivity growth has also been critical. Between 1960 and 1973, the average rate of growth in real GDP per capita for the OECD nations as a whole ranged from 3.5 to 4.0 per cent; between 1973 and the early 1990s, it fell below 2.0 per cent (Denny and Wilson 1993). The reasons for this decline are not well understood.[4] Nevertheless, the cumulative effect of several decades of sluggish growth on the standard of living of citizens and the fiscal capacity of governments in western nations has been significant.

Globalization, technological change, and slow productivity growth have generated powerful pressures on the welfare state. However, those pressures have been contradictory: they have simultaneously impelled western nations to increase their social expenditures on the one hand and to reduce their social commitments inherited from the past on the other. The expansionist dynamic flows directly from the social stresses generated by economic restructuring. Although some groups have prospered, average real incomes in many western nations have been stagnant for years; unemployment has risen; and growing poverty and inequality are reversing many of the social gains of the post-war period. The most simple and compelling measure of social stress is unemployment. Figure 2.1 tracks its relentless rise throughout OECD nations since the mid-1970s. Although some of this unemployment has been cyclical, the scale of the problem is the result of pervasive economic restructuring. Countless jobs have disappeared as a result of global trade competition, technological change, geographical movements in the location of production, and changes in employment practices within firms. One sign of this has been the growth in *long-term* unemployment. Over a quarter of the unemployed in advanced industrial nations has been unemployed for more than a year (OECD 1994a).

Another measure of social stress is the greater inequality in earnings of different kinds of workers. This trend exists in a wide range of western nations (see Figure 2.2). A more detailed survey by the OECD found a trend toward greater polarization of earnings in 12 of 17 countries for

FIGURE 2.1   Unemployment in the OECD Area

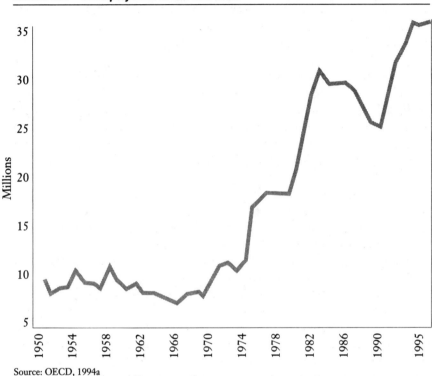

Source: OECD, 1994a

which information was available; it concluded that an important cause of
greater earnings inequality in the 1980s was an increase in the relative
demand for highly educated workers, which 'appears to be associated with
technological developments linked to shifts in the demand for products
and services and linked to changes in trade and investment patterns'
(OECD 1993a: 177).[5]

The social strains generated by unemployment and greater inequality
have put considerable stress on the redistributive instruments of the
welfare state. Much of the fiscal burden is automatic, as higher unemployment drives up the cost of unemployment benefits. However, rapid
economic change also creates strong political pressure for new forms of
state action, as individual citizens, industries, and regions seek protection
from global competition or help in adapting to it. In the social-policy
sector, governments face demands to expand retraining and adjustment
assistance and to provide special programs for particularly vulnerable
groups, such as older displaced workers and young people having difficulty
establishing a career.

FIGURE 2.2   Changes in the Dispersion of Earnings in Selected Countries

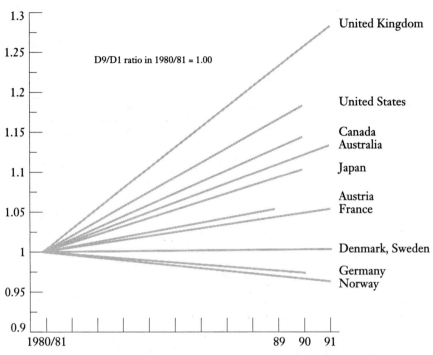

Note: This chart shows the change in the ratio between the earnings of someone at the bottom of the upper-
most tenth of all earners, and someone at the top of the lowest tenth (these are the top and bottom
'deciles' of the distribution, repectively). For many countries, this ratio increased between 1981 and
1991, indicating a widening in the distribution of earnings. This may correspond to gains at the top of
the distribution relative to the middle, or to losses at the bottom, or both.

Source: OECD, 1994a, Chapter 5

However, globalization simultaneously weakens the redistributive
capacity of the state. Governments are under pressure to redesign social
programs in ways that reduce rigidities in the labour market, enhance flexibility in the domestic economy, and reduce the fiscal burdens on the public treasury. This emphasis on adaptation and flexibility conflicts with the
emphasis on security and protection that was embodied in the historic
conception of the welfare state. In addition, given the greater mobility of
factors of production, especially finance, many countries have felt obliged
to lower the tax and regulatory burden on production in order to remain
competitive with other trading nations. Economic theory may suggest
that flexibility in exchange rates can compensate for differentials in production costs, thereby preserving the scope for distinctive national policy
choices. But, in the hard world of politics, domestic business interests

FIGURE 2.3   Unemployment, Canada, 1946–93

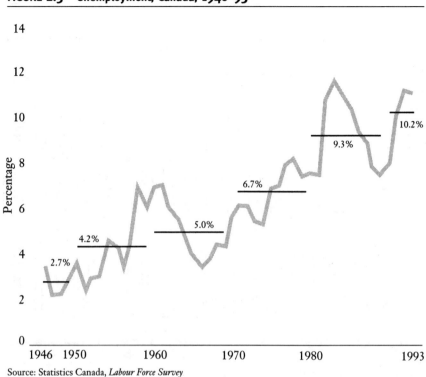

Source: Statistics Canada, *Labour Force Survey*

complain bitterly if they believe their taxes and regulatory costs are higher than those of their international competitors.

These contradictory pressures are all found in the Canadian case. Figure 2.3 tracks the steady rise of unemployment over the decades since the 1950s, and Figure 2.4 confirms that a growing portion of unemployment is for long periods. The real earnings of the average worker have virtually stood still since the 1970s, and average real family income has declined in the 1990s. There has also been greater polarization in the occupational structure, with the loss of middle-income jobs and the growth of jobs paying either very low or very high wages. The burden of economic adjustment has tended to fall most heavily on young workers and displaced older workers. Wages for new entrants to the labour force in particular have proved very flexible in a downward direction, and young families face particularly difficult times. The social stresses implicit in these figures are quickly passed on to the newest generation, as a survey of young Canadians aged 5 to 18 confirmed: 'Children live this. They have absorbed the feelings of insecurity, worry and fear that have come to characterize

FIGURE 2.4   Long-Term Unemployment, Canada 1976–92

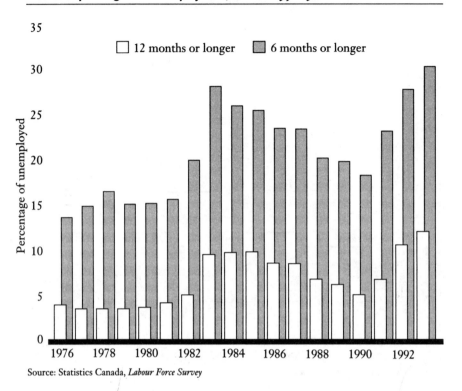

Source: Statistics Canada, *Labour Force Survey*

their parents' and families' world' (Insight Canada Research 1993).

On the other hand, Canada also feels all of the limitations on the redistributive power of the state inherent in globalization. Indeed, Canada's vulnerability is heightened by several factors. No other OECD country is as dependent on the market of another country as Canada is on the American economy. This export concentration makes Canada vulnerable to American protectionism, a danger that lay behind the negotiation of the Free Trade Agreement in the late 1980s, Canada's participation in the subsequent North American Free Trade Agreement in the early 1990s, and the trade frictions between the two countries since then. In addition, Canada's exposure to international economic forces has been increased by its reliance on foreign borrowing. As Figure 2.5 shows, Canada leads all other G7 nations in its net foreign indebtedness by a considerable margin, making this country particularly vulnerable to volatile global financial markets. Canadian foreign indebtedness has enfranchised international bond-rating agencies, making their pronouncements an important part of the country's fiscal politics. In the words of the federal Department of

FIGURE 2.5   Net Foreign Indebtedness of G7 Countries

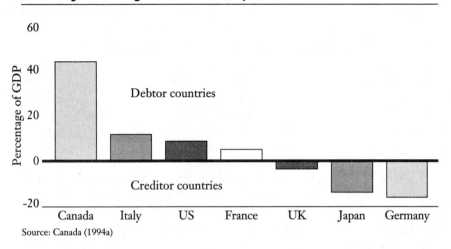

Source: Canada (1994a)

Finance, 'we have suffered a tangible loss of economic sovereignty' (Canada, Dept of Finance 1994a: 78).

Globalization clearly creates contradictory pressures on the welfare state. However, as noted at the outset, the way in which those contradictions are mediated depends in part on the internal processes of governments and the policy communities in which they are embedded. It is to those internal dynamics that we now turn our attention.

INTERNATIONALIZATION AND THE SOCIAL-POLICY PROCESS

Powerful changes in the circumstances in which governments operate transform the intellectual and institutional screens that public policy must pass through. These transformations take three forms: changes in the prevailing ideology that shapes the policy discourse; changes in the institutions of government responsible for public programs; and changes in the non-governmental stakeholders with which the government engages when shaping policy. In the case of Canadian social programs, internationalization is most evident at the ideological level, where the broad post-war consensus that supported the expansion of the welfare state is giving way to a polarized debate about the future of social policy. Internationalization is also evident in the structure and distribution of power among the political institutions responsible for social policy. In contrast, however, the key interests within the domestic social-policy community that the government consults have changed little. The result is a yawning gulf between the government and the social-policy community.

The Ideological Shift

Large social transformations cause ideological debates. Long-established ideas are contested; settled understandings about basic social, economic, and political relationships are challenged; and new paradigms emerge to define the world into which policy makers and citizens are moving. Such transitions are seldom tranquil. Alternative ideological prescriptions tend to multiply, each with a different interpretation of the changes under way, and the appropriate response to them. At such times social conflict is likely to increase, the sense of community to break down, faith in government and leaders to decline, and public policy to appear increasingly incoherent or contradictory.

Canada is living through such a transition. The diffuse ideological consensus that nurtured the post-war expansion of social programs has dissolved. During the decades after the Second World War, the prevailing assumption was that a redistributive state would complement a market economy: social policy would be an instrument of automatic counter-cyclical stabilization; it would ensure an educated and healthy work-force; and it would provide the social services and institutions essential to an urban economy. It was also assumed that Canada was a fully autonomous nation that could create its own version of the welfare state as it saw fit.

All of these assumptions are now subject to intense debate, and the globalization of economic life has been crucial to this unravelling of the post-war consensus. However, a new consensus has yet to emerge. There is considerable disagreement about how fundamental the international economic changes really are, the extent to which they limit the room for manoeuvre of individual states, and the desirability of the new order that is unfolding. From the welter of political voices competing for attention, at least three distinctive positions can be identified.[6]

Globalism: Globalists argue that international integration is a fundamental change from the past and that government policy should accept and complement the impulses implicit in this transition.[7] The powerful competitive pressures inherent in the emerging global market are beneficial because they sweep away inefficient industries and free up resources for high-quality, high-value-added enterprises that are competitive on a world level. The challenge for Canadians is to embrace the pain of change.

Globalists also tend to believe that the effective sovereignty of the nation state is now significantly reduced and that pressures for harmonization or at least convergence in social programs are narrowing the room for manoeuvre enjoyed by governments. In the long term, social policy that seeks to offset or delay adjustment can only lead to lower economic growth, long-term unemployment, and growing budget deficits.

Social policy should therefore facilitate change by enhancing flexibility in labour markets and should emphasize the development of human capital through education and training. Properly equipped, Canadians have no reason to fear the future.

Anti-Globalism: Opposition to globalism tends to be associated with the political left.[8] Anti-globalists agree that globalization constitutes a dramatic transformation, but they see it as a profound threat to equality, social justice, and democratic life. The shift of production to the Third World causes high unemployment in the west and facilitates the exploitation of workers in developing countries. For Canada, unrestrained global markets offer little beyond economic insecurity, the erosion of social programs, rising inequality, and a weaker sense of social solidarity. Anti-globalists also tend to agree with the globalists that international economic integration effectively undermines the sovereignty of the state. The enhanced mobility of capital limits the capacity of governments to tax corporate income, to engage in industrial policies and economic planning, and to chart distinctive national solutions to social problems. Moreover, these constraints have serious implications for the quality of democratic life in individual nations. If policy options are increasingly narrowed by external pressures, democratic governments become less able to carry out the wishes of their citizens, and the public grows more cynical about the political system.

Although anti-globalists agree with much of the analysis of globalists, they disagree strongly about what should be done. They argue that governments should resist further unrestricted integration into the global market and should insist that world trade proceed on terms compatible with social and democratic ideals. This strategy points to managed trade, controls on capital movement, the insertion of social requirements into international trading agreements, and the preservation of social programs to protect the victims of change.

Global Scepticism: Global sceptics are less convinced that the world economy is undergoing a sudden transformation. After all, they argued, the expansion of world trade has been continuous throughout the postwar period. Indeed, the present pace of change may well be less dramatic than earlier waves of innovation, such as those caused by the mechanization of agriculture and the urbanization of the population in the middle decades of this century. From this perspective, the strength of western nations is that they are always adapting to change, and the late twentieth century is no exception.

Global sceptics also challenge the assumption that economic restructuring necessitates a convergence of social policy. History, they argue, provides ample evidence that closer economic integration is consistent with a rich variety in social programs from country to country. Programs financed by taxes that reduce net real incomes rather than increasing the costs of production create no competitive problems; and programs that do increase production costs simply trigger a compensating change in exchange rates. In the words of one sceptic, 'what matters is whether the system provides what the citizens want, and in the most efficient manner. If the programs are right, then they can be as large and expensive as may be, and the exchange rate will adjust to keep trade and capital movements balanced without any need for Nordic and US values and programs to converge' (Helliwell 1994: 23).

Debate rages among these world-views. In the world of business, the dominant political parties, and the senior levels of the bureaucracy, the debate tends to be primarily between globalists and global sceptics. Within the external social-policy community, advocacy groups are much more inclined toward the anti-globalist perspective. Although the views of the wider public are less well defined and all three points of view have some support among the public, the public's highest priorities do not fit easily within the enthusiasm of strong globalists.

These patterns can be seen in surveys of the opinions of different segments of Canadian society conducted in the mid-1990s. A survey of 400 corporate executives, for example, found a general consensus that the Free Trade Agreement and the North American Free Trade Agreement would benefit their industries, and that government should play only a limited role in compensating for the social dislocations implicit in trade liberalization. Although the respondents favoured government leadership to upgrade workers' skills, they were divided over the idea of stronger benefits for the growing legions of part-time workers and overwhelmingly opposed to proposals to share employment more broadly through such as instruments as legislative limits on paid overtime. The survey concluded: 'In an ideological shift to the right, Canada's top business executives see government as the main barrier to growth. Like the general public, corporate executives once saw government as a helpful partner in the building the national economy. But, today corporate Canada embraces the radical free market view that government is no longer the solution, but the problem itself' (Compas 1995).

Other surveys have detected a growing divide between the élites more generally and the wider public. As Figure 2.6 shows, élite decision makers in both the public and private sectors give priority to international competitiveness and see only a minimal role for government in co-ordinating the necessary economic and social adjustments to this new world.

FIGURE 2.6   Values for the Federal Government

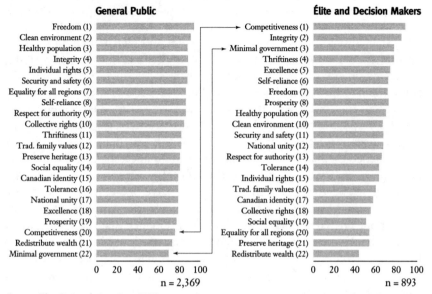

General Public | Élite and Decision Makers

Source: Ekos Research Associates 1995

The wider public, however, has different views. To be sure, Canadians are more cynical about government than in the past and have reduced their expectations about the state's capacity to solve complex social problems. There is also considerable acceptance of cuts to programs, such as welfare and unemployment insurance, that benefit only specific groups. However, there is no widespread public support for deep cuts in universal social programs such as education, health care, and pensions. Moreover ideals of international competitiveness and minimal government evoke little resonance with the wider public. In the words of the authors of one study of élite and public preferences, 'a chasm exists between those charged with governing our country and those being governed. Whether the élites are correct in their beliefs or not, they are clearly disconnected from the views of the mass public; and this disconnection serves to underline the growing rift between the comfortable and insecure segments of Canadian society' (Ekos Research Associates 1995: 13).

Institutions

The political institutions that shape social policy at the federal level have also changed in response to international forces. Canadian experience here follows an international trend for power to flow more strongly to

those agencies in closest touch with the global economy, such as the
offices of presidents and prime ministers, treasuries, and central banks,
and away from agencies identified with domestic clients (Cox 1994: 49).
The classic battles over social policy in the federal government have
always been fought out between the Minister and Department of Finance
on one side and the ministers and departments responsible for social
programs on the other.[9] This classic dispute remains. But the balance
among these contenders has shifted, there has been a large-scale reorganization of the social departments, and the domestic disagreements over
social policy are increasingly projected into international arenas.[10]

The fiscal and economic problems of the last decade have clearly
strengthened the hand of the Department of Finance, making it the dominant social-policy department in the federal government. Increasingly,
new policies have come from Finance and have been announced in the
budget by the Minister of Finance rather than by the ministers of relevant
social-policy departments. It is primarily in Finance that the implications
of globalization and the loss of economic sovereignty implicit in heavy
foreign borrowing are brought to bear on social-policy decisions. The
department has strong links to the international economy: its relationship
with the Bank of Canada and the rest of the Canadian banking system is
close; it consults widely with the business sector and is conscious of the
competitive trading pressures that confront the country; and officials of
the department, being responsible for the sale of federal government
bonds, are sensitive to the judgements of international financial markets
and bond-rating agencies. While the department is publicly discreet about
its views, the broad framework documents that it has produced in recent
years leave little doubt that the world has changed decisively, and that
Canadian governments must change with it (Canada, Dept of Finance
1994a, 1994b). Its assertion in 1994 that Canada has suffered a loss of
economic sovereignty is simply the most explicit form of its world-view
(Canada, Dept of Finance 1994a: 78).

In the case of social departments, their traditional structure gave way to
an extensive reorganization in the summer of 1993. The long-established
Department of National Health and Welfare was divided; its health components remained an independent but weaker portfolio, and the welfare
programs were combined with the old Department of Labour and the
employment elements of the old Department of Employment and Immigration to produce one super-ministry, the Department of Human
Resources Development. This department is responsible for a huge
agenda and half of all federal program expenditures. It owes its current
shape, orientation, and prominence to the changing world economy. Federal policy makers are convinced that the adjustment to the new global

order requires greater flexibility in the labour market, which in turn requires better integration of income-support programs, such as unemployment insurance, child benefits, and welfare on one hand, and labour-market programs, such as training, employment-readiness initiatives, and minimum wages on the other. By grouping all of the relevant policy instruments in one giant department, the federal government hopes to facilitate that integration and the rebalancing of programs that influence labour markets. The importance of international forces to this agenda was pointed out by the discussion paper that launched a major review of social security in the fall of 1994 (Canada, Dept of Human Resources Development 1994b). The case for sweeping reform was based on the changes created by the globalization of the economy, the world-wide liberalization of trade and investment, the decline of unskilled and labour-intensive manufacturing, the growth of Third World producers, and the importance of technological innovation. 'The world has changed faster than our programs,' the paper concluded (ibid: 7).

The internationalization of the Canadian policy process can also be seen in the efforts of the Department of Human Resources Development to participate more vigorously in international policy debates. Because of growing economic interdependence and the resulting pressures for greater co-ordination of economic and fiscal policies among industrial nations, the policy community has become more globalized:

> There is a transnational process of consensus formation among the official caretakers of the global economy. This process creates consensual guidelines, underpinned by the ideology of globalization, that are transmitted into the policy making channels of national governments and big corporations. Part of this consensus-formation process takes place through unofficial forums. . . . Part of it goes on through official bodies like the Organisation for Economic Co-operation and Development (OECD), the Bank for International Settlements, the IMF, and the G7. These shape the discourse within which policies are defined, the terms and concepts that circumscribe what can be thought and done. (Cox 1994: 9)

Traditionally, social-policy departments have been at a considerable disadvantage in this global policy community. Although senior departmental officials have always had some contact with international organizations concerned with social issues, such contacts were dwarfed by the domestic pressures beating on the door every day. Moreover, as in other western nations, links with agencies such as the OECD and representation at international meetings such as the annual summit of the G7 nations have tended to be dominated by the Department of Finance and the

Department of Foreign Affairs and International Trade (DFAIT). The situation is similar in other nations, and, as a result, international debate reflects the language and opinions of ministers of finance.[11]

Human Resources Development is trying to insert itself more vigorously into international networks. To establish an external presence requires considerable political and bureaucratic commitment, since the older departments are naturally reluctant to surrender their dominance over these links.[12] Nevertheless, the Human Resources minister is increasingly one of Canada's representatives at international meetings, such as the 1994 special G7 'jobs summit' in Detroit and the annual ministerial meeting that sets the direction of the OECD. The department now also commits more resources to preparing for international meetings and projects. Admittedly, the department is still finding its feet in the area, and has some distance to go simply to co-ordinate its own relations with different international organizations more effectively. Nevertheless, its efforts are a telling sign of the internationalization of policy discourse.

The OECD has a special place in this campaign. The OECD seeks to foster a common policy culture among industrial nations through its ministerial statements, research studies, and authoritative data comparing the performance of member nations. In the words of one Human Resources Development official, 'the OECD is the keeper of conventional wisdom'. Because OECD studies and recommendations influence policy debates in Canada, federal government departments attempt to use the OECD to promote their own domestic agendas vis-à-vis ministers, other departments, and the wider policy community (Wolfe, D. 1993). Although officials of Human Resources Development have long attended OECD meetings, the department is engaging in this process more determinedly, devoting more of its analytical resources to preparing for meetings, and contributing to the OECD's analytical studies. Although it is still not as well established in the process as the Department of Finance, Human Resources Development is attempting to inject a stronger social element into international debates.[13]

The politics of international policy analysis was neatly illustrated by the annual OECD ministerial meeting in 1995. Lloyd Axworthy, Minister of Human Resources Development, and Robert Reich, Secretary of Labor in the United States, met before the meeting to co-ordinate their approach. Both men were the leading spokesmen for social issues in countries moving in a conservative direction. They continually felt at a disadvantage in internal policy struggles because of the lack of hard, quantifiable measures of the effectiveness of social expenditures comparable to economic data on debts, deficits, and productivity. As Axworthy complained, 'Finance ministers have this incredible tool chest of hard information that they can use to frame a policy decision' (*Globe and Mail*, 15 May 1995). Accordingly, the two ministers pressed the OECD to develop more sophisticated measures of the value of investment in people. What is required, Axworthy told the OECD ministerial meeting, is 'the development of quantifiable performance measures that would demonstrate clearly how expenditures on human capital and social policy programming yield positive returns' (Axworthy 1995). The two ministers succeeded in convincing the representatives around the table from other nations, and the ministerial committee directed the OECD to examine the possibility of developing 'comparable and standard measures of human capital investment and common performance indicators of such investment' (OECD 1995a). Human Resources Development is contributing significantly to the analytical work for the study. The department hopes that it will provide a new, authoritative source of data with which social ministers can arm themselves when they march into the cabinet room.

The tension between Finance and the social departments is hardly new. Today, however, it is played out in both international and domestic arenas, in a bureaucratic analogue to the two-level game long familiar to diplomats engaged in bargaining among nations (Putnam 1988; Evans, Jacobson, and Putnam 1993).

The Social-Policy Community. The internationalization of the policy process at élite levels is increasing the distance between government and the domestic social-policy community to which government also belongs. The domestic social-policy community reflects the complex diversity of Canadian society. Contemporary politics—variously described as 'postmodern politics' or the 'politics of identity'—are characterized by the mobilization, politicization, and institutionalization of a wider range of social differences. The post-war assumption of a nation-wide citizenship has begun to crumble in the face of demands from newly mobilized collectivities for a 'less universalistic understanding of citizenship, and for categorical equity' (Jenson 1992: 197). This more fragmented society confronts the economic consequences of globalization most explicitly in the domain of social policy.

The diversity of the social-policy community can be seen in the range of groups with a direct interest in social issues. Although business interests occasionally take a position on the specifics of social programs, the most active groups represent the beneficiaries and providers of health, education, and welfare programs. Among the groups that take part in consultations on social policy are organized labour, the women's movement, associations of retired people, coalitions representing disabled persons, anti-poverty groups, aboriginal organizations, racial minorities, multicultural groups, church organizations, food banks, and the gay community.[14] The importance of this social diversity is reinforced by a new culture of participation in policy making. It takes considerable effort to recall that the major review of social-security programs held in the mid-1970s was conducted almost exclusively in closed federal-provincial meetings, and that interested groups outside of government were reduced to reading between the lines of vague communiqués. That world is gone. In its place is a new political culture: social groups demand active participation in the policy process, and deference to élite opinion is in short supply.

It is not easy, however, to integrate consultations with the social-policy community into a policy world defined by global economic constraints and the partial loss of economic sovereignty. Social-policy advocates are suspicious of the globalists' enthusiasm for economic adjustment. Though there is undoubtedly a diversity of views within the social-policy community, most advocacy groups accept the anti-globalist critique advanced by the political left; they fought hard against the Free Trade Agreement with the United States in the late 1980s, and they resist an emphasis on flexibility rather than on security in the redesign of social policy. In addition, the social-policy community in Canada is vigorously pluralistic, and advocacy groups have little capacity to work together in a situation of diminishing resources and hard trade-offs. These groups reject the notion that new social programs or increased activity in an established program must come at the expense of some other social program. As a result, government officials and advocacy groups increasingly talk past each other.

This tension was obvious in the community's response to the federal social-security review launched in the fall of 1994.[15] The vast majority of submissions to the parliamentary committee that held hearings across the country argued for the preservation of existing social programs, the development of new programs to respond to emerging problems, and the responsibility of the federal government to meet the social needs of Canadians (Canada, House of Commons 1995). Interestingly enough, there was something of a gap between the advocacy voices heard by the parliamentary committee and the views of the wider public as measured by opinion polls. Survey data available at the time pointed to a hardening of attitudes among Canadians generally towards unemployment insurance and social assistance (Tomlin 1994). However, the loudest voices in the debate expressed a strong commitment to the social needs of poor and vulnerable Canadians and a suspicion that 'globalization' and 'fiscal restraint' were simply code words for a highly conservative ideology that seemed to threaten the gains of the post-war era.

The social security review illustrates the contradiction between a vibrant consultative culture and diminished economic sovereignty. A public consultation process, by its very nature, echoes and intensifies domestic political demands. In the case of Canadian social policy, the groups that participate most vigorously in such a process are primarily concerned with the needs of the poor and other vulnerable groups that depend on the redistributive capacities of the state. As a result of these pressures, the government ends up striking a balance between the demands of such groups and hard constraints in ways that almost inevitably deny the preferences of the social-policy community. In a world of tightened international constraints, there is a danger that public consultations will heighten, not reduce, cynicism about the responsiveness of our political institutions.

The growing isolation of the domestic social-policy community is compounded by its limited engagement in international arenas. With the exception of organizations committed to development in the Third World, the leading Canadian social-policy groups tend not to take an active part in larger international networks and have not established strong links with international agencies. In part, this is due to the diversity of advocacy groups; the world stage does not have room for a multitude of small, single-issue groups. In part, the weak international profile is due to limited resources; in an era of declining financial support from governments, most social advocacy organizations are concentrating on survival. And in part, it is simply due to a lag in the community's response to the increasingly global context of social policy.

The strengths and weaknesses of non-governmental organizations, or NGOs, in this sector were illustrated by the United Nations Summit on Social Development held in Copenhagen in March 1995. Canadian social-policy groups did participate actively; over 60 organizations attended, and several representatives of NGOs were included in Canada's official delegation. However, international-development groups, which have more experience in such settings, tended to take the lead and to exert the strongest influence on the Canadian delegation and, through it, on the conference proceedings and recommendations. For many domestic social-policy groups, on the other hand, the summit was the first foray into international debates. Several of them attempted to use the forum as a platform to attack the Canadian federal budget, which had made large cuts to social expenditures a month before the summit, but their efforts had little effect on the proceedings and received scant press coverage even in Canada. Perhaps more important, there is little sign that the summit experience gave birth to a more co-ordinated coalition of Canadian groups capable of developing an effective international strategy. All of this stands in sharp contrast to the environmental sector, where high-profile international activism by NGOs is common.

Clearly, the internationalization of the Canadian social-policy process is only partial. At the ideological level, globalization has contributed to the erosion of the post-war consensus, but no new consensus has emerged. Although the globalist perspective clearly predominates, it is challenged on many sides. At the level of political institutions, the traditional struggle between the Department of Finance and the social departments continues in new organizational forms and is increasingly projected into the international domain. However, the fiscal constraints rooted in the domestic and international economies have driven a wedge deeply between government and the part of the policy community most actively engaged in social issues. As a result, this policy sector is divided. Ideologically and politically, it is a house divided against itself.

POLICY RESPONSES TO GLOBALIZATION

The response of governments in Canada and western nations generally to the contradictory pressures generated by globalization can be explored by examining three dimensions of social policy: total social expenditure; the restructuring of social programs; and the convergence between the social programs of different countries.

Social Expenditures

Every government in the west has had to struggle with powerful pressures on social expenditures: high unemployment caused partly by economic restructuring, aging populations, exploding health care costs, and growing public deficits. Every government has made painful changes in its benefit and tax regimes. The depth, speed, and configuration of benefit reductions have varied with the political circumstances of each country. Whatever the political style, however, there have been widespread reductions in benefits: governments have cut benefits directly, or indirectly by tightening the conditions of eligibility or by changing the formulas governing the indexing of benefits. Nevertheless, these reductions have not reversed the historic upward trend in total social expenditures. To be sure, the period of rapid growth in social expenditures in the 1960s and 1970s is clearly over. But the higher unemployment implicit in economic restructuring, together with demographic pressures, ensured that the share of GDP represented by social expenditures continued to creep up during the 1980s and early 1990s. Public spending on social protection in OECD countries outside of the European Union rose from an average of 18.2 per cent of GDP in 1980 to 21.2 per cent in 1990; within the European Union, the average rose from 21.6 per cent to an estimated 24.3 per cent in 1991 (OECD 1994b: Tables 1b, 1c).

TABLE 2.1   Changing Composition of Public Revenue in OECD Nations: Tax Revenue
for Major Taxes as Percentage of All Taxes

	1965	1975	1985	1991
Personal income	26.0	30.9	30.6	30.1
Corporate income	8.9	7.5	7.9	7.3
Social security (total)	18.0	22.9	23.5	24.0
Employee	5.9	7.1	7.7	8.1
Employer	9.9	14.3	13.7	13.6
Payroll	1.1	1.4	1.2	1.0
Property	7.8	6.0	5.1	5.4
Goods and services	38.0	31.4	31.1	30.4

Source: OECD (1993b)

At the same time public revenues have also been rising. Although governments have been reluctant to raise taxes dramatically to mitigate the social stresses implicit in rapid change, total tax revenues as a proportion of GDP continued to creep up from an OECD average of 35.1 per cent in 1980 to 38.7 per cent in 1991 (OECD 1993b). As Table 2.1 shows, this trend does mask shifts in the relative burden of taxation that have been caused by international economic competition. The capacity to tax depends on the relative mobility of different factors of production. As the most mobile factor, capital is the most difficult to tax; as a result, the proportion of total government revenues raised from taxes on corporate income is small and has declined throughout the OECD is recent decades. The same is true to a lesser extent of employers' social-security contributions. In comparison, individual workers are less mobile and have had to bear a growing share of the costs of the welfare state through taxes on personal income and employees' social-security contributions. And, of course, western governments have also relied on borrowing, thereby passing some of the costs of economic adjustment on to future generations.

These general trends are also found in Canada. Social expenditures continued to rise as a proportion of GDP throughout the 1980s and early 1990s, climbing steadily from 14.4 per cent of GDP in 1980 to 18.8 per cent in 1990 (OECD 1994b: Table 1b). Table 2.2 shows that the structure of taxation in Canada has followed the general trend in OECD nations. The proportion of revenue derived from taxes on corporate income has declined from well above the OECD average in 1965 to well below in 1991. The employers' social-security contributions did expand proportionately over this period, but the trend has been reversed by recent federal budgets that reduced employers' unemployment insurance contributions in the name of employment creation. At the same time, the biggest shift was the rapid rise in the weight of taxes on personal incomes, as the burden of the contemporary welfare state was shifted more firmly onto the shoulders of

TABLE 2.2   Changing Composition of Public Revenue in Canada: Tax Revenue for Major Taxes as Percentage of All Taxes

	1965	1975	1985	1991
Personal income	22.6	32.8	35.2	40.7
Corporate income	14.9	13.6	8.2	5.5
Social security (total)	5.6	10.0	13.5	15.3
Employer	3.5	6.1	8.6	10.2
Property	14.3	9.5	9.3	9.5
Goods and services	40.5	32.0	31.8	27.3

Source: OECD (1993b)

individual Canadians. Moreover, as noted earlier, by 1993 total public debt in Canada had risen to 70 per cent of GDP; and at the federal level, interest payments on the debt took up roughly 35 per cent of all government revenues, putting immense pressure on the other expenditures, including those for social programs (Canada, Dept of Finance 1994a: 11–12).

The Restructuring of Social Programs

Although the contradictory pressures on the social responsibilities of the state have not produced radical reductions in social expenditures, they have generated a new politics of restructuring. The prevailing discourse in governmental circles emphasizes the importance of adjustment to the changing economic order and the need to restructure social programs in ways that strengthen work incentives and facilitate rather than impede the adjustment to global economic forces. Organizations like the OECD and, increasingly, the European Commission preach the virtues of shifting resources from 'passive' programs like unemployment insurance, which simply provide income transfers, to 'active' programs that emphasize training and retraining, assistance with job searches, employment subsidies, and geographic mobility (Commission of the European Communities 1993; OECD 1994a). With the disappearance of millions of low-skilled jobs, retraining in particular has taken on a symbolic importance far greater than its capacity to improve the lot of the most vulnerable groups in western nations.

This agenda appears in different forms in different countries. In Europe, there is high unemployment, especially long-term unemployment. Europe's failure to match American and Japanese levels of job creation in recent years has generated a debate about structural unemployment, in particular labour market regulations and social policies (Commission of the European Communities 1993; OECD 1994a). In the United States, where labour markets are much less constrained by employment regulations and social programs, the politics of restructuring

TABLE 2.3 Convergence in Social Expenditures among OECD Countries, 1960–1980

Public Expenditure on Social Programs as Percentage of GDP

	1960	1964	1968	1972	1974	1980
Average	10.1	11.9	13.1	15.1	18.6	19.6
Coefficient of variation	0.36	0.34	0.35	0.34	0.31	0.30
Ratio of highest to lowest	4.47	3.51	3.70	3.76	3.28	2.75

Source: Calculated from data provided in OECD (1994b: Table 1a)

have centred on welfare, especially Aid to Families with Dependent Children (AFDC), which provides support mainly to single mothers and their children. The US debate takes on distinctive characteristics, owing to the politics of race, a strongly individualist culture, and alarm at the proportion of inner-city children born to single mothers, especially in the black community. Nevertheless, proposals for 'workfare' and the complete termination of benefit after a specified period are simply more radical versions of a shift from income security to work incentives.

The debate in Canada is similarly influenced by the ethos of the age, with its emphasis on a shift from passive to active programs. On occasion the shift in spending has been explicit, with some of the savings from reductions in unemployment insurance being transferred to training programs. This strategy was the basis of the 1994 discussion paper on social-security reform, which proposed to withdraw more money from income transfers to the unemployed (especially repeat beneficiaries such as seasonal workers) in order to enhance training and child benefit programs; to reduce associated payroll taxes; and to ease the large government deficit (Dept of Human Resources Development 1994b).

Convergence in Social Protection

As noted earlier, many observers insist that globalization is unleashing powerful forces for harmonization in the social-policy systems of western nations. But here the evidence is more mixed. It is important to note at the outset that convergence in spending levels has been a long-standing trend. As Table 2.3 shows, the coefficient of variation in social expenditures in OECD nations as a whole fell from 0.36 to 0.30 between 1960 and 1980, and that the ratio of the highest to the lowest expenditure levels fell from 4.47 to 2.75. Western nations were more similar at the end of the period of social-policy expansion than at the beginning.

During the 1980s, however, different regions of the west moved in different ways. Within the European Union, convergence in expenditure

TABLE 2.4   Convergence in Social Expenditures among European Union Countries, 1980–1991

Public Expenditure on Social Programs as Percentage of GDP

	1980	1983	1986	1989	1991
Average	23.1	25.1	24.7	24.3	25.7
Coefficient of variation	0.25	0.21	0.18	0.17	0.15
Ratio of highest to lowest	2.52	2.06	1.89	1.86	1.67

Source: Calculated from data in Commission of the European Communities (1994: Table 1)

levels remained strong. As Table 2.4 shows, the coefficient of variation and the ratio of the highest to the lowest expenditure levels fell steadily over the decade. A closer look, however, should allay some fears about the withering effects of a more competitive economic order. The convergence in expenditures within the European Union was due as much to considerable increases in the spending of southern countries like Greece and Portugal as to a slowing of expenditure growth in high-spending countries like Belgium, Denmark, and Germany (Commission of the European Communities 1994: 42–3). Moreover, underneath the convergence of total social spending lies a continuing diversity in the design of social programs, which is clearly rooted in the history and political cultures of the member states. A study by the European Commission could find no consistent pattern of convergence implicit in the program adjustments undertaken during the 1980s:

> There has certainly been a convergence of the problems to be solved, partly because all countries have had to confront the social and financial problems posed by slow growth and higher unemployment. . . . [However], there is no clear evidence of convergence of social protection systems in the Community in the 1980s. While a number of changes have worked in the same direction in specific areas. . . , others have worked in opposite directions. (Commission of the European Communities 1994: 9)

The pattern in North America during the 1980s provides even less evidence of convergence. Over the decade total public expenditures on social programs in Canada and the United States diverged further (see Figure 2.7). Both countries devoted comparable shares of their national resources to social programs at the beginning of the decade, but by the end of the decade the difference had grown sharply. As in Europe, the simple expenditure levels conceal a complex pattern of convergence and divergence in specific programs. In the case of a number of programs,

**FIGURE 2.7   Public Expenditure on Social Programs as a Percentage of GDP,
Canada and the United States, 1960–1990**

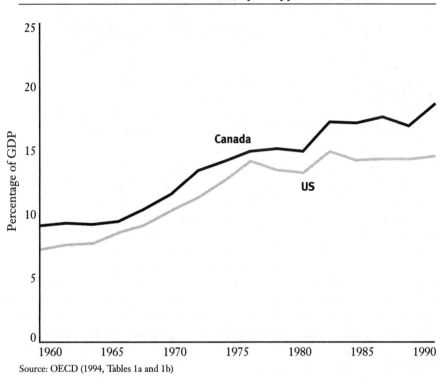

Source: OECD (1994, Tables 1a and 1b)

including health care, pensions, and social assistance, the 1980s and early
1990s were marked by mild divergence, that is, the incremental accentua-
tion of traditional differences between the two systems. Convergence in
program structure has occurred in some fields, most dramatically in child
benefits and to a lesser extent in unemployment insurance. In the case of
child benefits convergence had little to do with economic integration;
rather it was due to a common domestic debate about the nature of
poverty and the proper relationship between tax and transfer systems. In
the case of unemployment insurance, the pressures implicit in the wider
global economy, including the Canada–United States relationship, were
undoubtedly relevant. However, the changes were also due to the fiscal
weakness of the federal government and the wider international trend
from passive income transfers to more active programs. Even when full
weight is given to convergence in the case of child benefits and unemployment insurance, however, it is possible to argue that the two welfare
states are as different today as they were in the mid-1970s, the high-water
mark of the post-war welfare state.[16]

In the broadest terms, Canada and the United States have differed in the extent to which they have sought to offset the social effects of economic restructuring by political means. In the United States, the redistributive impulse faded during the 1980s, and government programs failed to offset the growing inequality resulting from market trends. As a result, the distribution of final income, which measures income derived from the market and government transfers, also became more unequal over the decade. In Canada, however, redistribution by the state continued to prevent income inequality from growing. Its larger system of income-security programs largely offset the changing pattern of market pressures, and the overall distribution of final income has remained essentially stable. This situation may not continue in the future as Canada comes to grips with a fiscal crisis more severe than that in the United States. Nevertheless, in the recent past there has been as much divergence as convergence.

The experience of both Europe and North America stands as a warning against an automatic assumption that economic integration necessitates policy harmonization. There has been a strong convergence in the problems that nations face and in the constraints under which they labour. Each nation must adjust to strong forces emanating from the international system, but the global economy does not dictate the precise ways in which each country responds. Policy is also shaped by domestic politics, and different countries are responding to a changing world with a different mixture of program adjustments. This process is painful; the quality of social protection established in the post-war period is declining. But the result is unlikely to be a harmonized international model of social policy.

CONCLUSIONS

The day is long past when social policy could be regarded as a simple expression of the domestic culture and politics of a nation. The restructuring of the international economy has placed enormous pressures on the welfare state, creating contradictory pressures for the expansion of the redistributive role of the state, and for its contraction and redesign. The ways in which these contradictions are mediated depends heavily on dynamics within the policy process. In the case of Canada, the internationalization of the social-policy process is incomplete. Although the conceptual lenses through which social issues are interpreted and the structures of policy making have shifted, the domestic social-policy community remains largely resistant to the arguments for global economic integration. The result is a divided policy sector, in which international and domestic pressures remain in contention. Although the social protection enjoyed by Canadians has clearly eroded, expenditures on the welfare state remain deeply entrenched in the system, and policies continue to be influenced by the internal dynamics of Canadian life as well as forces from beyond our borders.

The longer-term prospects of the welfare state will depend greatly on whether global forces erode our collective sense of community, our faith that Canadians are in some way a single people who care about each other. This sense of community is fundamental to the willingness of affluent citizens, enterprises, and regions to pay the taxes that enable governments to protect vulnerable individuals, groups, and regions of the country. In the United States, analysts have argued that corporate leaders and professionals are increasingly engaged in global markets and are losing their sense of connection with the rest of American society; they are retreating physically into well-protected suburban enclaves and withdrawing psychologically from a sense of civic obligation to less fortunate Americans (Reich 1991; Lasch 1995). Signs of a similar process can be seen in Canada in the vigorous attacks on social programs by business interests and the growing gulf between élite and public priorities for government. Moreover, Canadian social programs are strong instruments of inter-regional redistribution, expressing a long-standing commitment to the equalizing of opportunities and well-being among the regions of this diverse country. Here again, threats to the ties that bind us together can be seen in the strength of separatism in Quebec and the growing resentment of inter-regional transfers in many parts of the rest of Canada. Ultimately the future of the welfare state in Canada and other nations depends in large measure on whether the historic sense of community nurtured over the last century by the nation state can survive as the economic and social horizons of citizens spread farther and farther beyond national boundaries.

NOTES

1. I would like to thank Shelley Pilon for her excellent research assistance. I would also like to thank the editors of this volume, David Ross and other participants in the associated symposium, Harvey Lazar, Henry Milner, and Robert Wolfe for helpful comments on an earlier version of this chapter. Parts of the chapter build on Banting (1995a; 1995b).

2. For the most celebrated example of this form of analysis, see Esping-Andersen (1990).

3. There is also considerable debate about whether North American economies in particular have turned the corner to stronger productivity growth in the 1990s. For a sceptical view from the OECD on US productivity trends, see French and Jarret (1994). For conflicting views of the Canadian data, see Denny and Wilson (1993) and Fortin (1994).

4. The literature on globalization is now monumental. See, for example, Courchene (1992a, 1992b); Gill and Law (1988); Omhae (1990); Maxwell (1993); Porter (1990); Reich (1991); Stubbs and Underhill (1994).

5. A substantial literature on polarization in earnings has emerged in recent years. In addition to a special issue of the *Quarterly Journal of Economics* (No. 107, 1992), see Banting and Beach (1995); Beach and Slotsve (1994); Harrison and Bluestone (1988); Krugman (1990); Levy and Murnane (1992); Danziger and Gottschalk (1993); and Phillips (1993).

6. This section is heavily indebted to Brown (1994).

7. For Canadian globalists, see Courchene (1992a; 1992b; 1993); Lipsey (1993).

8. For Canadian examples, see Cameron and Watkins (1993); Grinspun and Cameron (1993); Warnock (1988).

9. For an interesting recent discussion of the influence of the Department of Finance on the development of social programs from 1940 to 1955, see Haddow (1995).

10. A full treatment of the evolution of political institutions would include an analysis of relations between the federal and provincial governments in this sector. However, such an examination is beyond the scope of this chapter. For a recent discussion, see Banting (1995c).

11. One sign of this predominance can be seen in the frequency of meetings of different committees of the OECD. The Economic Development and Review Committee, which is dominated by departments of finance, meets approximately 20 times a year, whereas the Education, Employment, Labour and Social Affairs Committee meets only twice a year. Both committees have sub-committees and working groups, and there are more meetings than either number suggests. Nevertheless, the interaction among departments of finance is continuous.

12. At the political level, the composition of ministerial delegations to international meetings is decided by the Prime Minister. At the bureaucratic level, Canadian representation to major international meetings is co-ordinated by the Department of Foreign Affairs and International Trade.

13. The privileged position of the Department of Finance can be seen in the composition of the staff of the Embassy to the OECD, through which all communication must flow. Finance is the only department to have one of its own officials posted to the embassy; all other departments must rely on DFAIT officials, who normally have little experience with their issues.

14. Haddow (1990). For an appreciation of the diversity of groups that constitute the social-policy community, see also the report of the parliamentary committee that held hearings on the federal government's discussion paper on social-security reform in 1994–95 (Canada, House of Commons 1995: Chap. III).

15. For a fuller discussion of the social security review, see Banting (1995b).

16. For a fuller exposition of this argument, see Banting (1992) and Banting (forthcoming).

3

Banking and Securities Policy

William D. Coleman and
Tony Porter

The financial-services sector comprises a wide variety of firms engaged in many different business activities. These activities extend from banking (credit giving and deposit taking), to the management of trusts and estates, the provision of insurance, the underwriting of securities, the selling of securities in secondary markets, and portfolio management and counselling. This chapter deals principally with banking and the various activities in securities markets. Since the early 1960s, globalization has considerably reshaped the political economy of banking and securities. In the process, the task of the state has changed from *protecting* domestic financial-services firms against external forces to *facilitating* adjustment of the domestic sector to a new neo-liberal, globalizing, ideological consensus about world finance. In Cox's words (1987: 253), this 'internationalization of the state' involves its participation in new global decision-making forums, the reorganization of domestic state structures to implement the consensus, and the redefinition of domestic public policies to conform with the consensus.

The concept of the internationalization of the state differs from the view, most often expressed by liberal economists, that the state has been, and should be, weakened as it is forced to adjust to the inexorable expansion of global market forces. It also differs from the contrary view, most often expressed by political scientists, that states have played a decisive part in bringing about globalization and could therefore reverse the process if they chose to do so. By contrast, the view of the internationalization of the state propounded in this chapter sees the state becoming stronger and more autonomous in relation to both its domestic population and individual market actors, but only by participating in global institutions, practices, and discourses, of which the neo-liberal consensus is a fundamental expression. At the same time, the nature of this participation is affected by the character of the state, including its institutions and its capability in relation to other states. Overall, however, if we define sovereignty territorially, as is conventional, then globalization involves paradoxically the strengthening of the state and the erosion of sovereignty.

This institutionalist perspective draws on previous work in which we argued that the way states respond to globalization are strongly affected by the character of the international institutions through which states act (Porter 1993), and by national differences in the institutional structure and capacity of states (Coleman 1996). Similarly, different types of financial systems may affect the ease or difficulty with which states adapt to globalization. Two factors appear relevant here. First, systems based on capital markets, to use Zysman's (1983) term, will have certain advantages over credit-based systems, such as those found in France and Japan, because of their highly developed securities markets. Second, systems that feature 'universal' banks (which offer fully integrated financial services) will have advantages over those with narrow banks because of the easier integration of banking and securities businesses.[1] The chapter addresses these two themes with respect to the internationalization of the Canadian state as it bears upon banking and securities markets.

More specifically, it begins with a review of the process of globalization in financial services and of the nature of the neo-liberal consensus on global finance. Next the chapter examines the Canadian state's participation in international forums where a consensus is formed on the need for globalized financial services. Attention then shifts to changes in public policy and in the organization of the state at the domestic level that are relevant to the process of adjusting to this consensus. The chapter concludes with an analysis of the new policy discourse, an assessment of the implications of growing policy complexity for state capacity, and an evaluation of changes to state sovereignty that have resulted from these changes.

THE GLOBALIZATION OF FINANCE: WIDENING AND DEEPENING

Several recent dramatic developments have highlighted in the popular imagination the degree to which the globalization of finance has undermined the ability of states to control financial markets. One is the high proportion of Canadian debt held by foreigners and the correspondingly heightened attentiveness of policy makers to the views of debt-rating agencies and foreign investors. The second was the peso crisis of December 1994 in which an estimated 12 per cent of foreign investment in Mexico fled in nine days (Lacayo 1995: 32). A third was the collapse of the Bank for Commerce and Credit International, which had concealed fraudulent activities through its complex arrangement of international offices, and the fall of Barings Bank, one of Britain's oldest, as a result of more than $1.32 billion worth of losses on international derivatives by a single trader in Singapore.[2] This image of the relentless, uncontrollable globalization of finance can be misleading if it leads to the conclusion that individual nation states have lost virtually all autonomy or control over markets. In fact, states continue to have significant power to regulate and supervise global finance. It is also clear, however, that the co-ordination of policy among states has become much more institutionalized over the past two decades. Thus the challenges to sovereignty caused by the globalization of finance are due as much to increased influence of inter-state institutions on national policies as to the increased autonomy of financial markets.

One reason that the influence of financial globalization on sovereignty is often overstated is our short historical perspective. It is often forgotten that through most of the present century states have had much more control over finance than in previous centuries. In the late fifteenth century, for instance, the Fugger Bank easily moved funds across Europe and played a decisive part in the election of Charles V as Holy Roman emperor. International debt crises date back to at least 1344, when the repudiation by the English king of his debts to Italian banks led to a financial crisis in Florence, and they have come at fairly regular 50-year intervals since the early nineteenth century (Suter 1992). Paper money, nationalized central banks, counter-trade, and effective exchange controls are relatively recent innovations by which states have enhanced their control over finance. Indeed, state control of global finance reached its zenith in the immediate post-war period, when large numbers of socialist states took total control of their economies. Even the architects of the liberal international order at Bretton Woods had consciously attempted to circumscribe sharply the role of international finance because of its apparent destabilizing effects (Helleiner 1994). Thus in some respects, the recent globalization phase of finance, at least the widening of markets, simply returns us to the situation that existed before the period of intense state building of the mid-twentieth century.

Certainly, a first feature of the contemporary phase of globalization is the widening of markets. Widening here refers to the expanding geographic reach of financial markets, partly through the dismantling of state barriers and partly through the expanded capacity of financial institutions to carry out transactions over great distances due to information technology. The widening of global finance has been continuous since the Second World War. It is evident in the progressive elimination of exchange and capital controls, first in the countries of the OECD (Organisation for Economic Co-operation and Development) and more recently in the Third World and former Soviet bloc. Since the 1960s, the rapid growth of the Eurocurrency markets—bank deposits in US dollars located outside the United States—has symbolized the increased divergence between the territorial organization of sovereign states and financial trans-actions. Access by financial firms to foreign markets, already well under-way by the 1980s, has been further liberalized by negotiations in the Uruguay Round of the General Agreement on Tariffs and Trade (GATT), European Union (EU), and the North American Free Trade Agreement (NAFTA).

A second feature of globalization, one that distinguishes the present era from earlier periods of globalization, might be termed the deepening of markets: the intensification of the role of finance in economic activity. That trend is readily apparent in national markets from statistics on the increasing proportion of financial assets to real assets (Goldsmith 1985: 136). It is also evident in the increased complexity of international finan-cial transactions. The simple bank deposits that were the basis of the early Euromarkets have been supplemented by a bewildering profusion of financial instruments, including Eurobonds; Euroequities; derivatives, such as futures and options; and currency and interest-rate swaps. Beneath this complexity is a constantly expanding application of sophisticated financial technologies for estimating and monitoring risk across borders. The rise of Euroequity markets, for instance, in which corporate stock is issued in more than one market simultaneously, presupposes a sophisti-cated set of decentralized institutions. These must be capable of making information available to dispersed investors about the likely future value of the ownership claims that they are purchasing. The rapid growth of global bonds, from their start in 1989 to a value of $78 billion in 1994, is significant not only because they are issued simultaneously in all major global markets, but also because they are moved freely from one domes-tic market to another (OECD 1994c: 55).

If globalization is distinguished from internationalization by the former's greater simultaneity, intensity, and common global norms and standards, then we can locate a point in the first half of the 1970s when globalization became more apparent. At that time the collapse of the Bretton Woods system of fixed exchange rates and the US decision to end controls on capital movements signalled the challenges to states posed by cross-border financial flows. The ensuing instability contributed to exces-sively risky behaviour by banks, which, in turn, stimulated the creation of the Basle Committee on Banking Supervision in 1974. From that commit-tee was to come the first serious effort to define global standards for the regulation and supervision of banks.

Canada has participated fully in this process of globalization, being always relatively open to international financial flows. In 1992, 30 per cent of the assets of Canadian banks were offshore, far more than comparable figures for the United States, Germany, or Japan—11 per cent, 15 per cent, and 18 per cent respectively (Clarke 1994: 28). Canada has been particularly active in the Euromarkets: from 1963 to 1970, 3.3 per cent of Canadian bonds were placed outside the United States and Canada, but the proportion had risen to 35.6 per cent during the 1981–7 period. For bonds issued by Canadian financial institutions, the comparable increase was from 0.6 per cent to 68.1 per cent (Lazar and Mayrand 1992: 7). This trend has continued: Canada accounts for 31 per cent of all global bonds issued as of mid-1994, far more than the next most frequent country, the United States, at 19 per cent (OECD 1994c: 59).

Both the widening and the deepening of financial-services markets correspond to a growing consensus on a neo-liberal financial order among national policy makers, who are themselves supported ideologically by large, transnational firms, that is, firms that operate in many countries. This consensus contains a number of elements. First, traditional international protectionist devices must be removed, whether they are exchange controls, controls on the movement of capital, or barriers to foreign entry into domestic markets. Second, international markets in banking, in longer-term debt and equity securities, and even in shorter-term securities are accepted as useful outlets for transnational corporations and banks and as alternatives to domestic markets that are slow to liberalize. Third, traditional barriers between market segments *within* domestic markets will be removed to ensure that these markets become more efficient sources of capital for the non-financial sectors of the economy.

The implementation of this growing policy consensus has required more intense co-ordination of policy on the international plane, the translation of the results of this co-ordination into domestic policy, and the reform of domestic financial-services markets along neo-liberal lines. The domestic state has a crucial part in each of these processes. Although there are still persistent differences among countries, with the United States and Japan retaining an unusual degree of separation between commercial banking and securities markets, there is a convergence towards a model of universal banking that has been the norm in Europe. At the same time, the Europeans have been adopting certain practices associated with competitive capital markets—such as insider-trading regulations—that long have been part of the US system.

The policy consequences of more competitive, efficient, and risky markets have forced the state to reorganize its supervisory and regulatory structures and to add significantly to its own professional expertise and competence. Ironically, as we show below, globalization has led to greater supervision by the state of financial-services markets than under previous, more protectionist regimes.

NEW INTERNATIONAL INSTITUTION BUILDING

International negotiations and the building of a consensus on neo-liberal policies on banking and securities markets have generally been pursued in two different kinds of forums, both of which are independent of the trade and foreign affairs ministries. The first of these is prudential regulation and supervision, which for banking has been carried out through the Basle Committee on Banking Supervision at the Bank for International Settlements in Basle[3] and for securities through the International Organization of Securities Commissions (IOSCO) in Montreal. Canada is represented on the Basle Committee by an official from the Bank of Canada and by the Superintendent of Financial Institutions or his delegate. Our representatives to IOSCO include the chairpersons of the Ontario and Quebec securities commissions. Negotiations at these institutions have also been supplemented with regional and bilateral arrangements.

The second set of negotiations, which concern market-access questions, are generally part of broader trade negotiations such as those concerning the Canada-US Free Trade Agreement (FTA), NAFTA, and the Uruguay Round. Even here, the Department of Finance appears to play the lead role. Although the issues dealt with by these two sets of negotiations overlap, there is a surprising degree of separation between them. Finally, when it comes to the building of a neo-liberal consensus on banking and securities matters, the Committee on Financial Markets has been an important forum for discussion (Harris 1995: 103–6). Canada's representatives to the committee come from the Department of Finance and the Bank of Canada.

Prudential Regulation and Supervision

The Basle Committee has had two particularly visible and concrete achievements, both of which have facilitated inter-state co-ordination of the supervision of international banks. First, faced with the increased risks to the stability of the financial system and to depositors' funds from liberalized markets, the member countries agreed to ensure that international banks do not use lightly regulated foreign jurisdictions to escape and undermine jurisdictions that have adequate regulatory standards (Basle Committee on Banking Supervision 1975). Several features of this first set of agreements contributed to enhanced control by regulators of multinational banks. The adoption of consolidated supervision in 1983 required a home regulator to obtain information on, and supervise, all the operations of the banks headquartered in its jurisdiction. This concordat clarified the division of responsibilities among regulators and made banks less able to escape regulation by shifting funds across borders.[4] This policy was reinforced in 1992 by the adoption of standards for adequate supervision and by commitments by home and host regulators to refuse entry by banks into markets that did not meet these standards. The Basle Committee has extended its influence beyond its own member states by encouraging the creation of similar but subordinate groups in other markets, most notably the Offshore Group, which includes previously lightly regulated jurisdictions such as the Bahamas and the Cayman Islands.[5]

The second major accomplishment of the Basle Committee was to agree upon a fairly complex and specific set of common standards for bank capital in July 1988. These standards were based on risk-weighted capital-asset ratios, a measure used by supervisors to ensure the viability of banks. National supervisors were expected to make the necessary modifications in their national regulations. Final and interim targets were set, including full compliance by the end of 1992. In September 1992, the Basle Committee noted that 'the capital agreement has now been fully incorporated within the supervisory framework of all member countries. . . . Virtually all countries outside the membership of the Basle Committee with international banks of significant size have introduced, or are in the process of introducing, arrangements based on the capital agreement' (Basle Committee on Banking Supervision 1992: 20–1).

Several features of the agreement show the degree to which it has strengthened regulators in relation to banks. First, by requiring capital to be a certain proportion of a bank's assets, capital standards limit the growth of banks.[6] Second, the requirement for higher levels of capital has shifted the burden of ensuring that banks are run prudently from supervisors to the shareholders of banks. This corresponds to a generalized shift away from the protection of individual depositors and banks to a concern with systemic stability on the part of regulators. Third, the establishment of a *risk-weighted* ratio of capital to assets allowed supervisors to increase their control over the lending practices of banks.[7] The Basle Committee continues to refine its agreement on capital adequacy, as in its subsequent efforts to incorporate new financial innovations and other types of risk. It has also pressured securities regulators to create international capital-adequacy standards for securities firms to ensure that the market does not shift transactions from banks to securities markets in order to avoid regulation.

The three most significant developments for Canada in international co-ordination of securities regulation are the Multijurisdictional Disclosure System (MJDS) in 1991, the memoranda of understanding on securities-law enforcement, and capital-adequacy standards for securities firms. Although IOSCO is the main multilateral forum for promoting the co-ordi-nation of securities regulation, most of the key initiatives come from else-where. In the case of the first two types of agreements, their actual negotiation remains bilateral. Indeed, unilateral initiative on the part of the US Securities and Exchange Commission has played a key role (Porter 1993). IOSCO has sought to play an important part in developing capital standards but with little result. In this respect, it has been outflanked by negotiations in the European Union (Coleman and Underhill 1995), and in the Basle Committee. The latter has turned its attention to this matter in order to avoid having its own standards undermined by more lightly regulated securities firms that compete with international banks.

International Trade in Financial Services
The most important trade-negotiation forums for Canadian banking have been the FTA, NAFTA, and the General Agreement on Trade in Services (GATS). All have worked in the direction of national treatment for finan-cial-services firms, thus concretizing further the neo-liberal policy con-sensus on global market structures. In the FTA, US banks were exempted from the ceiling on banking activity under the Schedule II category, which had been designed for foreign banks in the 1980 Bank Act.[8] In exchange, Canadian banks received the right to sell Canadian government securities in the United States, were promised that they would benefit from future US domestic liberalizing legislation, and were guaranteed that existing access to the US market would not be further restricted. NAFTA extended the concessions granted to the United States under FTA to Mexican banks in exchange for greatly expanded access to the Mexican market. At the time, it appeared that both US and Canadian banks had gained much more than they had given up because of the great potential for growth in the under-banked Mexican market. But the crisis that broke out in December 1994 has made Mexican financial markets considerably less attractive. The NAFTA also created a Financial Services Committee to replace the more informal provisions for consultation in the FTA. This committee is working out rigorous procedures for settling disputes under the Financial Services chapter of the NAFTA.

In the Uruguay negotiations, Canada generally agreed to offer national treatment to foreign banks, including the elimination of the ceilings on foreign ownership for trust and insurance companies and chartered banks.

As in NAFTA, the retention of a 10 per cent maximum on individual holdings of chartered banks will remain an impediment to foreign take-overs. In exchange, Canada received national treatment in the European Union, Switzerland, and several markets in east Asia. The European Union agreed to forgo the reciprocity provisions of its Second Banking Directive. A separate Understanding on Commitments in Financial Services, which includes a higher level of commitments for most OECD countries than does the agreement as a whole, requires the parties to try to remove geographic and functional barriers, even if non-discriminatory, such as the US Glass-Steagall and McFadden Act prohibitions against participation by commercial banks in securities markets and inter-state branching. As we note below, many of these kinds of reforms had already taken place in Canada. At present, however, the fate of the financial services provisions is not known: negotiators were not satisfied with the agreement and agreed to temporary commitments that are now being negotiated (Wilkinson 1994).

ADAPTATION IN THE DOMESTIC SPHERE

This section reviews the dramatic changes that have transformed the Canadian financial system over the past three decades. We note certain indicators of the internationalization of the state and observe how the institutional specificity, especially the federal nature, of the Canadian system shapes to an important degree the way in which this internationalization develops in Canada. We describe a shift from a nationally idiosyncratic system of segmentation of financial services towards a type of universal banking that has become increasingly the norm internationally. This change has involved a shift in economic power away from smaller nationally based firms that had relied on the segmented regime towards the large internationally active chartered banks. It also led to an enhancement of federal power, both in relation to financial institutions and in relation to provinces.

The cause of many of the changes is hard to determine because parallel developments are occurring domestically and internationally, often apparently autonomously from one another. Like the codification of international policy, domestic banking policy networks have shifted from a kind of 'esoteric' clientelism, to echo Moran's (1984) phrase, to a more formal pressure pluralism. By esoteric, he means that policy discussions tended to be private rather than public, informal rather than formal, and technical rather than political. Securities-policy networks have edged toward corporatism (joint industry-government agreements on regulation) and away from clientelism, with less supervision by the state.

In speaking of banking and securities policy communities, we understand them to have distinct sets of policy concerns. The banking policy communities are interested in the regulation and supervision of deposit taking and credit giving, the powers of, and ownership rules for, firms engaged in these activities, and the viability of the banking system as a whole. Securities-policy communities are concerned with the regulation and supervision of money and capital markets, the powers of, and ownership rules for, firms engaged in these activities, and the promotion of particular sites for these markets.

The *Status Quo Ante:* The 'Four Pillars'

Among the OECD countries, informal practice and state regulation between 1950 and 1970 yielded almost as many patterns of market segmentation of financial services as there were countries. These differences had deep historical roots in each country's formative stages of industrialization and in its experiences of financial crises. Over the course of the twentieth century, the Canadian pattern of market segmentation came to be organized loosely around what has been called the 'four pillars'. Each pillar represented a distinct policy community organized around a particular function, one type of financial institution, and a separate regulator. Loosely defined, these communities had formed around the functions of commercial banking (short-term lending and deposit taking for business), trust and estate management, underwriting of insurance, and investment banking (underwriting of corporate debt and equity securities).

Traditionally, commercial banking was the domain of the domestically owned chartered banks. By 1960 the chartered banks had added other activities, including consumer finance and term deposits. Trust companies, which emerged in the 1870s, took responsibility for a second basic function, trust and estate management. Like the chartered banks, trust companies added other activities, the most important being mortgage lending, long-term investment certificates, and term deposits.

Other types of financial institutions became marginal members of these two policy communities. Building societies, which emerged in the mid-nineteenth century, tended to evolve into loan corporations specializing in mortgage finance. In the twentieth century, many of these corporations became the property either of trust companies or of chartered banks. Still other financial organizations, which did not gain entry to either of these policy communities, gradually formed their own communities. Thus, financial co-operatives, which began to be formed around the beginning of the twentieth century, formed distinct policy communities at the provincial level. The strongest of these, the Mouvement Desjardins, emerged in Quebec, where a system of *caisses populaires* modelled directly on the German Raiffeisen financial co-operatives was set up. The local credit unions formed in the other provinces had a different structure and less coherent philosophy than their Quebec counterparts.

In effect, the cluster of activities around the two central functions of trust and estate management and commercial banking expanded throughout the twentieth century until the similarities in the business activities of the respective institutions—chartered banks, financial co-operatives, and trust and loan companies—began to overshadow the differences. But important political distinctions remained. Commercial banks, some trust and loan companies, and some aspects of interprovincial clearing arrangements for financial co-operatives were supervised by the federal government. But local financial co-operatives and the remaining trust and loan companies were supervised by the provincial governments. These regulatory arrangements helped keep the various 'banking' communities distinct, despite the diminishing differences in their business activities.

Finally, as was consistent with Anglo-American practice, a distinct policy community formed around the underwriting of corporate debt and equity securities. This function was the primary business of specialized investment dealers (Drummond 1987), commercial banks having withdrawn from this field early in the century. Commercial and investment banking were kept distinct because policy makers feared that conflicts of interest might emerge if an institution that was making commercial loans to a firm was also engaged in underwriting and selling that firm's securities.

Throughout the first two decades of the post-war period, securities markets were regulated by self-regulatory organizations that had received a mandate from provincial governments. These organizations—the Investment Dealers Association of Canada (IDAC) and the stock exchanges—were small private 'clubs' overseeing rather oligopolistic markets under the jurisdiction of small provincial securities commissions. In 1961 the largest of these, the Ontario Securities Commission (OSC), had a registry staff of only five (Porter Commission 1964: 345). In practice, this level of staffing meant that the provincial commissions had responsibilities without corresponding authority, and duties without corresponding privileges (Baillie 1965: 210). The crucial place of self-regulatory organizations in the securities-policy community distinguished it from the banking-policy communities throughout the globalizing era.

Common to the banking and securities communities was a style of politics that Moran (1984: 5) in his study of British banking describes as 'esoteric'. This characterization of financial-services politics also describes well the situation in Canada. Policy communities were exclusive and informal and were often dominated by financial-services firms themselves. Before the 1960s, reforms to the Bank Act were made after relatively quiet negotiations among the large domestic chartered banks, the Bank of Canada, and the Department of Finance. As other types of firms began to challenge the market position of these banks, the government gradually adopted a more formal policy process; the turning point was the Royal Commission on Banking in the 1960s. Successive waves of deregulation in the 1970s and 1980s were to expand these policy communities as Canada moved toward the universal bank model increasingly common in the OECD countries. This step also facilitated inter-state co-ordination of regulation and supervision.

The Desegmentation of Banking

The growth of 'international' banking markets in London during the 1960s and the liberalization of capital controls that began in the mid-1970s had a decided effect on domestic banking politics. The strongest financial-services firms began to urge the political authorities to remove long-standing market regulations in order to create a wider domestic market. Only by widening the domestic market, these firms argued, could Canada hope to remain competitive in the new international markets. Market desegmentation would permit domestic firms to evolve into universal banks, able to operate successfully in the deepening international financial markets and other domestic markets, both of which were increasingly accessible because of new information technologies. Some first steps toward desegmentation were taken in Canada in the late 1960s, and some further changes emerged in the amendments to the Bank Act in 1980. But the major reforms were to come at the end of the 1980s after a decade of debate and discussion.

In the late 1960s, the federal government took several preliminary steps that had the effect of blurring the distinctions between commercial banks and trust companies. It removed the 6 per cent interest-rate ceiling on bank-loan charges and permitted banks to enter more fully the field of conventional mortgage loans, the traditional segment of the trust and loan companies. It also set up a system of deposit insurance under the responsibility of a new body, the Canada Deposit Insurance Corporation (CDIC). By providing deposit insurance for both banks and federally regulated trust and loan companies, the federal government hoped that the trust companies could become more attractive to consumers and thus more able competitors of the chartered banks in deposit taking.

Nevertheless, market desegmentation in banking was far from complete as the 1970s began. Trust companies were excluded from unsecured lending and were thus kept largely out of business and consumer loans. The payments system continued to be run by the commercial banks' trade association, the Canadian Bankers' Association (CBA).

Competition from foreign banks was, in practice, prohibited, although foreign banks had set up companies under provincial companies laws and were undertaking some very limited banking functions.

The next round of reform began in 1974, when the Minister of Finance called for submissions on possible amendments to the Bank Act; the result was a new act in 1980. Under this legislation, responsibility for the clearing system was transferred from the CBA to a new Canadian Payments Association (CPA). Only the federally regulated chartered banks were required to join the CPA and to maintain reserves with the Bank of Canada. Trust companies and clearing corporations for financial co-operatives could apply to join if they wished. In fact, all the large ones, including the Mouvement Desjardins, did apply. The creation of the CPA marked an important step toward the creation of a single banking community.

The minister responded to requests from foreign banking firms for liberalization by requiring foreign banks that wished to do business in Canada to be regulated and chartered under the Bank Act (Pauly 1988). This amendment to the 1980 Act brought foreign banks formally into the policy community. Finally, the minister removed all remaining restrictions on chartered banks' activity in mortgage loans. Consequently, commercial banks were to become full competitors with trust companies and co-operatives in the residential mortgage field, reducing further the distinctiveness of the trusts and estates 'pillar'.

The increasing similarities in the business activities of chartered banks, trust and loan companies, and financial co-operatives led to demands for a 'level (regulatory) playing field', a common term in the neo-liberal discourse. This idea that similar institutions doing similar kinds of business should be regulated in a similar way added important impetus to the demands for desegmentation. Accordingly, after the 1980 Bank Act came into force, the federal government committed itself to 'modernizing' the legislation for trust companies and financial co-operatives. In effect, 'modernization' meant the reform of the legislation to make it more similar to the new legislation for chartered banks. A series of failures of trust companies in the early 1980s added impetus to this wave of reform, particularly as these companies had evolved away from the widely held ownership that characterized the chartered banks toward closely held ownership, often by non-financial firms. The latter kind of ownership introduced new regulatory questions about self-dealing and related-parties transactions.

The story of the long journey toward major reform cannot be told here.[9] It was to involve legislation, not only for trust and loans companies, but also for financial co-operatives and chartered banks. The process was to entail major, somewhat divergent, reform efforts by Ontario, Quebec, and British Columbia as well. In Quebec in the late 1960s, a young civil servant had chaired a task force that had taken a comprehensive look at financial services and had recommended far-reaching reforms, including desegmentation based on the idea of a comprehensive banking policy community (Quebec 1969). In the early 1980s, this same civil servant, Jacques Parizeau, was serving as Quebec's Minister of Finance. The old report was dusted off and became the unofficial guide to reform in that province.

In keeping with the principles outlined in the Parizeau Report, Quebec proposed that diverse financial services be integrated into a single policy community. Drawing on the state mercantilist tradition installed with the Quiet Revolution, the province designated financial services as a 'chosen sector' for economic growth. New laws were passed for insurance companies (in 1984), for trust and loan companies and financial co-operatives (in 1988), and for financial intermediaries (in 1989). These laws were distinguished by a fairly conservative approach to asset and liability management and by an innovative reworking of sectoral relationships in order to encourage the desegmentation of the financial sector (Quebec 1988). Somewhat in opposition to the federal government's thinking at the time, the Quebec authorities also explicitly endorsed the possibility of commercial or industrial corporations being majority owners of financial services firms (Quebec 1990). Taken together, the reforms were designed to promote such Quebec institutions as the co-operative Mouvement Desjardins, indigenous financial conglomerates (such as the Laurentian Group and Power Financial), and more broadly based conglomerates (such as Bell Canada Enterprises and Imasco).

Unlike Quebec and the federal government, Ontario resisted strongly the pressure from trust and loan companies and financial co-operatives for desegmentation. It preferred conservative policies that would prevent further failures of trust companies such as those experienced in the province in the early 1980s. Accordingly, the new trust and loan company legislation that came into effect in 1988 encouraged traditional market segmentation by setting limits on particular kinds of lending and tightly restricted transactions between shareholders and the company and between companies that belong to the same conglomerate. Unlike the Quebec legislation, it provided no specific encouragement to companies chartered by the province. And unlike both the federal and Quebec legislation it offered no incentives for the building of ownership links between the traditional four pillars.

Ontario took the further, extraordinary step of virtually forcing all trust companies, whether chartered in Ontario or elsewhere, to operate according to Ontario's rules. The new legislation, which was presaged by the

1983 White Paper (Ontario, Ministry of Consumer and Commercial Relations 1983) and endorsed by the report of a task force (Ontario, Task Force on Financial Institutions 1985), introduced the so-called 'equals approach' to regulation. The legislation stated that any trust company that wished to operate in Ontario must follow Ontario regulations and procedures in all its operations, whether in Ontario or not. This condition applied even if the company was incorporated under federal law or the law of another province. In practice then, the legislation was *extraterritorial*: any trust company that wished to operate in Ontario, regardless of where it received its charter, had to operate according to Ontario rules throughout Canada. Given other differences with the federal and Quebec governments, this legislation presented a significant obstacle to regulatory harmonization in Canada.[10]

The federal government finally tabled its own proposals in 1990; they became law in 1992, after a long debate and discussion. In proposing simultaneously amendments to legislation for chartered banks, trust and loan companies, and financial co-operatives, the federal government provided further momentum to the creation of a comprehensive banking community. The proposals narrowed the differences over ownership with Quebec by leaving room for two different ownership regimes, one based on the widely held chartered banks and financial co-operatives and the other on the closely held trust companies, foreign banks, and nascent domestic chartered banks. It demanded that trust companies raise the proportion of their shares sold publicly, a move designed to anchor a new internal control system over self-dealing. The government continued to endorse desegmentation by permitting commercial banks to set up subsidiaries in the trust and estates and the insurance businesses. Trust and insurance companies received similar privileges.

By the mid-1990s, therefore, the chartered or commercial banks could occupy freely all banking market segments either directly or through subsidiaries. Financial co-operatives in Quebec and British Columbia had similar rights. Trust companies certainly had more freedom than they had in 1980, but the Ontario regulatory regime, together with traditional approaches to asset management in Ontario and Quebec, put some limits on their choice of business activities. Regulatory and supervisory systems for trust companies and financial co-operatives continued to vary from one jurisdiction to another. The commercial-banking and trust- and estates-management pillars had largely crumbled.

Market Desegmentation in Securities

Historically, Canada's commercial banks, trust companies, and financial co-operatives had not participated in all areas of securities markets. The chartered banks did engage in a range of securities activities: they traded in federal government treasury bills and bonds, provincial government bonds, provincial utilities bonds, municipal bonds, bonds of foreign governments, debt obligations of financial institutions, and such money market securities as commercial paper (Stransman and Greenwood 1989: 34). Banks could also register with provincial securities commissions to enter the mutual fund business. But banks did not participate in the underwriting of corporate debt and equity securities, in secondary-market trading of equities, or in portfolio management and investment counselling. These latter activities were the preserve of a distinct securities-policy community comprising investment dealers and brokers who came under the regulatory ambit of the provinces and various provincially approved self-regulatory organizations. Foreign firms were also prohibited from owning these independent securities firms.

Throughout the 1970s and early 1980s, securities markets in the OECD countries had deepened with the rapid introduction of a series of innovative products that permitted buyers and sellers to hedge their risk in the new liberalized international monetary and financial systems. Other short-term or money-market securities, such as commercial paper and banker's acceptances, grew to become competitive substitutes for short-term commercial bank loans (Bryant 1987). Both of these developments in global markets increased the interest of banking firms in having full access to securities markets. In addition, the widening of world securities markets with the attendant increased risk dictated that independent securities firms increase their equity capital.

These pressures existed in Canada, as elsewhere, precipitating the usual skirmishes around the edges of regulation. In 1983 the Toronto Dominion Bank proposed setting up its own in-house discount brokerage service, triggering an investigation by the Ontario Securities Commission. The same year, Daly Gordon Capital proposed creating a special subsidiary to circumvent the restrictions on public ownership of securities companies, leading to another OSC review (Harris 1995). As the barrier between banking and securities came under increased scrutiny, in the fall of 1986 the Bank of Nova Scotia applied for and received permission from the Commission des valeurs mobilières du Québec to register a securities subsidiary in that province. The bank used a little-known provision of the Bank Act that said such a subsidiary could be set up temporarily.

In December, faced with the possibility that all banks would register securities subsidiaries in Quebec, the Ontario government announced its intention to open up ownership of securities houses to foreign firms and to permit banks and trust companies to own securities subsidiaries. This announcement coincided closely with the federal government policy paper of December 1986, in which it too expressed its wish that banking firms should be able to enter the securities sector fully, thus becoming universal banks. After several months of further discussions, Ontario and the federal government agreed that the traditionally exempt securities activities of federally regulated institutions could continue to be conducted by these firms in-house under federal supervision. They also agreed that portfolio management and investment counselling and discount brokerage, which had formerly been proscribed, could now be done in-house under federal jurisdiction. In return, federally regulated institutions would need to set up subsidiaries under provincial supervision to conduct the primary distribution of corporate debt and equity securities, secondary-market trading in equity securities, and those aspects of portfolio management and investment counselling not covered by federal law (*Financial Observer* 1987, no. 39: 388–9). Canada's 'little bang' followed on 30 June 1987 with the promulgation of new Ontario regulations and federal amendments to the Bank Act. The subsequent federal reform legislation of 1992 completely opened portfolio management and investment counselling as an in-house activity to federally regulated institutions.

Within three years, the chartered banks had become universal banks: five of the 'big six' had purchased one or more independent securities dealers, and the sixth, Toronto Dominion, had set up its own investment-dealer subsidiary. As a result, the banks became members of the Investment Dealers Association and the stock exchanges, broadening significantly the securities-policy community. In fact, within three years, the banks accounted for over 80 per cent of the corporate underwriting business (Boreham 1990). In the face of globalization pressures requiring higher levels of capital to counter risk and favouring universal banking, the investment-banking pillar had also collapsed.

Administrative Reform

As Cox (1987) anticipated, the implementation of the neo-liberal policy consensus has also required changes in administrative arrangements. These changes centralized supervision at both the federal and provincial levels, while adding significantly to the policy expertise and supervisory staff of the relevant agencies. On the international plane, Canada was thus better equipped to take part in co-ordination arrangements between countries, particularly in banking. Questions remained, however, about the co-ordinating capacity *within* Canada, a point to which we return below.

As late as the 1970s, banks, trust and loan companies, financial co-operatives, and securities firms exemplified esoteric politics, working under a 'wink and nod' regulatory system, to quote a senior federal official (Estey Commission 1986: 154). The Office of the Inspector General of Banks, the federal commercial banking regulator, relied on bank auditors to do its work. In 1978, it had but 13 employees, six of whom were analysts or inspectors (Estey Commission: 46). Similar, if not lower, staff complements existed at the provincial level.

After a number of trust companies and chartered banks had failed during the early 1980s and policy thinking on desegmentation had advanced further, not only these staffing levels, but also the division of responsibilities among the several federal agencies with jurisdiction in banking came into question (Coleman forthcoming). In the face of these problems, the federal government introduced several changes in 1987. Recognizing the growing desegmentation between commercial banks and trust companies, it established a new regulatory and supervisory office, the Superintendent of Financial Institutions (OSFI), by amalgamating the Office of the Inspector General of Banks and the Department of Insurance (the regulator of trust and loan and insurance companies). The superintendent assumed responsibility for chartered banks, federally chartered trust and loan companies, insurance companies, investment companies, and co-operative credit associations. The new office was given considerable autonomy[11] and expanded powers, and it quickly enlarged its staff. Similar consolidation occurred in the provinces.

In the same legislation, the Canada Deposit Insurance Corporation received a revised mandate and was given the power to appoint members of the private sector to its board of directors. Crucial to this mandate was the requirement that it promote standards of sound business and financial practices among all insured firms, whether regulated federally or provincially. It too expanded its staff and assumed a greater role in developing new procedures and then in assessing risk portfolios in insured institutions, except some firms chartered in Quebec.[12] Finally, the legislation created a senior committee, comprising the Department of Finance, the Bank of Canada, OSFI, and CDIC, which was expected to co-ordinate responses when the financial system was threatened.[13]

The administrative changes in securities brought increased co-ordination among the provinces and a stronger federal presence. With the commercial banks and trust companies now permitted to engage in a full range of securities transactions, the federal regulator, OSFI, joined the provincial securities commissions and self-regulatory organizations in the securities-policy community. In 1988 OSFI signed formal memoranda of understanding with the Ontario and Quebec securities commissions to establish a framework for information sharing and consultation on changes to capital adequacy. In the same year, the provincial securities commissions further institutionalized their own co-operative procedures. Their organization, the Canadian Securities Administrators, which met twice a year, set up a series of working sub-committees that were to meet more often. These committees helped speed up the development of national securities regulations, regulations that all provincial authorities agreed to implement at the same time.

These changes, however, were not well-adapted for international co-ordination. Canada has been in the somewhat embarrassing situation of sending several representatives from different provinces to international meetings like those of the International Organization of Securities Commissions. All other countries, of course, were represented by their national governments.

CHANGES IN POLICY DISCOURSES, POLICY COMPLEXITY, AND STATE CAPACITY

Policy Debates and Policy Complexity

The greater international co-ordination among states and the deregulation of domestic financial-services markets have been accompanied by both a changing policy discourse and more complex policies. In the two decades following the Second World War, there was widespread public concern about the need for stability and reconstruction based on the nation state in order to restrict the destabilizing effects of financial flows and to prevent excessive concentrations of economic power. These concerns led to nationally specific discourses about regulation, which advocated that domestic systems be insulated from international finance and envisioned a careful segmentation of markets. Stability and safety were the dominant goals: they took precedence over competitiveness and efficiency. In Canada, as elsewhere, the preservation of domestic control of the financial system was valued both as an end itself and a way of enhancing stability.

With the breakdown of the Bretton Woods arrangements,[14] territorial differentiation of policy discourses by national markets has been replaced by a differentiated but integrated set of distinct discourses along neo-liberal lines that cut across borders. Political concerns have been separated from and subordinated to economic ones. A discourse about financial services as tradable and potentially subject to GATT-like rules has been created and separated from an increasingly technical discourse about the appropriate techniques for achieving systemic stability. Complex market-based practices for coping with risk, such as options, swaps, and futures, have expanded and now co-exist with the more modest stabilizing practices of regulators. And a series of similar bilateral memoranda of understanding creates a network of highly specific commitments between securities regulators carefully insulated from the political monitoring that would come with ratification of treaties. Being 'globally competitive' and maximizing 'efficiency' have propelled most of these discourse shifts.

Cutting across these nested discourses, as in other sectors, is a remarkable shift towards more market-oriented solutions, the deployment of ever more sophisticated and specialized bodies of abstract technical knowledge, and more codified procedures and rules. Both nationally and internationally, regulators have become more interested in systemic stability and less interested in protecting individual depositors or firms.

These changes in policy discourse thus coincide with a significant increase in policy complexity in the present globalizing era. In a typically perceptive analysis, Moran (1984: 5–8) observes that policies can be complex in three ways. First, policy problems may be intellectually complex because of the difficulties policy makers have in gathering information and understanding its implications. Second, it may be socially and politically complex to formulate and implement policy because of the large number of diverse actors involved, including many very large, transnational firms skilled at subverting if not avoiding policy rules. Third, the institutions required for sectoral governance may become administratively complex as decision makers seek to increase their means of control in order to cope with both the intellectual and social complexities of policy.

The politics of complexity describes well the situation in contemporary financial services. The rapid innovation in products, the quickening of links among markets, and the importance of international markets less susceptible to control by nation states—all of these factors multiply the information required by policy makers and create constant puzzles. As our review of policy changes in Canada shows, markets have become more socially complex: long-familiar firms are changing their market strategies and structures; new market intermediaries are dealing in products based not on assets directly, but on expectations about the future of assets; and unfamiliar, foreign firms, many of which are large and transnational, are entering Canadian markets and competing with the familiar domestic firms, which themselves are growing larger. As Moran (1984: 8) remarks, the extraordinary capacity for financial-services firms to innovate and adapt, particularly in order to avoid public controls, forces the creation of more complex administrative arrangements. 'New financial practices have created novel problems of regulation. As a result both the rules, and the ways in which they are administered, have become progressively more complicated.'

State Capacity
Accordingly, the globalization of financial-services markets must not be equated with the withdrawal of the state from making policy concerning

financial services. To the contrary, as Cerny (1993) observes, desegmentation has involved extensive *re-regulation*. Complex new rules have been devised to redraw the markets. The widening and deepening of financial-services markets have also required more complex safety nets in the form of deposit insurance and investor-protection funds. These changes have forced policy makers to devise new prudential rules for capital adequacy, related-parties transactions, and state intervention in troubled firms. The increasingly internationalized Canadian state has actually increased its presence significantly in financial-services policy. Yet state capacity in Canada remains limited by two further factors: one is the dependence of financial-services supervisors on firms for expertise and information; the other is the obstacles to the co-ordination of information sharing and supervision *within* Canada. We examine each of these factors in turn.

The Canadian state, like others in the OECD, has grappled with the complexity of financial-services policy by attempting to rationalize its administrative processes. It has designed policy instruments and drawn up memoranda of understanding in order to generate new sources of information. In doing so it has had to use more elaborate and systematic gathering techniques and rely on more expert administrative personnel. Technical information and knowledge have become an even more important source of power. But to gather and understand this kind of information requires close collaboration with the financial-services firms themselves. Not only do these firms possess the information needed by the state, but they also have the expert knowledge necessary for interpreting and codifying the information. Government officials must be able to learn from the experts working in the markets.

Nowhere is this dependence more apparent than in some of the newer derivative securities. Derivatives, 'financial instruments that derive their value from that of an underlying asset or index' (Steinherr 1994: 14), help large investors and borrowers to cope with the instability of the global financial system. They permit investors to change the risk characteristics of securities and to pursue the most advantageous investment or borrowing opportunities. It is important to note, however, that they do not *reduce* the amount of risk in the financial system; rather, they *transform* and *reallocate* it.

Those who regulate financial services have come to worry more than in the past about potential threats to the financial system as a whole from these developments (IMF 1994: 3). They worry that deposit insurance and the lender-of-last-resort facilities available to banks have provided an implicit guarantee for the rapid expansion of derivatives markets. More important, they wonder whether banks, investment firms, and officials like themselves really understand these products and how to evaluate the risks involved. They realize that derivatives establish links between individual firms that are difficult to identify. Many of the sophisticated information-sharing procedures and more frequent auditors' reports that came with desegmentation are ill-suited to overseeing derivatives. As the recent collapse of Barings in the United Kingdom shows, derivatives transactions can be so large and rapid that a collapse can take place in a matter of weeks. Policy making is indeed complex.

In a curious fashion, this very complexity means that policy making for financial services in the globalizing era is still esoteric, but in a new way. Policy making is no longer a matter of informal understandings, moral suasion, and clubby relationships among bankers and politicians. Rather, as Moran (1991: 13) notes and we have described, it is more formalized, juridified, and institutionalized. The banking- and securities-policy communities expanded with a more formalized membership during the 1980s. The banking-policy network was transformed from an informal clientelist relationship to a more formal pressure pluralist network. The securities-policy community took on a more formal corporatist character (Coleman 1994).

But the complexity of the new rules and the technical rationality upon which they are based creates a new esoteric world. When one examines these policy networks carefully, it becomes apparent that only the privileged few can really participate; those few are the professionals working for financial-services firms and government agencies, usually finance ministries and central banks. Globalization encourages a 'limited democracy' at the level of the nation state, since some crucial aspects of economic policy are deemed too technical and complex for the world of politics (Cox 1994: 51).[15]

In Canada state capacity remains limited not only by the continued dependence of officials on financial firms for information and expertise, but also by administrative arrangements themselves. The widening and deepening of markets has placed a premium on timely and full sharing of information. In Canada, however, information sharing among regulators and politicians is often hindered by federal-provincial jealousies. Even at the federal level, relations among the CDIC, the OSFI, and the Bank of Canada may be difficult to co-ordinate.

First, the new mandates of OSFI and the CDIC have raised new questions about overlapping responsibilities. This issue came to a head in the early 1990s after more failures of trust and loan companies. After the failure of Central Guaranty Trust, the House of Commons Finance Committee held hearings and issued a report. In this report, it criticized the OSFI and the CDIC for a kind of 'buck passing'. The committee wrote:

It is the opinion of this Committee that the supervisory system should bear much of the blame for the ultimate cost of the Central Guaranty failure. While it is undoubtedly true that the recession had a role to play in the deterioration of the company's assets, our concern is with the relaxed attitude these two agencies took to the deterioration of Central Guaranty Trust's health (Canada, House of Commons 1992: 9).

The federal government has responded with a new White Paper that proposes to increase the powers and leadership role of the OSFI (Canada, Dept of Finance 1995b).

Co-ordination in banking policy between the federal and provincial levels has also not come easily. The Western provinces did meet in the spring of 1988 and agreed to improve the exchange of information and to consult on further policy changes. Quebec, which welcomed this agreement, convened a meeting of all relevant provincial officials in October 1988, and succeeded in having the agreement expanded to include all provinces. Since that time, provincial regulators and supervisory departments have met regularly. This agreement did not, however, establish any permanent co-ordinating body like the Banking Advisory Committee of the European Union, a step recommended by the then president of the Canadian Bankers Association (MacIntosh 1988) and by the Senate Banking Committee (Canada, Senate Standing Committee on Banking, Trade and Commerce 1990). Nor did it include the most important regulatory authority, the federal government. In addition, unlike Europe, the Canadian regulatory authorities do not all recognize each other's competence and have thus delegated primary responsibility to a firm's home regulatory authority (Coleman 1992). In fact, Ontario's 'equals approach' suggested the opposite: it was not willing to trust any regulatory authority but itself.

The expanded mandate received by the CDIC in the 1987 federal legislation did represent another avenue for increasing harmonization among the banking authorities. In 1989 CDIC set up a standards subcommittee to develop standards of sound business and financial practices. Chaired by a senior official of OSFI who sat on the CDIC Board of Directors, and composed of government and private-sector representatives, the committee worked well into 1992 before it could get agreement. Once agreement was obtained, there was still the task of persuading the provinces to follow the standards.

Co-ordination also proved difficult to achieve in securities. First, the Canadian Securities Administrators did not include the federal authorities, which, as we have seen, have additional important responsibilities in securities. Second, although securities markets were, in effect, national in scope, firms still had to register in each province, and the rules of the game continued to differ from province to province. Faced with these co-ordination problems, in 1993 the premiers of the Atlantic provinces recommended to the federal government that it consider the creation of a national securities commission. Ontario agreed and studies began. In the spring of 1994, Quebec withdrew from the discussions. The federal government persisted, presenting a draft proposal to the provinces in the late spring. Ontario, British Columbia, and Manitoba did not like the proposal, and the issue stalled. In contrast, by 1993, Europe had agreed on a Community-wide framework for securities and common rules for capital adequacy (Coleman and Underhill 1995).

CONCLUSIONS: GLOBALIZATION AND SOVEREIGNTY

When adaptation in both the international and the domestic forums is considered, the effects of globalization on state sovereignty appear to be mixed. Trade negotiations fit with the popular view that the globalization of finance has led to diminished state control and increased freedom for corporations to move across borders. Regulatory co-operation, by contrast, has allowed states to regain considerable control over private firms. Involvement in the process of co-operation has also required states to relinquish a variety of regulatory and supervisory instruments that would be available if there were no need for international co-ordination.

Overall then, we are seeing as much a change in the techniques of regulation as a loss of control by the state as a result of deregulation. Regulators no longer rely on informal relations with a community of national financial-services firms; instead, more and more of the regulations, are codified, and several are standardized across states. Sovereignty has become somewhat shared through commitments to other states. Such sharing becomes more possible as domestic financial markets are deregulated and the differences in market structures and administrative arrangements between states are reduced. Co-ordination and sharing are a means of recovering some of the control over financial services lost to transnational firms operating in international markets. Clearly the two processes are related: inter-state co-operation is needed in order to respond to the economic power of private international firms. Co-operation in forums like the Basle Committee and IOSCO, coupled to market desegmentation at the domestic level, serves to shore up national sovereignty over domestic markets.

In addition, changes in sovereignty do not affect all countries equally. In both trade and regulatory negotiations, there are examples of powerful states that have anarchically pursued policies that they consider to be in their national interest, a type of interaction upon which the prevailing realist approach to international relations has traditionally focused. For instance, the United States introduced 'fair trade in financial services' legislation at a crucial point in the Uruguay negotiations; this was a threat to exclude particular countries from US Most Favoured Nation (MFN) status in order to obtain more liberal access in those countries' markets.[16] More generally, the United States promoted trade in services in the trade negotiations as a way to benefit from its comparative advantage in service industries, including financial services. According to one US official (Power, L. 1993: 83), the United Sates would not have agreed to NAFTA if financial services had not been included.

Similarly, at a crucial point in the negotiation of the Basle Committee on Banking Supervision's most important agreement, that on risk-based capital-adequacy standards, the United States temporarily defected from the multilateral process. It concluded a bilateral accord with the United Kingdom that effectively threatened to exclude its negotiating partners from the world's two largest financial markets. In this way the United States was able to expedite the negotiations. Reducing the competitive advantage of more lightly regulated jurisdictions and of Japan was a stated goal for the United States in its practice in the Basle Committee.

These examples of power politics show that globalization is not simply an autonomous process that originates from outside and affects all states equally. Indeed, globalization is, in part, a set of policies that more powerful states impose on weaker ones. In addition, globalization benefits some financial-services firms more than others. Those that are large, have experience in a number of different domestic and international markets, and are backed by powerful states have more to gain from globalization. The combination of private and political power must be considered in any assessment of the effects of globalization on sovereignty. These effects can be expected to vary across states and financial services firms. In many respects the Canadian regulatory regime and Canadian financial-services firms have become stronger from initiatives taken in response to globalization. The relations between international regulatory practices, international firms, and the convergence of national regulatory regimes, as suggested by the concept of the internationalization of the state, have strengthened state capacity, eroded sovereignty, and also further attenuated the democratic character of financial policy making.

NOTES

The authors wish to thank the editors of this volume and Nick Le Pan for his comments on an earlier draft of this chapter. Research was supported in part by the Social Sciences and Humanities Research Council Grant 410-88-0629.

1. A bank will be said to approach the universal bank model to the degree to which it is involved in the following six broad activities:
   (a) holding liquidity reserves and financial savings and investments
   (b) providing facilities and instruments for direct credit and loans
   (c) operating in new-issue markets for money-market instruments, longer-term instruments such as bonds, and equity and equity-linked instruments
   (d) engaging in secondary-market trading in money markets, note and bond markets, equity markets, and foreign-exchange markets
   (e) providing brokerage services for the buying and selling of financial instruments
   (f) providing investment services including trusts and estates management, portfolio management, investment advice, and other related services
   Conversely, a firm will be said to approach the narrow bank model when it concentrates on the first two activities only.

2. The official Bank of England report on the collapse blamed Barings' management as well as Nick Leeson, the bank's head trader in Singapore.

3. The Basle Committee on Banking Supervision consists of bank regulators from the Group of Ten (G10) industrialized countries plus Luxembourg. It has played a leading role in developing a regulatory framework for international banks. It was set up by the G10 central bank governors in 1974 in response to bank crises involving inadequate control and monitoring of international transactions.

4. For information on the concordat and its implementation see Pecchioli (1983: 98) and various issues of *Report on International Developments in Banking Supervision* published by the Bank for International Settlements.

5. This does not mean that fraudulent activity, like those at the Bank for Commerce and Credit International (BCCI), has been completely eliminated. It does, however, make it considerably less likely. On the BCCI scandal, see Makin (1991) and the Bingham Report (United Kingdom 1992). The 1992 revisions of the concordat were in large part a response to this scandal.

6. Because capital—most of which is equity—is more expensive than deposits as a source of funds, capital standards restrained the strategy of rapid growth and high volume that had been followed by most international banks.

7. Banks have tended to concentrate their lending in high-return high-risk activities. 'Risk weighting' refers to the requirement for higher proportions of capital to be held for riskier loans. For instance, the agreement specifies that no capital needs to be held for loans to OECD governments, whereas there must be capital equal to 8 per cent of loans to corporations. Before the agreement, banks with less risky loan portfolios were finding themselves unable to compete with banks that had concentrated in risky high-return sectors, since both types of banks would have to pay the same amount for deposits.

8. Schedule I banks are chartered banks for which a maximum of 10 per cent ownership for an individual investor and 25 per cent for all foreign investors had been required. The United States was exempted from the 25 per cent limit, leaving the 10 per cent limit as the means of keeping the chartered banks in Canadian hands.

9. Some analysis can be found in Coleman (1992) and Coleman (1996).

10. British Columbia, the third major province in the financial services field, announced its reforms in 1989. These tended to be closer to the Quebec than the Ontario position (Coleman 1996).

11. The superintendent was appointed by the Governor-in-Council for a seven-year term, and the office was given the designation of 'separate employer', which allowed it to assume responsibility for its own personnel policy.

12. Quebec is the only province to have set up its own deposit insurance agency, the Régie d'Assurance-Dépôts du Québec. This agency insures the deposits of financial co-operatives, provincially chartered trust companies held in Quebec, and some federal and extra-provincial trust companies held in Quebec.

13. The Bank of Canada does not take a direct part in the regulation and supervision of financial services. In this respect, it differs from some other central banks, notably the Bank of England and the Federal Reserve.

14. The most visible sign of the collapse of the Bretton Woods system was the abandonment of fixed exchange rates in the early 1970s. More fundamental, however, was the abandonment of the compromise between the desire for liberalized trade and measures designed to protect domestic populations from the adverse effects of international markets. An important degree of insulation between national financial markets was one aspect of this compromise (Helleiner 1994; Ruggie 1982).

15. In a comment on an earlier draft of this chapter, Michael Hart argued that the shift toward more explicit rules promulgated by democratic states make the current regimes more democratic than previous alternatives. We feel that, unfortunately, the complexity of discourses and institutions will continue to outweigh these positive features of the present regimes until new processes for enhancing public involvement are developed.

16. This is similar to the 'reciprocal' national-treatment standard embodied in the European Union's Second Banking Directive.

—4—

Telecommunications Policy

Richard J. Schultz and Mark R. Brawley

Over the last three decades, the telecommunications industry has been radically transformed. Where once the defining characteristic of the industry was monopoly, in almost all segments competition now prevails. Regulation, once the primary instrument of public policy, is today much less important. The transformation from monopoly to competitive telecommunications has been most pronounced in the United States and has been emulated, in varying degrees, by other countries, not the least of which is Canada.

Although Canada began its transformation later, and at first lagged behind the United States, more recently we have leap-frogged ahead. We embrace competitive markets as the norm, not the exception, for structuring and generally governing telecommunications services (Globerman *et al.* 1995; Schultz 1995b). Regulation, also hitherto Canada's primary policy instrument (together with public ownership), is likely to be of secondary importance in the future.

The transformation culminated in a series of international agreements, starting with the Canada-United States Free Trade Agreement, then the North American Free Trade Agreement (NAFTA), and especially the recent General Agreement on Trade in Services (GATS). These agreements entailed a progressive reorientation of the goals and instruments of public policy. They subject domestic policy makers to rigorous and extensive international disciplinary forces. What had once been an exceptionally closed domestic policy sector, based on the tenet that it was the 'sovereign right of each country to regulate its telecommunications' (ITU 1982), was converted into just another 'normal' economic trading sector with sovereignty much more attenuated, if not largely displaced (Noam 1989).

The obvious question raised by Canada's emulation of the American telecommunications market and policy model is the part which external forces, principally but not solely American, played in causing such a dramatic transformation. Does Canadian telecommunications-policy making now depend on forces outside the country?

There are those who would answer with an unequivocal 'yes'. For its part the American government, in the 1980s, supported by American multinational enterprises, began to urge both international organizations and individual countries to adopt the American model. Cowhey argued, for instance, that US firms 'became the most prominent exponents of regulatory reform . . . [and] in the 1980s, a transnational corporate coalition for reform emerged as firms in other countries wanted to match the terms offered to US companies' (Cowhey 1990: 188). With respect to Canada in particular, Aronson and Cowhey (1988: 153) suggested that American competition was contagious for Canada, in part because Canada's interests in the equipment industry would lead it to make concessions 'to avoid a confrontation over telecommunications trade issues'. In the face of American pressures, John Meisel, then Chairman of the Canadian Radio-televi-, sion and Telecommunications Commission (CRTC), concluded that 'as surely as Coca-Cola and satellite footprints, not to mention apple pie, the American push to deregulation is crossing the international border,' and that Canada would succumb to this push (Meisel 1982: 5–27).

There are many obvious reasons why one could have predicted that Canada would embrace the contemporary American telecommunications model. Our two economies are among the most enmeshed in the world, and our two telecommunications systems are the most integrated in a number of ways; for example, we are the only two countries to share a single system of telephone numbers. Moreover, the extent of American foreign ownership in Canada (Smythe 1996), including control of the second-largest telephone company in Canada, would obviously result in a constituency that would press for such a move. Furthermore, the size of the Canadian-American telecommunications market (for example, approximately 30 per cent of AT&T's international switched minutes of service and almost 25 per cent of its revenues from international services in 1985), underlines the importance of this market for international business (Kwerel 1994: 79).

Three final considerations would appear to reinforce the power of the American model for Canada. First, Canada-US telecommunications relationships are outside the purview of the International Telecommunications Union and are therefore more amenable to bilateral forces. The second consideration was the desire of Northern Telecom (now Nortel), the telecommunications-equipment manufacturing arm of Bell Canada (now BCE), to become a major player in the world market. This desire was partly satisfied in the early 1980s because of the growth in Northern Telecom's American sales, but to a certain extent Northern Telecom was a potential hostage to American pressures. Finally, the election of the Mulroney Conservatives in 1984 with their ideological predisposition to deregulation, privatization, and generally free-market economics, would suggest that the transformation of Canadian telecommunications was a foregone conclusion.

The interesting question about the Canadian transformation would appear not to be 'Why?,' but rather, 'Why did it take so long?,' given the strength of the forces of internationalization in the early 1980s. Reality is far more complex, however, than this straight-line projection would suggest. It would be foolhardy to deny the influence of the modern American telecommunications model, in Canada or universally for that matter (Wellenius and Stern 1994). However, it would be equally erroneous to confuse cause and effect in explaining the Canadian transformation. The thesis of this chapter is that American developments and pressures were at best a catalyst, through the power of ideas and arguments as well as allies, rather than the cause of this transformation. The Canadian telecommunications system proved to be remarkably resistant both to the lure of the American model and to the concomitant calls for change. A large number of hurdles had to be removed or lowered before change could be effected. Moreover, a dramatic reshuffling and repositioning of almost purely domestic actors, both within the telecommunications user community and the structure of the state, was needed before any significant change took place in the Canadian telecommunications sector. In short, while international forces provided the conditions conducive to change in domestic Canadian policies, the primary causes of the changes that ensued were domestic.

We present our explanation of why and how Canadian telecommunications policy changed over the last two decades in three sections. The first will provide an overview of both the traditional telecommunications-policy model and then the major changes that were introduced in the United States, along with some of the consequences of those changes for both international and domestic telecommunications. The second part will describe and analyse the Canadian reactions to the American changes. The final section will describe our conclusions about internationalization and the Canadian telecommunications sector.

TRADITIONAL TELECOMMUNICATIONS AND THE AMERICAN CHALLENGE

Overview

Until the recent wave of technological change that is leading to the convergence of telecommunications and communications media more generally, the basic components have been relatively straightforward and comprehensible.[1] Traditional telecommunications consists of equipment for transmitting, switching, and receiving and transmitting, i.e., telephones. More specifically the system comprises equipment on the customer's premises, lines at either end connecting to local switching centres, and lines to long distance switching centres. Until recently, despite the plethora of technological changes, these basic components have not essentially changed.

As a public-policy construct, the traditional characteristics of the telephone system have similarly been fairly straightforward, reflecting a long-standing consensus. The essential features of the telephone provisioning throughout the world, with some qualifications pertinent to North America to be described below, have been the following: (1) public ownership of telecommunications companies and all facilities, including equipment on the customer's premises, which was leased to the subscriber; (2) territorial monopoly for all telecommunications services, including local, toll, and international calls; (3) local and long distance pricing based on some combination of distance, duration, time of day, and day of the week; (4) value-of-service rather than cost-of-service pricing; and (5) subsidization of local calls by long distance calls, rural by urban subscribers, and residential by business subscribers.

The essential elements of the international telecommunications regime complemented the domestic regimes. The first was referred to above, namely the unqualified sovereign right of each country to regulate its own telecommunications. In other words, the interconnection of national telephone systems and participation in the International Telecommunications Union did not affect the regulatory and political control by individual nations. The second was that interconnectivity was between domestically closed systems that agreed to co-ordinate the links between national facilities and services (Schultz 1990; Globerman *et al.* 1992). Finally, actual services and facilities are constructed through bilateral or, because of the growth in costs, increasingly through jointly owned multilateral arrangements.

Public policy for telephone service in Canada and the United States was premised on the same foundations with the following major exceptions. Both countries opted mainly for private ownership of telephone companies. The exceptions were the three Prairie provinces, Teleglobe Canada (Canada's overseas carrier, which was wholly owned by the federal government from 1949 until 1987), and Telesat Canada (the satellite carrier, which was a joint venture, of which, until 1992, one-half was owned by the federal government and the other half in varying amounts by the major telecommunications companies). To compensate for private monopoly ownership, North American governments employed independent regulatory agencies to police and otherwise supervise the telephone companies.

The third major North American difference was that monopoly provisioning was built on sub-national territories rather than on a national basis.[2] In the United States, for example, while AT&T provided all long distance services, local service was provided by hundreds of companies of vastly different sizes within specified regions of the country. Similarly in Canada, sub-national units, which were usually but not solely built on provincial boundaries, were the territorial unit for the provision of telephone service. The final major difference was that for the most part North American carriers charged flat rates for local service, rather than charging per call. This fact (in combination with the extensive cross-subsidization of that service that had developed over the years) weighed heavily on subsequent public-policy debates. And, notwithstanding their membership in the ITU, Canada and the United States exempted their bilateral agreements from the ITU regime.

In North America therefore, public policy rested on five principles: (1) monopoly provision; (2) public regulation; (3) end-to-end service, from transmission to reception; (4) universal service; and (5) affordability. The latter two principles depended on the extensive practice of cross-subsidization. Building on these principles through a complex set of relationships involving national and sub-national governments, regulatory authorities, and particularly private telecommunications companies, both Canada and the United States were able to construct a telecommunications network and policy system that went through two stages, to use Noam's typology. The first was the 'cost-sharing network whose growth is based on the sharing of costs and increasing the value of interconnectivity'; the second was the 'redistributory network which grows through politically directed expansion and through transfers from some users to others' (Noam 1995: 4).

One measure of the power of these principles and the concomitant policy system is the fact that few other countries have matched the universality of telephone service found in both Canada and the United States. In Canada over 98 per cent of the population has telephone service, and in the United States approximately 94 per cent. Nor do any other countries have such inexpensive local service. It should not be surprising that any deviation from the principles or practices that had helped construct affordable, universal telephone service would be viewed with apprehension.

Changes in US Domestic and International Policy

Over a 25-year period, the theoretical basis of the American telecommunications sector was challenged on several fronts, and eventually the system and its public-policy framework were radically altered. The United States then sought to have the larger international system and individual countries match the American changes, which obviously had implications for the Canadian telecommunications-policy system.

If defenders of the traditional system had to rank the basic principles, they would probably give priority to the tenets of monopoly provision and end-to-end service ('system integrity'). Starting in the late 1950s, both of these principles were to come under attack. The roots of the challenges lay in the development of the microwave and its application to the transmission of telecommunications signals. The rapid growth in service was largely due to the introduction of microwave technology, which dramatically lowered the cost of long distance transmission. As a result, the traditional practice of using local service to subsidize long distance was reversed. Greatly augmented revenues from long distance or toll service markets were used to keep local telephone rates down and so to extend service to a larger proportion of the population.

The first material change that threatened the traditional monopoly provision of service came in 1959, when the US Federal Communications Commission (FCC) in its 'Above 590' decision permitted large users to provide their own internal long distance service using microwave systems instead of relying on traditional common carriers. In itself, this did not cause a substantial change in the telecommunications system, but the traditional operators of that system and most of the regulatory community opposed the decision as being the 'thin end of the wedge'. Their fears were not unfounded, for within a decade, MCI, a new operator designated 'a specialized carrier' as opposed to a 'common carrier' such as AT&T, successfully petitioned the US courts for permission to offer private-line microwave service to any customer, over the opposition of the traditional carriers and the FCC. Within a decade, MCI (soon joined by others) had overridden, again through legal action, the opposition of both traditional carriers and state and federal regulators to its offering the equivalent service to that offered by AT&T. Where monopoly had prevailed only two decades earlier, now fully competitive markets were found, at least in principle. It took the MCI-induced, court-ordered divestiture in 1984 by AT&T of its local telephone service to turn long distance into a competitive market in practice. From a high of more than 98 per cent of the public long distance market in the 1970s, AT&T's share had fallen to less than 70 per cent by the 1990s.

At almost the same time as the emergence of public switched voice competitors, AT&T faced a second challenge—namely that from the resale and sharing of bulk leasing of its public long distance transmission facilities. Starting again in the 1970s, as it did in the long distance segment of the market, the FCC sought to confine resale and sharing to private, not public, line services. Over time this distinction was to disappear, however, and soon AT&T faced competition both from facilities-based competitors such as Sprint and MCI, and from a myriad of resellers, without any constraints on what the new entrants could offer.

One of the main aspects of the debate over permitting the resale of telecommunications services pertains to a second major technological change that was occurring during this period: the merging of communications and data processing. As a result of the rapidly growing capacity and sophistication of computers and their introduction into both transmission networks and switching systems, a new set of regulatory issues arose. This was because AT&T was prohibited by its 1956 consent decree from engaging in businesses other than rather narrowly defined common-carrier communications services. New entrants wished to provide 'enhanced services' through the resale and sharing of AT&T's public long distance facilities. At the same time, relying on the consent decree, they wished to prevent or at least inhibit AT&T and its affiliates from offering the same services. It is vital to note that most of the users of such services were large corporations, the very market that the new facilities-based carriers initially targeted.

If the preceding two challenges were not enough to cause stress to the American telecommunications regulatory and policy system, a third front was opened. Insisting on the principle of 'end-to-end' service, American and foreign telephone companies had always refused to allow equipment not provided by the telephone company itself to be connected to the telephone system. This prohibition included simple hearing aids and answering machines, as well as any form of network addressing device. Anyone who tried to attach any such device was threatened with termination of their telephone service—a sanction that was supported by the regulators.

The telephone companies' end-to-end service monopoly was overcome in the late 1960s and had effectively disappeared within a decade. With the 'Carterphone' decision in 1968, the wall was breached, despite efforts by the telephone companies to impose coupling devices and then rigorous technical standards. All such efforts failed. As a result the market for customer-premises equipment (including not only telephones and answering machines but also private branch exchanges or switching systems within offices and factories) was fully competitive within a decade.

From our perspective, the 1982–4 mandatory divestiture by AT&T of its local operating companies was the death knell of the traditional telecommunications policy system. Faced with competitors in almost all of its hitherto closed markets, and prevented by its 1956 consent decree from entering the new computer-based telecommunications services markets, AT&T secured the relief from the 1956 agreement that it needed if it was to be able to adapt to the new realities. Henceforth, market-driven and customer-determined and -designed telecommunications services and systems would replace monopoly-based, end-to-end telecommunications controlled by the telephone company.

It took a few more years before the second phase of the transformation, namely the redesign and redirection of the traditional regulatory supervisory and support system, was complete. But within a few years, detailed profit or rate-of-return regulation was gone. It was replaced by less intrusive price-cap regulatory systems, social contracts, and, in many states, outright dismantling or deregulation. It is unlikely that an observer from the 1960s would recognize the regulatory regime of the 1990s.

It is essential to note that the American remodelling of telecommunications policy did not stop at its borders. After all the segments of the domestic telecommunications market had been opened up, corporate users, service providers, and regulators turned their attention to the international telecommunications system. In the first instance, liberalization, deregulation, and competitive market approaches were extended to the American component of the international system. Previous regulatory barriers, protection for individual segments and players, and price controls were reduced or eliminated (Kwerel 1984, 1994; Chiron and Rehberg 1986; Drake 1994; Noam 1989; Schultz 1990). Competition, liberalization, and deregulation were the goals as US federal decision makers sought to 'mirror domestic policies in the international market' (Chiron and Rehberg 1986).

But rather than seeing their own image abroad, Americans found, for the most part, the reverse: a determined effort not only to maintain the telecommunications status quo within individual countries but, if possible, to reverse the American push for competition in international telecommunications. Only Japan and the United Kingdom took some steps to accommodate or match the American initiatives. Others, including major trading partners of the United States such as France and West Germany, sought measures through the ITU to constrain the growth of competition internationally (Stern 1989).

The United States was worried about the foreign reaction for several reasons. In the first place, American firms were troubled by the failure of other countries to match the lower prices they were now paying, both for their domestic services and their international calls that originated in the United States. They were also angry because they were being denied the quality and range of services to which American firms were becoming accustomed. For its part, the US government's aims went well beyond simply defending domestic corporate interests.

The United States had to confront the negative consequences for the country as a whole of its recent regulatory decisions. One problem was that the unilateral liberalization of its equipment market, combined with the opening up at the time of the AT&T divestiture of the previously closed Bell Operating Companies, almost immediately transformed a US trade surplus of $1.5 billion into a deficit of $2.5 billion (Cowhey 1990: 191). Of equal importance were the consequences for the balance of payments of the reductions in US international telephone rates. In 1975, the United States had a deficit for international telephone service of $37 million. By 1987, that deficit had grown to $1.4 billion (Stanley, 1988; FCC 1988; Schultz 1990).

The explicit forces of internationalization in the telecommunications sector arose in this period. The United States, supported and encouraged by corporate users of international telecommunications, most of which were based in the United States, launched a three-pronged assault on the traditional international system. In the first place, the United States, along with Japan and the United Kingdom—with Canada as a lukewarm supporter (Stern 1989)—fought to prevent the ITU from extending its regulatory ambit to limit the growth of international competition. Secondly, the United States, through the state and commerce departments, tried to persuade individual countries to liberalize. The FCC backed up these efforts by imposing reciprocal obligations on foreign telecommunications companies that wished to operate in the United States.

Perhaps the most important development was the decision by the United States to redefine the entire issue, thus moving telecommunications from the narrow purview of the ITU to the domain of the General Agreement on Tariffs and Trade (GATT). Within GATT, telecommunications would be but one, though an important one, of the trade-in-service issues to be negotiated in upcoming trade talks. The United States was the force behind the initiation of a GATS that would govern telecommunications trade, among other sectors. The purpose, as explained by one of the American trade negotiators, was to establish, both domestically and internationally,

> the right of private business users (a) to purchase telecommunications equipment from any supplier and to attach such equipment to the public network, (b) to lease private lines, (c) to establish a private network by linking together leased lines, privately owned lines within the premises of the firm and privately controlled computer switching facilities, (d) to interconnect private networks with other private networks or public networks. (Feketekuty 1989: 1)

In other words, the United States tried to recreate the international telecommunications system and that of individual countries within that system to resemble the American model as it had developed over the past two decades. As we shall see below, in addition to its effort through GATT, the United States sought to use bilateral trade negotiations, as in the Canada-United States Free Trade negotiations and the trilateral NAFTA process, to achieve similar, indeed reinforcing, objectives.

In summary, the following general points need to be noted regarding the changes in the telecommunications sector generally, and particularly in their role in setting the stage for the Canadian response. Starting in the early 1980s, the American push for liberalization and competition in both international and the domestic telecommunications sectors of its trading partners was clearly established. The combination of governmental and corporate American interests working to impose the American telecommunications model was a potent force.

Moreover, as the American domestic experience had demonstrated, technological change was also a major force in its own right. Two technological changes were particularly important to the transformation. The first was the decrease in the costs of long distance transmission, as a result, first, of microwave systems, then of satellites, and above all of fibre optics. The second was the greater use of computerization in both transmission and switching.

Nevertheless, it is important to avoid suggestions of 'technological determinism', not only in the case of the American restructuring but, as we shall see, in Canada's case as well. In fact we reject the argument that the changes in policy were determined or explained by technological change, even of the magnitude experienced in the telecommunications sector and even when combined with the American push for change. At best, technological change opened the possibility for restructuring.

In the first place, the initial cost-cutting series of changes helped undermine the traditional values, assumptions, and, especially, the commitment of some telecommunications users to the traditional telecommunications-policy system. This undermining applied especially to the extensive cross-subsidization that came to be at the heart of that system as a result of decreases in the cost of long distance transmission. Consequently, the traditional political coalitions became destabilized as corporate long distance users rebelled against being the primary source of the subsidies or the 'tax' that regulators imposed on long distance calls.

These corporations rejected the 'redistributory network' and eagerly welcomed the chance to leave that network that in-house and private-line carriers such as the early MCI offered them (Schiller 1982; Horwitz 1989). Furthermore, they supported the push for further reforms coming from the new entrants. The new entrants wished to remove the restraints on the services they offered in order to provide the fullest possible range of services at prices that did not contain the same commitment to cross-subsidize other groups of telecommunications subscribers. This was the first step in the development of what Noam calls the 'pluralistic network'. In this network 'the cohesion of the unitary network breaks apart because the dynamics of expansion and redistribution lead to a divergence in the interests of its participants that can no longer be reconciled within one network' (Noam 1992: 43).

The second generation of technological changes, those due to the growing use of computers in switching, transmission, and terminal equipment, further destabilized the traditional telecommunications-policy system. In large part, the first generation of change made one sector of long distance users unwilling to continue subsidizing local calls, certainly at what had become the accepted level. The second generation of change led to a profound reassessment of the place of telecommunications services in both the wider economy and individual firms.

The dramatic decreases in costs, combined with corresponding increases in the diversity and particularly the capacity of telecommunications services, helped produce a radical redefinition of the significance of telecommunications for corporate users (Barr and Borrus n.d.; Keen 1988; Janisch and Schultz 1989). Telecommunications, once considered exclusively a cost item over which corporations had little control, became a source, first of intra-corporate efficiency and finally of substantial competitive advantage.

Corporate users were no longer prepared to be subject to telecommunications objectives and decisions driven by the telephone companies. They wanted to be active participants in a system driven by the customer. Technological changes gave them the incentive both to reassess the traditional system and their place in it and to join with other like-minded corporate users to insist that telephone companies and governments either restructure the telecommunications-policy system to recognize their interests better, or at least allow them to do so on their own.

INTERNATIONALIZATION AND THE CANADIAN RESPONSE: FROM RESISTANCE TO ACCOMMODATION

In the light of the American push for restructuring, the technological changes in telecommunications, and the multitude of contingent factors cited earlier, Canada was undoubtedly a prime candidate to restructure its telecommunications system in the early 1980s. The surprise is not that it happened but that it took more than a decade before the extensive resistance of a variety of state and social forces was overcome. Even when major changes did take place, they were not a foregone conclusion, since opposition to such changes continues to this day.

Change required not only that large, domestically oriented corporate users organize to counter-balance the social resistance to the adoption of the American model, but also that there be a substantial realignment of governmental actors. For a variety of reasons, governmental actors sympathetic to the American approach became ascendant in Ottawa. This part of the chapter describes the conflicts and the processes that caused the resistance to give way to accommodation. We will concentrate on the decisions that we believe are central to our argument that restructuring resulted more from domestic than from international forces.

Early Skirmishes and Victories, 1976–1982

Two decisions made within a year of each other suggested that Canada would be at the forefront of countries adopting the American telecommunications model. The first was in 1979, when the CRTC approved an application from CNCP Telecommunications (now Unitel) to interconnect its private voice and public data lines with those of Bell's switched system. This decision was comparable to that made in the United States in 1968. The second decision was in 1980, when the CRTC permitted customers to attach their own equipment, both terminals and switching devices, first to Bell Canada's system and then to BC Tel's. (Those were the two telephone companies regulated by the federal government.) The decisions about terminals mirrored the American decisions made a decade earlier. These represented a rejection of some aspects of the traditional telecommunications model and appeared to herald a radical restructuring that was destined to copy the new American approach.

The prediction that Canada was following the American model proved to be too optimistic, at least in the short term. The other aspect pertains to the forces that led to these decisions. Although American forces were encouraging other countries to take similar initiatives, there is no evidence to suggest that either American governmental or corporate interests influenced these decisions. They were the result of a unique confluence of Canadian domestic forces and factors that would not be repeated for more than a decade. A brief analysis of each of the decisions will support this view.

The CNCP interconnection decision resulted from an application first made in 1976 by CP Telecommunications and subsequently joined by its corporate partner, CN Telecommunications, in 1977. The application resulted from a number of strategic decisions by the applicants. In the first place, they waited until the spring of 1976, when responsibility for telecommunications had been transferred to the CRTC from the Canadian Transport Commission, because they assumed the new regulator would be much more receptive to their arguments. They were to be encouraged by the first statement made by the CRTC on assuming its responsibilities, when it suggested that it was discarding the conservative approach of its predecessor and would interpret its mandate 'in the widest terms' (CRTC 1976). The second strategic decision was to apply only for private-line interconnection and not interconnection with the most lucrative part of the market, public voice transmission. It is instructive to note that, simultaneously, MCI was moving into the latter market in the United States. But CNCP deemed it too radical a first step. Related to this narrow focus was the fact that CNCP based its application, not on some general public-interest argument in defence of competition, but on the narrower charge that Bell Canada was abusing its monopoly power both to stifle competition and to threaten a competitor's viability (Surtees 1994).

CNCP's application was opposed by all the telephone companies in Canada, by all provincial governments, with the exception of Ontario, which was ambivalent, and by the various communications trade unions. It was supported by the Canadian Anti-Combines Directorate; business associations like the Canadian Business Equipment Manufacturers Association and especially the Canadian Industrial Communications Assembly, which was an association of large and small corporate telecommunications users; and public institutions like hospitals and universities. The application was also supported by specialized corporate users and groups like the Ontario Hotel Association and Canadian Press. In general, more groups supported the application than opposed it. Although American firms were among the members of the various business associations and other groups, they were not at the forefront of the public debate, nor do they appear to have been notably active in promoting a competitive model to their associates.

Bell Canada and its allies argued that the application was only the thin end of the wedge of competition and, as such, threatened the universal availability of affordable telephone service. Bell predicted that, if the application were allowed, the company would lose $325 million within two years and that its partners would suffer indirect losses because of the effect on the telephone companies' settlement system.

The anti-competitive case lost for several reasons. The first is that the CRTC did not believe Bell's predictions of the long-term implications. Its own forecast, which proved to be much more accurate, was that the losses for Bell would be less than $46 million. Secondly, Bell lost considerable sympathy when it appeared to have coerced the Royal Bank of Canada into withdrawing its support for the application. This resulted in a subpoena compelling the individual executives of the bank to give testimony in support of the application that the bank had withdrawn (Surtees 1994: 89–91). The third reason (and closely related to the previous) was that Bell had been admonished by the regulator only two years earlier for abusing its power by driving a very small competitor into bankruptcy (CRTC 1977).

The second major pro-competitive decision by the CRTC in this period allowed customers to attach their own equipment to Bell Canada's system (CRTC 1980). In the first half of the decade, Bell had strenuously prohibited any type of 'foreign attachment', including answering machines. It threatened both individuals and large firms, such as the Bank of Montreal, with termination of service if any equipment not supplied by Bell was used. Although owing to regulatory pressure, Bell had gradually allowed non-network addressing equipment to be connected, it was adamant that terminals such as telephones and private branch exchanges (PBXs) were not allowed. To pre-empt these developments, Bell applied to the CRTC in 1979 to change the rules to permit customers to attach extension telephones but not the primary telephone, which would still have to be leased from the telephone company.

The same sets of antagonists lined up on this application. The telephone companies and their allies argued that loss of the rentals would undermine universal service and that equipment not belonging to the phone company might cause technical harm to the network. The various business and user groups argued for complete liberalization along the lines of the US model. Again it is instructive to note that American suppliers of telephone equipment, which had a large stake in the issue because of the closed nature of the Bell Canada–Northern Telecom relationship, were not at the forefront of the debate. The main proponents were the Consumers' Association and the various corporate user groups, including American firms located in Canada.

Bell Canada could not sustain its argument of technical harm in the face of American evidence to the contrary. Nor was the CRTC persuaded by the threatened loss of revenues, which it ruled once again was greatly exaggerated. Consequently, it not only rejected Bell's application for limited liberalization, but in almost all respects adopted the policy of unlimited ownership and attachment by customers that had been adopted by the United States 10 years earlier.

One of the surest signs of the apparent attractiveness of the American telecommunications model for Canada was the rejection by the federal cabinet of appeals by Bell Canada. Bell's appeal of the CNCP interconnection decision was supported by all the other telephone companies and six provincial governments; yet the newly elected Conservative government summarily rejected it in just two days. Similarly, the CRTC's terminal-liberalization decision was upheld in 1980, this time by a Liberal government. Both governments justified their decisions by arguing that competition was beneficial both for Canadian telecommunications and for the economy generally.

In short, although not as the result of any direct corporate or governmental 'push' from the United States, Canada appeared by the early 1980s to have become an enthusiastic supporter of the modern American telecommunications model. Competition in two market segments, private-line services and equipment, had been introduced. A wide coalition of domestic customers, both corporate and residential, had been able to overcome determined opposition from the Canadian telephone industry and its small number of supporters, namely the trade unions and provincial governments. Any doubts about the attractiveness of the American model appeared to have been dispelled when successive federal governments, Conservative and Liberal, endorsed the pro-competitive decisions of the CRTC. It appeared to be only a matter of time before further steps would be taken toward competition and liberalization in telecommunications.

Reaction and Retrenchment, 1983–1990

Those steps were taken quickly when Canada adopted the American model of duopolistic rather than monopoly licensing for cellular telephone service, the latest technological advance. So confident was CNCP that the trend to market competition was irreversible that it applied to the CRTC for full public voice competition, which had become the norm in the United States in 1978. Reinforcing this optimism was a decision by the CRTC in 1984 to adopt a liberal definition of enhanced services similar to that of its American counterpart, as well as to permit resale and sharing of basic telephone services, both local and long distance, for the purpose of providing enhanced services. It also announced that it would not regulate the provision of enhanced services by non-telephone companies. (Enhanced services are 'those services which, in transmission, modify the form, content, or delivery of the information. The most common are e-mail, voice-mail, videoconferencing, and electronic stock trading' (Cowhey 1990: 190).)

CNCP's confidence was misplaced, however, for a number of decisions and efforts were made by regulators and politicians, not only to stall, but if possible to reverse the trend towards competition. Increasingly, Canadian policy makers were concerned about the disruption and conflict caused by the 1984 divestiture of AT&T (Janisch 1986). Three CRTC decisions in particular stand out during this period: the 1985 decision to preserve public voice services as a telephone monopoly; the attempt to restrict growth in the resale and sharing markets; and the failure to act on rate rebalancing, which all commentators thought to be a prerequisite for further competition.

The CRTC's denial of the CNCP application for public voice long distance competition surprised almost everyone concerned (CRTC 1985; Surtees 1994). Although the commission was fulsome in its praise of the virtues of competition in the abstract, it nevertheless rejected the application on the narrow grounds that the applicant's business plan did not provide confidence that it could survive if it entered the market on the terms proposed.

The second reversal came when Bell Canada sought and won a decision from the CRTC to terminate the services of a major provider of resale and enhanced services for the Montreal and Toronto corporate communities on the grounds that its service was not sufficiently 'enhanced' (CRTC 1987; Hancock 1991). In making this decision, the commission moved away from its earlier commitment to extending this form of competition in lieu of facilities-based competition, given that it had earlier refused to allow CNCP to offer such services (CRTC 1985). The CRTC moved away from its initial commitment on the grounds that providers of enhanced services must not be permitted to offer anything that threatened to intrude on the public voice markets. Had this decision been allowed to stand, competition in resale and sharing would not have been possible. The process leading to the reversal is discussed in the next section.

The third major decision in this period involves the CRTC's promise to freeze the amount of the subsidy flowing from long distance to local service at its 1985 level before holding a hearing on rate rebalancing and introducing measures to accomplish this goal. Although such a hearing was held in 1987, the CRTC opted not to introduce any specific form of rebalancing or any measure to replace universal subsidization with more targeted subsidies similar to those introduced in the United States after the AT&T divestiture (CRTC 1987; Schultz 1989). In fact, the CRTC permitted the opposite of what it had promised: rather than impose a freeze, it allowed the cross-subsidies to grow (Schultz 1995a).

The explanation for these developments, which indirectly demonstrate the weaknesses of the internationalization thesis, is to be found in a realignment of domestic forces in which the anti-competitive constituencies gained the upper hand. The most important development was the disintegration of the initial alliance favouring liberalization and competition. In particular, residential customers, represented by such groups as the Consumers' Association of Canada, the National Anti-Poverty Organization, and the Public Interest Advocacy Centre, now strongly opposed the extension of competition and any rise in local rates.

The residential-customer groups supported the claims made by the carriers that hundreds of thousands of people would be forced to give up their telephones if competition were allowed, since this would, in their eyes, cause local rates to increase dramatically. They also invited consumer advocates from the United States to describe the apparent disasters that had befallen American consumers in the wake of competition. Their former opponents, the trade unions, engaged in a massive letter-writing campaign to the federal Minister of Communications, as well as airing television commercials in which Ralph Nader warned of the horrors of competition. The unions also launched court challenges, which were ultimately successful, to the CRTC's decision to forebear from regulating CNCP and resellers as 'non-dominant carriers'.

In addition, the senior political and departmental officials in the Department of Communications turned against further competition. Influenced in part by the apparently massive opposition expressed in letters to the minister, but also attempting to placate the provincial governments (which were almost unanimously opposed to competition), the Minister of Communications, Marcel Masse, warned the CRTC that rate rebalancing was unacceptable to Canadians and therefore to the government. In his first speech on telecommunications in 1985, Masse went so far as to offer his condolences to the United States for what he called 'déréglementation brutale' and promised that such a situation would 'not be repeated in Canada' (Masse 1985). Two years later, as part of the long-term effort to reach a federal-provincial accommodation on telecommunications, Masse and his provincial counterparts endorsed a set of principles that were premised on the explicit rejection of future inroads by the American model in Canada. The first of those principles declared that 'the future development of the industry presents uniquely Canadian challenges requiring uniquely Canadian answers' (Canada, Dept of Communications 1987).

The final loss to the original pro-competition forces was the CRTC itself, or at least its senior members. Charles Dalfen, the outspoken and aggressive vice-chairman who was responsible for its early decisions favouring competition, was replaced by a career public servant who was much more in tune with the prevailing mood of the government. In fact, one of the reasons for the curious nature of the CRTC's 1985 decision—which praised competition in principle but in its final pages condemned the competitor—was that the vice-chairman had rejected the draft decision, written by the staff, recommending that the application be approved. As there was no time to rewrite the entire decision and the staff was not prepared to do so, the negative decision was simply grafted onto the original report. A subsequent statement by the chairman, André Bureau, on the rate-rebalancing issue demonstrated that the commissioners had heard the political message. In his annual report, Bureau wrote that even if only

1,000 subscribers 'drop their telephone service because of an increase in local rates, it would be 1,000 too many' (CRTC 1987–8: xii).

If the forces opposed to competition were much stronger in this period, it is partly because the pro-competition alliance was weakened not only by its loss of allies but also by its much more muted approach. There was no corresponding public campaign mounted by the corporate users to defend competition. Corporate users confined themselves largely to appearing before the regulatory agency to demonstrate their support. In addition, the voice of the corporate users was muted because its primary association, now the Canadian Business Telecommunications Alliance, had a very diverse membership of large and small businesses and public and private institutions. Some of the members were less enthusiastic than others in their support for competition.

Two measures taken by the federal government during this period appear to conflict with the anti-competitive trend. They are the privatization of Canada's overseas carrier, Teleglobe Canada, and of its 50 per cent ownership in Telesat Canada. It would be inaccurate, however, to interpret either privatization as part of the debate about telecommunications policy or as a response to pressures from the United States. Both sales were due almost solely to the Conservative government's preoccupation with the budget deficit. In the case of Teleglobe in particular, the fact that Teleglobe was given an 'exclusive franchise' for at least five years to offer Canadian gateways to overseas traffic, and that firms were prohibited from using Canada-US lines to go overseas, are both evidence of the continuing commitment to closed markets and an unwillingness to adopt the American model for international traffic and services. Aside from these provisions, telecommunications-policy issues were distinctly secondary, if not irrelevant, in the decisions to privatize (Schultz 1988).

Embracing the Competitive Model, 1990 to the Present

By the late 1980s, the adoption of the American competitive or market-oriented telecommunications model appeared stalled, if not reversed. Appearances proved deceiving, however, for within a few years the momentum had been regained and it would be safe to say that by the mid-1990s the competitive model was well-entrenched in Canada. In several respects, Canada has embraced competition even more strongly than the United States.

The renewed commitment to the American model came in a series of regulatory and governmental decisions and actions. The forces driving this renewal were largely domestic, including a more focused and strengthened push for change by the corporate users and, within the federal government, a shift in the balance of power towards support for the American model. Finally, unlike the two previous periods, when domestic forces were almost exclusively at work, in this period international actors (primarily but not solely American) played a major role.

The strength of the anti-competitive coalition was already threatened in the late 1980s, particularly as federal politicians and bureaucrats challenged the hegemony of the Department of Communications and the CRTC. Reference was made above to the effort made by the CRTC, at Bell Canada's request, to restrict seriously the competitive potential of emergent resellers. One particular target of this effort, Call-Net Canada, did not accept the rebuff from the CRTC, but instead began lobbying the federal bureaucracy; ultimately it achieved a victory in the cabinet (Hancock 1991; Surtees 1994).

In the appeal process, the Department of Communications supported the CRTC's decisions to order the termination of Call-Net's services on the grounds that they were not sufficiently 'enhanced' and were little more than modified public voice services, which in its 1985 CNCP decision the CRTC had sought to preserve as a telephone monopoly. Cabinet had the final word, however, and the Department of Communications and the CRTC found themselves opposed by other departments, including Consumer and Corporate Affairs, Trade, Industry, Privatization and Regulatory Affairs, and above all Finance.

These departments supported Call-Net specifically, but more importantly, the extension of competition generally. They were less committed to a concentration on universal service; instead they emphasized the role of telecommunications in making Canada more competitive both domestically and internationally. Consequently, they were able to persuade cabinet to give Call-Net a series of reprieves and ultimately complete victory when the CRTC announced that it would defer to the cabinet's wishes and liberalize the resale and sharing markets. This pro-competition alliance in Ottawa had had an earlier victory in 1988, when the other members were able to persuade the Minister of Finance to vote against a proposed federal-provincial agreement. This agreement had been negotiated solely by the Department of Communications (DOC), which would have seriously entrenched provincial opposition to, and opportunities for, frustrating telecommunications competition.[3]

It was after the first series of cabinet reversals that the Minister of Communications began to waver in his opposition to the American model and defence of the status quo. In a speech in June 1989, Masse was critical of his provincial counterparts' opposition to competition and the continued fragmentation of both the Canadian regulatory and market systems. He asked, 'Given the unified markets of our major trading partners, which are also our major competitors, can we afford not to move toward a significant simplification and unification of our own?' (Masse 1989). He also quoted approvingly a statement from one of the industry groups advocating the competitive model, the Information Technology Association of Canada, that 'the current regulatory regime is a direct threat to the international competitiveness of Canadian companies.'

After deferring to political authorities in 1985, the CRTC, undoubtedly reading the new political directions, reversed itself in 1992, when it authorized a request by Unitel (the renamed CNCP) to enter the public long distance voice market (CRTC 1992). This decision was remarkable for a number of reasons. First, this application was little different in substance from the earlier application. Unlike the 1985 decision, which was highly paternalistic, the CRTC in 1992 put the onus on shareholders for any losses that might result. Second, and far more important, the CRTC imposed no restrictions on competition, whether it was national or regional, facilities-based or resale. The market was now to be open to anyone.

The 1992 decision was the result of a number of forces. One already mentioned was the influence of new governmental actors sympathetic to competition on the Minister of Communications, if not on his less responsive departmental officials. Secondly, Unitel adopted a high-profile public relations strategy to generate and demonstrate public support for their application, at least among corporate users. In a series of informal regional CRTC hearings, the supporters of competition overwhelmingly outnumbered the opponents (Surtees 1994). In addition Unitel commissioned several public opinion surveys to show that there was more general support than consumer groups had suggested.

The resurgence of support among independent corporate users was also highly influential. Canadian corporate users now echoed their American counterparts in their demands for user-controlled and -driven telecommunications as a source of competitive advantage. They completely dismissed the telephone companies' promises to match American prices if the application were rejected because the primary corporate goal was now freedom of choice, rather than price.

The strength of the demand by corporate users was due to a restructuring of the corporate user community. Instrumental in this restructuring was the Royal Bank of Canada and the banking community generally. Officials in the Royal decided that freedom of choice in telecommunications was vital to their corporate performance, especially their competition with non-Canadian financial institutions. Consequently, senior management persuaded Allen Taylor, the bank's chairman, to lead the corporate crusade. The bank commissioned a public-policy paper (Janisch and Schultz 1989) that was widely distributed after a speech by Taylor in Toronto calling for competitive telecommunications.

Perhaps more important, the Royal Bank was instrumental in establishing what Surtees (1994: 188) called a 'user revolt' in the form of a lobby group, the Competitive Telecommunications Coalition (CCC). This group was modelled after a similar American group whose only function was to pressure for unlimited competition in telecommunications. Unlike the more broadly based business-user group, the CBTA, the CCC was limited to the largest corporate telecommunications users. The membership fee was $50,000 a year, and the initial membership contained some of Canada's largest corporations, a majority of which were Canadian-owned. American firms were among the members but were not among the most active in plotting strategy or developing positions, although they used their American contacts to facilitate the preparation of a report on American experiences, which is described below.

One of the indications of the high profile that the new group intended to adopt was the appointment of William Davis, the former premier of Ontario, as honorary chairman. This time the business groups were determined not to let Bell Canada intimidate them collectively or individually, as it had done in 1979. One measure of the commitment was the release by the Canadian Bankers Association, during the Unitel public hearing before the CRTC, of a lengthy report based on interviews with American telecommunications providers and users illustrating the 'success' of the American model (Canadian Bankers Association 1991). Subtitled 'The Power of Choice', the report so infuriated the president of Bell Canada, Jean Monty, that he threatened legal action against the authors.

Business groups were also supported by the director of research and investigations of the Competition Bureau in the Department of Consumer and Corporate Affairs. Not only did the director support Unitel's application, but he also intervened in the proceeding and retained a leading American economist, Robert Crandall, to report on the American experience and defend the case for competition. Earlier, the director had commissioned a study to refute allegations by consumer groups of a threat to universal service in the United States (Schultz 1989). Partly for that reason, and partly because of internal difficulties, the Consumers' Association was no longer an opponent of competition in the regulatory proceedings.

The 1992 CRTC decision to allow public voice competition showed the strength of the domestic corporate push for competition, which had overcome the opposition of the telephone carriers and their supporters, the unions, and of the weakened consumer groups. For their part, the CRTC commissioners hearing the application were, with a single exception, also much more sympathetic to competition, both because of personnel changes and undoubtedly because of the changed political climate in

Ottawa. Having been forced to retreat in its opposition to liberalized resale and sharing, the commission had a clear signal of the prevailing consensus in Ottawa, both politically and bureaucratically.

Among the factors that shaped that consensus were the international trade negotiations that Canada had been undertaking all through this period. These negotiations provided the first evidence that international forces and actors had a direct role in Canada's adoption of the American model. Over the period of eight years, from the beginning of the negotiations on the Canada-US Free Trade Agreement to the signing of NAFTA in 1992, and to the General Agreement on Trade in Services in 1994, Canada was involved in major talks on international aspects of telecommunications that had a direct relevance to domestic developments (Janisch 1987; Hylton 1994). The fact that Canada was engaged simultaneously in both domestic and international processes inevitably had an effect on the outcome of the negotiations.

It would be easy to underestimate the significance of the Canada-US Free Trade Agreement for Canadian telecommunications because of the limited, mostly symbolic reference to the sector in the agreement. Traditional national practices were 'grandfathered', and basic (as opposed to enhanced) services were not subject to the agreement. The FTA defined an enhanced service as 'more than a basic' service but allowed each country to establish its own definitions of the two types of services. As noted above, this permitted the CRTC and the DOC to develop a much more restrictive regime than that found in the United States.

One should be careful, however, not to dismiss the significance of the FTA for subsequent developments, in particular, for domestic policy processes. The FTA was important as a symbolic act because it acknowledged the integration of international telecommunications services and because it was the first international agreement to cover services. As such, its influence was immediately felt in subsequent negotiations. It was also important in that it reinforced the users' awareness of the domestic regulatory system and the need for change.

Finally, in domestic policy-making circles the FTA legitimized, and indeed demanded, the expansion of the membership of those with an interest in domestic regulatory issues. Before the FTA, the DOC and the CRTC were able to dominate the process and keep their governmental critics, such as Consumer and Corporate Affairs and the Office of Privatization and Regulatory Affairs, at bay. As a result of the redefinition of telecommunications from a narrow regulatory to a broader trade issue, the latter two departments gained important allies, including the Trade Negotiations Office and the departments of Industry and Finance. When the Department of External Affairs was expanded to include international trade and renamed the Department of Foreign Affairs and International Trade, this simply reinforced for telecommunications matters, as for others, the breakdown of traditional departmental and interest-group boundaries, not to mention zones of exclusion.

The defeat of the DOC-CRTC campaign to limit competition in the enhanced-service market is a prime example of the emerging power of the broader set of government actors in this field. A second illustration came from the remarks in 1990 by a senior executive of Teleglobe Canada who complained that Teleglobe had to hire a firm in Washington to discover the Canadian position in the GATT and GATS negotiations, even though the president of Teleglobe was on the Sectoral Advisory Group on communications that was purportedly advising the trade negotiators on Canadian positions.[4]

The Teleglobe official had reason for concern, as did other members of the traditional telecommunications-policy sector. Although the United States had not been particularly aggressive in pushing its model in the FTA negotiations, this was far less true in the case of NAFTA and the GATS. In NAFTA, the negotiations dealt only with enhanced services, but these were now defined, and thus the discretion of the Canadian regulatory authorities was limited. The objective was much more expansive than the FTA in that, for NAFTA, the objective is to 'maintain and support the further development of an open and competitive market for the provision of enhanced services and computer services.' Finally, trade principles were made much more explicitly applicable to telecommunications services. The three primary principles or obligations were Most Favoured Nation treatment, national treatment, and transparency.

The GATT negotiations that culminated in the signing of the GATS show the further internationalization of telecommunications while underscoring the relative shift in influence in Canada of the domestic actors influencing Canadian policy. The central feature of GATS concerning the issues under consideration here was not the increase of obligations, for they remain what they were under NAFTA, but rather the extension for Canada of telecommunications services from the trilateral NAFTA to the multilateral GATS and the World Trade Organization.

The scope of GATS is at present limited to enhanced services, which are not defined, although the NAFTA definition would undoubtedly apply. The GATS also requires signatories to eliminate anti-competitive conduct by domestic monopolies arising from their control over basic services. Finally, and of considerable significance for further internationalization, is the commitment to undertake negotiations providing for the liberalization of basic services, traditionally the most protected of all service areas both nationally and especially internationally. That commitment is now being honoured by Canada and a number of other countries, including the United States. This last initiative is perhaps the most persuasive evidence of the transformation of the Canadian telecommunications policy sector over the past decade from both the perspective of changes in market structures and the internationalization of the domestic-policy sector.

CONCLUSION

Clearly it would be obscurantism to deny that internationalization played a major role in the transformation of the domestic telecommunications regime in Canada. In the first place, without the changes introduced primarily in the United States, but elsewhere as well, it is unlikely that the Canadian regime would have changed. Moreover, the American changes provided the alternative and arguments to be employed by those demanding similar changes in Canada. Finally, the American push to have telecommunications, in particular, included in an international agreement regulating trade in services had an influence on subsequent Canadian debates and decisions.

But it would be fallacious to argue that international forces, particularly American, were the primary cause of Canadian developments. There was substantial and, for a time, effective resistance to the displacement by the American market-driven model of telecommunications of the traditional public-utility monopoly model. The ability of the defenders of the status quo to resist demands for change was impressive. Only in the area of customer-owned equipment and private-line services was there immediate emulation of the American model. In the most important section of the market, public long distance voice, Canadian resistance was highly effective.

To overcome that resistance required that large corporate users be joined by a coalition of governmental actors who, for various reasons, began to push for the reform of Canadian telecommunications. The redefinition of telecommunications from a purely domestic to an international trade issue was the primary force that gave strength to the domestic coalition.

The changing nature of the domestic regulatory regime was influenced by several international factors. First, the American experience gave an idea of the alternatives that existed. Indeed, we have referred to the telecommunications regulatory regime that embraces competition as the 'American model'. As gains were made by American firms, increasing their domestic and international competitiveness, Canadian businesses took notice and began to reassess their own view of telecommunications and its regulation.

Second, the United States successfully redefined international telecommunications from a sector governed by special rules to one trade issue among many. International trade negotiations accelerated the restructuring that had already begun by empowering new bureaucratic actors that were much more receptive to the American model. While several other departments had already voiced their support for greater competition in telecommunications, their ability to influence decisions had been limited. This was most apparent when CRTC decisions had been appealed to cabinet. All that these other departments could do was argue about those decisions that reached cabinet on appeal. With the redefinition of telecommunications in the trade negotiations, other agencies had a more legitimate influence on policy, which they began to exercise actively. Perhaps this is seen most clearly in the most recent major CRTC decision (CRTC 1994), which, by accepting both local competition and competition between cable and telephone systems, put Canada ahead of the United States for the first time in the adoption of the competitive model. Canada had out-Americanized the Americans!

Third, international agreements have now entrenched the American model in Canada. It would be difficult to reverse the decisions made thus far without violating international obligations. Just as the older ITU and bilateral agreements had complemented the domestic regulatory regime based on domestic monopolies, the FTA, NAFTA, and GATS complement and reinforce a domestic regulatory regime based on competition.

With these three points in mind, it is important to underscore our argument that the internationalization of Canadian telecommunications policy resulted primarily from the actions of domestic actors. To be sure, the American transformation supplied powerful weapons, especially ideas and models, as well as important allies. But domestic actors used the American experience, and international agreements, to their own ends.

NOTES

1. The discussion in this paper is limited to 'traditional telecommunications' as they are understood and does not address the contemporary convergence of telecommunications, computers, and various communications media commonly called the 'information highway'.

2. It should be noted that in the early years of telephony, there was local service competition in both countries, but by early in the twentieth century such competition had disappeared. See Babe (1990) for a discussion of this period.

3. Other departments as well as domestic groups were also influential in curbing some of the efforts by the Department of Communications to secure a larger role in regulating telecommunications after a new Telecommunications Act was substantially rewritten to remove or otherwise diminish the questionable

provisions. For a discussion of the development of the new legislation, see Janisch (1995), and the sources cited there.

4. The executive was André Lapointe, then senior executive vice-president. His remarks were not published but were made available to the authors.

—5—

Environmental Policy

Glen Toner and Tom Conway

Over the past 30 years, the focus of Canadian environmental policy broadened from local and regional issues to include global issues. The issues of urban air quality and local water pollution in the 1960s were followed in the 1970s by acid rain in eastern North America and the joint management of regional bodies of water like the Great Lakes. In the 1980s there was a growing concern with global issues, such as ozone depletion, ocean- and air-carried toxic pollution, global warming, and the loss of biological diversity. Our recognition of these biophysical changes was the result of advances in environmental science that shed light on both the nature of the problems and the definitions of the solutions. Indeed, scientific evidence, together with advances in telecommunications and computerization and the rise of free trade, have combined to globalize the environmental policy framework. Thus, in the environmental policy field globalization is a biophysical phenomenon which is influenced by technical and economic factors.

Globalization has caused a shift in policy discourse toward new understandings of common-property resources (from local air and bodies of water to the planetary ecosphere)[1] and the long-range impact of industrial activity.[2] A related trend is the internationalization of domestic environmental policy. There has been a dramatic growth in the number and scope of international institutions, protocols, conventions, and agreements; as a result, in almost every area of environmental policy, some aspect of domestic policy becomes contingent upon or affected by forces, institutions, or actors beyond the territorial boundaries of the state. Consequently, Canadian environmental issues in the 1990s are seldom strictly local, regional, or national; rather, they have become complex transboundary matters that must be addressed in partnership with other nations. Even bilateral Canada-US environmental problems have to be addressed through formal negotiated agreements, some of which are part of broader multilateral agreements.[3]

Because of the scientific recognition that environmental problems and solutions are in fact international and global, governments have been willing to sacrifice sovereignty to international institutions and agreements. Though a scientific consensus is a fundamental precondition to a political consensus, it is not in itself enough. Domestic and international political and economic interests will influence the pace at which a political consensus on collective action emerges. Climate change, stratospheric ozone, smog, acid rain, hazardous wastes, pollution of the oceans, biological diversity, toxic air contaminants, endangered species, and the Antarctic environment are all trans-boundary issues that are now dealt with through international agreements.

While Canadian environmental policy has always been influenced to some degree by international developments and the demands of foreign policy, there is little doubt that the internationalization of environmental-policy formation in Canada has reached a new permanent importance. Few domestic environmental policies can now be developed without taking international factors into account. Environmental policies are also more difficult to forge since they require consideration of international and domestic factors, and each policy change involves a dense array of players both within and outside national boundaries. For example, the growth of free trade as the dominant global economic approach is both a domestic policy and an international phenomenon that has the effect of internationalizing all policy domains that affect the way products are produced and consumed, such as environmental policy.

This chapter is divided into two sections. The first discusses the ideas, associational actors, institutions, and instruments that are central to understanding the process of internationalization. The second section assesses the implications of internationalization for environmental-policy making in Canada.

IDEAS AND POLICY DISCOURSE

Sustainable development, with its emphasis on interdependence and integration, is inherently an internationalizing idea. Moreover, the implementing of sustainable development practices forces countries to think internationally. Though the idea of sustainable development emanated from international discussions in such forums as the International Union for the Conservation of Nature and Natural Resources (IUCN) and the World Commission on Environment and Development (WCED), also known as the Brundtland Commission, it has subsequently become a stated goal of Canadian environmental and economic policy. It is a primary goal in major pieces of environmental legislation, such as the Canadian Environmental Assessment Act (CEAA) and the revised Canadian Environmental Protection Act (CEPA). It is increasingly relevant to legislation, regulations, and programs in economic departments, such as Agriculture and Agrifood, Natural Resources, and Industry. The same process is underway throughout all the OECD countries as they seek to integrate environment and economic policy in line with sustainable development and pollution prevention.

Sustainable development is economic and social development that respects ecological integrity, so that the current generation meets its needs without compromising the ability of future generations to meet theirs (MacNeill, Winsemius, and Yakushiji 1991). The WCED Report *Our Common Future* argued that the current patterns of development could not continue and that greater equity between the developed and developing world was required. It went on to state, 'In essence, sustainable development is a process of change in which the exploitation of resources, the direction of investments, the orientation of technological development, and institutional change are all in harmony and enhance both current and future potential to meet human needs and aspirations' (WCED 1987: 46). Thus, every one of a government's activities—from procurement of goods and services to the construction of taxation, regulatory, and investment regimes—ought to establish incentives that encourage citizens, businesses, and governments to make environmentally sustainable decisions in their day-to-day activities (Cairncross 1991; Jacobs 1991).

While sustainable development and other internationally generated ideas have clearly influenced Canadian policy debates, if sustainable development is to be more than a slogan, it must become entrenched in the practices of public- and private-sector institutions in individual countries. The Liberal Party argued in its 1993 election manifesto that the convergence of economic and environment policy had not happened quickly enough under the previous, Conservative, government: 'The national environmental agenda can no longer be separated from the national economic agenda. It is past time for the federal government—across all departments—to act on this understanding by adopting economic and environmental agendas that converge' (Liberal Party of Canada 1993: 63–4).

The Department of the Environment (DOE)[4]—Environment Canada— has been struggling with this convergence of policies since the late 1980s, when it first became seriously involved with policy environment-economy linkages in the development of the Conservative's sustainable development framework known as the Green Plan (Canada, Dept of the Environment

1990; Toner 1994). Two recent government-wide initiatives by the Liberal government are intended to address two serious weaknesses of the Green Plan. The Liberals' Greening of Government Operations program is intended to improve the federal government's environmental stewardship by requiring that all departments minimize their use of water, fuel, and electricity and their production of waste in the operations of their buildings, fleets, and lands. They will also be required to take environmental impact into account when purchasing goods and services. The intent is to use the government's procurement muscle to aid the development of environmentally progressive Canadian technologies and industrial practices, which will be competitive in export markets (Canada, Dept of the Environment 1995b).

A wide range of government policies across several departments can influence public- and private-sector decisions that affect the environment. To ensure that federal policy encourages the efficient use of natural, manufactured, and social capital,[5] the Liberals are appointing a commissioner of environment and sustainable development. This independent officer of Parliament will operate out of the Office of the Auditor General, and the Auditor General Act will be amended to 'formally incorporate the environment and sustainable development into the Act and enhance the auditing of the implementation of the government's sustainable development policies and practices' (Canada, Dept of the Environment 1995a: 25). Each minister must regularly submit departmental strategies for sustainable development to Parliament. These strategies will outline the department's concrete goals and plans to further sustainable development. In generating their strategies, the economic, social, and foreign policy departments will be required to assess their existing policies, programs, and operations for their effect on the environment and sustainable development. The commissioner will evaluate each department's progress in implementing sustainable practices and policies.

This convergence of the environmental and economic agendas is also being driven by a desire to avoid costly clean-up measures by *preventing* pollution. The need to start preventing pollution so that damage to ecosystems does not occur in the first place has been emphasized by the Green Plan, *Creating Opportunity*; the House of Commons Standing Committee Report on CEPA, *Its about Our Health! Toward Pollution Prevention: CEPA Revisited*; and the recent reorganization of DOE.[6] Since this process of economic and environmental integration is taking place within the context of globalization and, in particular, the growing integration of national economies, countries will have to improve environmental practices and design economic activity to prevent pollution rather than bear the high costs of remediation and loss of economic competitiveness.

Furthermore, Canada, again like its competitors, is trying to develop economic and environmental efficiency innovations, and front-runner and spin-off advantages for its emerging billion-dollar environmental-industry sector.[7]

As economic, environmental, and even social policies[8] converge, there is a greater need to ensure that Canadian policies are integrated with developments in international forums and markets. Because of its emphasis on interdependence and integration, sustainable development is inherently an internationalizing concept; the institutionalization of sustainable development at the domestic level in Canada pushes Canadian policy makers and industries to ensure that Canada influences developments in the international arena, and that Canadian policies reflect international trends.

Interests and Associational Actors
Environmental policy has been the subject of some fierce battles amongst environmental groups, industry, and government over the years. With the dramatic increase in formal consultations for virtually every change in legislation, regulations, and even programs, the field has become increasingly open and democratized. Indeed, it has also become the scene of some interesting collaboration between governmental and non-governmental interests (Hoberg 1993). Both sets of actors are more and more interested in international events and the way they interact with domestic policy. Because of globalization, both environmental organizations and industry increasingly want to see national and even international standards established to level the playing field for all players. The result has been a greater importance for the national level in domestic environmental and economic policy since it is the federal government that negotiates international agreements.

Business groups will continue to expect Canadian delegations to be involved in international environmental activities for at least three reasons: (1) an international convention or protocol may be seen as the best means to resolve an environmental problem (this was the case for the Montreal Protocol on Ozone Depleting Substances); (2) in cases where an industrial sector opposes an international agreement, Canada can either help to prevent an agreement from being made or influence an agreement (this was the case with the negotiations for a convention on global climate change during 1993–5); and (3) to shape trends in international standard-setting forums, such as the Organisation for Economic Co-operation and Development (OECD) and the International Standards Association (ISO). This interest of business in international developments will place major internationalization pressures on domestic policy processes.

In industrial sectors, such as mining, fishing, forestry, and energy, which have a serious effect on the environment, there is some pressure to create international agreements regarding the production practices of the industry. This is of direct interest to these industries because it affects both their production costs and their markets. For example, the British Columbia forest industry has been worried about consumer boycotts of its products in Europe caused by criticism of its logging practices by Greenpeace and others. Increasingly, Canadian companies want to keep environmental issues out of the international trading system, and therefore they are willing to go along with international environmental agreements and to change their practices voluntarily.

In these cases the industry associations of the sectors will want to take part not only in the domestic processes that lead to decisions to change their practices, but also in the international negotiations. Canadian policy makers in the economic and environmental departments will thus be urged to be active in international debates, and in so doing they will internationalize domestic policies and processes.

Environmental groups insist that policies be made openly and with the participation of a broad range of interest groups (Conway 1992; Toner 1991). This is increasingly true also for international environmental policy. Strong precedents were set by the environmental scrutiny levelled at the North American Free Trade Agreement (NAFTA) and the Rio UNCED process. In many ways NAFTA, Rio, and the events leading to the recent conventions and protocols, such as those on biodiversity and climate change, have internationalized the groups far more than ever before. As Cooper and Fritz (1992: 816) argue, 'The heightened effort by government to raise the level of its commitment with respect to the environment helped to shape a more cooperative relationship between government and NGOs throughout the UNCED negotiations.' Whereas the World Wildlife Fund, Greenpeace, and Friends of the Earth have always been active internationally, many smaller, domestic groups were internationalized by their participation in the Rio process and were financed in their participation by the Canadian International Development Agency (CIDA), the International Development Research Centre (IDRC), and DOE.

The international capacities of environmental groups have been further enhanced by new communications technologies, such as the Internet. The groups can now exchange information at very low cost. More and more often, Canadian ministers and officials will find themselves encountering environmental groups around the world who are well-informed about Canadian environmental performance. Greenpeace, for example, has a World Wide Web home page that allows anyone in the world to obtain information on environmental issues from around the world. Other groups can download information on any number of topics and suggest to Greenpeace additions of other information for their home page. Furthermore, nothing prevents other environmental groups from establishing their own Web home pages to distribute information at very low cost.

As a result of these strengthened international connections, Canadian environmental groups will be better able to hold federal and provincial governments accountable for their performance. Environmental non-governmental organizations (ENGOs) will continue to use the media to pressure ministers and delegations to agree to and meet international obligations. They will insist that the Canadian government be involved in all key international negotiations, and they will demand that they be involved in both the domestic and international processes associated with the negotiations. For example, the new World Trade Organization (WTO) is under growing pressure to engage environmental expertise in the dispute-settlement process (de Jonquières and Boulton 1995). As Cooper and Fritz (1992: 798) argue: 'As Canada's international environmental policy has been reshaped to meet emerging international and domestic policy challenges, the role of the NGO has taken on a different significance. While some NGOs remained completely outside (and highly critical) of the decision making dynamic, others became more integrated into the environmental policy making process.' The increased international influence of ENGOs will present challenges for environment policy makers according to the National Round Table on Environment and Economy (NRTEE 1993).

As a result of the creation of international organizations such as the United Nations Sustainable Development Commission (UNCSD) and the North American Commission for Environmental Cooperation (NACEC) under NAFTA, member governments must submit reports on their environmental policies. ENGOs will use these reports to pressure Canadian governments that are lagging behind other countries by arguing that Canadians are being less well protected than citizens of other countries.

The adoption of a science-based ecosystem approach to trans-boundary environmental problems will require international co-operation. Since Rio there appears to be a better understanding among these organizations that the resolution of these problems requires complex forms of co-operation among many countries. Still, Canada's domestic economic interests will be a major determinant of Canada's international positions, even when the scientific evidence is solid (Doern 1993).

Institutions

The number of international institutions that have environmental mandates or environmental or sustainable-development programs has increased substantially in the last 20 years. Consequently there is considerable pressure on countries to work with these institutions to pursue their environmental goals. As Boardman argues, 'the international level is a germination area for environmental policy ideas. Only a small minority of the proposals aired at international meetings find their way into international law or the programs of governments. But some set the themes of national environmental debates' (1992: 226). The more of these international organizations that Canada belongs to, the wider will be the range of ideas animating the domestic policy discourse.

These international institutions influence the context within which individual countries' economic and environmental policies evolve. Therefore, each country must decide how much to invest in the activities of the different organizations (Hurrell and Kingsbury 1992). A number of factors enter into Canadian calculations. Given that Canada cannot resolve trans-boundary and global environmental problems itself, it will join organizations concerned with trans-boundary and global problems that affect Canada. If an organization is able to create binding international agreements to prevent or resolve specific environmental problems, it will be in Canada's self-interest to join. An example is the United Nations Economic Commission for Europe (UNECE) and the work it is doing on developing protocols for heavy metals and persistent organic pollutants. While the ISO's work on an international environmental-management system is voluntary and not binding, the ISO standards could become essentially a trade barrier, if, for example, European countries and leading companies began to require compliance with the ISO 1400 standards. Both of these international initiatives will have a significant impact on Canadian industries.

If an institution is a good forum for enhancing Canadian capacities in science, knowledge, and innovation, Canada will want to be involved. An institution for sharing the most advanced knowledge on the prevention and resolution of problems that effect Canada's environmental and economic interests will be a good investment. This will particularly be the case if this knowledge could not be obtained in Canada without commitments of resources far exceeding the costs of participating in the institution. The work of the OECD on risk assessment of chemicals is an example of pooling of research that has improved Canadian environmental-policy capacity.

In some cases, the solution to a trans-boundary or global environmental problem that may become the subject of an international convention or protocol requires an intense international scientific effort co-ordinated by an international institution suited to that specific purpose. Canada may want to be involved in that institution to contribute to and influence the scientific evidence that will be generated. One such institution is the World Meteorological Organization, which has played such a role in the study of ozone depletion and global warming.

TABLE 5.1   International Organizations with Environmental Mandates

Institution	Organization and Mandate	Activities and Programs
United Nations Environment Program (UNEP)	The UNEP emerged out of the 1972 Stockholm Conference with a mandate to promote environmental co-operation, review the world environmental situation, and report on implementation of environmental programs. It is the United Nations institution with the largest role in the area of environment and sustainable development.	UNEP has programs on environmental law, protection of the ozone layer, environmental impact assessment, hazardous waste, potentially harmful chemicals in international trade, trade and environment, and industry and environment, among others. Several important international activities and programs also involve UNEP, including the Montreal Protocol, the Basel Convention, the International Register of Potentially Toxic Chemicals (IRPTC), the International Program on Chemical Safety (IPCS), and the Intergovernmental Forum on Chemical Safety (IFCS).
United Nations Economic Commission for Europe (UNECE)	The UNECE comprises both western and eastern European countries, as well as Canada and the US. Its mandate is broadly economic, but it became a forum on environmental issues such as the Convention on the Long Range Transport of Atmospheric Pollutants (LRTAP). It continues to have a major role to play on air pollution issues in scientific, technical, and policy terms.	The UNECE is the forum for preparatory work for protocols on persistent organic pollutants (POPs), heavy metals, and sulphur emissions.
United Nations Conference on Trade and Development (UNCTAD)	UNCTAD, with 188 member states, is the principal organ of the United Nations in the field of trade and development. UNCTAD pursues its mandate through policy analysis, intergovernmental discussions, consensus building and negotiation, and technical co-operation.	UNCTAD has undertaken to consider a topic on trade and environment issues, and sustainable development issues, at each of its annual sessions.

TABLE 5.1 Continued

Institution	Organization and Mandate	Activities and Programs
United Nations Commission for Sustainable Development (UNCSD)*	The UNCSD was established to follow up the results of UNCED. The commission reports to the UN Economic and Social Council (ECOSOC). The commission is composed of representatives from 53 UN Member states, who are elected by ECOSOC for three-year terms.	The commission's functions are to increase information flows and improve dialogue on environment and development issues; co-ordinate and analyse reports submitted by relevant UN bodies, national governments, international organizations, and NGOs on activities to implement Agenda 21; prepare a comprehensive review of such activities for submission to the UN General Assembly by 1997; review the adequacy of funding and financial mechanisms as well as the actual financial resource and technology flows between donor and recipient countries for sustainable development efforts; and make recommendations to the United Nations General Assembly on environment and development.
Organization for Economic Cooperation and Development (OECD)	The OECD is primarily an economic research and science and technology organization of the 24 most economically developed countries, though Mexico is now a member. Among its many working committees it has an active Environment Policy Committee (EPOC). The EPOC was founded in 1970 to bring governments together to work co-operatively towards shared environmental objectives and to promote sustainable development and a high quantitative and qualitative standard of living throughout the OECD countries.	EPOC's programs and activities include: promoting the integration of environmental and economic activities, developing and providing tools to assist member countries in protecting environmental resources, reducing the overall pollution burden, assessing environmental performance, and improving international comparative data and information on environmental issues. EPOC is composed of the following subsidiary groups: Chemicals Group and Management Committee of Special Program on Control of Chemicals, Chemicals Program, Environmental Performance, Economic and Environment Policy Integration, Pollution Prevention and Control, Air Management Policy, Waste Management Policy, Energy and Environment, and Technology and Environment.

TABLE 5.1   Continued

Institution	Organization and Mandate	Activities and Programs
World Meteorological Organization (WMO)	The WMO promotes world meteorological co-operation, information, and research. It evolved in the 1980s from an essentially technical and service agency to a global research organization concerned with acid rain, the ozone layer, and global warming.	The WMO's activities are scientific and technical, related to trans-boundary and global air issues.
International Maritime Organization (IMO)	The IMO promotes standards in marine safety and navigation, including pollution from ships.	The IMO has been involved with international environmental agreement setting, including the 1973 International Convention for the Prevention of Pollution from Ships, and the 1978 Tanker Safety and Pollution Prevention Convention.
International Union for the Conservation of Nature (IUCN)	The IUCN is primarily a non-governmental body seeking to influence and guide societies throughout the world to conserve the integrity, productivity, and diversity of nature and to use natural resources appropriately and sustainably. Its membership includes governments and scientific, professional, and conservation organizations from around the world.	The IUCN's activities are targeted at increasing the capacity of societies to understand the factors that control the productivity, diversity, and resilience of the earth's major ecosystems, the way in which they may be safeguarded, and the basis for ensuring that human use of natural resources is sustainable.
World Bank	The World Bank provides development funding to less developed countries. Environmental issues have become a larger concern for the Bank since the Rio UNCED.	The World Bank has become involved in environmental monitoring and providing financing for environmental projects. For example, the bank participated actively in the development of the Environmental Action Plan for central and eastern Europe that was endorsed at the UNECE Ministerial in April 1993.

TABLE 5.1   Continued

Institution	Organization and Mandate	Activities and Programs
Global Environment Facility (GEF)*	The GEF was developed in 1990 before the Rio UNCED. However, at Rio the GEF was assigned an important role for administering multilateral environmental aid under the auspices of the World Bank. The focus of the aid is in support of various international environmental agreements.	The GEF's activities support adjustment projects in less developed countries which are required by international environmental conventions and protocols, such as the Climate Change Convention, Biodiversity Convention, and the Montreal Protocol.
North American Commission on Environmental Co-operation (NACEC)*	The NACEC was established by the North American Agreement on Environmental Cooperation (NAAEC). The NAAEC supplements NAFTA and commits the parties to a series of obligations and institutions intended to advance both environmental protection and the environmental sustainability of NAFTA-related trade.	The NACEC has a range of responsibilities, including co-operation and capacity building for the development and implementation of environmental policies; public inquiry and comment concerning the fulfilment of environmental goals in the NAFTA countries; and encouraging the enforcement of national laws in the area of the environment.
Group of Seven (G7) Economic Summits	The G7 economic summits bring leaders from Britain, Canada, France, Germany, Italy, Japan, and the United States together to address pressing issues of the day and advance the process of finding solutions to them. Over the past 20 years environmental issues have appeared more frequently on the G7 summit agendas.	Sustainable development, international institutional reform, and related issues of trade and environment were chosen as important issues for consideration during the 1995 G7 Summit held in Halifax. G7 governments also held their third stand-alone meeting of environment ministers in Hamilton between 29 April and 1 May 1995. The ministers focused on environment-economy integration, global environmental priorities, and international institutions relevant to environmental issues.

TABLE 5.1   Continued

Institution	Organization and Mandate	Activities and Programs
World Trade Organization (WTO)*	The WTO was formed out of the Uruguay Round of trade negotiations for the General Agreement on Tariffs and Trade. The WTO is responsible for administering the GATT and the other trade agreements that came out of the Uruguay Round.	A Trade and Environment Committee was established under the WTO to investigate the relationship between GATT trade rules and environmental standards. There are a range of complex and technical trade and environment issues on the Committee's agenda.
International Standards Organization (ISO)	The ISO is an international standard-setting body based in Geneva, whose membership comprises the principal standardization body in each of approximately 90 countries. Its mission is to promote the development of standardization and related activities in the world with a view to facilitating the international exchange of goods and services, and to developing co-operation in the spheres of intellectual, scientific, technological, and economic activity.	ISO's work results in international agreements which are published as international standards. ISO standards are well recognized around the world and are often adopted for national rules and regulations. ISO is completing standards for environmental management systems, the so-called ISO 14000 Series. Other standards under development include life-cycle analysis, environmental labelling, environmental-performance evaluation, environmental auditing, and environmental aspects in product standards. It is expected that it will also be asked to develop standards for site remediation, environmental-risk assessment, environmental-performance reporting, and resource and conservation management.
World Health Organization (WHO)	WHO is based in Geneva and has 170 member states. Its basic goal is the attainment by all peoples of the highest possible levels of health.	The WHO's activities include the work on hazardous substances under the International Program on Chemical Safety (IPCS), environmental protection, and occupational health and safety issues. The WHO has also developed a strategy for Health and the Environment.

TABLE 5.1 Continued

Institution	Organization and Mandate	Activities and Programs
Organization of American States (OAS)*	The OAS is the oldest regional organization in the world and has 35 member states. The mandate of the OAS is essentially to strengthen the peace and security of the continent, promote and consolidate representative democracy, and promote co-operation for economic, social, and cultural development.	The Summit of the Americas held in Miami in December 1994 resulted in the OAS having an increased hemispheric environmental role. As a result, the OAS is establishing a new Environment Unit. The unit will stress co-operation and capacity building in the conservation and sustainable use of natural resources
International Joint Commission (IJC)	The IJC was established by the 1909 Canada-US Boundary Waters Treaty. The commission has six members with a mandate to follow the treaty as they work to prevent and resolve boundary water disputes. More than 20 boards, made up of experts from Canada and the US, have been established to help the IJC carry out its responsibilities.	When asked by governments, the IJC investigates pollution problems in lakes and rivers along the Canada-US border. The governments can also ask the commission to monitor situations and to recommend actions. Most of the IJC's work has focused on the Great Lakes-St Lawrence River system. However, in addition to water issues, the governments have asked the IJC to bring to their attention, or to investigate, air pollution problems in boundary regions.
United Nations Development Programme (UNDP)	The United Nations Development Programme was created in 1965 and is the world's largest multilateral source of grant funding for development co-operation. The UNDP has three overriding goals: to help the UN nations become a powerful and cohesive force for sustainable human development; to focus its resources on poverty elimination, environmental regeneration, job creation, and advancement of women; and to strengthen international co-operation for sustainable human development and serve as a major resource on how to achieve it.	The UNDP has a range of environmental programs targeted at building environmental protection capacity within less developed countries.

* New institutions or institutions with relatively new environmental mandates.

Like other developed countries, Canada is looking for opportunities to advance the economic prospects of its environmental industry. If an international institution can provide such opportunities, Canada would view it as promoting both environmental- and economic-policy goals. International standard setting under the ISO and co-operative initiatives under NACEC could serve such a purpose. In some cases, Canada's prime motive for being involved with an international institution will be defensive, to protect its economic interests with respect to environmental and economic decisions made internationally or in other countries. Canada's interest in an international sustainable-forestry agreement is, at least in part, to avoid being boycotted.

Because of its membership, composition, and bureaucratic character, an international organization may be able to achieve some international goals but not others. Countries will therefore make various calculations as to which agency they might want to be involved with either to speed up or slow down a particular environmental measure. For example, it is more difficult to reach a consensus in UNEP than in the relatively homogeneous OECD or UNECE. International organizations are also easily bound up in dense realms of international bureaucracy, which varies in degree among organizations.

Canada may want to support an organization in order to maintain long-standing, well-established relationships or to form new relationships in newer organizations, such as the Asia Pacific Economic Cooperation (APEC) and NACEC. Thus, there are a number of reasons for Canada to join international organizations active in the environment and sustainable development areas. Moreover, as the number of trans-boundary and global issues grow, so do the number of international organizations, conventions, and protocols to address them. These two factors combined lead to a stronger pull on domestic policy makers to take international considerations into account in domestic environmental policy.

Recent Domestic Policy Reviews

During its first 15 months in power, the Liberal government subjected all federal departments to a systematic program review, which culminated in the February 1995 budget. In 1994 it undertook a major review of foreign policy. In June 1995 the House of Commons Standing Committee released its statutory review of the Environmental Protection Act. These two reviews combined to raise the importance of the international dimension in domestic environmental policy at the same time that questions were being asked about policy capacity after the budget cuts that resulted from program review.

The foreign-policy review placed considerable importance on international sustainable development issues. Indeed, Canada committed itself to making sustainable development a pillar of Canadian foreign policy. If it fulfils that commitment, there will be increasing pressure on DOE and economic-development departments to be involved in foreign policy initiatives. Departments will be held accountable by the Environmental Commissioner for the international activities that are a part of its sustainable-development mandate.

The review acknowledges that Canada's international image has been tarnished by bad publicity about the way it has been treating its own environment. For example, domestic policy regarding forestry practices, fisheries management, and environmental assessment, often at the provincial level, has had an influence on international trade and foreign policy. The chapters of the review on shared security argue that domestic policies on environment, trade, and development assistance have an effect on international security by influencing international developments. Building shared security involves creating a long-term international trade and investment agenda that focuses the WTO's attention on issues such as agricultural export subsidies, labour standards, anti-dumping actions, and other domestic practices that harm the environment.

The emergence of free trade as the dominant global eonomic strategy means that economic policies that influence the environment-economy relationship now have international significance. Canada's strong commitment to Canada-US and North American free trade, as well as its support for broadening freer trade arrangements in the hemisphere and globally, means that Canada has to develop its environmental policies with an eye on the standards and regulatory approaches of its trading partners. Harmonized standards developed in international standard-setting bodies, such as the ISO, and international obligations under international trade agreements, such as GATT and NAFTA, are important. Governments also have to pay attention to budgetary and subsidy practices and reforms in competitor countries (IISD 1994). In each case, domestic environmental policy is influenced by international trade and economic factors; so, in turn, Canada must try to influence international developments in order that they will promote rather than hinder domestic environmental goals. This requires a substantial, ongoing and co-ordinated international role and domestic interests will push the Canadian government to be directly involved.

In the chapter on sustainable development, the foreign-policy review notes that the basic elements of an international system of rules and institutions on sustainable development have begun to emerge since UNCED.

As more and more decisions about what and how we produce and trade are governed by international rules, Canadian business interests are promoting the development of common rules on trade and the environment to protect Canada from any trading partner that might be tempted to use the environment as a pretext for erecting protectionist barriers. On the other hand, environmentalists want to ensure that trade rules do not unnecessarily restrict environmental policies. To strike a balance between these two positions, the bilateral, regional, and multilateral institutions that promote sustainable development must be strengthened, and these institutions must be made efficient and accountable (CCME 1993). This will require strong alliances and new approaches to common problems, as domestic environmental and industrial interests push the Canadian government to be active in, and indeed in the forefront of, such international activities. Yet Canada may be prevented by fiscal pressures from meeting the growing costs of its international environmental obligations.

Paradoxically, the range of international environmental issues requiring action by the federal government has grown significantly at the same time as budgets have been cut. Simultaneously, the policy capacity of all departments is being challenged by changes in the nature of policy process with pressure for more pre-decision consultation, formal multi-stakeholder follow-up, and consistent linking with related issues across government (Canada, House of Commons, Standing Committee on Environment and Sustainable Development 1995). Such changes require increased expenditures and staff time during a period of budget cuts. For example, the 1994 program review and 1995 federal budget resulted in cuts of 32 per cent to Environment Canada's budget and staff over the 1995–8 period. For the same period, the cuts for Industry Canada were 45 per cent, Fisheries and Oceans 28 per cent, Natural Resources 50 per cent, Agriculture and Agri-Food 20 per cent, and Foreign Affairs and International Trade, 18 per cent (Canada, Dept of Finance 1995c: 9).

With the decline in fiscal resources and the review of the Environmental Protection Act, the federal government has had to reassess the federal role in environmental protection in relation to that of the provinces. Although there are still unanswered questions about how national standards on toxic substances will be set and enforced, the federal government will likely continue its commitments to international environmental policy, scientific research, federal leadership in pollution prevention, and integration of environmental matters into economic and social policy at the federal level. The 1995 budget, like the foreign-policy review, referred to international policy as one of the areas where the federal government can make a large contribution to environmental protection and sustainable development.

Its about Our Health! listed a broad range of domestic environmental and economic issues that are causing environmental policy to be increasingly internationalized. While international commitments on air and water pollution, hazardous wastes, biodiversity, and trade were identified as *pulling* Canadian environmental policy internationally, policies on the North, biotechnology, the management of coastal zones, and toxics are *pushing* Canadian policy in the direction of internationalization. *Its about Our Health!* reasserts the need for a strong federal presence in this area.

There is little doubt, however, that it will be difficult to persuade the provincial governments to agree. 'While the federal government acts as Canada's representative in multilateral bodies, and as the authoritative actor for the negotiation of international environmental agreements, the provinces have responsibility for the implementation of international agreements where the subject matter falls within their sphere of legislative jurisdiction' (Boardmore 1992: 242; Doern and Conway 1994).

This is a particularly Canadian conundrum. The constitution does not explicitly give jurisdiction over the environment to either the federal or the provincial governments. Hence, jurisdictional authority has to be inferred from the division of powers that are explicitly enumerated in the constitution. Section 92 outlines a number of provincial powers, such as local works and undertakings, property and civil rights within the province, matters of a local or private nature, and authority over provincially owned lands and resources. In a 1982 amendment, the provinces were given exclusive jurisdiction over the development, conservation, and management of non-renewable resources in the province, including forests and hydroelectric facilities.

The federal authority over the environment rests on its responsibility for federal lands and facilities and on powers enumerated in sections 91 and 92(10), such as trade and commerce, sea coasts and inland fisheries, navigation and shipping, Indian lands, and interprovincial and international transportation. Federal criminal law and the 'peace, order and good government' powers have also been relevant to environmental protection. Given the increased importance of trans-boundary environmental issues and the globalization of trade, it is likely that federal powers over international trade and commerce will become an increasingly important lever to allow the federal government to meet international commitments.

Nevertheless the importance in the Canadian political economy of resource development and provincial jurisdiction over resource development means that provincial interest in international environmental issues is likely to continue to grow. However, the degree of provincial government concern will depend on what the international obligations might imply for change at the provincial level, and on the local importance of the issue being addressed internationally (Harrison 1994). Working with the provinces will also require increased commitments of resources as provinces urge the federal government to take particular positions in international forums.

Increasingly, federal officials are required to consult and brief business and environmental groups and provincial officials before, during, and after international negotiations and activities. Business, environmental groups, and various provinces may also expect to be represented on the delegations to international meetings. DOE, Foreign Affairs, Fisheries and Oceans, Agriculture and Agri-food, and Natural Resources, for example, will have to become more sophisticated at managing these demands, which are part of conducting sustainable-development policy in the 1990s. Such demands from domestic interests push domestic environmental policies and processes further in the direction of internationalization.

Instruments

In the international arena environmental relations are governed by bilateral and multilateral agreements. An international agreement can be something as basic as a statement agreed to among ministers or as formal as a convention or protocol. Conventions are international pacts in which the signatories commit themselves to long-term principles and some initial actions. Conventions may at first contain detailed provisions, but later become frameworks within which one or more protocols are negotiated. Protocols contain even more precise commitments backed up by some form of sanction and implementation regime. Some are created under the auspices of existing international organizations, whereas others create the need for a new institutional actor (Birnie and Boyle 1992).

Political efforts to address global and trans-boundary issues have resulted in the creation of a range of international agreements. Canada is a signatory to over a hundred legally binding multilateral and bilateral agreements that have important implications for domestic environmental and economic policy. Such agreements are increasingly important as the globalization of environmental stresses and economic actors dictates the need for trans-boundary solutions. As Tables 5.2 and 5.3 show, more and more decisions about the production, consumption, transportation, trade, and management of economic and environmental resources are being influenced by international agreements. This underscores the need for Canada to be involved so as to influence these international decisions and prevent injury to domestic interests. Such a requirement necessarily draws Canadian public- and private-sector decision makers further into the international orbit, thereby further internationalizing domestic policies and their processes.

As Tables 5.2 and 5.3 show, during the past decade the setting of conventions, protocols, and other agreements has become a prominent feature of international environmental relations. Canada takes part in such arrangements for a variety of reasons. If the problem being addressed has significant environmental or economic effects on Canada, Canadian decision makers will want to decide if the agreement provides the best means to achieve Canadian policy goals, including protection of the global commons. This assessment is balanced against the environmental and economic costs of not being party to an international agreement.

The processes surrounding these agreements are complex, time-consuming, and expensive (see Table 5.4). Once created, the agreements are managed by international institutions, and involvement with them tends to beget further international involvement. All of these agreements put pressure on domestic policy makers to find the money and staff to administer them, and all establish a new set of international constraints on domestic policy. The many stages in the development and implementation of international agreements require the involvement of the appropriate federal technical department as well as Foreign Affairs and International Trade (DFAIT), and likely Environment Canada. Such processes clearly demand a long-term commitment.

As well as these formal arrangements, there are informal arrangements that affect Canada's international commitments and therefore our domestic environment policy. Various loose alliances of countries emerge around environmental issues. While these alliances are not the solid blocs characteristic of security matters or trade agreements, they nevertheless become important at various stages of international policy development and sometimes lead to the establishment of new international instruments (Porter and Brown 1991).

The various international-agreement-setting processes discussed above tend to create coalitions and alliances. On some issues Canada may find itself in the OECD block with Japan, the EC countries, and the United States. On other issues Canada will line up with Australia and New Zealand, or with those countries and Japan and the United States, or even with one or two countries from the G77 group of developing countries. The alliance will depend on the particular hazard being dealt with and how it affects different countries.

Something as widespread as global warming, unlike a more regional issue like acid rain, is unlikely to produce a simple or stable coalition for Canada to work with. In the case of acid rain, Canada, as a receiver of US emissions, found a natural alliance with the Nordic countries, which were on the receiving end of acid rain from Britain and Europe. Indeed, over the years, Canada has often been in alliance with the Nordic bloc.

TABLE 5.2   Selected Multilateral Conventions and Agreements

Title	Objective
1. United Nations Framework Convention on Climate Change, Rio de Janeiro, 1992.	Stabilize the concentrations of greenhouse gases in the atmosphere at a level that impedes human interference with the climate, enables ecosystems to adjust naturally, and ensures their perpetuity.
2. United Nations Biodiversity Convention, Rio de Janeiro, 1992.	Ensure the preservation of biological diversity, sustainable use of its components, and fair and equitable sharing of the profits generated by exploiting genetic resources through, for example, adequate access to these resources and appropriate transfer of related techniques that take into account all rights to these resources and techniques, and adequate funding.
3. Declaration on Protection of the Arctic Environment, Rovaniemi, 1991.	Establish, in the framework of an Arctic Environment Protection Strategy, a joint-action plan in the areas of scientific co-operation, assessment of the possible effects of development on the environment, and application of measures to control pollutants and reduce their harmful effects on the Arctic environment.
4. Basel Convention on the Control of Transboundary Movements of Hazardous Wastes and Their Disposal, 1989.	Minimize the production and trans-boundary movements of hazardous wastes, regulate exports and imports of hazardous wastes by enforcing the requirement to obtain official consent from the importing country, and establish a monitoring system from point of production to point of disposal.
5. Vienna Convention for the Protection of the Ozone Layer, Vienna, 1985.	Protect human and environmental health from the harmful effects of changes in the ozone layer.
6. Montréal Protocol on Substances that Deplete the Ozone Layer, 1987.	Protect the ozone layer by taking measures to regulate global emissions of substances that deplete it, in the context of the Vienna Convention for the Protection of the Ozone Layer.

TABLE 5.2 Continued

Title	Objective
7. Convention on Long-range Transboundary Air Pollution, Geneva, 1979.	Make every effort to limit as much as possible and prevent air pollution, including long-range trans-boundary air pollution.
8. Convention on International Trade in Endangered Species of Wild Fauna and Flora, Washington, 1973 (amended at Bonn in 1979 and at Gaborone in 1983).	Protect specific endangered species from over-exploitation through a system of import and export permits.
9. Convention on the Prevention of Marine Pollution by Dumping of Wastes and Other Matter, London, Mexico, Moscow and Washington, 1972 (amended in London in 1978 and 1980).	Combat marine pollution resulting from dumping operations and promote regional agreements to complement the existing convention.
10. Convention on Wetlands of International Importance Especially as a Waterfowl Habitat, Ramsar, 1971 (amended in 1982).	Halt encroachment into and progressive loss of wetlands, taking into account the basic ecological functions of wetlands and their economic, cultural, scientific, and recreational value.

TABLE 5.3 Selected Bilateral Conventions and Agreements

Title	Objective
1. Memorandum of Understanding (MOU) between Environment Canada and the Ministry of Environment of Germany in Collaboration in Environmental Policy, 1990.	Promote co-operation on environment policy and complement the joint scientific and technical activities under the Science and Technology Agreement.
2. MOU between the Department of the Environment of Canada and the National Environmental Protection Agency (NEPA) of the People's Republic of China on Cooperation on Environmental Matters (1993).	Broaden the scope of existing environmental co-operation with China, especially in the context of the MOU on meteorology signed in 1986 between AES and the State Meteorological Agency of China. Specifies nine sectors of co-operation, including pollution control, development of policies and programs on sustainable development, integration of environmental priorities and economic development, and education and public awareness regarding the most pressing environmental matters.
3. Framework Agreement on Commercial and Economic Cooperation between the Government of Canada and the Commission of the European Community (1976).	Scientific and technical interchange in various sectors, including the environment.
4. MOU between Environment Canada and the Minster of Environment of France on co-operation in the Field of Environment, 1991.	Provide opportunities for upgrading knowledge and understanding of environmental problems.
5. MOU between Environment Canada and the Hong Kong Planning, Environment and Lands Branch on Environmental Co-operation, 1992.	Promote interchange of environmental technology and policy and programming expertise.
6. Agreement between the Government of Canada and the Government of Japan on Cooperation in Science and Technology (1986).	Facilitate co-operation in science and technology, specifically in the environmental sector.

TABLE 5.3 Continued

Title	Objective
7. Agreement on Environmental Cooperation between the Government of Canada and the Government of the United Mexican States (1990).	Harmonize Mexican priorities for environment management with Canadian expertise and technology and provide outlets for Canadian environment industries to market Canadian goods and services in Mexico.
8. MOU between Environment Canada and the Ministry of Housing, Physical Planning and the Environment of The Netherlands on Environmental Cooperation (1988).	Facilitate co-operation in areas of common interest, such as assessment of environmental impact, ecotoxicology, soil contamination, air pollution, and water quality.
9. Agreement between the Government of Canada and the Government of the (former) Soviet Union concerning Environmental cooperation (Moscow 1989), renewed in 1993.	Develop bilateral joint projects in pollution-technology transfer; water contamination; management of natural and biological resources; environmental-policy and environmental-impact assessment; and relations between humans and the environment.
10. Agreement between the Government of Canada and the Government of the United States of America on Air Quality.	Framework for co-operation for solving trans-boundary problems related to air quality and acid rain. Includes objectives for sulphur dioxide and nitrogen oxides.
11. MOU on Transboundary Control of Hazardous Wastes, (Canada–United States, 1986).	Ensure that hazardous wastes crossing the US-Canada border comply with each country's regulations.
12. Canada–United States Agreement on Great Lakes Water Quality (1972, 1978 and 1987).	Re-establish the chemical, physical, and biological integrity of the waters in the Great Lakes ecosystem.
13. Treaty relating to Boundary Waters (Canada–United States, 1909).	Address water flows and water quantity of shared watersheds; provide for management of boundary and trans-boundary waters; establish an order of precedence for use; prevent trans-boundary pollution; and provide for arbitration by IJC on issues of concern.

TABLE 5.4   Typical Stages in the Decision Process for Conventions and Protocols

1. Early awareness and scientific identification of the hazard	Dominated by scientists, can last for several years as debates occur among scientists and as political and economic interests decide how far to push or resist solutions.
2. Global recognition of problem and convening of meetings to develop a convention	This involves formal international political recognition of the problem, typically through a UN General Assembly resolution to negotiate a convention.
3. Development of a formal convention	Negotiations can take several years and tend to revolve around devising a set of workable principles and determining just how general versus specific various countries' commitments can be or should be. The further negotiations proceed into a protocol-setting stage, the more likely domestic economic, environmental, and political interests are to demand detailed study and take part in extensive lobbying, thereby internationalizing the domestic policy process.
4. Development of regulations and control strategy	Involves the development of regulatory and control mechanisms, which are developed in complex technical and policy meetings to obtain a practical sense of what overall kind of control regime is needed and likely to work. Attention paid not only to formal negotiating sessions (which may culminate in several weeks of negotiation), but also to the numerous interim meetings of technical and economic experts and lawyers. These groups develop agreed-upon data bases, formulas for reducing or controlling emissions, and timetables for reductions. Domestic business and environmental groups increasingly want to ensure that some of their members are on the accredited negotiation team, and preferably in the room and at the table.
5. Development of protocols	Involves the negotiation of a protocol, which itself can take a number of years.
6. Development of funding mechanism	Such mechanisms can involve complex negotiations to resolve funding ceilings and formulas, institutional modifications, or entire new institutions, such as GEF.

TABLE 5.4 Continued

7. Implementation	Formal implementation of the convention or protocol involves three steps: a signature phase; ratification, which is a formal legal step which, among other things, ensures that a country has made the necessary statutory changes to give effect to its commitments and the entry-into-force stage. Agreements do not take effect until specified conditions are met, such as ratification by the minimum number of countries with appropriate shares of production.
8. Enforcement	Processes are put in place to ensure, not only that commitments are honoured, but that momentum for the advancement of environmental change is maintained. Evaluation and review lead to new research findings, new control regimes, and the discovery of new or related hazards. This in turn leads to future renegotiations of the treaty to improve its stringency and operation.

However, on most environment and economic issues, the Nordic bloc has ceased to exist since Sweden and Finland joined the European Union (EU).

Indeed, the EU is another important bloc in its own right. Even though it is based on a formal treaty and in international trade negotiations speaks more or less with one voice, there are often disagreements within its own ranks on environmental issues. Indeed, on environmental matters, the division of powers between the EU and its member states is not clear-cut, and thus it can be difficult to deal with the EU. Canada's confrontation with Spanish trawlers off the Grand Banks of Newfoundland was formally a Canadian dispute with the EU members of the North Atlantic Fisheries Organization (NAFO), though divisions emerged in the EU ranks as countries which had themselves had problems with the Spanish fishing fleet expressed their sympathy, though informally, with the Canadian government.

Still, the EU is increasingly acting as a bloc, for instance within the OECD. The EU is environmentally conscious on some issues such as climate change. As an energy importer, it favours demand-side strategies on energy-management issues. Thus on climate change, within the OECD and elsewhere, Canada finds itself aligned with Australia, New Zealand, Mexico and, uncomfortably for some Canadian negotiators and interests, with the United States.

On global issues, such as ozone depletion and hazardous wastes, where there is a fairly clear North-South split, the G77 group of developing counties will become a more relevant group for Canada to deal with. This alliance has existed for some time but is now making its presence felt on environment and development issues. On most global issues the position of Third World countries is quite clear. The rich developed countries have the responsibility to reduce pollution since the majority of such pollutants were and are produced by the North. The global clean-up of toxic chemicals, ozone-depleting substances, and greenhouse gases and the preservation of forests and biological diversity should not be done at the expense of the South's development prospects.

The developing countries believe that when they must alter their industrial methods for environmental reasons, they should be subsidized financially or should be given technology that will allow them to develop while avoiding the old polluting technologies the North is now replacing. Though the G77 is not itself a fully coherent bloc on environmental foreign policy, there is little doubt that large countries in this bloc, such as China, India, and Brazil, and coalitions of smaller countries will have important international influence (Hurrell and Kingsbury 1992).

In spite of the increasingly dominant position of the EU in international environmental politics, as far as Canada is concerned the dominant player is still the United States. Because of its shared border, Canada has had more experience in dealing with its giant neighbour than with any other country (Munton and Castle 1992). This relationship has ranged from successful and co-operative programs such as the North American Water Fowl Management Program to the contentious acid rain case, in which it took well over a decade to achieve a credible agreement. The fact that Canada shares so many water, land, and air ecosystems with the United States and yet is one-tenth its size in population and economic terms, has meant that Canada has often been a 'policy taker' where the US is concerned, often emulating American policies (Howlett 1994; Hoberg 1991; Moffett 1994).

Such shifting alliances on various environmental and economic issues draw Canada farther into the international sphere and expose domestic policy to internationalizing influences. Canada's environmental foreign policy has often focused on broad multilateral initiatives. Yet, even while acting multilaterally, Canada must, in practice, keep its eye firmly fixed on concrete bilateral actions with the United States. For biophysical reasons and because Canada's economic and trade relations are firmly rooted in a powerful continental embrace, it is Canada's bilateral environmental relations with the US that will matter most, even as multilateral deals are struck.

IMPLICATIONS

Ideas and Policy Discourse

As a result of globalization and the emergence of a policy discourse influenced by the ideas of sustainable development and pollution prevention, there is a growing understanding that the environmental welfare of nations is as tightly linked as national economies. This interdependence has meant that governments have increasingly been willing to sacrifice sovereignty to international institutions. As the foreign policy review noted, the recognition of shared biophysical problems has helped reconfigure security concerns to notions of 'global security', 'common security', or 'shared security'. In this context, sovereignty concerns have diminished, and ecological interdependence has become more important than independence. However, just as in trade agreements in which governments have ceded sovereignty over economic policy to international organizations, the national economic self-interest and the material considerations of powerful domestic interests will have a profound influence on national positions.

Because Canada is often a 'policy taker' rather than a major influence in shaping the international policy agenda, it cannot always choose which international activities it will be involved in. Many of Canada's international environmental activities are intended to protect Canada's economic and environmental interest from the environmental policies of other larger countries or blocs of countries, such as the United States and the European Union. This reality conflicts with the proactive strategies that many environmentalists, in particular, would like to see Canada pursue.

Interests and Associational Actors

Globalization and internationalization have without a doubt expanded the perspective and activity of the business and environmentalist members of the Canadian environmental policy community. Business-interest associations are now heavily involved in environmental policy, both at home and abroad. Economic integration through formal trade agreements such as the FTA, NAFTA, and GATT and the growing importance of environmental considerations in their deliberations as the principles of sustainable development begin to become institutionalized are of great concern to domestic business interests. So is the increasingly integrated international approach that governments are taking to a broad range of industry activity, from the emissions of toxic wastes and greenhouse gases to new standards for products and processes. Canadian firms want to be sure that the harmonizing of such standards does not put them at a competitive disadvantage.[9] For process standards, industry's lobbying efforts will have a domestic focus since both the federal and provincial governments have relevant regulatory powers. For product standards they will also target international organizations like the ISO in the interests of establishing common international standards (CSA 1995).

Environmental NGOs (ENGOs) have always had a complex relationship with governments—acting both as partner and watchdog. Internationalization has opened up new opportunities for both co-operation and conflict. Federal departments have often made it possible for ENGOs to be part of Canadian delegations at the same time that ENGOs have used this access and their connections with other nations' environmental groups to hold the government to a higher level of accountability.

Co-ordinated campaigns by Canadian, European, and American environmental groups have been successful in influencing the international market for Canadian products. European campaigns have forced the federal and provincial governments and industry to alter trapping, forestry, and pulp and paper manufacturing processes. US ENGOs have persuaded many American municipal and state governments to require that newspapers contain a specific percentage of recycled fibre, thus directly affecting Canadian pulp and paper exporters. Domestic groups will continue to form coalitions with ENGOs in other countries to challenge industry and governmental decisions at home that they consider deleterious to the environment. They will be helped by global communications systems, even if their revenues fall as a result of government cutbacks or a decline in membership.

The requirement that each department create a sustainable-development strategy which the minister should table in Parliament as part of the environmental commissioner initiative will provide the ENGOs in the policy community with unprecedented access to departmental planning. They will have the opportunity to help shape strategy as departments will be required to consult broadly with stakeholders and clients in the development of their strategies. This will also provide an opportunity for ideas generated by the internationalization debate to affect directly the activities of departments. It may also provide an occasion for conflict between the business and non-business interests in the policy community.

Institutions

From the Stockholm Conference on the Human Environment (UNCHE) in 1972 to the World Conservation Strategy in 1980, to the Brundtland Commission in the mid-1980s and the Rio Earth Summit in 1992, Canadians have been centrally involved in international environmental initiatives.[10] In the last decade, numerous structures and measures have been put in place to facilitate Canada's efforts to develop sustainable practices. The multi-sectoral Projet de Société has catalogued hundreds of these initiatives, both governmental and non-governmental (Projet de Société 1995). The Rio Summit Agenda 21 document called on all countries to prepare national sustainable-development strategies.

The institutionalizing of sustainable development will have practical implications for the international activities and related domestic support activities of all federal departments. In particular, officials must balance environmental and economic considerations in Canadian positions taken to international forums. This involves significant commitments in time and resources to develop the necessary analytical capacities within departments; consult and negotiate among environment and economic departments, provincial governments, industry associations, and others; and manage delegations comprising people from different departments and non-governmental actors who bring various interests to the negotiations (Doern and Conway 1994).

Environment Canada has never had much influence in the federal government, and on those rare occasions where it has enjoyed some power, it has encountered strong bureaucratic resistance from other departments. Moreover, in a context of sustainable development as opposed to environmental protection, Environment is just another department. The mandates and statutory obligations of the big land-holding departments like National Defence, Transportation, and Indian Affairs and Northern

Development and the economic-policy departments like Finance, Industry Canada, Fisheries and Oceans, and Natural Resources are as important as Environment Canada's. Nevertheless, for a host of reasons related to technical expertise, history, and practicality, Environment finds itself involved in most international issues. In fact, at present, it often has to try to represent, in addition to its own interests, the interests of other federal departments, the provinces, and non-governmental stakeholders.

It is particularly difficult to agree on environmental goals and strategies in a country with strong regional, constitutional, and functional divisions. This is especially true when the technical expertise and legal and statutory jurisdiction rest with provincial governments or several different federal departments (Toner 1996). An example is the recent difficulty in trying to develop a Canadian negotiating position for the UN climate-change meetings in Berlin in March 1995 (Leblanc 1995). Canada will also face internal disputes about the development of the protocols on persistent organic pollutants (POPs) and heavy metals at UNECE. POPs are an important issue for Canada, but heavy metals are much less so. The EU may demand progress on heavy metals before conceding any action on POPs. It is likely that Environment Canada will have serious disagreements with the Departments of Industry and Natural Resources, the provinces, and the mining, chemical, and metal-fabrication industries.

In fact, there is a question as to whether Environment Canada is the right unit to build interdepartmental consensus on positions to be taken to international forums. Some departments doubt that Environment Canada can do this fairly since its job is to stress environmental protection in the federal policy process. There is a great need to build trust among departments. Canada can no longer afford to have delegations from various departments looking over each other's shoulders before, during, and after international meetings. The economic departments are afraid that the agenda will move too fast and exceed the capacity of Canadian industry to adjust in a global market context. For that reason Environment Canada will be under increasing pressure to move to non-regulatory ways of setting environmental standards. Business and economic departments often prefer non-regulatory approaches because they allow business to adapt more efficiently to the environmental expectations and competition in a global market.[11]

Since none of these interdepartmental disagreements are new, however, it is clear that Foreign Affairs needs to assume much more responsibility for developing interdepartmental consensus on international policy and strategies for furthering environmental goals. Whereas Canada's environmental priorities have to be determined by departments that have the scientific and technical capacity to do so (for example, Environment and

Health in the matter of toxic chemicals), DFAIT has to rely on different skills and a different location in the policy process than the scientific departments.

If DFAIT is to take more responsibility for co-ordinating international positions and strategies, its environmental expertise needs to be upgraded. There is a strong sense that there is a role for the department that is not now being filled. If DFAIT were to assume this role in a concerted way, there would probably be beneficial spin-offs for the integration of economic and environment matters in other Canadian foreign policies where the main issues are concerned with the economy or security but where the environment should be given greater consideration than it has been in the past.

Instruments

In the presence of internationalizing forces, the federal government will be under increasing pressure to take part in international environmental activities and in domestic activities that support international agreements; at the same time there will be fiscal constraints and resistence from various departments, the provinces, and industry. Moreover, because of all this international activity and the financial commitments that result from international agreements, as well as the domestic costs of developing and implementing policy, the internationalization of Canadian environment policy is expensive.

It is therefore important that greater attention be paid to efficiency and effectiveness. The main task is to ensure that Canada can continue to be effective. Efficiency requires that Canada strengthen its capacity to monitor what its contributions are accomplishing and to decide whether to continue various activities. Though Canada will have to take a hard look at new international initiatives in light of the fiscal situation, there are always strong pressures to be involved.

While the principle of pollution prevention is beginning to emerge as a guide to action, there is nevertheless the legacy of past environmental degradation to be addressed. Remedial measures are often very expensive, and governments forced to reallocate scarce funds away from other desirable social activities will end up interjecting environmental issues into social and economic policy debates (Paehlke 1989).

The growth in the use of multilateral and bilateral agreements based on sanctions leads to a greater reliance on regulatory and quasi-regulatory instruments in domestic environment policy—a trend that is in opposition to the broader deregulatory tendency in other fields of public policy. The report of the House of Commons Standing Committee, while not government policy, calls for an even stronger federal regulatory role, in part to meet international commitments (Matas 1995).

Yet, because of the increasingly competitive international economy, integrated environmental-economic policies must be developed with a sharp eye on international developments. Canada, like other developed countries, is slowly considering the use of economic instruments, such as charges, taxes, and tradable permits as a way to increase environmental efficiency. However, Canada cannot afford to internalize the economic costs of environmental protection more quickly than its major trading partners unless such developments achieve efficiency gains, or unless environmental goals override the goal of economic competitiveness (Canada, Task Force on Economic Instruments and Disincentives to Sound Environmental Practices 1994; Runnals and Cosbey 1992).

Similarly, Canada can no longer develop regulatory approaches without being aware of competitiveness issues, regulatory issues in important export markets, and harmonization of trade rules on technical barriers to trade. Perhaps the most important attempt to reconcile the trade and environment relationship is the creation of the North American Commission on Environmental Cooperation (NACEC). The commission will make it more difficult to forge domestic environmental policies, since both international and domestic constraints and pressures must be considered. Canada is affected by trans-boundary and global environmental problems that can be solved only by co-ordinated international efforts. For example, any effort Canada makes to reduce its contribution to global warming by reducing its use of greenhouse gases would affect Canadian industry and consumers and could be rendered irrelevant by energy-consumption practices in China and other developing countries. This realization is driving the development of the joint-implementation approach (Hassan 1995; UNCTAD 1995a). Similarly, efforts by Canada to conserve migrating fish stocks can be pointless if other fishing nations act independently and in opposition to Canada's conservation regulations.[12]

Conclusions

Though there have always been international influences on Canadian environmental policy, advances in environmental science in recent years have taught us more about the ecological damage that is resulting from human activities. Changes in the international marketplace and technological breakthroughs in telecommunications have added to our knowledge of the trans-boundary dimensions of the problems and placed greater pressure on the international community to respond. The result has been an expansion of activity in international organizations and the creation of new international policy instruments. This has led to the internationalization of domestic policy as more and more domestic policies are subject to international forces and agreements.

None of these pressures is likely to abate over the next decade. The management of toxics, climate change, biodiversity, and trade and the environment are four of the issues that will dominate the international stage at the turn of the century and require responses at the domestic level. On some global issues such as climate change, the political will to act has been slow to emerge. When the parties to the UN convention on climate change met in Berlin in May 1995, virtually all countries had fallen short of their reduction targets. However, as the scientific consensus in the International Panel on Climate Change continues to strengthen, pressure will continue to build for a political solution (Lemonick 1995). International markets may step ahead of the political consensus by establishing market instruments that will complement regulatory changes. For example, tradable emission permits for carbon emissions may be trading on international stock markets by early in the next century (UNCTAD 1994a, 1995b). And as part of extensive joint implementation initiatives emitters in the First World may invest in environmental safeguards in the developing world in exchange for concessions in developed countries (UNCTAD 1995a).

As new protocols on heavy metals, persistent organic pollutants, and other toxic contaminants work their way through the international system, there will be ramifications for the way in which individual countries handle their own toxic issues. One indication of how efforts to tighten standards will stimulate domestic controversy is the opposition by the federal departments of Industry and Natural Resources and the business community to the Parliamentary Standing Committee's recommendations for strengthening the Canadian Environmental Protection Act (Matas 1995). The Rio Biodiversity Convention will require countries to review their current practices, as DOE is now doing as it attempts to pass Canada's first Endangered Species Act.

The connection between trade and the environment will continue to be a major issue into the next century. From the trade point of view, critics will continue to insist that new environmental policies must not be used for protectionist purposes. From the environmental point of view, the critics argue that current and emerging trade rules must not restrict countries from adopting environmental policies appropriate to their needs. There could be friction between trade and environment policies on a number of fronts. For instance, as countries move to new forms of environmental taxes and charges, there will be a desire to adjust border taxes on imported products so as not to put domestic industries at a disadvantage. It is ᴧow such measures would be regarded under trade rules. Another sou.   of friction will be the increased use of life-cycle assessment, cradle-to-grave, and product-stewardship concepts in environmental policies. As foreign products are increasingly subjected to these policies, questions will be asked about the extraterritorial application of domestic environmental policies under trade rules (de Jonquières and Boulton 1995).

All of this international activity and Canada's obligations that result from it will be a challenge to the federal government. The pressures the federal government faces from its own political and bureaucratic elements as well as from the provincial governments and the organizations in the policy community to be active across the broad spectrum of environment-economy issues will come up against the restrictions of smaller budgets. There will have to be greater efficiency in administration and perhaps reallocations of remaining resources to issues and areas driven by internationalization. This may result in further turf wars and resource battles within and between departments. The forces of internationalization are probably irresistible, and it is an open question as to whether we have the institutional arrangements, the resources, or the international influence to rise to the challenge.

NOTES

1. 'Ecosphere' refers to the entire global ecosystem that comprises atmosphere, lithosphere, hydrosphere, and biosphere (the latter meaning all the Earth's organisms) as inseparable components. 'Environment' is defined by the United Nations Environment Programme as that outer biophysical system in which people and other organisms exist. The term is handy for referring to whatever surrounds and influences organisms as long as we remember that the verbal separation—'organisms' and 'environment'—is not a real division (Canada, Dept of the Environment 1991).

2. A stark example is the 'pristine' Arctic ecosystem, which is polluted by acid rain, soot, PCBs, pesticides, heavy metals, radionuclides, and other contaminants that originate in industrialized regions of Europe, Asia, and North America thousands of miles away. These contaminants are carried to the Arctic by winds, rivers, and ocean currents. Inuit mother's milk has been found to be high in PCBs because the Inuit eat local fish and animals that absorb contaminants from distant sources.

3. This shift in focus does not mean that local and regional issues are no longer important—they are of crucial importance to the health of the ecosystems of which they are a part.

4. A Department of the Environment has only existed in Canada since 1970. That is also the period when most provincial governments created environment departments. In 1974, the Department of the Environment became

Environment Canada, as part of the Trudeau government's effort to incorporate bilingual terminology into the federal lexicon. However, the old acronym, DOE, continues to be used. For an historical overview of DOE see Doern and Conway (1994).

5. We are slowly beginning to change the way we think about the meaning of wealth, capital, and development. In a 1995 study, the World Bank for the first time attempted to measure the wealth of nations by including natural and social capital as well as manufactured capital or 'produced assets', such as machinery, factories, roads, and other infrastructure required for industry. Natural capital comes from the natural bounty of a country and includes not only minerals but water, land, and other environmental resources. Social capital consists of the human resources of a nation and reflects the levels of people's health and education. The potential for economic development is higher in countries with healthy, well-trained populations and abundant resources. 'Richer countries are generally those that invest more in human resources' and guard their natural capital. 'Good environmental policies are good economic policies and vice versa.' In the World Bank's ranking Canada placed second, after Australia (Zagorian 1995).

6. Environment Canada underwent a major reorganization after the Canadian Parks Service was transferred out of the department in the June 1993 reorganization of government departments. At that point a Pollution Prevention Directorate was created in the department's Environmental Protection Service. It has five branches: Air Issues, Commercial Chemicals, Hazardous Waste Management, Industrial Sectors, and a National Office of Pollution Prevention. The goal of the Pollution Prevention Directorate is to create a culture and milieu that promotes and reinforces responsible decision-making and encourages pollution prevention and environmental protection.

7. The Canadian environmental industries sector is growing at 6–8 per cent a year. Comprising approximately 4,500 companies, it generated $11 billion in economic activity in 1994, of which $1 billion was exported. It is expected to be a $20 billion industry by the end of the century (S. Hart 1995).

8. There is a growing realization that social policies, as well as economic policies, can have serious effects on the environment. For example, unemployment insurance has maintained high levels of marginal seasonal employment in the fishery, and this overcapacity has helped to deplete the fish stocks on Canada's east and west coasts. Conversely, when natural resource sectors such as the fishery have to be shut down or reduced for conservation reasons, real hardship is created for the displaced labour force and their communities (Yaffe 1995).

9. For two recent assessments of the changes business faces in the international economy as a result of changing attitudes and practices regarding the environment, see Business Council for Sustainable Development (1992) and Paul Hawken (1993).

10. Individual Canadians have been prominent in various international agencies and events in this area. They include Maurice Strong, UNCHE, UNEP, and UNCED; Jim MacNeill, OECD and WCED; David Munro, IUCN; Elizabeth Dowdeswell, UNEP; Jim Bruce, WMO; and Len Good, World Bank.

11. Even then, Environment Canada will face contending pressures from industry as there is no consensus among business interests. The Canadian Environmental Industry Association is concerned about the government's movement away from the regulatory approach to a reliance on 'voluntary initiatives' and 'economic instruments'. The environmental-industries sector has grown rapidly and is now one of the top five industries in Canada. It is concerned that the environmental regulations which have driven technology innovation have been so weakened that the growth of this sector may be undermined (Canadian Environment Industry Association 1995).

12. Environmental problems could also affect Canada indirectly. International peace and security could be threatened by trans-boundary disputes over declining global natural resources, like fish and fresh water. The dispute between Canada and the European Union over the Atlantic fishery is a mild example of the problems that could affect parts of the developing world in particular. See for example Myers (1995: A7).

6

Agricultural Policy

Grace Skogstad

INTRODUCTION

In the mid-1990s the Canadian agri-food sector is more subject to market forces than it was a decade ago and is certain to wear less of a 'made in Canada' label in the future. The change has been wrought by a series of reforms in domestic policy. In 1985 Canada's grain and oilseed producers received government subsidies to export their grain, and farmers' gross returns from grain and oilseed sales were stabilized with the help of government financial transfers. By mid-1995, the export subsidies had been eliminated, and the Canadian government's contribution to the cost of stabilizing grain farmers' incomes had shrunk significantly. In 1985, Canada's dairy, poultry, and egg producers enjoyed a virtual monopoly in the Canadian consumer market. A decade later they still had little foreign competition, but they faced the prospect of having to become more efficient and responsive to the market.

The transformation of Canadian agricultural policy over the past decade took place alongside the enhanced regionalization and internationalization of Canadian agriculture. Discussed more fully below, the regional integration of the Canadian agri-food sector into the US political economy and the signing of international trade agreements have undoubtedly hastened the reform of domestic policy. However, it is difficult to separate the effects of these international developments from domestic pressures for neo-liberal policies. Foremost among the latter is the declining fiscal capacity of Canadian governments. In this era of highly mobile capital,[1] debt-laden governments, like Canada's, face enormous pressures to cut spending. Thus, the trade agreements that prohibit expenditure policies like export subsidies clearly work in conjunction with freer financial capital markets to produce more market-oriented agricultural policies in

Canada. But the retrenchment of expenditure policies has been greater than international trade agreements alone would dictate, suggesting that the strongest impetus has been budgetary. However, internationalization and regionalization have propelled agricultural policy reforms. They have made such reforms appear to be inevitable and have reduced the opposition to them.

The first task of this chapter is to trace how internationalizing developments have helped to diminish the role of Canadian governments in the agri-food sector. International trade agreements are shown to have directly curbed the Canadian state's legal authority, removing fiscal and regulatory policy instruments or rendering them ineffective. Regional-market interdependence and competition have simultaneously induced powerful pressures for the convergence of policy instruments in international agreements. Has Canada's effective sovereignty thereby been diminished? To answer this question is the second objective of the chapter. The answer requires that a sharp distinction be drawn between regionalization and internationalization. The trade agreements that Canada has entered into with the United States—the Canada-US Free Trade Agreement (FTA), and the North American Free Trade Agreement (NAFTA)—and which have intensified trade interdependence and tensions, pose a hazard to Canada's autonomous choice of domestic policy instruments. There is increasing evidence of pressures for Canada to redesign its policies along American lines. The internationalization of domestic policy also limits the choice of domestic policy instruments; some programs must be eliminated, others altered to make them legal under the terms of the General Agreement on Tariffs and Trade (GATT). However, the GATT regime also offers the prospect of increasing the sovereignty of small and medium-sized countries. By establishing well-defined rules that bind all signatories equally, GATT may ensure 'meaningful sovereignty' by providing sanctuary from the unilateral and retaliatory trading practices of the super powers (Courchene 1992c: 122).

The internationalizing and regionalizing developments that have narrowed the scope of Canada's governments for independent action have not left internal political relationships and decision making unchanged. The third purpose of the chapter is to document how three political relationships pivotal to agricultural policy making have been altered over the past decade and how the nature of governance in the agricultural sector has thereby been affected. The first of these relationships is within the Government of Canada, between the Department of Agriculture and Agri-Food and the departments responsible for negotiating and implementing trade agreements. The second is between the federal government and the provincial governments. The third is between government officials and private interests. Within the Government of Canada, trade and agricultural policies are now inextricably intertwined; fiscal responsibility for agriculture has been decentralized to the provinces and producers; and the composition and function of policy networks have been transformed. Producer groups have been drawn more closely into policy decision making, even while having to share their influence with non-producer agri-food interests, which now have a higher place on the policy agenda. The cumulative result is more pluralistic governance in the agri-food sector.

The fourth and final purpose of the chapter is to assess what the example of agricultural policy reveals about the behaviour and policy capacity of state officials in the face of internationalization. The case confirms the generally strong policy capacity of Canadian governments. State officials expedited the changes in domestic policy making and politics by serving as 'transmission belts' for the idea that change in a more market-oriented direction was necessary, and ultimately, inevitable, in the agri-food sector. As intermediaries between the international and domestic arenas, they carried ideas of market liberalism and the necessity for change from the international arena to the domestic agri-food community, enabling these ideas to acquire some legitimacy, and reconciling a broad segment of the agricultural policy community to the idea that a more market-oriented agriculture with less government support was inevitable.

INTERNATIONALIZATION AND REGIONALIZATION

The internationalization that characterizes Canadian agriculture in the mid-1990s differs in kind from that which prevailed from the 1950s to the 1980s. The importance of export markets for Canadian commodities, especially wheat and other cereals, meant that Canadian governments always framed domestic agricultural policies with an eye to the international marketplace and the agricultural programs of other countries. Accordingly, Canadian grain growers were assisted with transportation subsidies, an export marketing board, and other policies to help them compete in the international marketplace. Others that could not, including dairy and poultry producers, were equipped with policy instruments like import quotas and supply management to shield them within the domestic market.

Canada's relative autonomy to devise domestic agricultural policy was consistent with the practices of other countries in the Organisation for Economic Co-operation and Development (OECD). This was because agriculture was largely outside the GATT regime. The original 1947 GATT accord made only a modest attempt to limit trade barriers.[2] It did not prohibit export subsidies. Article XI allowed countries to restrict imports providing they managed the supply of the commodity internally. However, the effectiveness of GATT as a regime that would liberalize trade by telling 'countries . . . what they could and could not do to intervene in domestic [agricultural markets and sectors]' (Avery 1993: 2) was quickly undermined. In 1955 the United States obtained a waiver from Article XI and most of its GATT obligations concerning agriculture. After that, other countries tended to follow the US practice of insulating their domestic agriculture from foreign competition. Although there were some exceptions, most OECD countries formulated their agricultural policies to meet domestic interests. The Common Agricultural Policy of 1962 effectively insulated the European Community's producers from foreign competition and subsidized their sales in external markets. The GATT rules presented few constraints to domestic policy making, and where they did, these rules were often ignored.

The wide latitude Canada enjoyed to fashion its agricultural policy came to an abrupt halt in the mid-1980s. Since then Canadian agriculture has been faced with formidable trade competition abroad and been buffeted by developments beyond our borders. The wave of US trade protectionism that began in the mid-1980s and its trade war with the European Community forcibly exposed Canada's grain sector to greater trade competition. Subsequently, the 1989 FTA and the 1995 Uruguay Round of GATT have caused our agri-food markets to become more regionally integrated and have further intensified the competition that faces Canadian producers and processors in foreign markets.

The greater interdependence of the Canadian and US agri-food markets is seen in the heightened importance of the US market for some significant agri-food exports. In 1984, 30 per cent of Canadian agri-food exports went to the United States; by 1993, increases in exports of live animals, meat (beef), and beverages had pushed the figure to 55 per cent (Canada, Dept of Agriculture and Agri-Food 1994).[3] Imports from the United States also grew over this period, rising from 55 per cent of total Canadian agri-food imports in 1984 to 61 per cent in 1993. With the intensification of Canada-US trade since 1989, when the FTA came into force, Canada has become increasingly dependent upon this single market. Canadian agri-food exports to all other countries have declined from 46 per cent of total agri-food exports in 1984 to only 22 per cent in 1993.[4] The important exceptions to this greater regionalization of markets are grains and oilseeds. Grain and oilseeds markets remain international, though more highly concentrated today than in the past, and strongly competitive (Saskatchewan Agriculture and Food 1993: 12).[5] Canada's overall trade vulnerability is demonstrated in its declining share of world agri-food markets since the early 1980s (Canada, Dept of Agriculture and Agri-Food 1994: 18, 21).

Behind these market developments lies the fact that sectors previously shielded from competition, notably the dairy, egg, and poultry sectors, are now required under the terms of the FTA and GATT to compete with more imports. Collectively, the regional integration of agri-food markets and international trade agreements have regionalized and internationalized Canada's agricultural policy. Domestic policies and policy instruments are determined by developments in the US political economy as well as in the wider international political economy.

INTERDEPENDENCE AND COMPETITIVE TRADE PRESSURES: THEIR DIRECT EFFECTS

For Canada, with its close ties to the American market and economy, the conundrum has been how to respond to the two elements of American trade policy: protectionism and 'aggressive unilateralism' (Bhagwati and Patrick 1990) on the one hand, and the rhetoric of market liberalism on the other hand. From the mid-1980s on, the United States championed free trade abroad, aggressively pushing other countries to open their markets. At the same time it spearheaded the Uruguay Round of GATT, with the intent of establishing rules for sectors previously outside international trading rules. US actions and rhetoric here have often been sharply at odds with its practice of protectionism at home. Canada's response to the American Janus-faced trade policy, to pursue fairer trading rules equally binding on all signatories, has not been an unqualified success.

The Lessons of Excessive Protectionism

The first in the chain of events that has led to the greater external competitiveness and interdependence of Canadian agriculture was the US quest to recapture its 'lost' markets from the European Community (EC); this was signalled by the Export Enhancement Program (EEP) for wheat in the American 1985 Farm Bill (Libby 1992). The American mercantilist trade policy from the mid-1980s onward and the ensuing US-EC grain trade wars revealed fully the deleterious consequences of excessive protectionism. This protectionism lent momentum and legitimacy to ideas of market liberalism abroad and underlay Canada's support of trade agreements designed to curb it: the bilateral Free Trade Agreement with the United States and the multilateral Uruguay Round Agreement of GATT. It is correct to regard these trading agreements as offshoots of globalization in the sense that they were propelled by ideas of market liberalism, which were gaining ascendancy across the western industrialized world. Agri-cultural-market liberalism was championed by an epistemic community based in the OECD and in think tanks in the United States, Canada, and Australia; their objective was to redefine the roles of governments and markets along more market-oriented lines.[6]

Regionalization: The FTA

At first blush, the bilateral Canada-US Free Trade Agreement, which came into effect in January 1989 and which was broadened but not appre-ciably altered with the passage of NAFTA in late 1993,[7] appears to be of minor significance for Canadian agriculture. Its agricultural provisions are restricted to the dismantling of the remaining tariffs on a few agri-food items (horticultural products are those most affected); removing tariff and non-tariff barriers to cross-border trade in red meats; eliminating discrim-inatory provincial policies on wine distribution, listing, and mark-up; and freeing cross-border trade in grains, grain products, and oilseeds.[8]

The limited scope of the agricultural provisions in the FTA shows the extent to which domestic social pressures, when joined with strategic state interests, were able to limit the regionalization and internationalization of Canadian agricultural policy in the late 1980s. For its part, the US was unwilling to discuss any major dismantling of non-tariff barriers in agri-culture in the FTA, since its primary 'liberalizing' target was the European Community. Moreover, commodity sectors, like sugar and peanuts, that were opposed to trade liberalization mobilized to prevent this. On the Canadian side of the border, federalism and well-organized domestic producer groups succeeded in thwarting any significant direct interna-tionalization of Canadian agricultural programs. The scope of the agree-ment was limited by the constitutional-legal constraint that allows Ottawa to negotiate international trade agreements but not to implement provi-sions that fall under provincial jurisdiction.[9] The FTA trespassed very little on provincial jurisdiction and left protected sectors like dairy and poultry largely exempt. The latter industries were able to mount an effective campaign to maintain the status quo (Skogstad 1992).

A major reason that Canada pursued free trade with the United States was to curb the American trade protectionism to which Canadian agri-food exports had been prone (Skogstad 1992; Rugman 1986). One of the mech-anisms deemed necessary to do so, a mutually acceptable set of trade rules, including clear definitions of what constitutes a subsidy and dumping, was, of course, not realized. In its place, a bi-national dispute-settlement mechanism to replace US appellate bodies was agreed to; it was heralded by Canada as a review mechanism that would curb the discretion of US trade administrators to interpret US trade law in a protectionist fashion.

In a detailed case study of bi-national panel decisions, Boddez and Trebilcock described them as 'a significant procedural improvement over the pre-FTA system of judicial review' (1993: 151). However, it should not be thought that the bi-national panel mechanism transferred the power to make decisions about trade from the nation to a new supra-national institution. Under the terms of the FTA, US trade laws continue to apply to Canadian exports and the United States can amend its trade-remedy laws without Canada's consent. It must specify, however, that an amendment or a new law will apply to Canada.[10] American laws are to prevail even if they conflict with the FTA, but they are subject to broad judicial review to determine whether they have been applied correctly.[11] In short, the US Congress retains sovereignty over American trade law and can change it as it sees fit, notwithstanding the FTA or NAFTA.

The FTA's modest *direct* effects on governments' agricultural policy instruments and legal authority stand in sharp contrast to other consequences that were far more important. The FTA has, first, integrated Canadian agriculture more fully into the US market and political economy; second, destabilized private-sector relationships in Canada and shifted bargaining power to non-producer interests; third, given a boost to liberal ideas; and fourth, put pressure on Canada to align its policies and policy instruments with those of the United States. The first of those consequences is dealt with below; the other three are discussed later in the chapter.

The FTA has further *regionalized* Canada's agri-food trade. Canadian and US agriculture are now more economically interdependent than they were before the FTA took effect in 1989. US-Canada agri-food trade has been 'growing over 15 per cent annually since 1988' (Canada, Dept of Agriculture and Agri-Food 1994: 30), and since 1992, in a reversal of the historic pattern, Canada has enjoyed a positive agri-food trade balance with the US (Quebec, Ministry of Agriculture, Fish and Food 1994: 38–9).[12] The greater economic integration of the two agri-food sectors, in conjunction with the fact that the FTA and NAFTA left pre-existing, potentially protectionist American trade remedy processes and laws intact, has created new bilateral trading tensions and caused others to persist.[13]

The 1994–5 dispute over Canadian wheat exports to the United States demonstrates how Canadian access to the US market continues to be limited by the American domestic political economy.[14] The political and administrative framework within which American trade-relief administrators and members of Congress function ensures that both will be highly responsive to complaints by local interests that foreign competitors are trading unfairly. The intent of American private and public officials is clearly not just to prohibit the entry of competitive imports and preserve the American market for American producers and industry. Rather, trade-relief actions are also efforts to discredit foreign practices and policy instruments that differ from their own. This is evidenced by American efforts to eliminate the Canadian Wheat Board and, failing that, to have its monopoly as the sole export agency for Canadian wheat and barley removed. The Canadian Wheat Board is labelled an unfair trading practice by Americans; it is certainly at odds with their system of oligopolistic private grain traders.

The wheat dispute, the American recourse to an 'extraordinary challenge' of Canadian pork imports in 1991,[15] current trade controversies over other commodities—all these indicate the enormous pressures to bend to American demands and conform to American practices and programs in order to gain access to the US market. Domestic policies have already been abandoned—red-meat price-stabilization programs, for example—to bring them in line with American definitions of what constitutes 'fair trade'. In this sense, Canadian agricultural policy has already been regionalized; anticipation of the reaction of political actors south of our border has ruled out domestic policy initiatives.

Internationalization: The GATT Uruguay Round

Concluded in December 1993 and brought into effect in January 1995, the Uruguay Round GATT accord inaugurated a new era in domestic agricultural policy making. The explicit goal of the Uruguay Round (1986–93) was to limit the sovereignty of governments in the realm of agricultural policy—with respect to all trade-distorting measures: export subsidies, import barriers, and all domestic measures that distort trade. Although its provisions on all three accounts fall far short of what was hoped for by the proponents of liberal trade, the principle that agriculture trade should be subject to the rules of a multilateral regime is a major departure from the past. It initiates the internationalization of agricultural policy by restricting countries' use of certain regulatory and expenditure policy instruments, and it presages a further internationalization of agriculture.

First, GATT requires countries to reduce their domestic and export subsidies.[16] It is the forced reduction of export subsidies—36 per cent in value over six years—that is the most significant for Canada's dairy and grain sectors. Subsidies levied to finance the export of surplus dairy products are affected, as are freight rate subsidies for grain (the Crow Benefit), which have kept down producers' costs of exporting grain.

Second, with the elimination of Article XI.2.c., quantitative import controls that have protected supply-managed commodities must be converted to tariff equivalents and reduced by 15 per cent for each product over six years. However, they have been set high enough to afford protection from imports into the foreseeable future.[17] Imports must be gradually increased as well.

The FTA and NAFTA destabilized private-sector market relationships in the supply-management sectors. The loss of GATT Article XI.2.c. will do so even more. Although the dairy and poultry marketing boards were explicitly exempted from the FTA and NAFTA, the removal of tariffs on *processed* dairy, egg, and poultry products opened a wide cleavage between domestic food processors that use cheese and other dairy or poultry products to produce their foodstuffs (such as pizza, TV dinners), on the one hand, and processors and producers, on the other hand. The profitability of food processors has, of course, been threatened by cheaper American imports. Canada's attempt to extend protection to dairy-product manufacturers (by replacing the lost tariff protection for Canadian yogurt and ice cream with restrictions on imports) was unsuccessful. But that failure did not strike a lethal blow to supply management. After a GATT panel ruled the import restrictions illegal in December 1993, the dairy industry found another solution, one that effectively required producers to limit their own profits by restraining prices, to enable further dairy processors to remain competitive.

The elimination of Article XI has enormous potential to change the logic of supply management and to shift the system from one in which provincial boundaries and political bargaining determined domestic market share to one in which market power and economics dictate where commodities will be produced. Under Article XI.2.c., countries had to control between 80 and 85 per cent of their domestic production if they wished to limit foreign imports. This external constraint dictated a logic of negotiated market sharing under a supply-management system in which the larger provinces received more market share in order to keep supply management intact and avoid an influx of cheap imports. Under the new GATT agreement, however

> the maintenance of tariff protection for dairy, poultry, and eggs is not dependent upon the maintenance of a supply management system. The external threat is ended (tariffs remain no matter what happens internally) and a single province cannot make a threat to open the flood gates to cheap foreign products. If a breakdown in supply management occurs, there can be an internal fight among the provinces in Canada over market share. Bargaining power will eventually shift toward the most cost efficient producer. (Rosaasen *et al.* 1995: 2–3)[18]

Third, the creation of the World Trade Organization (WTO) to implement and enforce the GATT accord offers the first real possibility of an effective body to police and advocate a liberal, more open trading regime. The WTO will operate with clearer and stronger trading rules. These include new subsidy and dumping codes that clarify which subsidies are permissible and which are not and that outline the criteria for determining dumping and injury to industry.[19] The new codes ought to make it more difficult to use countervail and anti-dumping actions for harassment. In addition, there are new dispute-settlement procedures which should ensure that no single nation can dictate when the GATT rules will and will not apply. A major innovation is that new dispute-settlement rules make it harder for any signatory to block panel judgements.[20]

But the promise offered by GATT to *increase* Canada's 'effective sovereignty' (Courchene 1992c: 122)—by imposing equal constraints on nation states and realigning sovereignty 'upward' to an effective international body—is yet to be realized. Whether it ever will be depends upon which trade agreement, NAFTA or GATT, takes precedence. The July 1996 interim ruling of a trade dispute panel bodes well for GATT's priority. The ruling centred on the long-running US endeavour to open Canada's borders to American dairy and poultry exports. The United States has challenged Canada's imposition of high tariffs on poultry and dairy products on 1 January 1995. The United States declared the new tariffs, allowed under the GATT, to be illegal under NAFTA. It argued that NAFTA restricts signatories from imposing new tariffs on bilateral trade without the consent of the other parties to the agreement and commits Canada to eliminate existing tariffs. Canada countered that the tariff equivalents were consistent with both NAFTA and GATT, and maintained that in any event GATT takes priority. Canada was unwilling to negotiate an end to the dispute, and it was referred in July 1995 to a bilateral panel. The July 1996 interim ruling of the trade panel unanimously upheld Canada's tariffs.

There were two issues at stake in the panel's ruling. The first was the fate of Canada's supply-managed industries. Had the panel ruled that the United States was correct, that NAFTA takes precedence over GATT, Canada's dairy and poultry producers would have been subject to full American competition in as little as four years. The broader consequence of such a ruling would have been to draw Canada further into the vortex of the American political economy. Regionalization would have been given its strongest boost yet—and the possibility that internationalization might equalize Canada's bargaining power *vis-à-vis* the United States would have been undermined. Canadian agricultural policy instruments would then have converged in the direction dictated by US political interests, rather than around the (more favourable) GATT requirements. Now that the panel has ruled in Canada's favour, that GATT takes precedence over NAFTA, the United States will have to decide whether to continue treating GATT rules as subject to US law, rather than vice versa. Were the US to use 'GATT to gain access to the markets of others and US law to protect its own industries and markets' (Rosaasen *et al.* 1995: 1), regionalization would also gain the upper hand over internationalization.

DOMESTIC RESPONSES: ACCOMMODATION AND INSULATION

As the 'crucial nodal point' (Underhill 1994: 37) between the international arena and domestic society, the nation state has a different place in the contemporary international political economy than during the era of embedded liberalism (Ruggie 1982, 1994). In Cox's (1994: 49) words, the state has ceased to be 'the bulwark defending domestic welfare from external disturbances' and is now 'an agency for adjusting national economic practices and policies to the perceived exigencies of the global economy.' The necessity for, and capacity of, nation states to play the role Cox ascribes to them is thrown into sharp relief both *during* trade negotiations *and after* them.

Trade Policy

In Cox's terms, Canada's agricultural trade policy shows plenty of evidence of the state's continuing to act as 'the bulwark defending domestic welfare from external disturbances'.[21] The Government of Canada reacted to the US-EC grain trade wars in a traditional, defensive fashion. Its response was to shore up the grain producers' incomes, which had plummeted when world grain prices were intentionally driven downward by the American 1985 Farm Bill. Subsequently, in both the bilateral and multilateral trade negotiations, Canada tried to secure more access to other countries' markets for export-dependent grains and oilseeds, even while attempting to maintain border protection (and internal market control) for domestic dairy and poultry producers and processors. This two-pronged strategy was consistent with the difference in the consequences of liberalization of agricultural markets for the different commodities: beneficial for the Western Canadian export-oriented grains, oilseeds, and cattle sectors; harmful to the central Canadian supply-managed commodities.

Does Canada's inability to produce a logically coherent agricultural trade strategy display a lack of state autonomy and policy capacity? Perhaps. However, as pointed out below, the incoherent trade strategy owes much to Canada's federal system. Moreover, an examination of the parallel domestic reforms that the Government of Canada embarked upon shows more evidence of state autonomy and capacity for an anticipatory approach to agricultural policy. State officials proved willing and somewhat able to act as 'transmission belts' for promoting the adjustment of domestic sectors to the exigencies and new 'realities' of the international arena.

The Domestic Policy Reform Debate

In late 1989, the Conservative Minister of Agriculture, Don Mazankowski published a framework for the future direction of Canadian agricultural policy. Entitled *Growing Together*, the document's publication was followed by consultations with the agri-food policy community that included the formation of several task forces. The purpose and mandate of the task forces varied. However, in those sectors most likely to be affected by international trade developments and foreign competition—grains and oilseeds, poultry, and dairy—the objective was clearly to achieve a consensus for policy reforms that would require farmers to be more responsive to the market and more self-reliant.

The Government of Canada's attempts to reform domestic policies remind us that international trade strategies are often used to expedite the resolution of intractable domestic problems.[22] In the grains sector, the government's major income-stabilization program was financially bankrupt. In the supply-managed sector, changing consumer tastes, long-term interprovincial skirmishes over domestic market share, chronic complaints about the inefficiency of the marketing boards, and the vulnerability of food processors in the wake of the GATT panel ruling all created domestic reasons for a reform of agricultural policy reform (Skogstad 1993). Without these domestic reasons, it is unlikely that the international developments alone would have led to the reformist dialogue.

None the less, the additional impetus of American protectionism and international trade agreements has been a necessary ingredient in the wide-ranging debate in the agricultural community about the future of Canadian agricultural policy. American trade protectionism and the Mulroney government's initially defensive response to it had the ultimate effect of expediting the reform of domestic policy. The government expenditures that were needed to protect Canadian farmers from other countries' aggressive protectionism were so enormous that Canada could not continue to practise 'tit for tat' financial protectionism over the long term. This recognition, combined with the trust the Canadian government 'bought' for itself with its financial protection, was sufficient to persuade the grains and oilseeds sector to discuss new, less expensive income-protection programs.

The debate about domestic reform produced some modest changes. New income safety nets in the grain sector conform to the Canadian government's desire to reduce its expenditures and have provinces and individual producers assume more responsibility for farm income security. Less progress has been made in the supply-management sectors, although there has been more in the dairy industry than in the chicken and egg industries.[23] In the poultry sector, governments have opted to hand over the principal responsibility for reform to private interests in the sector. The results have been meagre: six years of talks have produced little evidence of greater economic efficiency and market responsiveness in poultry supply management.[24] The predominantly reactive strategy in poultry supply management and the limited success of an anticipatory strategy in grains and oilseeds stalled the realignment of domestic policies along liberal lines until the successful conclusion of the Uruguay Round of GATT. The prohibitory provisions of GATT, plus broader public support for fiscal and budgetary retrenchment, meant that the most significant policy reforms in the grains sector came only with the 1995 Martin budget. The adjustment of the poultry sector to internationalization will likely be propelled disproportionately by market forces rather than led by government.

CHANGES IN DOMESTIC POLICY MAKING AND INSTITUTIONS

Internationalization and regionalization, as realized through the two-step process of international trade agreements and subsequent changes in domestic policy, have altered the relations between Canada's two levels of government and between governments and agri-food groups and firms. The centrality of trade negotiations on the political agenda for virtually a decade and the domestic process by which these trade agreements were negotiated internally heightened the role of provincial governments and private interests in trade matters, including agricultural matters. The domestic reforms which have accompanied, and been a response to, the trade agreements have also affected intergovernmental relations and relations between state and society, although in different ways. Domestic reforms have tended to weaken the ties between the farm community and the Canadian government and to strengthen those between agri-food interests and provincial governments as Ottawa has decentralized fiscal responsibility for farm income support to the provinces.

Inter-bureaucratic relations in the Government of Canada appear to be the least affected by internationalization. There is little evidence that the Department of Agriculture and Agri-Food has suffered a decline in its responsibility for agriculture; its expertise is vital to officials in the Department of Foreign Affairs and International Trade. Because of the continuation of trade tensions in the wake of the FTA and NAFTA, like those surrounding Canadian wheat exports in 1994, and the necessity to resort to diplomacy to solve such disputes,[25] the two ministries responsible for agricultural policy and trade work closely.

Intergovernmental Relations
a. Trade Negotiations and Disputes. In all countries, as Aho (1988: viii) reminds us, 'trade negotiations are as much domestic negotiations as they are negotiations among countries.' This is because domestic policies must be reconciled with the goals of trade policy. The Canadian government has displayed considerable innovation in creating structures to co-ordinate its trade policy internally (across expert line ministries like Agriculture and trade ministries) and to receive ideas and information from provinces and sectoral groups (Skogstad 1992). These structures have undoubtedly strengthened its policy capacity and helped to manage internal disagreements. However, policy capacity should not be mistaken for policy autonomy. The outcomes of trade negotiations demonstrate that the Government of Canada does not have a free hand on agricultural trade policy.[26]

The latitude of the federal government to develop agricultural trade policy is appreciably narrowed by the authority of provincial governments and by well-organized farm and agri-food lobbies linked closely to the federal and provincial governments. Not only is the approval of provincial governments necessary for the implementation of trade agreement provisions that fall within provincial jurisdiction, but provinces have considerable advisory and informational responsibilities concerning trade policy generally (Winham 1990, 1994; Brown 1988, 1991; Doern and Tomlin 1991; Skogstad 1990, 1992; Cooper 1992).[27]

Over the past decade it has become clear that trade policy is *de facto* a matter of shared jurisdiction. In this sense, the prominence of international trade agreements over the past decade has decentralized Canadian federalism by allowing the provinces to enter into what was an exclusively federal domain, at least until the Tokyo Round of GATT. The federal-provincial co-operation that characterizes both the negotiating of trade agreements and the management of trade disputes[28] indicates that the provinces' contribution to national trade policy does not follow exclusively from their legal authority, but also from their expertise and close links to their farm communities. The co-operation is also a recognition that even when trade agreements do not directly impinge upon provincial subjects, as they have tended not to do without the provinces' consent, the economic well-being of the provinces is invariably affected indirectly by trade accords that curtail national powers and policy instruments.

The provinces' role in the 'domestic negotiations' over trade policy as 'a privileged, even partnering role with the federal government' (Brown 1991: 114), and the incorporation of agricultural officials and agricultural interests[29] into formulating national trade policy, have mitigated regional tensions and prevented divisive internal political discord. The two-pronged strategy was certainly criticized, by western Canadian grain interests and the Saskatchewan Conservative premier, who argued that grain growers' interests were being undermined by Canada's inconsistent negotiating stance. But the Government of Canada has shown itself to be rather deft in devising a trade policy that avoids pitting regions against one another. Its insistence on not being forced to choose between the supply-managed commodity sectors based in central Canada and the export-dependent grains and oilseeds sector on the Prairies was again apparent during the wheat dispute with the United States in 1994—and again with success (Skogstad 1995a).

b. Domestic Policy Making after Trade Agreements. As noted earlier, internationalization and regionalization have joined with budgetary constraints to cause all of Canada's governments to re-evaluate their agricultural policies. Ottawa's program changes have resulted in the devolution of considerable fiscal and program responsibility to provincial governments. The Government of Canada's share of total expenditures in the agri-food sector declined from 66.5 per cent in 1987–8 to an estimated 55 per cent in 1994–5. At the same time, the provinces' costs have risen. The expenditures of the Quebec government, which were larger than Ottawa's in 1987–8 (Quebec's share was 60 per cent), grew to account for two-thirds of total farm program costs in 1994–5. In Saskatchewan, whereas federal expenditures amounted to 83 per cent of total farm cash receipts in 1987–8, by 1994–5 they accounted for 65 per cent (Canada, Dept of Agriculture 1995: 34).

The devolution of significant financial responsibility for income support to the provinces is clearly decentralizing. As a result ties between provinces and producers are reinforced. In several provinces, internationalization has motivated provincial governments to embark on their own parallel strategic exercises. The governments of Quebec, Saskatchewan, and Alberta have all consulted their farm communities widely in an effort to develop agri-food strategies that are more market-oriented, rely more on processed foodstuffs and less on bulk commodities, and are based on a more diversified agriculture.[30] In the case of Quebec and Saskatchewan, these endeavours have been province-wide and cross-sectoral, incorporating the full range of stakeholders (producers, processors, retailers, distributors, financial institutions, and government officials) into the discussions.

Only the Government of Canada has international status when it comes to negotiating and signing treaties and handling trade disputes. The internationalization and regionalization of Canadian agriculture thus ensure that Ottawa will remain prominent in matters of food and agriculture. However, because of its reduced financial responsibilities for agriculture, Ottawa's leadership will probably continue to weaken. Linked less and less to the farm community by its expenditure programs, and perhaps even by its regulatory instruments, Ottawa's capacity to build public support for itself will likely decline. As food products are traded less and less between provinces, and more and more across our southern border, those who predict the weakening of east-west ties and the undermining of national political integration may well be proved correct (Simeon 1987: 205).

Relations with Interest Groups and Clients

Embedded in well-established policy networks, groups representing producers and other agri-food interests must be part of any trade negotiations. Canada's two-pronged trade strategy clearly reflected the force of domestic interests: export-oriented grain sectors pushing for trade liberalization and domestically oriented supply-managed commodity groups resisting internationalization. The extensive consultations that the Government of Canada engaged in with domestic farm lobbies, combined with the international lobby that domestic commodity and farm organizations launched to bring other nations on side (Cooper 1992), demonstrate that private-interest associations have an important influence on trade negotiations. Moreover, as the outcomes of the FTA and GATT reveal, that influence is likely to impede trade liberalization and internationalization.

The active and consultative role of farm organizations during the bilateral and multilateral trade negotiations (1985–93) along with the *Growing Together* task forces have transformed the function of interest organizations in the domestic agricultural policy community. First, they created an expectation on the part of agricultural groups that agricultural policy making will henceforth be a collaborative exercise between governments and farm groups. The task force in the grains and oilseeds sector that was mandated to devise new income-support programs changed the function of farm interest groups. Rather than being policy advocates, proffering advice from outside the decision-making circles, they became co-designers with government officials of the new programs.

Second, and somewhat inconsistently, there is a greater recognition that non-producer interests (processors, further processors, financial institutions, retailers, and consumers) must be involved in the formulation of agri-food policy. This recognition stems in part from the greater importance the government now attaches to marketing as compared to the traditional emphasis on production (Canada, Dept of Agriculture and Agri-Food 1994). It also derives from the fact that groups and interests traditionally at the margins of agricultural policy making were invited to be a part of the *Growing Together* task forces.

Third, by re-designing policy networks in a pluralist fashion, provincial and national governments have undercut the leadership of traditional farm organizations, augmented the influence of commodity groups with fewer members, and subsequently contributed to the segmentation of the farm community. The fragmentation occurs along philosophical lines and is intensified by the altered market relationships that follow on the region-alization of Canada's grain and cattle trade. At home a division has grown between those ready to meet American demands for policy harmonization and those urging the government to stand firm in support of Canadian grain-marketing practices and other indigenous policies. The two views reflect the more fundamental cleavage in the Canadian agriculture commu-nity between market-oriented farmers and commodity groups, on the one hand, and proponents of orderly marketing, on the other hand. Discord in the farm community has grown as the numbers in the former group have swelled, caught up with the ascendant ideas of market liberalism.

CONCLUSION

Domestic agricultural policies and policy making have been altered over the past decade, as Canada's agri-food sector has encountered greater foreign competition and international trade agreements have been signed. Agricultural policy making is no longer the preserve of the federal Department of Agriculture, provincial departments of agriculture, and farm organizations. New state actors, notably those responsible for trade matters, now exercise considerable influence on agriculture. So, too, does the Department of Finance. Financial and other elements of agricultural policy are now significantly shaped by departments whose primary mandate is not agriculture. However, although Agriculture and Agri-Food Canada must share the responsibility for agricultural matters, because of its technical and substantive expertise as well as its links to the farm community, it continues to have a large part in policy formation.

The confluence of internationalization, domestic budgetary pressures, and a philosophical change in the farm community has also left its imprint on the design of policies. The balance of ideas and values in the farm community has changed. In place of the traditional discourse of state assis-tance, collective bargaining, regional equity, and fairness for producers, the new discourse highlights market responsiveness, individual self-reliance, competitiveness, and efficiency. These new, neo-liberal ideas have always had their adherents in the farm community, but until recently they represented a minority view. The growing ascendency of the neo-liberal perspective can be traced to some extent to internationalization: neo-liberal views were the force behind the Uruguay Round of GATT and have been incorporated into the new accord, although more in principle than in substance.

What of the future? Do the internationalization and regionalization of Canadian agriculture mean that neo-liberalism and the consequent retreat of governments from agriculture are inevitable? Yes and no. Regionalization and the American pressure on Canada to realign its regulatory policies along American lines—that is, to dismantle regulated market structures—are proving very difficult to resist. Moreover, deficits and debts at both levels of government give provincial and federal decision makers strong incentives to practise the same divestiture policy with respect to expenditure programs. Thus, the neo-liberal current may be difficult to swim against. However, it is possible that the current will shift. Although international trade agreements have stripped Canadian governments of some of their legal authority and domestic policy independence, the World Trade Organization (WTO) may yet restore meaningful sovereignty to Canada and other smaller powers. If the WTO proves to be an effective international policeman of world trade, it will provide an antidote to regionalization by curtailing American aggressive unilateralism. If the WTO succeeds in bringing American trade law and trading practices under its purview, Canada will surely benefit. This is because the WTO will uphold the rules and principles of GATT: namely, modest neo-liberalism that continues to allow for a role for government.

However, it is not internationalization alone that will determine the future of Canadian agricultural policy. Domestic institutional factors and developments remain important. The same institution—federalism—that hampered a coherent trade policy will continue to prevent the state from withdrawing fully from the agri-food sector. Agriculture is of such economic and political importance in provinces like Saskatchewan and Quebec to rule out the full endorsement of neo-liberalism. Thus the road ahead for Canada will probably involve a mixture of neo-liberal and state-assisted policy instruments. Such a mixture would reflect the dual forces at play in Canadian agricultural policy: neither immunity from external forces nor complete subordination to international and regional developments.

NOTES

1. Although used to describe European states' latitude for devising independent domestic social policy, Rhodes' (1995: 21) characterization of domestic policy makers as now 'hostage' to international financial opinion is apt.

2. Cohn (1993: 21) points out that GATT Article XVI, which allows export subsidies, providing they do not permit a country to gain 'more than an equitable share of world export trade' (Article XVI: 3), and even Article XI, were written largely to take account of existing US legislation. The US Agricultural Adjustment Act permitted the US Secretary of Agriculture to use export subsidies. Section 22 of that Act allows import controls to be placed on entering commodities when they raise the cost of domestic price-support programs.

3. The Department predicts the United States will account for 65 per cent of Canada's agri-food exports by the year 2000.

4. Ministère de l'Agriculture, des Pêcheries et de l'Alimentation du Québec, *Commerce international du Canada et du Québec: Produits agricoles, alimentaires et marins : Bilan statistique 1984–1993*, 27, 37.

5. China and the former Soviet Union purchase one-half of Canadian wheat exports. *Future Directions*, on p. 30A, observes that many markets for bulk grain exports 'have become more self-sufficient or cannot afford purchases.' Further, Canada's value-added exports are 'static outside the US, especially in Asian markets where there is growing demand.'

6. Haas (1992: 3) defines an epistemic community as 'a network of professionals with recognized expertise and competence in a particular domain and an authoritative claim to policy-relevant knowledge within that domain or issue.' Its members included experts in agricultural trade policy in the Australian Bureau of Agricultural and Resource Economics; the International Agricultural Trade Research Consortium, an informal association of mainly North American university and government economists; and the International Policy Council on Agriculture and Trade, formed in 1987 'to develop and examine policy alternatives' to help governments to address global agricultural problems. The latter was composed of 26 agricultural economists, farm leaders, government officials, and businessmen from 16 countries in the developed and developing world.

7. NAFTA does not alter the terms of agri-food trade between the United States and Canada that are provided for by the FTA. It does introduce some obligations for all three countries in the areas of rules of origin, safeguards, and sanitary and phyto-sanitary standards. Agri-food trade between Canada and Mexico is comparatively small, and the provisions regarding agri-food trade between the two countries are similar to those for Canadian-US trade. Before NAFTA, over 85 per cent of Canadian agricultural imports entered Mexico duty-free. NAFTA requires all tariffs to be phased out over 10 years and for non-tariff barriers not permitted under GATT to be eliminated or converted to tariffs. Canadian exports of livestock and cereals to Mexico are expected to grow. See Hufbauer and Schott (1993: 58); and Josling and Barichello (1993).

8. More details can be found in Skogstad (1992) and Canada (1987).

9. It is assumed that Ottawa had to jettison those parts of its trade agenda that fell within provincial jurisdiction when it could not get provincial support for them. See Brown (1992: 96–7), Doern and Tomlin (1991).

10. Doern and Tomlin (1991: 186–99) specify that any changes in US law that name Canada are subject to review by a bi-national panel to determine

whether they are consistent with the FTA and GATT. Laws are also assessed for their effects on prior panel decisions.

11. See Doern and Tomlin (1991: 186–99), Clark (1992: 42), and Sinclair (1993: 226). Article 1902.1 states that the legality of US anti-dumping and counter-vailing duties will be judged on the basis of US law rather than GATT laws. Article 1902.2 gives the United States the right to change such laws without Canada's agreement.

12. Exports of beef and cattle, wheat, and beverages have risen.

13. It should be noted that the persistence of trade disputes can be traced, at least in part, to the fact that the FTA left many non-tariff barriers intact (such as Canadian supply management and US sugar and peanut import quotas) and failed to achieve dumping and subsidy codes.

14. A fuller discussion can be found in Skogstad (1995a).

15. A fuller discussion can be found in Boddez and Trebilcock (1993: 147–52).

16. GATT requires domestic subsidies to be reduced by 20 per cent over six years from a base period of 1986–8. However, no reductions are required in Canada (or in the European Union or the United States) since all three had already reduced domestic program spending by this amount. Export subsidies must be reduced 21 per cent in volume and 36 per cent in value from 1992 levels and over six years. If a country's exports have increased since the base period of 1986–90, it may use 1991–2 levels as the starting point for the reductions in export subsidies. The latter provision means that Canada will not realize significant gains in the early years of the agreement since EU and US export subsidies will not drop significantly.

17. Schmitz *et al.* (1995) argue that the tariffs, combined with the increases in the minimum access requirements for butter, ice cream, turkey, and eggs under the GATT agreement offer more protection for these sectors than they had before the Uruguay Round Accord.

18. The 'market power' muscle flexing by Ontario's chicken industry in 1994 lends credence to the prediction by Rosaasen *et al.* Frustrated with a quota that left it unable to provide the province's processors with the chicken supplies they needed, Ontario increased its own production beyond its quota allocation in 1994. Its 'unilateral' action was sanctioned by government officials and, once Ontario conceded some ground, was grudgingly accepted by other provinces (NFPC, 1994a, 1994b).

19. The new subsidies code provides for a more rigorous test to prove material injury and to link it to subsidized products: the threat of material injury must be demonstrated and not based on allegation or possibility. Sunset provisions ensure that anti-dumping and countervailing duty penalties will generally expire within five years unless a review proves their continuation is necessary to protect the importing country from injury. There are clearer rules for anti-dumping investigations.

20. With respect to dispute panels, the important departure from past GATT panels is that individual countries would normally no longer be able to block

the formation of a panel to hear a dispute or to block adoption of a panel's report. In the past, countries could effectively block implementation of a panel judgement for years by refusing to accept it (the United States was a major culprit). Under the new Uruguay Round rules, a country can block the adoption of a panel's report only if it has served notice of its intent to appeal. The adoption of appellate reports (which can uphold, modify, or reverse a panel's findings and conclusions) cannot be blocked by a country. In short, dispute settlement will 'be much more automatic' (Ontario, Ministry of Agriculture and Food 1994: 2).

21. Using slightly different language, Cooper and Higgott (1993: 135–6) describe Canada's trade policies as 'defensive', seeking 'to preserve or reinforce existing arrangements' and its domestic adjustment policies as constituting 'a defensive transactional approach'. By comparison, Australia has reacted to the same developments in the international political economy 'offensively, by creating new arrangements more suited to changing arrangements'.

22. Winham (1994: 485) observes that free trade negotiations are often undertaken, not only to achieve greater and more secure access to key markets, but also to provide states with 'a rationale for initiating and continuing domestic economic reform that would have been much more difficult to effect politically without the crutch of a bargained relationship with a larger trading partner.' See Paarlberg (1993), as well, on the US GATT strategy.

23. A fuller discussion of developments in the grains and oilseeds sector can be found in Coleman and Skogstad (1995). For a discussion of the supply-management reform see Skogstad (1995b).

24. There are three explanations for the different outcomes of the consultations in grains and oilseeds, on the one hand, and in supply management, on the other. First, it is easier for the Government of Canada to change financial policies than to rescind regulatory policies. Second, when the government launched the consultations, it said it was committed to retaining supply management. The intricate web of instruments that constitutes dairy supply management makes it difficult to change one without affecting the others. And third, the undetermined future of Quebec in Canada makes dairy support measures more difficult to reduce than grain support payments.

25. The US attempt to restrict imports of Canadian wheat is not a countervailing duty claim and did *not* hinge on establishing that Canadian wheat exports were subsidized by Canadian governments. Rather, the authority to impose import restrictions rested with the President, following a non-binding recommendation by the US International Trade Commission. The President acts when he is persuaded that imports have impaired or interfered with (driven up the costs of) US farm-support programs.

26. The legal authority of the provincial governments and their political influence on national trade policy help explain why Canadian negotiators pressed hard—and successfully—to have all provincial subsidies automatically deemed 'specific' and removed from the final text of the Uruguay Round GATT accord (Ontario, Ministry of Agriculture and Food 1994: 2).

27. There is little doubt that the combined pressure of dairy producers, the Quebec farm union, the Union des producteurs agricoles, and provincial governments persuaded the government to hold firm on Article XI.2.c. until the dying days of the Uruguay Round and then to insist upon very high tariff equivalents to replace the border protection that Article XI.2.c. had allowed.

28. I disagree with Robinson's (1993a) characterization of the FTA and NAFTA as centralizing, owing to the extent of the federal obligation to enforce the FTA and NAFTA, as well as the federal exclusive authority to request dispute-settlement panels and name Canada's members on the panels. Robinson (1993: 217) argues that the obligation on the Government of Canada to take *all necessary measures* to enforce the FTA and NAFTA means that 'federal intrusions into provincial jurisdictions can be expected to increase in scope.' Moreover, because the Government of Canada, not the provinces, decides when to seek resolution of trade disputes through bi-national dispute-resolution mechanisms, as well as who Canada's panel members will be, 'provincial governments have no place in any of the dispute resolution processes set out in the (NAFTA) agreement' (1993a: 207). Provincial governments may have no *formal* status when it comes to resolving Canadian-American trade disputes, but provincial premiers and agriculture ministers have confirmed that they were fully informed of federal negotiating strategies and developments throughout the 1994 wheat dispute with the United States.

29. Winham (1994: 502) notes the 'substantive contributions' of line departments like Agriculture to the NAFTA negotiations.

30. In June 1992 the Quebec department of agriculture, with the agreement of the farm organization UPA, held a summit to outline a way to obtain a consensus on a strategy for improving the competitiveness of Quebec agriculture. The subsequent discussions have been highly structured. They include 19 working groups involving 400 persons. Some of the working groups are quite specialized, dealing with farm credit and income protection; others are seeking ways to improve the competitiveness of particular commodities. There is an oversight committee (Comité de Suivi), which advises the Minister of Agriculture and is responsible for important matters like supply-management review, and market development. For further information, see Quebec (1992).

    Saskatchewan's 'Agriculture 2000' strategy began in November 1993, its intent being to provide a blueprint for a more diversified, value-added agricultural sector where the emphasis is on partnerships among public and private segments of the industry. As part of devising the blueprint, the provincial agriculture department struck a Farm Support Review Committee, staffed with 32 farmers, to devise a new long-term farm-income-support program (Saskatchewan Agriculture and Food 1993, 1994a, 1994b).

    Alberta's consultations in 1994 included discussions with the 'grassroots' as well as farm leaders and farm organizations. One of its goals was to devise safety-net policies and a business plan for the provincial department of agriculture, (*The Western Producer* 1995: 1; Paszkowski 1995: 7; Wilson 1995: 50–1).

Trade-Industrial Policy

G. Bruce Doern and Brian W. Tomlin

Canadian trade and industrial policies have always been intertwined, but for much of the post–Second World War period, analysts and governments often treated them as separate. Trade policy is aimed at influencing the nature and extent of Canada's exports and imports of goods and Canada's general trading relations with other countries. Industrial policy is aimed at promoting the development and competitiveness of Canadian industry (especially the manufacturing and resource sectors) and guiding its regional location and distribution within Canada. While these are broad definitions, it is clear that internationalization has always been a feature of the twinned policy realms. Trade policy was the international context within which industrial policies ultimately were made (Doern and Phidd 1983; McFetridge 1986).

However, these two policy fields have become even more closely linked in the last decade, and thus for the purposes of this chapter we refer throughout to trade-industrial policy.[1] The making of trade-industrial policy continues to be ever more internationalized, partly through the elaboration of existing international agreements such as the General Agreement on Tariffs and Trade (GATT) and the creation of new ones, such as the Canada-United States Free Trade Agreement (FTA) and the North American Free Trade Agreement (NAFTA) (Woodside 1993). It is also internationalized through the normal pressures and actions of other countries, especially the United States, by far Canada's major trading partner. However, internationalization is intensified even more by the direct effects on industry of globalization, which is defined here as the linked results of the telecommunications-computer revolution, escalating global financial capital flows, and flexible world production sourcing (Best 1990).

In what follows we first trace the change in policies and policy ideas emanating from the Department of Foreign Affairs and International Trade (DFAIT) and Industry Canada (and their predecessors) over the past 15 years. The emphasis here is on what is new or different about recent internationalization compared to the earlier forms. These policy changes are then examined further in relation to their interplay with the trade-industrial policy process looked at in three arenas and processes of adaptation, support, and resistance: interdepartmental and jurisdictional politics (within the federal government and between federal and provincial governments); associational politics; and a growing arena of client politics, which results partly from changes in the kind of policy instruments available to policy makers.

Internationalization has intensified the relationships between DFAIT and Industry Canada, not only making new forms of co-operation essential, but also generating new disagreements over which department plays the lead role and how each interprets the policy agenda needed both to support and to resist internationalization. Jurisdictional politics are not only interdepartmental, but also federal-provincial. These broader adaptations have partly centred on new approaches to eliminating internal trade barriers, the trade analyst's name for provincial 'industrial' policy.

For our purposes associational politics refers to a fast-changing and quite dense array of both traditional, vertical industry-sector interest groups and newer, horizontal industries for which groups may only be emerging or whose creation must be actively fostered by both DFAIT and Industry Canada. Associational politics regarding human capital interests and consumers is also being forged in traditional ways.

Client politics refers to the impact of internationalization and globalization on business firms as autonomous actors, as distinct from sectoral interest groups. These impacts and relations are linked especially to changes in the policy instruments available, especially the shift from spending and subsidies to knowledge and service roles by both departments (Doern 1994a).

POLICY CHANGE: BEYOND INCREMENTAL LIBERALISM

Since about 1980, trade-industrial policy has undergone significant change both in Canada and elsewhere (Hart 1993; Wade 1990). In one sense, Canadian policy since the Second World War can be seen as the pursuit of the long-term goal of general trade liberalization, and from this perspective it has had a 'freer trade' trajectory (McFetridge 1985; Blais 1985). There have been five major changes in policy: (1) an accelerated adoption of free trade, primarily through bilateral and regional agreements but also through GATT; (2) the extension of liberalized trade rules to goods, services, and some aspects of investment 'over the border'; (3) the re-energizing and deepening of trade- and export-promotion policies; (4) the decline of the tariff and of spending as policy instruments and the adoption of knowledge and service-delivery instruments; and (5) the growing attention to business framework laws. All of these changes were made in the context of a larger and often intense debate over both sovereignty and economic liberalism with the latter ascendant and the former on the defensive or in the process of being redefined.

The pursuit of free trade *per se*, first under the FTA and then under NAFTA, is clearly the first major change in policy. This change was all the more significant because it involved a shift to a bilateral and regional approach to trade policy from the multilateral GATT-centred emphasis of the earlier post-war years (Stone 1984). Even with Canadian participation in, and support for, a new GATT agreement in 1994, there is little doubt that trade policy shifted to a more regional approach over the period as whole (Hart 1993; Doern and Tomlin 1991).

The second change in trade-industrial policy involved a conception of free trade that extended considerably beyond tariffs and measures applied to goods 'at the border' to include more intrusive rules 'across the border' that would be applied as well to services and trade-related investment. Such policies were endorsed under the general concept of promoting national treatment (undertakings to treat incoming goods and investment no differently than domestic ones). Inevitably they involved changes to, and partial collisions with, many other policies that had previously involved domestic-policy levers in other, non-trade policy fields, from agriculture to intellectual property and from foreign investment to the environment and health and safety standards (Boddez and Trebilcock 1993).

The third change in trade-industrial policy was a renewed emphasis on the trade-promotion function of government, accompanied by a redefinition of traditional trade-promotion activities. In one sense, this was a renewal of an old policy emphasis with roots going back to the formation of Canada's Trade Commissioner Service (TCS) in the earliest days of the old Department of Trade and Commerce (Phidd and Doern 1978; Williams 1983). However, the focus of trade promotion was new because the TCS would have to adapt in order to service firms that are either going global or being globalized because of incoming competition. As we see later in the chapter, this would require new specialized expertise and an attention to knowledge and service delivery to firms.

Trade-industrial policy has also changed in a fourth way. The tariff, the earliest instrument of trade-industrial policy and the centre-piece of John A. Macdonald's National Policy, has been virtually eliminated. Furthermore, procedures to review the use of subsidies and trade remedies significantly limit the ability of governments to favour national firms or industries (Harris 1993; Eden and Molot 1993).

In the 1950s and 1960s, federal trade-industrial policy supported a more liberal international trade regime, even as it developed programs for various sectoral and infrastructure-based targets of policy, including the 'managed trade' package known as the Auto Pact. This took place at a time of high but declining tariffs, moderate subsidization, and relatively high government revenues. In the 1970s and early 1980s, while tariffs went down further and some new non-tariff barriers went up (for example, import quotas and voluntary export-restraint agreements), federal trade-industrial policy was cast much more explicitly in terms of regions and sectors (Savoie 1986). As tariff protection went down, subsidies and grants went up, at least as long as federal money was available. The provinces too, seeking to create regionally vital industries in the name of province building, played the spending version of sectoral and regional industrial policy (Tupper 1986).

By the mid-to-late 1980s, as the FTA was being negotiated, federal trade-industrial policy shifted into its present form. When the federal Department of Industry, Science and Technology was formed in 1987, it was given a micro-economic mandate that to a greater extent than ever before focused upon international competitiveness based on technology. The Conservative government of Brian Mulroney also announced that its new flagship department for the micro-economy was to base its work much more on good analysis and the dissemination of knowledge than on subsidizing weaker industries or trying to pick winners (Doern 1990). It was also to become, within the government, an advocate for industrial competitiveness—in short, a more aggressive horizontal agency.

Fifth, federal trade-industrial policy is once again emphasizing business framework laws. Such laws on competition policy, intellectual property, corporate governance, and the like have always been a part of domestic policy. However, the new emphasis, especially since the NAFTA and GATT agreements of the 1990s, is on how to link and harmonize international framework regimes in these areas to traditional trade policy (Doern 1995; Hart 1995).

Recent analyses suggest that these regulatory framework laws are rich in potential for international capitalist 'system frictions'. System friction is the term given by Sylvia Ostry to a new form of international discord, which, she argued in 1990, was much broader than earlier kinds of protectionism (Ostry 1990, 1993). The term 'underlined that there were several different market models *among* capitalist economies, the differences stemming from both historical and cultural legacies as well as divergence in a range of domestic policies' (Ostry 1993: 2). These different models influenced the international competitiveness of firms, where competitiveness was the product of an 'interaction between the firm's own capabilities and the broad institutional context of its home country' (Ostry 1993: 2). These frictions had to be reduced through harmonization of those policies that affected a firm's innovative capability. Ostry went on to argue that the emphasis would have to be on ensuring 'effective market access,' a concept, which she acknowledged to be 'soft and even slippery' and which, at its core, was at the blurred boundaries of competition, trade, investment, intellectual property, and 'high tech industrial policy'. Ostry was referring to relations among 'the Triad' of trading and political blocs: the European Union, the US-North America, and Japan-Pacific. These system frictions involve regulatory framework laws which are directed not at governments *per se*, but rather at firms (Albert 1993; de la Monthe and Paquet 1993). They are often in areas of policy that practitioners consider to be largely 'domestic' and that are embedded in different national capitalist traditions. However, these areas are already partly covered in the new GATT agreement and will certainly be covered even more fully in the next GATT-WTO (World Trade Organization)[2] round. Many, if not most of these framework areas are now, in departmental terms, under the jurisdiction of Industry Canada. It is worth noting that DFAIT is also being urged to make changes in the international rules about framework business laws. This is already happening directly, but it is also manifested through similar pressures *within* various international and regional bodies, such as the Organisation for Economic Co-operation and Development (OECD), the WTO, and various international sectoral regulators and regimes (Doern and Wilks forthcoming 1996).

Although those changes in trade-industrial policy are important, a mere list of them does not convey the intensity of the debate that accompanied them. Indeed, one of the main reasons why recent internationalization is different from earlier forms is that it evoked a more polarized debate about economic liberalism and national sovereignty. Broad economic liberalism had been a part of the long-term goal of federal policy, but globalization was now intensifying political concerns, as was the regional, especially Canada-US, nature of the change.

Sovereignty can have many meanings (Camilleri and Falk 1992). It can be a synonym for nationalism, a loose description of actual independent power possessed by national or sub-national governments, or a legal concept denoting the capacity of the nation state to decide and pass laws.

There is little doubt that the decision of the Mulroney government in 1985 to undertake free-trade negotiations with the United States brought the contending ideas of economic liberalism and sovereignty to the forefront of political disputes. It was an explicit part of the political struggle, particularly as portrayed by the broadly based anti-free-trade coalition that formed (Doern and Tomlin 1991; Drache and Gertler 1991). For its part, the pro-free-trade coalition presented the FTA as a progressive international initiative in which Canada was taking the lead; it portrayed its opponents as small-minded and timid nationalists who lacked confidence in a strongly entrepreneurial Canada. Although the sovereignty debate addressed the alleged loss of sovereignty that would result from the FTA as a whole, it centred on specific policy areas, concerning culture, energy, health care, and foreign investment. This concern about internationalization was widespread because the FTA dealt with Canada-US relations in one all-inclusive negotiation, and hence raised fears about American domination. It was also a time when the capacity of national governments to withstand the pressures of globalization was being debated, especially in Canada, and an argument could be made in favour of national strategies to support sovereignty (Pammett and Tomlin 1984).

By the time the policy debate over NAFTA was revived in the 1993 federal election campaign, their was considerably less concern about sovereignty, and, when expressed, it was often by different coalitions than previously. When sovereignty arguments were raised on the issue of the NAFTA side-deals on labour market and environmental policy, for example, it was the political left in Canada that allied itself with the Clinton administration to urge the Canadian government to accept the side agreements. This meant, ironically, that domestic Canadian interests were using Washington to influence the federal government in opposition to the Canadian business class, which, this time, was using the sovereignty argument (although mildly) to assert that the side deals had no place in a trade agreement.

There are two reasons for the change in the intensity of the concerns about sovereignty. First, NAFTA was presented as the 'FTA plus Mexico', simply a fine-tuning of the FTA. As a result, NAFTA generated less emotion, though not less opposition, than did the FTA (Robinson 1993b). Second, and more important, the globalization that was emerging in 1985 had accelerated by 1993; as a result it was realized that governments could not escape its effects. Even though public opposition to NAFTA was often greater than to the FTA, the arguments about sovereignty and against free trade were simply less credible, or relevant, by 1993. This decline in the credibility of the sovereignty argument can be seen in the adoption by the Chrétien government of an overtly aggressive free-trade agenda, which included the establishment of free trade not only in the Americas, but also with Asia-Pacific and the European Union. This Liberal trade policy represented a fundamental change from the party's opposition to the

Mulroney free trade agenda in the latter half of the 1980s (Doern and Tomlin 1991), opposition that continued right up to the 1993 election.

While this brief description captures the major changes in trade-industrial policy over the past 15 years, there are many important parts of this trade-industrial policy that moved at different rates and in different directions. For example, policy on research and development, intellectual property, or the agri-food sector may not have marched to the same drummer, or in response to the same international influences, as policy at the aggregate level.

DEPARTMENTAL AND JURISDICTIONAL POLITICS

With the changes in policy and ideas as background, we proceed now with a necessary second stage of analysis, namely, a discussion of the two lead departments involved. We must also assess broad changes in jurisdictional politics within Canadian federalism. While this section will emphasize the relations between the DFAIT and Industry Canada, it must be stressed that trade-industrial policy making has always involved the Department of Finance as well (Phidd and Doern 1978). This is partly a result of the latter's influence in all matters economic, but also because Finance has jurisdiction over tariffs, banking, international finance, and deficit reduction.

A further important factor is that parts of the trade function, especially trade policy and the Trade Commissioner Service, were transferred in 1982 to the then Department of External Affairs (Doern 1987; Keenes 1992). Before that, these key trade areas were in the hands of the industry departments. With the acquisition of the trade function, External Affairs, then renamed External Affairs and International Trade, became a decidedly more 'economic' department than it had been. The transferring of the trade function to External Affairs was one factor (among many) that moved the issue of free trade with the United States to the top of the policy agenda (Doern and Tomlin 1991). In short, this particular form of North American internationalization was supported by External Affairs officials and ministers, who advanced the free trade file through the Ottawa policy system.

For its part, Industry Canada, in 1982 called the Department of Regional Industrial Expansion (DRIE), almost immediately had to find ways to reinvent its trade-policy function, though on a much smaller scale. With a new, combined regional-national industrial mandate, DRIE was considered by many to be a protectionist department. And regional issues did dominate its ministerial priorities; nevertheless, the department was also increasingly involved, as a repository of knowledge, in the Sectoral

Advisory Groups on International Trade (SAGITs) that played a crucial consultative role during the negotiation and implementation of the FTA, and later NAFTA.[3]

But DFAIT (renamed in 1993) is still fundamentally a foreign-policy department, with varied bilateral, multilateral, and regional strategic, foreign-policy, and diplomatic responsibilities (Nossal 1989). Its main spending function is through development assistance programs administered by the Canadian International Development Agency (CIDA). It is to these central responsibilites that the trade function is appended. Compared to the Minister of Foreign Affairs, the Minister of Trade is the junior portfolio, though an important one.

The predominance of the foreign-policy function is not quite so apparent at the ministerial level. In the Chrétien government's Foreign Policy Statement, trade issues and the then Trade Minister MacLaren's aggressive promotion of trade and free trade had a prominence that belies the trade function's status as an appendage to a foreign-policy department. However, this may be because a clearly defined and forcefully expressed foreign policy is a scarce commodity in the post-Cold War world, and hence trade issues win the policy day by default.

DFAIT's involvement in trade issues has also been affected by the changes in the nature of those issues in the global political economy of the 1990s. While DFAIT continues to be involved in the implementation of the FTA, NAFTA, and GATT, and the Trade Minister appeared anxious to negotiate new trade agreements, the lead role of the department is continuously contested by the Department of Finance. In addition, the department must increasingly deal with 'over the border' issues that involve other departments which possess most of the expertise, and which do not see the issues exclusively in trade-industrial policy terms. DFAIT claims that it must have jurisdiction in all matters related to foreign affairs and international trade, including control of diplomatic communication and the negotiating of agendas and approaches to negotiations. However, such authority is much more difficult to assert as the number of domestic policy fields related to trade grows to include issues, such as agriculture, competition, intellectual property, telecommunications, and investment, that require specialized expertise. In the latter area, for example, DFAIT is responsible for negotiating bilateral investment treaties (Foreign Investment Protection Agreements, or FIPAs), but that mandate was itself the subject of intense interdepartmental debate.

On the industry side, Industry Canada is now a department with a three-fold mandate, especially after the changes made in 1993 and after the program review in 1994–5 (Doern 1995a). The newly reorganized department incorporated a wider set of policy tools and mandates by absorbing such areas as consumer-policy and business-framework law, including competition policy, from the former Department of Consumer and Corporate Affairs; telecommunications policy and research from the former Department of Communications (Doern 1995b); and investment policy and research, plus investment review, from Investment Canada. (Responsibility for investment development went to a new Investment and Technology Bureau in DFAIT.) In addition, the changes in the policy environment that had promoted the change from subsidization protection to international competitiveness in 1987, at a time when the FTA negotiations were underway, were now more obviously in place, and this reinforced the fundamental shift that had occurred in trade-industrial policy.

Industry Canada sees itself first as the chief micro-economic adviser to the government, a claim that may receive additional credibility from the fact that virtually the entire micro-economic component of the Department of Finance disappeared as a result of the 1994–5 program review cuts. Second, it emphasizes its mandate concerning business framework rules but set in the context of its new service function of supplying industry with knowledge rather than grants. Third, it is an industrial-sector developer, again through information and services rather than through subsidies.

From the perspective of Industry Canada, there are also new areas of overlap, and tensions, in the interdepartmental relationship. During the run-up to the reorganization of federal departments in 1993 by the short-lived Conservative government of Kim Campbell, Industry Canada (then ISTC) tried to have the trade function transferred back from DFAIT. As one senior official of Industry Canada put it, 'trade and industrial policy are the same thing, and we wanted to be able to use the full tool kit.' It was felt that more effective policy responses could be made if issues were resolved in a single industry-trade department. DFAIT, however, turned back the Industry Canada initiative.

More important, after the 1993 reorganization, Industry Canada was determined to put an end to its reputation as a protectionist department; it was helped to do so by its absorption of the more outward-oriented Investment Canada. Industry Canada was now committed domestically to advancing the pro-market micro-economic agenda of the government, and internationally to eliminating any rules or conditions that inhibited Canadian business access to other markets. In this latter endeavour, Industry Canada still views DFAIT first as a foreign-policy department and only secondarily as a trade and economic-policy department. Thus there are bound to be some disputes over who will have the lead role or whose views will prevail within the federal government.

Questions of jurisdiction in trade-industrial policy are also found in the federal-provincial arenas. Recently the combined effects of international-ization and globalization have made the internal barriers to trade within Canada much more important. Provincial governments have argued that commerce between provinces is a matter of provincial jurisdiction. The federal government, on the other hand, backed by constitutional powers over interprovincial trade and commerce, argues that an economic union must be finally established. In support, business interests have argued that Canada cannot prosper as a free trading nation if it does not have free trade internally.

Internal trade barriers refer broadly to non-tariff barriers to trade within Canada that result from federal or provincial policies and actions that distort trade through local preferences or discrimination (Ontario, Legisla-tive Research Services 1991). While federal policies are certainly part of the problem, the emphasis in recent years has been on barriers erected by provincial governments. These barriers were established by various governments in the name of provincial industrial policy, or simply as an element of 'province building'. Some were overt, such as beer and liquor regimes and hydro procurement policies, but many others were less visible.

The importance of these barriers and their competitive harm to Canada as a whole was recognized in the early 1980s (Safarian 1980). Indeed, the establishment of the Macdonald Commission in 1982–3 was premised on the need to preserve and enhance the Canadian 'economic union'. Estimates have put the cost of internal trade barriers at 1 to 1.5 per cent of GNP.[4] These estimates, however, fail to capture the larger economic losses that occur because the web of barriers and policies affects the practices of firms and industries. In many respects, the practical polit-ical and institutional problem in Canada is exactly the same as the subsidy situation internationally, namely how to persuade (domestic) semi-sover-eign political jurisdictions to give up the 'industrial policy' policies and practices that are seen by them, or by local interests, as useful tools of protection (Brown, Lazar, and Schwanen 1992).

The first significant policy response to the internal debate over trade barriers was the establishment in 1987 of the Committee of Ministers on Internal Trade (CMIT) (Ontario, Legislative Research Services 1991; Industry Canada 1994). Composed of federal and provincial ministers responsible for internal trade, CMIT is supported by a small secretariat at Industry Canada. The barriers to be identified and dismantled are decided at meetings of CMIT; all decisions must be approved by first ministers or provincial cabinets. Hundreds of barriers have been identified, but progress in removing them has been slow. After a burst of more intensive negotiations, a modest Agreement on Internal Trade was signed by first ministers and announced on 18 July 1994 (Industry Canada 1994a). The agreement includes a general statement of principles; an affirmation of constitutional rights; a general-rules section and a specific-rules section for the sectoral chapters; sections on administration and dispute resolution; and exceptions. The agreement is a step forward, but there is still a long road to the realization of free trade within Canada.

A brief discussion of internal trade barriers does not do justice to the intricacies of the jurisdictional politics of trade-industrial policy. Internationalization and globalization are generating newer 'bottom-up' regional-local networking theories of how knowledge-based competitive industries ought to be developed (Wolfe 1993c; Paquet and Roy 1995). These theories are being applied in several provinces, including Ontario, Quebec, British Columbia, and New Brunswick. Although their roots can be traced to earlier concerns about regional policy, the movement has accelerated because of the requirements of new trade agreements, new communications technologies, and the need to attract investors who have many countries and many regions and locales within countries to choose from (Roy 1995).

There can be little doubt, therefore, that both interdepartmental and jurisdictional politics have been altered significantly by intensified internationalization. But before the varied form of these changes can be examined further, we first need to understand the related changes in the associational politics of trade-industrial policy and how these are connected to policy formation.

ASSOCIATIONAL POLITICS

Associational politics refers to the sectoral and horizontal groups and latent interests that are a part of the trade-industrial policy process. We differentiate this from client politics, examined in the next section, which refers mainly to individual firms and businesses, which are the intended beneficiaries of the new emphasis on service and knowledge in trade-industrial policy.

Analyses have shown that in traditional industrial-policy formation, which emphasized active sectoral policies, there was little chance of success in Canada because the inherent structure of business interest groups ran counter to the institutional needs for such concerted and co-ordinated policies (Atkinson and Coleman 1989). Not only were there no overarching 'peak associations' of business in Canada, but even sectoral groups were rarely capable of reaching any consensus.

On the DFAIT side of the associational-politics arena there are also diverse interests and associations represented in the foreign-affairs community. The recent foreign-policy review showed an even broader range than has been typical, partly because of the interest among Canadians of various ethnic origins about the new nationalisms and independence of former Soviet republics and Eastern European countries. Although our subject in this chapter is the associational politics of trade-industrial policy, the larger foreign-policy community cannot be separated completely from the analysis, because these groups compete for DFAIT's attention and resources.

When one looks more closely at the associational arena, the new complexities become evident. For example, until quite recently, Industry Canada's sector branches were the main link with interest groups and were the analytical core of the department. These branches used to deal with largely vertical industrial sectors (such as automobiles and chemicals), but by the 1990s, with the addition of telecommunications, strategic materials, environmental industries, and bio-technology, they dealt increasingly with a mixture of vertical and horizontal sectors. In some of the new horizontal sectors, there was a need to create or foster associations.

The central job of the sector branches is, in general, to know their industries 'both analytically and experientially', as one senior official put it. In recent years, the sector branches have produced competitiveness framework studies, analyses of how a particular Canadian sector compares with those in other countries, and some custom-tailored analyses. This analytical work was seen as the strength of the branches. Far less developed was their ability to use, recombine, and impart the information that the government had collected and that could be of use to industry. This information included the potential or actual service aspects of some of the new business and consumer framework law. All of the above was, accordingly, tied to knowledge roles and hence to the new technologies of information delivery. In this sense, the internationalizing influences were accelerated by globalization, both through its effects on industry and by the new information technologies that changed the way Industry Canada had to function.

Industry Canada's associational world now consists of over one thousand associations of various vertical and horizontal configurations. In developing policy, the department certainly consults major business groups, such as the Business Council on National Issues, the Canadian Manufacturers' Association, the Canadian Chamber of Commerce, and the Canadian Federation of Independent Business. However, because of globalization, these consultations are insufficient for the requirements of developing trade-industrial policy. Moreover, slicing through the process is the world of service delivery, which is very client-based and characterized by a dense mixture of specific sub-clients, and even important re-definitions of clients, a point to which we return below.

The effect of internationalization on the changing associational mix in Industry Canada is also illustrated by the recent formation of a new sectoral group for the 'entertainment industry'; until recently, such a group would have been unthinkable. Cultural industry was the name given to the film, publishing, magazine, and related arts industries. These sectors and sub-sectors were seen as the protectionist preserve of other departments. This is no longer the case. Protection still exists and in many cases can still be justified, but there are also business opportunities for a Canadian industry that can be promoted internationally as an entertainment business.

A further crucial feature of associational politics is that it has been largely focused on, and disciplined by, the succession of trade negotiations over the past decade—the FTA, NAFTA, and GATT. Central to these negotiations were the Sectoral Advisory Groups on International Trade (SAGITs), which involved individuals from large industry associations as well as other representations made through both DFAIT and Industry Canada officials on the various negotiating teams. The great disciplining force of these negotiations was the fact that everyone knew that there were real deadlines and that crucial deals would be struck. This differs fundamentally from typical associational politics, which involves endless 'lobbying without deadlines'. This discipline was especially important in the FTA, when groups really confronted the realities of the global agenda. By the time of the NAFTA and GATT negotiations, many of these lessons had already been learned by industry sector groups.

An important issue for the near future is whether this form of associational politics will persist with no major new trade negotiations on the horizon. Without the discipline imposed by such negotiations, the various parties may simply fall away or look for other federal (and provincial) departments to lobby. Those who feel especially threatened by internationalization and globalization may hope to find a more hospitable climate in these other departments.

A related feature of associational politics in a period of enhanced internationalization is that cross-border or international alliances of interest groups are forced out into the open. In fact, DFAIT and Industry Canada have become involved directly in forming or encouraging these alliances. For example, the Canada-US trade dispute over softwood lumber generated strategic alliances between Canadian producers and American home builders and consumers against the producers of US softwood lumber. The same was true more recently for Canadian wheat producers and

American manufacturers of pasta, an alliance that was encouraged and facilitated by DFAIT. Of course, trade agreements that provide rules and objective procedures for settling disputes are intended to depoliticize trade-industrial policy; they seek to remove associational politics from trade-industrial policy by making protectionism more visible and thus less likely to be practised.

Another important arrangement of associational politics concerns what can be called human-capital interests. Industry Canada and its predecessor departments undoubtedly saw business groups as their main constituency. But because of internationalization and globalization, there is now a need, in Industry Canada in particular, to address human-capital issues and interests. At first glance, this suggests that the department should be dealing with unions and organized labour, but that is not happening because unions do not consider Industry Canada to be an ally. Nevertheless, at the sectoral level and across the government, Industry Canada is having to invent ways of relating to human-capital interests.

A recent example emerged in the very first micro-economic policy paper that the new Industry Canada submitted to the Chrétien government in the fall of 1993. The point stressed in the micro-economic paper was the need for far better social and human-capital policies for enhancing the mobility, training, knowledge, and flexibility of workers and professions at all levels. In the 1990s specific sectors of the department were already encountering many situations where, at the sectoral level, relations had to be established with educational institutions and local workers, both unionized and non-unionized. A further manifestation of this kind of change can be found in the recent 'lines of business' that each sector branch is now instructed to be involved in for its sector: investment, innovation, markets, and 'human resource development'.

A final point should also be noted about the associational politics of consumers. When Industry Canada inherited the responsibility for consumer policy as a result of government reorganization, consumer interests were institutionalized in that department; previously they had resided in the Department of Consumer and Corporate Affairs. Many consumer lobby groups saw this as the lamb wandering into the lion's den. But internationalization, as manifested in free trade agreements and free trade economics is, almost by definition, a pro-consumer policy. To this must be added in Industry Canada the new telecommunications presence, where conflict between issues of protection versus choice and competition (the medium versus the message) are endemic. Consumer interests are notoriously difficult to mobilize, for all the usual free-rider reasons, but they must not be lost sight of in the new trade-industrial policy nexus. Indeed, under the influence of ideas such as Michael Porter's competitiveness strategies, tough and informed domestic consumers, both individuals and firms as consumers of input products, are seen to be crucial to national competitiveness in the modern globalized economy (Porter 1990, 1991).

CLIENT-SERVICE POLITICS AND CHANGES IN POLICY INSTRUMENTS

In the previous section we suggested the prospect of the emergence of a more concerted emphasis on client-service politics. As noted above, the term 'client' may refer to interest groups, but, more important, it refers to individual firms and businesses that are seeking information as they adjust to the international realities of both policy and the global marketplace. To understand why this is happening we need to examine more closely some specific changes in the use of policy instruments. Basic policy instruments, such as spending, taxation, regulation, and persuasion or the dissemination of information (Doern and Phidd 1992), are one kind of tool a government uses to solve problems. In other words, they are an important means of actually changing the behaviour of citizens, firms, and interests. But internationalization has made some policy instruments more available and restricted the use of others. As a result, federal decision makers have moved in new policy directions where the new, or newly emphasized, policy instruments have redefined the relations, not only with associations or groups, but also with clients.

The first obvious change is the greatly reduced use of spending on subsidies and an emphasis on providing information and services. This shift in policy instruments was reinforced in the Liberal government's 1994–5 program review, which was itself undertaken partly because of international financial pressures to reduce the deficit. Thus, Industry Canada was given an enhanced mandate to promote sector development 'by providing services to the private sector to assist in increasing the competitive capacity of industry' (Industry Canada 1995: 2). This mandate became even more compelling after the program review resulted in a 42.5 per cent cut in the budget of Industry Canada. In fact, only 11 of the department's 54 funded programs survived the 1995 cuts (Industry Canada 1995: 3).

If spending was going down, then industrial policy would have to rely more on supplying information and service roles, especially for small and medium-sized enterprises (Paquet and Roy 1995). The other instrument available was the new business framework laws that Industry Canada had inherited in 1993 from the former Department of Consumer and Corporate Affairs. But even though these instruments were regulatory, they were also the base on which the department could perform its function of providing knowledge and service since it was felt that these laws yielded much information which was useful for business and which could be disseminated as a service to firms.

This new service orientation has also been influential in the promotion of Canada's exports, which is largely a DFAIT function. Of course, trade promotion has always been used to some extent, but its scope and nature have increased in importance in recent years. Promotion must now extend to many firms and industries that previously were not exporters, or that were not as subject as they now are to competition from imports. Export markets, moreover, are more varied (they include the Pacific Rim, South America, and Eastern Europe) or require more intensive information and penetration (sub-regions of the United States and Mexico). As internationalization has transformed this policy instrument, so policy has shifted towards a much more aggressive use of business-development activities in support of the export efforts of Canadian firms. This has required the department to develop new, specialized expertise in the following areas:

1. Understanding the new ways in which firms will conduct their business in a system of global firms and networks, where many 'Canadian' companies will operate as outer-circle firms, concentrating on developing alliances and networks.

2. Assisting firms in their efforts to obtain foreign technology and identifying and matching potential sources to the technological requirements of Canadian industry.

3. Understanding the issues and principles surrounding financial flows, investment, and financing in order to find investment opportunities for Canadians and foreign investment capital for Canadian ventures.

4. Requiring trade commissioners to undertake more thorough, sector-specific investigations in order to provide sophisticated market information to clients.

5. Encouraging trade commissioners to develop geographical and area specializations, combining language ability with a sophisticated knowledge of markets.

6. Ensuring trade commissioners understand trade policy and market-access issues in order to ensure fair competitive conditions for Canadian industry in domestic and foreign markets.[5]

The government also established the International Trade Business Plan (ITBP), a mechanism to co-ordinate international business development.[6] In June 1995, the Ministers of Industry and International Trade submitted a memorandum to cabinet that proposed means of expanding the capacity of the federal government to co-ordinate assistance to Canadian companies seeking major international contracts and of mobilizing sector specialists across government to develop sector strategies and disseminate information to client firms. These initiatives included the establishment of an International Business Strategy to co-ordinate the activities of the various government departments and agencies operating in this area; National Sector Teams to work with sectoral clientele to develop and implement sector trade strategies; Regional Trade Services Networks to integrate the delivery of domestic-trade development services; an International Business Advancement Team to co-ordinate government interventions abroad to secure major offshore contracts; and a Trade Opportunities Sourcing Unit, subsequently dubbed the International Business Opportunities Centre (IBOC), that would match Canadian firms with business leads identified by DFAIT officials abroad. The IBOC is staffed by officials from DFAIT and Industry Canada, and is located in DFAIT.

The influence of these new service and client relations can be further seen by briefly noting the example of the Canadian Intellectual Property Office (CIPO). This office is now part of Industry Canada. It manages the regulatory (business-framework) law processes for various kinds of intellectual property, such as patents, trademarks, copyright, and integrated circuits. In the 1990s CIPO has adopted a much broader definition of its mission, and of its customers and clients. The important point is that the pressure for a new service emphasis, even though CIPO is primarily a regulator, is coming from new international constraints and from the revised Industry Canada mandate, both of which have been transformed by internationalization and globalization.

Thus, CIPO's business plan stresses many of the converging developments inherent in trade-industrial policy. In its discussion of the forces affecting intellectual property, CIPO first cites the success of the Japanese model of economic development and then goes on to stress the NAFTA and GATT trade imperatives and identify global pressures for harmonization. CIPO states that 'despite fiscal limitations' government can improve the competitiveness of industry 'by granting intellectual property rights and by actively acquiring and disseminating intellectual property information' (Canadian Intellectual Property Office 1994: 10). Accordingly, CIPO has been reorganized to emphasize its clients and its product lines. The language of service rather than regulation is prominent.

Interestingly enough, the clients of CIPO, in order of importance, are 'current and future creators of intellectual property; the employers of intellectual property—the innovators who capitalize on its economic potential; and agents that facilitate acquisition of intellectual property rights,' such as patent and trademark agents (Canadian Intellectual Property Office 1994: 12). Since creators and inventors can come from any part of society, CIPO stresses the need to increase the knowledge of intellectual property within Canada's education system.

With respect to the second client group, the employers of intellectual capital, CIPO says that it must do more to discover who they are and what they need. With respect to agents, its 'third client group', CIPO notes that they are 'by far the most visible client group' and that of paramount importance to them is a system of intellectual property administered in a way that 'provides a high presumption of validity—credible and defensible intellectual property rights' (Canadian Intellectual Property Office 1994: 12). As recently as five years ago, this description of clients would have appeared in reverse order and would have been much more confined and regulatory. CIPO is but one part of the Industry Canada's realm, but the shift to a world of client and service politics is paralleled elsewhere.

The above examples suggest that if trade-industrial policy really does emphasize the knowledge and information role of government, almost all of this information will be given to firms. Whether firms, as opposed to interest groups, actually *want* to use the information remains to be seen. Sectoral interest groups are thus, to some extent, being put out of their traditional political business, namely fighting for tariffs or subsidies. We have stressed the need to look both at associational and at client politics precisely because client politics in a world of 'trade-industrial policy as knowledge service delivery' becomes more important. It is much more firm- and client-specific than previous industrial-policy spending programs. If it is not client-focused in a global economy, it will be less useful for decisions by firms about investment and product development. Another possibility is that sectoral or horizontal associations, in combination with new knowledge-based firms, will themselves become so good at supplying this kind of client-based, competitiveness-relevant information that DFAIT and Industry Canada's own functions as disseminators of knowledge will be made redundant or will simply not be commercially useful.

CONCLUSIONS

This chapter has set out the changes in Canadian trade-industrial policy since the early 1980s, and has examined the ways in which internationalization, including globalization, has been supported, resisted, and reconfigured in key arenas and aspects of the trade-industrial policy process. Internationalization has always been an essential feature of trade-industrial policy but it has increased markedly in the last decade because of the increase in the depth and scope of trade agreements like the FTA, NAFTA, and GATT. It has also accelerated because of the impact of globalization and internationalization on industry.

The nature of the policy change is not difficult to detect. Canadian trade-industrial policy has continued on its broad post–Second World War trajectory of liberalization, but with a much greater emphasis on regional free trade through the FTA and NAFTA. More important, trade-industrial policy has 'crossed the border', embraced services and some aspects of investment, and engaged a host of policy fields which, in the past, were relatively more domestic. Trade promotion, different in magnitude and kind from traditional activities, is also more important in Canadian efforts to expand markets. Because subsidization is severely restricted, trade-industrial policy stresses information services to enable Canadian firms to compete in international markets. It also focuses more than in the past on business framework laws. Such framework policies are regulatory and hence a source of potential new 'system frictions' among countries or trading blocs as capitalist systems and cultures duel with each other.

When seen through the dynamics of interdepartmental politics between DFAIT and Industry Canada, internationalization is producing mutual co-operation, as in the SAGIT processes of the FTA and NAFTA negotiations, as well as conflicts over mandate. Partly because of the uncertainties of the post–Cold War era, and partly because of the pace of recent changes in trade policy, DFAIT may well wish to slow down and consolidate the many recent changes. Industry Canada, on the other hand, may prefer to move faster to break down barriers caused by some of the international business framework rules. This could produce considerable conflict over which department has the high ground on trade-industrial policy.

Jurisdictional politics in the trade-industrial policy field also involves federal-provincial relations. The debate and negotiations over internal trade barriers have witnessed both increased federal determination to eliminate such barriers and a considerable capacity by the provinces to slow down such processes in order to preserve some minimum capacity for provincial industrial policy. Newer 'bottom-up' regional and local kinds of industrial development are also being formulated as a result of internationalization and globalization; these may call into question the function a federal industrial policy can usefully serve in the decade to come.

With respect to associational politics, the chapter reveals three interesting problems. First, a complex new mixture of vertical and horizontal sectors is in place, making it even more difficult to practise the older arts of industrial and regional policy. These changes, which are a direct result of internationalization and globalization, have created a constituency of business interests that is undoubtedly more outward-looking or favourable to free trade. Second, we have shown that the FTA, NAFTA, and GATT negotiations provided a real discipline to traditional interest-group politics. With the conclusion of these agreements, it is questionable whether industrial-sector groups will, in fact, be able to continue to coalesce around DFAIT, as they have done recently. They may turn their attention to other line departments and ministers, but these agencies are themselves less able to deliver the largesse that made 1970-style industrial policy so attractive to these groups. Lastly, in the realm of associational politics we have noted that internationalization and globalization elevate the importance of human-capital and consumer interests, neither of which have been the natural clientele of either trade or industrial policy makers. Also added to the associational mix are horizontal sectors, including new cross-cutting industries, such as environmental industries, strategic materials, and the like, where new modes of interest articulation and consultation have had to be created and fostered.

Finally, internationalization and globalization have helped generate a separate form of client politics in trade-industrial policy making and implementation. The shift in policy instruments from spending to delivering knowledge and services is directed at firms. This does not mean that the individual firm had no role earlier, but rather that service and knowledge delivery must necessarily be directed at people who make real decisions about investment and product development, something that sectoral and other interest groups, as groups, do not.

With respect to changes in broader policy instruments, the decline in the use of the tariff and subsidies is apparent in the analysis. While the decline in the use of the subsidy is also the result of budgetary deficits, the impetus for budget cuts is itself strongly driven by the forces of global change. Finally, trade-industrial policy is also becoming more regulatory, especially as the WTO acquires more teeth and as the framework laws of different countries become more harmonized.

NOTES

1. Inevitably in such a combined discussion of trade-industrial policy, many important features of the field are not examined adequately. For example, the chapter does not do justice to regional economic policy or to such essential elements of business framework policy as competition and consumer law (Doern and Phidd 1983; Savoie 1986; Doern 1995b).

2. The successor organization to GATT.

3. By this time, in 1987, DRIE had become the Department of Industry, Science and Technology in yet another reorganization.

4. The commission's estimate is 1.5 per cent; the Canadian Manufacturers' Association puts the figure at 1 per cent. See Whalley and Trela (1986).

5. See the following papers for discussions of the specialized expertise that will be required of the Trade Commissioner Service: 'Death of the Salesman?: Making the Trade Commissioner Service Relevant for the Future' (internal DFAIT paper); 'The Trade Commissioner Service and Canadian Competitiveness' (internal DFAIT paper); 'Commentary on the Trade Commissioner Service from Marketplace 89 Clients' (Sector Associates, July 1990); 'Highlights of the Trade Commissioners' Conference', September 1992; 'From a Trading Nation to a Nation of Traders' (DFAIT Policy Planning Staff Paper no. 92/5); and 'The Trade Commissioner Service in the Year 2000' (Report from the Conference Board of Canada, March 1990).

6. The ITBP is managed by an interdepartmental steering committee chaired by DFAIT and comprising DFAIT, Industry Canada, the Canadian International Development Agency, the Department of Agriculture and Agri-Food, the Department of National Defence, and the Export Development Corporation.

8

Investment Policy

Elizabeth Smythe

INTRODUCTION

This chapter examines how the globalization of production and the increase in capital mobility have affected Canadian policy on foreign direct investment (FDI) since the early 1980s. It argues that globalization has internationalized the investment-policy process, reshaping ideas on the role and impact of FDI, transforming the policy-making process, and ultimately redefining investment policy.

Globalization has been closely associated with the rise of multinational enterprises and the increase in foreign direct investment in the post-war international economy. The term globalization describes a process, in the last two decades, of increasingly integrated systems of production where large firms have been able to organize a global division of labour within a single corporate entity (Office of Technology Assessment 1993: 1). Part of this process has been the enhanced mobility of capital. This enhanced mobility of capital and globalization are the product of two sets of factors. The first involves organizational and technological changes in communications and production processes. The second involves the post-war decisions of the larger market economies to remove many barriers to the movement of capital and goods by restoring currency convertibility, removing restrictions on capital flows, eliminating or lowering tariff barriers, and removing barriers to foreign direct investment. In addition, the greater openness of financial markets and changing technology accelerated the speed and increased the size of capital movements. Large firms now compete on a global basis with a greater ability to respond to changing competitive conditions.

Although this process of globalization rested on an increasingly liberalized set of rules of international economic exchange, liberalization has not been complete or uniform among states. Nor has it resulted in a convergence of economic policy. In fact, the impetus for firms to become multinational in the post-war period was the varying degrees of openness of national economies. For example, FDI was, in many cases, a response to high tariffs.

Many of the moves to liberalize the rules of international economic exchange were made through varying kinds of state-to-state negotiations. Powerful actors, both governmental and non-governmental, attempted, sometimes successfully, to influence state actors with the implicit or explicit threats to impose significant economic costs. In the case of FDI these costs were partially a result of the incapacity of many states to find other sources of capital. Thus globalization should not be taken to imply that broad, inexorable, and neutral external forces, detached from specific interests and power relationships, have determined state policy. Yet globalization does affect the policy process, as this volume argues. In the case of FDI, this chapter illustrates how globalization internationalized Canadian investment policy in the 1980s and 1990s.

While it is possible to identify an international trend toward the removal of barriers to FDI (UNCTAD 1994: 293), states continue to try to influence the investment decisions of firms in order to maximize wealth and employment in their own countries. They do that because, whereas capital is increasingly mobile, workers are not. Nor have individual countries opted for pure policies of either adjustment or resistance to changes in global markets. Rather, they have adopted a mixture of policies according to their willingness and capacity to influence international economic transactions.

As a result of capital mobility, an increasingly integrated global system of production, shorter product cycles, and the high cost of research and product development, both competition and co-operation among firms have intensified. One result has been more complex links (strategic alliances) among firms and new forms of investment, which blur the nationality of firms (Reich 1990). The size and speed of capital movements and the flexibility of production processes have further limited the effectiveness of certain state policy instruments to influence investment and have limited the state's ability to predict their economic impact.

A second consequence of globalized production has been the increase in intra-firm trade, now estimated to be more than one-third of all trade (UNCTAD 1994). Intra-firm trade enables goods and services to cross national borders as transactions within a single corporate entity. This poses a number of problems for states if they try to influence trade flows and regulate corporate activity. Moreover, the growth of intra-firm trade means that trade policy has become increasingly linked to, and influenced by, investment flows.

The greater openness of national economies and the greater integration of national markets has also fostered both co-operation among states on policy and competition for investment as states have become more sensitive to one another's policy changes. As a consequence of the limited effectiveness of various national policy instruments and increased policy interdependence, investment policy is being made more and more at the international level. Virtually all of the changes in Canada's regulations dealing with inward FDI have, since the creation of Investment Canada in 1985, been the result of international trade negotiations, either bilateral or multilateral.

This chapter traces the ways in which globalized production and capital mobility have internationalized Canadian policy on FDI. It begins with an overview of the changing nature of Canada's investment position. However, it also highlights the growing dependence of the Canadian economy on access to the United States market, which has significantly influenced Canadian policy on FDI since the early 1980s. The third section of the chapter shows how these changes have reshaped the ideas and policy debate in Canada on foreign direct investment. It shows that increased capital mobility has led to a re-evaluation of the costs and benefits of FDI, has raised doubts about the attractiveness of Canada as an investment location in the 1980s, and, in conjunction with trade dependence, has resulted in a redefinition of investment as a policy area. No longer is FDI seen as a discrete policy issue, but rather as a part of a broader trade policy. This section also outlines the evolution of the Canadian investment-policy community (comprising groups, social movements, and parties) and its efforts to influence investment policy in the 1970s and 1980s. The changes in policy discourse and in the policy community help to explain why the liberalization of Canadian investment policy, though dramatic, was incomplete, despite the international influences and predominance of investment liberalization ideas in Canada since the early 1980s.

The fourth section of the chapter examines one of the main ways in which Canadian policy on FDI has been internationalized through the increased use of bilateral and multilateral agreements. Canada's role in their negotiation and their impact on Canada in shaping the policy process and the choice of policy instruments are discussed.

The fifth section of the chapter examines the institutional impact of these internationalizing forces by looking at the responsibilities of departments and agencies for formulating and implementing Canadian investment policy. It highlights the decline in the power of regulatory agencies and departments concerned with domestic industrial development and the enhanced role of departments with a trade focus and mandates to negotiate international economic agreements—a reflection of the extent to which investment issues have been linked to, and subsumed by, trade and competitiveness concerns. The final section summarizes how and why investment policy has become internationalized, and the implications for state sovereignty and democracy.

CAPITAL MOBILITY, TRADE DEPENDENCE, AND THE INTERNATIONALIZATION OF INVESTMENT POLICY

The premise of this volume is that what hitherto were largely domestic policy issues have, in recent years, been more and more influenced by external forces. Canadian policy on FDI, unlike perhaps some other policy areas, has always been shaped partly by external elements. Like trade policy, Canadian policy on FDI has sought to maximize the economic benefits to Canada from inward direct investment by firms based elsewhere, primarily in the United States. Thus the success of Canada's investment policies has always depended on external forces, be they states or corporations.

In the 1980s however, significant changes occurred in the nature of this relationship that have reshaped Canada's ideas about the nature of FDI, the goals of Canadian policy, and the choice of policy instruments.

As a result of lower tariffs and enhanced capital mobility, Canada, which was largely an importer of FDI in the 1950s and 1960s, became, in the 1970s and 1980s, increasingly an exporter of capital. By 1994 the stock of FDI in Canada had reached $148 billion, about two-thirds of which was based in the United States (Statistics Canada 1995). This proportion had dropped from the three-quarters provided by the United States in 1985, largely as a result of increased Japanese and European investment (Industry Canada 1994c: 239). At the same time, the stock of Canadian direct investment abroad has now reached over $125 billion after growing rapidly, particularly in the early 1980s (Statistics Canada 1995). Most of this investment has gone to the United States, although in recent years it has diversified into other areas, including Europe and Latin America.

Open investment policies in the early post-war period, attractive opportunities for American firms in the resource sector, and decisions in the early 1970s not to impede seriously the expansion of established foreign firms, have created persistently high levels of foreign control despite changes to investment flows. While foreign ownership and control slowly declined from their peak of 36 per cent in the early 1970s and then stabilized in the 1980s at about 24 per cent, these levels are still unprecedented in any of the other Group of Seven (G7) countries (Industry

Canada 1994c). Since 1989, foreign ownership and control have been slightly increasing. In some sectors, such as manufacturing, foreign control has been even higher, reaching, for example, over 64 per cent in chemical industries and 68 per cent in electronic industries in 1994 (Statistics Canada 1995: 126).

Canada's share of world flows and stocks of FDI has also altered dramatically since the earlier post-war period. In essence, Canada has lost its pre-eminence as a destination for FDI. In 1967 Canada held over 18 per cent of the global stock of FDI. During the 1970s and early 1980s Canada's share fell dramatically to 10 per cent by 1980 and 6.6 per cent by 1990 (Industry Canada 1994c: 240), as Europe and the United States became magnets for new FDI. This change came to be interpreted as a measure of the declining attractiveness of Canada as an investment location.

Stocks of FDI in an economy can increase in a number of ways. Established foreign firms or their subsidiaries can expand, new firms can be formed by incoming investors (often called greenfield investment), or established Canadian firms may be acquired or taken over by foreign investors. In the early post-war period, greenfield investments were the predominant mode. Since the late 1960s much of the growth in FDI has occurred through expansion of established foreign firms or by acquisitions. Acquisitions as a form of entry for foreign capital pose particular political problems for Canada. Most industrialized countries have intervened in foreign acquisitions of domestic firms since they are often seen to increase foreign ownership with little in the way of offsetting benefits.

Aside from the shift in Canada's role as a host (importer) of foreign capital to its role as home (exporter), there has been a change in the nature of Canada's post-war trade relations that has had major consequences for investment policy. The most significant by far has been the increase in trade dependence on the United States market, which continued despite state efforts to diversify markets in the early 1970s. By the mid-1980s over 75 per cent of Canada's exports were going to the United States, up from 59 per cent in 1955 (Statistics Canada 1983, 1994). By 1993, as a result of further bilateral trade liberalization, the figure was over 80 per cent (Statistics Canada 1994). The combination of high levels of American FDI and the increasing openness of the two economies has resulted in more intra-firm trade.

Thus globalization, in Canada's case, has really meant ever closer economic integration with the United States in the 1980s and 1990s. In the light of the great disparities in the size of the two economies and their dependence on trade, this trend has given the United States additional means of influencing Canadian policies in the event of investment disputes.

INTERNATIONALIZATION AND INVESTMENT POLICY

In order for these changes in Canada's trade and investment relations to have an influence on policy, they must be interpreted and assigned meaning. The resulting ideas, along with institutions, will shape the political agenda, particularly the way in which the issue or problem of FDI is defined, what solutions are seen as viable, what policy instruments are seen as feasible alternatives, and whose voice is heard in the policy process.

Public-policy analysts have also pointed to the importance of the nature of policy communities for an understanding of the relationship between the state and civil society. Policy communities have been defined to 'include all actors or potential actors with a direct or indirect interest in a policy area or function who share a common policy focus and who, with varying degrees of influence shape policy outcomes in the long run' (Coleman and Skogstad 1990: 25). The focus on policy communities allows for a disaggregation of the state itself and the possibility of variations in both state autonomy and capacity across issue areas.

We begin by examining the changing ideas about inward FDI and how they have been reflected in a changing discourse on investment issues. Until the 1980s Canadian investment abroad was relatively small and thus policy attention to and action on outward FDI has been much more recent and will be discussed at the end of this section.

Any discussion of political discourse on investment issues in Canada must relate them to the fundamental structures and dominant ideas of Canadian liberal capitalism, which defines a limited realm of state intervention and the central role of the market. Canada's history, however, has been one of selective state intervention in a number of areas of the economy—sometimes direct, as in culture and transportation; sometimes less direct, as in manufacturing; and in many cases, not based on any kind of coherent plan or industrial strategy. Yet the Canadian state, like many others, was under pressure in the post-war period to intervene in the economy to secure economic well-being for its citizens in a country where major economic assets are privately owned and, in the case of FDI, externally controlled. Thus policy discourse on FDI has centred on the issue of state intervention and economic well-being. The fact, however, that so much investment in Canada was, and is, externally linked raises the question of state sovereignty.

Sovereignty is generally defined in the international-relations literature as the 'institutionalization of public authority within mutually exclusive jurisdictional domains.'[1] A sovereign state thus has final authority within a defined territory. Increasingly however, theorists have argued in favour of unbundling the concept or principle of sovereignty and examining its variation across states and issues. One of the main sources of the erosion of state sovereignty over economic matters since the war has been the increased movement of capital, in the form of both short- and long-term investment. The debate on FDI and sovereignty in Canada is part of this broader debate.

The concern about FDI has evolved substantially since it emerged as a policy issue in Canada in the late 1950s. At that time, sovereignty and the extent to which growing foreign ownership and control would erode the capacity of the Canadian state to implement policies and exercise authority over the behaviour of foreign firms was a central issue. Concerns over FDI included the possibility that externally based firms might come under the authority of foreign states (extraterritoriality), that firms would internalize cross-border transactions and elude regulation by the host state (e.g. transfer pricing), and that subsidiaries would be required to promote corporate interests that ran counter to the interests of the host country.

At the same time, FDI was also thought to provide significant benefits in the form of investment capital, technology, and market access. The potential loss of sovereignty was thus partially offset by economic gains. Early policy action included attempts to raise the level of Canadian ownership by discouraging acquisitions;[2] regulations excluding or limiting investments in banking and the media; and the creation of Crown corporations (such as the Canada Development Corporation). Until the late 1960s, however, dissension in the Liberal cabinet precluded much effective policy action.

A series of attempted high-profile take-overs of Canadian resource companies in the late 1960s and the reports of two task forces, one by experts outside government and the other internal, altered the policy discussion and presented the performance of foreign-owned subsidiaries as a problem as serious as any loss of sovereignty.[3] The objections to foreign ownership included poor export performance, inefficiency, low levels of research and development in Canada, and subsidiary sourcing policies that discriminated against Canadian suppliers. The crucial question was whether to correct these problems through regulation of foreign investors, through domestic economic reforms, or both. With the leaking of the 1970 interdepartmental recommendations to cabinet, the public debate very quickly centred on a cabinet recommendation to regulate the entry of foreign investors, using case-by-case bargaining between officials and investors. Two other options were largely excluded from the debate. The first was to refrain from any control over FDI, an option that was never suggested, even by business groups. The other was to repatriate the Canadian economy through extensive regulation and state ownership; such a policy was advocated by a group in the New Democratic Party but ultimately rejected as party policy.

The deliberations on investment policy in the early 1970s were at first led very much by the government. The cabinet's decision to take action was co-ordinated by the Privy Council Office and handed over to a task force under the direction of the Minister Herb Gray. A number of groups, provinces, and opposition parties competed to influence the process. As a result of internal divisions, the Liberal cabinet decided that the Department of Industry, Trade and Commerce would screen only acquisitions. But the leaking of the task force's report to cabinet, the minority government situation in which the Liberals found themselves in 1972, and the persistence of a nationalist wing within the Liberal party resulted, in 1973, in legislation creating broader screening of new investment and expansion of subsidiaries by a separate agency. Thanks to the confidence of officials in Canada's attractiveness as an investment location, the phased-in screening of new investment and EFC expansion, the narrow definition of EFC, and the exemption of much of their investment activity, there was sufficient cabinet consensus to implement the policy. The possibility that the screening might deter investment remained a continuing concern, especially for the business community, and was monitored by the Foreign Investment Review Agency (FIRA) over the years.

The general screening policies were accompanied by a series of sectoral regulations and the creation of state corporations. However, none of these policies were ever incorporated into a broader industrial strategy or co-ordinated with other economic policies to address systematically the issue of foreign ownership.

Further changes to investment policies were proposed in 1980 to strengthen FIRA and repatriate the energy sector. Again, there was little outside consultation until the legislative stage. In the case of FIRA, however, the proposals never got beyond the cabinet table. The groups opposing investment screening had begun to change by the 1980s. Business opposition was much more unified and vocal,[4] while the cabinet, less confident of Canada's bargaining position with manufacturing firms (as opposed to energy firms) was divided (Doern 1983: 220). In addition, provincial complaints about FIRA were many, and opposition to giving it more power was unified. Moreover, strong government and business opposition emanating from the United States formed an important ally to Canadian business groups seeking to limit state intervention and regulation of investment.

The different context of FDI policy making in the 1980s was directly due to the impact of Canada's changing investment and trade situation on ideas about FDI. Doubts were expressed about Canada's attractiveness as an investment location and the costs of investment screening. By 1982 the Liberal government had decided to make changes in investment-screening regulations to expedite some cases. In 1984 the newly elected Conservative government eliminated the screening of greenfield investment and undertook a vigorous campaign to attract new FDI, yet retained the screening of major acquisitions, including indirect ones. Special restrictions were retained for cultural industries and the oil and gas sector. Decision makers and officials had clearly come to view FDI and Canada's investment requirements somewhat differently.

In essence, the further lowering of tariff barriers as a result of the Tokyo round of the General Agreement on Tariffs and Trade (GATT) negotiations and the resulting requirement for further restructuring to maintain competitiveness strengthened the view that Canada would need new capital and technology. Lower tariffs also meant that FDI would not be attracted or retained solely to serve a local market. Furthermore, the world-wide recession had slowed the growth of FDI and increased global needs for capital, resulting in more competition among countries to attract FDI. These ideas were disseminated through international organizations such as the Organisation for Economic Co-operation and Development (OECD) and were repeated in Canada both by government agencies and by research bodies with business links, such as the C.D. Howe Institute and the Conference Board,[5] along with advisory bodies like the Economic Council and the Royal Commission on the Economic Union (Macdonald Commission). The conclusion drawn was that Canada was less and less attractive to investors, a view that appeared to be confirmed by weaker inflows of FDI and higher outflows of investment capital, especially to the United States. The decline in Canada's attractiveness undermined the strategy of bargaining with investors over entry in exchange for enhanced economic benefits.

The strong US government and business opposition to Canada's investment policies also helped to change ideas about screening FDI. The opposition of the United States to investment screening and performance requirements by the host state had resulted in the extension of US trade law to include unfair restrictions on investment as a basis for trade retaliation. This reinforced the consensus in the federal government that Canada could no longer 'afford' investment screening since it would jeopardize Canada's trade relationship with the United States (Canada, Dept of External Affairs 1983).

Nevertheless, the sovereignty issue never completely disappeared, and the acquisition of Canadian firms by foreign buyers remained controversial, and likely to offend the opposition parties, nationalist organizations, and public opinion. As the Industry Minister Sinclair Stevens (1984) so eloquently put it in introducing the 1984 Investment Canada legislation, 'Industrialized nations do not simply throw their door open and invite others to take over the components of their economic, cultural and political sovereignty.' However, the continued screening of acquisitions may have been at least in part more apparent than real since Investment Canada approved all applications, leading one nationalist to call it 'the world's most expensive rubber stamp' (Watkins 1994: 19). In some cases, approvals were given after various undertakings had been obtained from the investors. But at the same time in various bilateral and multilateral trade negotiations, Canada appeared to be bargaining away the power to impose these performance requirements.

Doubts about Canada's ability to compete as a location for FDI were seen in the creation of Investment Canada in 1985 with its new emphasis on promoting investment. The agency, which was given a mandate to seek new investment, began a vigorous promotional campaign, including investment seminars, the creation of a data base on investment opportunities in Canada, glossy publications, and the recruitment of business people to promote Canada abroad.

Yet the announcement that Canada was open for business increasingly came into conflict with public opinion, especially in the case of acquisitions. While take-overs are politically troublesome for many countries, it is the issue of culture and foreign control in Canada that goes beyond the legal question of sovereignty and touches on the sensitive question of national identity. It was an issue, therefore, that even the most zealous advocates of investment liberalization approached with caution. The dilemma of culture and the liberalizing of investment regulation can be seen in Canada's policy on book publishing. The Baie Comeau policy, limiting FDI to joint ventures and requiring divestment in the case of indirect acquisitions, split cabinet and departments in the first major attempt to enforce it, the case of Prentice-Hall in 1985. The messy case coincided with a large-scale investment-promotion effort then underway in the United States and exasperated the Canadian ambassador, Alan Gotlieb.

Such cases have proved troublesome for governments because they arouse intellectuals, artists, nationalists, and the media. At the same time, the United States has increasingly come to regard entertainment as an important service industry where it enjoys a comparative advantage, and it is willing to pursue aggressively the interests of large entertainment conglomerates in trade negotiations.

The dramatic, but incomplete, shift from broad screening to limited screening of acquisitions and the energetic promotion of inward investment is only one side of the change in investment policy. The other side was the dramatic rise in outward flows of FDI, especially in the late 1970s and early 1980s.

As might be expected, this change has had an influence on investment policy as the interests of Canadian firms and large subsidiaries have become increasingly involved in investment outside Canada. This has caused the corporate community to take an interest both in access to other markets for their investment activity and in enhanced security for investments, particularly in Eastern Europe. These concerns have been reflected in bilateral and multilateral agreements. In addition, however, Canadian government agencies have limited corporate risks in two ways. For many years investment insurance for specific projects has been provided through the Export Development Corporation. More recently, the Department of Foreign Affairs and International Trade (DFAIT) has been negotiating Foreign Investment Protection Agreements (FIPAs), mainly with Eastern Europe and developing countries.[6] These agreements cover such issues as the treatment of investors, expropriation, and processes for resolving disputes. They are part of a growing international trend.

In recent years Canada has been pursuing FIPAs more aggressively. A new kind of FIPA has been approved by cabinet, and guidelines developed to establish priority countries for FIPAs. The guidelines are based on the level of current Canadian direct investment in a country, the potential for future investment, and the risk for such investments. The opinions of Canadian firms about the investment policies of foreign countries have also been solicited by DFAIT. Canada has also been active in agreements to open Eastern Europe to further FDI through the Energy Charter Treaty and attempts to develop a code on investment in the Asia-Pacific Economic Co-operation Forum (APEC).

With the rapid development of Canadian direct investment abroad (CDIA) has come a new assessment of its significance. In 1985, the government claimed that such flows were capital flight and showed that Canada's desirability as an investment location was waning (Stevens 1984). More recently, these flows have been viewed much more favourably as part of the process of globalizing production which would ensure that Canadian firms maintained their competitiveness. CDIA is now believed by economic analysts in and outside government to be contributing to further export development, improving Canada's current account balance, and not diverting domestic investment (Industry Canada 1994c). In fact, the rapid growth of CDIA has received scant public attention. The exceptions are the few cases where transfers of production have led to job losses in Canada, or firms have invested in countries with poor human right records or in projects with deleterious environmental effects.

The policy community dealing with outward investment is very small; it consists essentially of those firms with CDIA and a small number of departments or agencies. The reason there are so few firms is partly that the bulk of CDIA is so concentrated in a few firms. The largest 159 Canadian multinational enterprises, according to a 1994 study, accounted for 50 per cent of all CDIA. Of that amount, 80 per cent is accounted for by the largest 20 firms (Industry Canada 1994c: ii). These firms have had a direct influence through consultations with officials on investment barriers and through organizations such as the International Chamber of Commerce and the Canadian Council for International Business.

As this discussion has shown, the changes to ideas about the significance of both inward and outward FDI have been a result of Canada's changing relationship to international capital. But major changes to Canada's FDI regime in the late 1980s and the 1990s have also been caused by a number of bilateral and multilateral agreements. This is perhaps the most significant aspect of the internationalization of investment policy, and it is to this which I now turn.

INTERNATIONAL AGREEMENTS AND CANADIAN INVESTMENT POLICY

Because of Canada's trade dependence on the United States, globalization has meant that investment policy became linked to, and ultimately absorbed by, trade policy. Canada's dependence on the US market and the US opposition to investment screening set the stage for a trade-off of screening for enhanced security of access to the US market. This process was encouraged by an increasingly organized and unified Canadian business community.

Trade negotiations have also led to the transformation of the investment-policy community through the development of a trade-policy network of formalized, federal consultation mechanisms with the provinces and the business community, the latter modelled on the US process. But in a country with a British form of parliamentary government, these structures have privileged the access of business to decision makers and largely marginalized the opponents of liberalized investment.

The most significant negotiations for Canadian FDI policy have clearly been those relating to the Canada-US Free Trade Agreement (FTA) and the North American Free Trade Agreement (NAFTA). Since these two agreements and the negotiations involved have already been the subject of intensive scrutiny, I will focus instead on the way these agreements have affected investment policy and the policy community, and the precedents they have set for further international negotiations on investment.

These two agreements, however, should also be placed in a broader context of international norms and agreements on FDI which preceded them. The behaviour both of multinational corporations and of states seeking to control foreign investors has been the subject of negotiations in the GATT, the United Nations, and the OECD.

Negotiations have centred on three basic issues: first, the right of access, that is, the ability of capital to move in and out of countries freely; second, the treatment of foreign firms, once established in a host country; and third, expropriation by a host state of foreign assets. The founding charter of organizations like the OECD and the GATT, which reflect their neo-liberal origins, emphasize the minimizing of barriers to the movement of goods and capital, free access, and national treatment. While the taking of private assets for a public purpose (expropriation) has been a long-accepted element of state sovereignty, the issue in this case has been what constitutes fair and adequate compensation for investors.

The positions of individual countries on these issues have depended on whether a country is an importer or exporter of FDI; that was especially the case in the 1960s and 1970s, when those roles were clearer and cross-investment less prevalent. The pre-eminent home state for much of the post-war period has been the United States, followed, in the 1980s and 1990s, by Europe and Japan. As a major exporter of capital, the United States has long been in favour of free access, national treatment, and compensation, especially after a wave of expropriations in developing countries in the 1960s. In contrast many capital-importing countries, particularly in the Third World, sought international recognition of the right of host states to control inflows of FDI, apply discriminatory treatment where necessary, and ensure that all investment disputes were dealt with under the host state's jurisdiction. Such states were more influential in the UN General Assembly in the mid-1970s, and as a consequence the United States looked to other organizations, such as the OECD and GATT, to further its investment interests.

The OECD embodied the principle of freer movements of capital in its Code on Capital Movements. Because of the extent of FDI in the Canadian economy, Canada did not sign this binding code in the 1960s, although many states signed only to lodge reservations (or exemptions) for a number of domestic policies. With the threat of UN action on a code dealing with multinational enterprises in the early 1970s, the United States pushed hard at the OECD for a code that combined guidelines on multinational enterprises with precedent-setting commitments of countries to remove barriers to FDI and to accord national treatment to foreign firms (Smythe 1994: 411). In this effort it was supported by the Business and Industry Advisory Committee, the international business lobby at the OECD, which included Canadian business organizations as affiliates.

Although the resulting code was only partially acceptable to Canada, it was non-binding, and Canada adhered to it with a reservation on national treatment. This led to extensive efforts by the OECD over the next 20 years to monitor the investment practices of its members, scrutinize their policies, encourage policy transparency, and work toward the elimination of barriers to FDI. The failure of the efforts by the developing countries to challenge the neo-liberal hegemony at the United Nations was reflected in the inability to negotiate an investment code (Krasner 1985). As a consequence, the OECD and GATT have been the organizations in which international rules on FDI are being made.

In the early 1980s, the United States began to consider the implications for trade of the proliferation of performance requirements imposed on US firms abroad. The United States tried to have the matter addressed at GATT, where the influence of Third World host states was weak and the potential for enforcing rules through trade retaliation was greater. However, the inability of GATT to agree to hold a new round of negotiations and the growing foreign-investment dispute with Canada led the United States to launch a GATT case against FIRA in 1983. The case was partly successful for the US in that it established that certain requirements on sourcing were in violation of Article III on national treatment. This set a useful precedent, and with some arm twisting the United States was able to ensure that trade-related investment measures would be part of the trade negotiations that began in Uruguay in 1986.

It is within this context that the United States demanded that investment issues be part of the free trade negotiations, even though changes had already been made in Canada's investment screening in 1985. US calls for national treatment and the elimination of investment screening were no surprise to Canadian officials (Canada 1986), although they had hoped to confine the US demands to trade-related measures. The demands were finally put forward by the United States in April 1987. The dilemma for Canada was how many concessions to make on investment in return for securing market access (that is, restricting the application of American trade-remedy laws) without arousing the ever-present concerns about sovereignty in negotiations that were already so controversial.[7]

Formal structures of consultation with the private sector and provinces were established for the trade negotiations in 1986. The private-sector structure took the form of an International Trade Advisory Committee (ITAC) and Sectoral Advisory Groups on International Trade (SAGITs). These groups allowed the Canadian federal negotiators to manage domestic interests, get advice on sectoral impacts when necessary, and manage the flow of information (Doern and Tomlin 1991). This was necessary partly because of the complexity and scope of the negotiations and the confidentiality required. The ITAC was intended to have labour representation as well, but since the Canadian Labour Congress refused to participate, the committee was dominated by business. Legislators were largely excluded from the process as well, and the information provided to the media was carefully controlled. These kinds of negotiations ultimately result in a package deal, which, in the case of trade issues, has become increasingly complex. It is the package as a whole that goes forward to legislators for approval. Investment measures are then only a small part of the package.

Concessions were made in the final negotiations for the FTA, which raised the threshold of reviewable acquisitions over a five-year period to $150 million, eliminated the review of indirect acquisitions, and accorded US firms national treatment. Exceptions were made for some industries, particularly culture, uranium, and oil and gas. Although Canada retained the right to screen major acquisitions, the agreement limited the scope of performance requirements that were permitted. For example, it excluded domestic sourcing, while the national-treatment commitment limited equity requirements. The whole purpose of reviewing acquisitions, however, had been to create a bargaining situation where access could be traded off for enhanced performance. But by 1987 Canada's priorities were in the area of new technology and in ensuring that foreign-owned subsidiaries in Canada were given world product mandates. These were still permitted under the agreement.

In contrast to the FTA policy process of 1987, the foreign-investment-policy process of the late 1960s and the early 1970s concentrated on the control of FDI as an issue in itself. Even the Gray Report was leaked early enough to allow for public debate. Parties and interest groups, such as the Committee for an Independent Canada and the Chamber of Commerce, lobbied the government for some time before action was finally taken.

In the case of the FTA in 1987, there was a polarized public debate over the trade deal. Investment was only one aspect, however, and it could not be separated from the rest of the agreement. The package as a whole was approved as a result of the 1988 election.

The FTA was quickly followed by the NAFTA negotiations, which built upon the FTA both in terms of the consultation process and the investment provisions, although the definition of FDI was significantly broadened. Mexico adopted a threshold for screening acquisitions similar to Canada's. Canada also kept the cultural exemption but unilaterally lifted the restrictions on oil and gas acquisitions in March 1992, in the midst of the negotiations, largely for domestic reasons. Although NAFTA imposes further restrictions on performance requirements, Investment Canada was exempted from the restrictions pertaining to technology and world product mandates. What is new in the NAFTA relates to investment security and dispute resolution and is due largely to the fact that both Canada and the United States, as capital exporters, have interests in Mexico. NAFTA also follows the pattern of the OECD and GATT in making barriers to investment more explicit: each country has to subscribe to the norm of national treatment and then list all exceptions within two years or lose them. This has had the effect of limiting new measures and of clearly identifying the existing ones, which can be chipped away at in future negotiations.

The NAFTA negotiations were underway during the Uruguay Round of GATT negotiations, which meant that Canada was involved in constant trade negotiations from 1986 to 1993. It ought not to be surprising, therefore, that as investment policy has become part of the trade package, the policy-development process has changed. In the case of NAFTA, the split in the Liberal Party and the severe recession ensured that the agreement as a whole did not play as central a role in the 1993 election as the FTA had in 1988. The investment aspects were subject to some economic analysis (Rugman and Gestrin 1994) but to even less public discussion than those of the FTA. The minor modifications made to labour and environmental aspects after the agreement was signed did not significantly alter the deal or affect its investment provisions.

In 1993, the final act of the Uruguay Round also included a new agreement on trade-related investment measures (TRIMs), which, unlike issues such as agriculture, aroused little public interest or debate in Canada. The TRIMs agreement formed but one small part of a very broad, complex package which had been negotiated over seven acrimonious years, involving a much more diverse group of countries. The agreement on investment was modest in comparison to the investment provisions of NAFTA or the FTA. It prohibited performance requirements that violate Article III of the act dealing with national treatment (WTO 1994). It required all members to notify the World Trade Organization (WTO) of any trade-related investment measures (the agreement lists five, including domestic sourcing, import limits tied to exports, and foreign exchange restrictions) and to eliminate them within two years (five for developing countries). Investment also falls under the strengthened dispute-settlement provisions of the WTO, which allow for retaliation against violators. However, the measures fell far short of the ambitious US efforts to eliminate a broad range of performance requirements and are not as inclusive or restrictive as the NAFTA investment provisions. This is clearly only the beginning of what will be a continuing process to negotiate stronger multilateral agreements on investment. Canada, along with other OECD members, has concluded that such an agreement is needed, and OECD ministers agreed to launch a process in May 1995 (OECD 1995b).

The growing number of bilateral and multilateral agreements defining the limits of state control over foreign investors raises a number of questions about investment policy. First, to what extent are the hands of states now tied on investment matters? Have states lost the power to control FDI? Clearly, as international investment agreements become part of trade agreements, they put constraints on states since violation of the agreement brings on trade retaliation which may have significant economic costs. But not all of a state's capacity to deal with FDI has disappeared as a result. Many formal barriers to FDI, that is, explicit measures restricting foreign investors' access to domestic markets (the route Canada chose) or discriminating against foreign-based subsidiaries, have been removed by states.

Canada has few informal barriers in the structure of its firms or financial markets that would limit FDI (Industry Canada 1994c: 276). Nor has Canada claimed a national-security justification to exempt its FDI regulations from international discipline, as some other countries have done. As a result, Canada's FDI regime has come under scrutiny and had to be adjusted in GATT in 1983 and exempted from the OECD Code on Capital Movements which Canada signed in 1984. In the case of the FTA and NAFTA, changes to FDI regulations were part of the concessions necessary to reach agreement. Although these agreements may limit the use of some policy instruments or raise the cost of using them, it does not preclude the more aggressive use of other existing instruments or the development of new ones if there is a desire to manage FDI.

The increased importance of international investment agreements raises a second question about what effect the trend of dealing with investments in international agreements has had on the policy process. It is to this latter question I now turn.

INSTITUTIONS AND INVESTMENT POLICY: THE RISE AND FALL OF INVESTMENT CANADA

When the Foreign Investment Review Agency (FIRA) was established in 1974, it was based on the premise that a separate agency reporting to cabinet would be able to function more effectively in bargaining directly with investors, developing expertise, and making the necessary trade-offs than the economic departments, which were likely to be favourable towards incoming FDI. When the decision was made in 1985 to liberalize investment screening and to promote inward investment more vigorously, the separate agency was retained, although with a change in its name and mandate. While the number of cases the agency dealt with declined, this was offset by expanded responsibility for promoting investment and for advising on investment policy.

After 1985, however, investment issues were increasingly addressed through formal agreements between countries, most of which involved trade negotiations. As a result of a reorganization of departments in 1982, the international trade function was moved to External Affairs from the former Department of Industry, Trade and Commerce. With the exception of the Trade Negotiations Office, which was created for the FTA negotiations, it is the Department of Foreign Affairs and International Trade (DFAIT) that has played an increasingly significant role in investment issues.

In the NAFTA negotiations led by DFAIT's international trade division, the vice-president of Investment Canada, Alan Nymark, headed the Canadian side of the investment working group. Since then, however, the responsibilities of the agency have diminished.

In 1993, as a result of the streamlining and a reorganization of government departments, the Investment Development Division of the agency (a crucial part of its new mandate in 1985), was transferred to DFAIT. With the reduced number of acquisitions cases to review as a result of the FTA and the loss of investment promotion, Investment Canada's role had become so limited that its progressive absorption into the Department of Industry in 1993 and its disappearance as a separate agency in 1994 are not surprising. Though Industry and Finance are still consulted and their ministers must consent to changes in investment policy, DFAIT now takes the lead in all aspects of trade and investment, as well as in international negotiations. When trade was transferred to External Affairs in 1982, it was feared that the trade commissioners would be overwhelmed by the diplomats, but the trend in the past decade would suggest the opposite.

With the development, beginning in 1992, of an annual International Business Plan to support the international business development of the private sector (Canada, Dept of Finance 1995: 42-c), the regularized consultation with the ITAC and SAGITs and their role in the promotion of inward and outward FDI, a veritable DFAIT Incorporated has been created. It raises the question as to what extent Canadian foreign economic policy is being driven by private business interests and what weight other interests and issues are being given along the way.

We must also ask to what extent policy on FDI is being made piecemeal, international agreement by international agreement. DFAIT's objectives for the 1995–6 fiscal year include the further development of a statement on Canada's interests in international investment (Canada, Dept of Finance 1995: 21-b), suggesting that as yet there is no clear policy to guide negotiations. This was a complaint that Investment Canada itself had made about the GATT negotiations on TRIMs in 1990. Canada's slowness in developing a position, given the aggressive proposals coming from the United States, the European Community, and Japan, caused concern about Investment Canada and the fear that its slow response would limit 'Canada's ability to influence the final TRIMs agreement if Canada did not put forward an agreed position soon' (Labbé 1990).

Thus, as a result of the internationalization of investment policy, an externally oriented department plays the lead role in investment issues with little in the way of a guiding policy, while the primary agency and department that had a domestic focus is being progressively dismantled.

CONCLUSION

Canada clearly joined the ranks of capital-exporting countries in the 1980s and has been part of a post-war process of technology change and declining barriers to the movement of goods and capital resulting in globalized production. Canadian officials accepted the idea that these movements are keys to competitiveness and economic growth. This view has been reflected in the liberalizing of investment regulation and vigorous attempts to attract inward FDI and promote outward FDI. But the process has been incomplete.

The liberalizing of investment regulation has continued in a world of sovereign states with varying (though perhaps diminishing) capacity to influence the international distribution of capital and production. Governments will thus need to continue developing policies that seek to maximize the benefits to Canada's economy of inward and outward FDI. Yet while policy makers have embraced the view that multinational enterprises of whatever nationality can bring new technology and strengthen the competitive positions of various industries (Eden 1994), the sovereignty issue will not disappear.

The level of foreign control of the Canadian economy remains high and appears likely to increase marginally. Several large Canadian firms have themselves become major MNEs. Yet two problems remain that will continue to be troublesome for the Canadian state. One concerns the distribution of benefits that result from the activities of MNEs. Even competitiveness gurus like Michael Porter (1991: 30) have argued that there are more advantages for a country in having MNEs that are headquartered in the country than in having subsidiaries. Concern about the role of subsidiaries, especially in a context of continental free trade, remains, and DFAIT has now taken on Investment Canada's old responsibility for 'working with foreign subsidiaries to increase their investments and mandates in Canada' (Canada, Dept of Finance 1995: 24-b).

Equally or perhaps more troublesome is the issue of acquisitions, particularly those of firms in high technology or cultural industries. The dilemma is that, as Canada removes its formal barriers to, and promotes, incoming FDI, in the absence of other structures in the economy or regulations to limit it, much of that FDI will be in the form of take-overs of Canadian firms. There have already been several cases, for example, Connaught Biosciences and Lumonics in 1989 (Crane 1992: 130; Canada, Industry Canada 1994c: 272). In many instances these firms were in financial difficulties or were searching for new capital. In other cases, such as Ginn publishing, they are the outcome of indirect acquisition (in Ginn's case, of Prentice-Hall, as discussed above), the continuing pressure of US firms and their government, and the financial difficulties of the Canadian publishing industry. Yet even nationalist organizations have recognized that the answer does not lie in general screening and that mobility of capital is a reality. The Liberal Party approached the problem warily in its 1993 election platform, which focused mainly on the promotion of small and medium-sized enterprises that 'are primarily Canadian owned' (Liberal Party of Canada 1993: 23) and the development of pools of capital to create a Canadian Investment Fund. Other nationalist groups have advocated similar funds, clearly modelled on Quebec's *caisses* (Crane 1992; Barlow and Campbell 1991).

Canada will continue to need an investment strategy, since even with the removal of formal barriers to capital mobility, all economies are not equally open to FDI and countries can continue to influence the location of capital flows and investment. Yet one of the other aspects of the internationalization of investment policy has been the proliferation of international agreements. The Liberal government has retained the formal structures of trade consultation established for the FTA, in particular the International Trade Advisory Committee. In addition, three new task forces, dealing with trade policy, international business development, and trade and the environment respectively, have been added. None of these groups, however, has a specific mandate to address investment issues. While the scope of representation has broadened somewhat, these groups are still heavily dominated by representatives of the corporate sector.[8] Investment-policy making has received low priority and is increasingly taking place within a relatively closed and selective trade-policy consultation process.

Making policy on foreign direct investment through international agreements appears to be the wave of the future for Canada. It need not mean a loss of sovereignty if Canada is able to influence the rules that are created to ensure that they operate in a way that works to the overall benefit of Canadians. Such policy can serve the interests of Canadians, however, only if a clear understanding of what Canada's interests are is established through a policy-development process that is more open and inclusive.

NOTES

1. John Ruggie, as quoted in J. Samuel Barkin and Bruce Cronin (1994: 107).

2. For example, the proposed take-over tax on acquisitions that was part of Walter Gordon's ill-fated 1963 budget. For a discussion of this period see D. Smith (1973).

3. *Foreign Ownership and the Structure of Canadian Industry* (popularly known as the Watkins Report) (Ottawa: Privy Council Office, January 1968) was written by a group of academic economists headed by Mel Watkins. *Foreign Direct Investment in Canada* (known as the Gray Report) (Ottawa: Privy Council Office, 1972) was the result of a task force of officials under Minister Herb Gray.

4. For a discussion of the fierce lobbying by the Canadian Manufacturers' Association, the Chamber of Commerce, and the Business Council on National Issues, see 'Extraordinary Business Lobby', *Vancouver Sun*, 12 Aug. 1980.

5. The Conference Board studies were financed partially by the federal government, and their release was timed to coincide with the legislation. See Barrett and Beckman (1984) and McDowell (1984).

6. Since 1989, agreements have been reached with Argentina, Czechoslovakia, Russia, Uruguay, Hungary, and Poland.

7. According to Michael Hart (1994: 236), the US demands were so sweeping and controversial that if the United States had insisted on them, they might have been fatal to the negotiations as a whole.

8. ITAC currently consists of 25 members, 16 of whom are drawn from the corporate sector, including major banks and interest groups such as the Business Council on National Interests and the Canadian Manufacturers' Association. Three represent trade unions, four are academics (in law, business, economics, and political science), one is a farmer, and one is a consumer representative. The task force and sectoral committees are even more heavily business-oriented. See DFAIT (1995).

9

Human Rights and Security Policy

Andrew F. Cooper and Leslie A. Pal

The internationalization of human rights is one of the most visible aspects of the new agenda in world politics.[1] The collapse of communism and apartheid and the spread of democracy in Latin America are prominent examples, as are the international women's and environmental movements. Rights-based discourse has become a pre-eminent form of policy debate, and new regimes for the protection of human rights have been extended through multilateral negotiations (Donnelly 1986; Forsythe 1985; Glendon 1991; Mandel 1994; Morton 1992). The internationalization of human rights represents the cultural dimension of globalization through the spread of universal norms, such as those enshrined in the Universal Declaration on Human Rights. As Kincaid notes, 'globalization is not genuinely multicultural. It is almost entirely Western in origin and orientation, and is dominated by the characteristics of Western modernity' (1993: 73).

The scope of human rights is so broad that it seems to defy definition as a policy field in itself. In essence, however, rights are claims of protection or support that individuals may make against their community or government to sustain their fundamental dignity as persons. Government policy with respect to rights therefore concerns the following: (1) the definition or list of recognized rights and their sources, (2) their degree or inviolability, (3) their interpretation, (4) their scope, and (5) their enforcement. The Canadian Charter of Rights and Freedoms, adopted in 1982, for example, lists what might be considered universal rights in democratic regimes (for example, free speech) along with rights peculiar to Canadians (for example, minority language rights). It is part of the Canadian constitution and is therefore deeply entrenched in law, is interpreted by the courts, and governs virtually every piece of Canadian government legislation. The 'internationalization of human rights' entails the attempt, through foreign policy, to establish a definition or list of recognized rights that has its source in international law; and the attempt, through domestic policy, to ensure that that definition or list governs domestic programs and practices. The more that human rights are internationalized, the greater the impact of external standards on domestic policy and the less sovereignty, in the classical sense, is exercised by domestic governments.

This chapter examines the dynamics of international human rights in Canadian foreign policy, with special attention to the changing concept of security. Only by setting the human rights issues in the context of the new security environment after the Cold War can we understand the extent of the transformation in thinking and practice. Human rights have been a subject of Canadian foreign policy for decades, but rarely at its centre. Indeed, it is tempting to dismiss human rights as mere window dressing for really important things like trade and investment. If human rights is set against the backdrop of evolving security considerations, especially the last decade's turbulent realignment of the international balance of power and set of alliances, a very different picture emerges. For one thing, security is being redefined in altered circumstances where there are 'threats without enemies' (Smith and Kettle 1992; Cooper 1995). Enemies still exist, of course, but the modern threats to security come as much, if not more, from environmental catastrophes, civil wars, and unstable regimes. For another thing, whereas security has traditionally been thought of as something that citizens achieve through a strong state that can defend itself against external enemies, it is now increasingly being thought of in 'horizontal' terms which stress the pattern of governance and adherence to universal norms (Halliday 1994: 143). Vertical security demands a strong, autonomous, and sovereign state in order to ensure internal stability and protection from external enemies. Horizontal security demands that states adhere to universal norms. It is the difference between being secure *through* one's state, or secure *against* one's state. The new concept of security challenges traditional rationales for state sovereignty and is in part the foundation for the insistence that governments adhere to universal human-rights norms.

As befits this book's theme of internationalization, the changing place of human rights in Canadian foreign policy is linked to changes in domestic policy as well. The internationalization of human rights involves the spread of universal norms to which domestic policy must be subordinated. Domestic policy actors, citizens, interest groups, and the media pay more attention to international violations of these norms than they did in the 1970s and 1980s (CNN lets them watch it live!) at the same time that they struggle to have those norms apply to Canadian domestic policy. Thus the dual feature of the internationalization of this policy field is the changing prominence and role of rights and security in foreign policy proper, along with growing constraints on everything from language policy to social policy in the domestic sphere.

This chapter explores the dual themes of human rights and security considerations in Canadian foreign policy, and the mechanisms by which international standards are applied on the domestic plane. We begin with a brief sketch of the international context for human rights policy, followed by sections that trace the domestic-policy responses in relation to ideas in the policy field, actors and interests, and institutions. With respect to ideas, we trace how the discourse on security in Canadian foreign policy has evolved in the last decade, and the place of human rights within that wider security discourse. In terms of interests, we first examine the role and structure of non-governmental organizations (NGOs) in the foreign-policy community, and then deal with how human rights NGOs have changed organizationally in the last decade along with their new modes of policy intervention. On institutions, we seek to answer the following questions. What are the organizational vehicles for the management of international human rights in Canadian government? What has been the pattern of Canadian government participation in international forums that reflect changing security issues and human rights concerns? What has been the pattern of Canadian adherence to international human rights instruments in the past decade, and how is that adherence administered with the provinces? What other institutional conduits exist domestically for the interjection of international norms into domestic-policy making?

The answers to these questions should cast considerable light on the dynamics of Canadian diplomacy dealing with the 'social agenda' of international relations. The human rights area demonstrates the usefulness of the notion of 'two-level games' in capturing the simultaneous 'interactions between domestic and international politics' (Moravcsik 1993). As with many other (although predominantly western) countries, the Canadian government is forced to balance both international and domestic concerns in a process of double-edged diplomacy. This presents a fundamental paradox, in that at the same time as the heightened forces of internationalization constrain governmental action they also invite 'new possibilities for creative statecraft' that encourage governments to interact in more imaginative ways with domestic policy communities (Moravcsik 1993: 16). Human rights policy presents abundant opportunities for a new form of multifaceted diplomacy.

THE INTERNATIONAL CONTEXT

Human rights have been a central theme in western political discourse since the eighteenth century. The American and French revolutions popularized the idea of the universal, natural rights of man, and the language of rights infused both the American Declaration of Independence and its Bill of Rights. This was the age of democratic revolution, and the inherent and inviolate rights of citizens to speak, think, worship, associate, and vote as they wished were the perfect instrument to limit government. The nineteenth and early twentieth centuries also saw the growth of international human rights movements around workers' rights and unionization, the abolition of slavery, and the right to vote. The place of human rights in international diplomacy, however, was relatively limited. The International Labour Organization, founded in 1919, was intended to foster workers' rights and encourage international standards, but the League of Nations, founded in 1919 and a precursor to the United Nations, did not even mention human rights in its founding document. This history points to a theme developed in other chapters in this book: internationalization of this policy field was evident before the modern wave of globalization.

The modern era of international human rights begins with the San Francisco conference of 1945 that led to the establishment of the United Nations (Burgers 1992). As early as 1941, President Roosevelt had argued that the United States was entering the war to secure four freedoms: freedom of speech, freedom of worship, freedom from want, and freedom from fear. The US delegation in San Francisco was accompanied by over 40 NGOs (Interim Committee of the Nongovernmental Organizations for Consultative Status with the United Nations 1949), and it was they that assured the prominence of human rights in the founding charter of the UN. The charter, for example, said that one of the objectives of the new organization was to promote and encourage 'respect for human rights and for fundamental freedoms for all without discrimination as to race, sex, language, or religion'. Article 55 reaffirmed the objective of 'universal respect for, and observance of, human rights and fundamental freedoms.' The 1948 Universal Declaration of Human Rights, which was only a declaration rather than a treaty in international law, carried this theme further in stating that it contained a 'common standard of achievement for all peoples and all nations'. Though it took until 1966 to ratify them, two covenants were eventually agreed upon as treaty instruments for the fulfilment of this purpose, the International Covenant on Civil and Political Rights and the International Covenant on Economic, Social and Cultural Rights. Both treaties came into effect in 1976, when each had been signed by the requisite 35 countries. The former contained classic civil and political rights, such as freedom of thought, expression, religion, association, and political participation. The latter contained what were referred to as 'second-generation' social and economic rights, such as social security, work, rest, adequate standard of living, and education.

Ironically, these two human-rights instruments, as well as the hundreds that followed in the UN system and other regimes, were inspired by the Cold War. Western democracies championed traditional civil and political rights, knowing full well that those rights were routinely ignored in Communist states. The Soviet bloc, for its part, took the opportunity to condemn capitalist states for their social and economic inequalities. Outside the shadow of this superpower rivalry, however, other human rights regimes continued to grow. Principal among them were the American Declaration of the Rights and Duties of Man (in 1948), the Convention for the Protection of Human Rights and Fundamental Freedoms (in Europe in 1950), and the European Social Charter (in 1961). Another of the most important developments in this series was the 1975 Helsinki Accords that brought NATO and the Warsaw Pact countries (as well as some others) together in the Conference on Security and Cooperation in Europe (CSCE, now known as the Organization for Security and Cooperation in Europe). The 'human dimension' of the Helsinki Accords, elaborated at periodic meetings, provided the basis for a large number of human rights–monitoring groups throughout Eastern Europe. The CSCE consolidated this activity, *inter alia*, through the establishment of the position of High Commissioner on National Minorities.

These developments signalled the gradual institutionalization of overlapping human rights regimes around the world. They were accompanied and amplified by a series of other developments as well. First, the international NGO community changed substantially in the 1960s. It grew in numbers, scope, and capacities as it whittled away at barriers in the UN system to participation by NGOs (Steiner 1991). Second, human rights were gradually being institutionalized and extended domestically through the passage of human rights codes and the willingness of courts to read programmatic rights into social legislation, particularly in the United States and Canada (Howe 1991; Horowitz 1977; Melnick 1994). Third, the technologies of communication and transportation were rapidly making it possible for people in one part of the world not simply to hear about abuses of human rights in other places but actually to see them taking place. As Elkins points out, this is of great significance, since it allowed the creation of 'virtual communities' or networks of individuals bound, not by territory, but by mutual interest or allegiance to a principle (Elkins 1995: 198–206).

The concept of territory of course brings us back to the state. While the progress of international rights over the post-war period is undeniable, it is also clear that the progress occurred in a world dominated by states, and two rival systems of states to boot. It was also a time when domestic economic policy could still control some of the effects of international forces, such as currency trading and the practices in multinational corporations. Human rights were therefore consistently overshadowed by considerations of military security and trade and economics. Other chapters in this book have outlined the growing globalization of economic forces in the post-war period. By the late 1960s, the whole concept of security had to be redefined as well.

DOMESTIC RESPONSE

Ideas and Foreign-Policy Discourse

The collapse of the Soviet Union in 1991 brought with it a host of important changes: the disappearance of the rivalry between the United States and the Soviet Union that had marked the international system during the Cold War; and a need to reconsider the future shape of the international order and the nature of national security in the post–Cold War world. These changes, not surprisingly, have sparked a 'defence debate' in virtually all countries which had predicated their national defence policies on the bipolar rivalry that emerged at the end of the Second World War. In these countries, governments are considering the implications of what are invariably described as the 'challenges of the changing world order', the 'transformation of the international system', and the 'new security architecture' of the post–Cold War era.

The orthodox security debate in Canada follows that trend, as the government examines what it spends on defence and, more important, why. To be sure, such governmental reconsiderations are driven to a considerable extent by the relentless cost cutting and deficit reduction, and a belief that a handsome 'peace dividend' could be realized from the transformation of the international environment. But the current rethinking of security also stems from a widespread belief among policy makers that the international system has changed so radically since the 1980s that policies and programs designed for Cold War conditions are simply no longer suitable.

Beside this official debate on security, however, lies another vigorous, if often fragmented, unorthodox discourse about security. Here Canadian security is examined through a very different lens. Orthodox Canadian policy views security in a traditional state-centric fashion, which gives primacy to the notion that governments should and must act as guardians of a 'national' interest (Bull 1977). The proponents of the unorthodox conception of security, on the hand, wish to elevate social issues to the apex of the security agenda; they view these issues as necessary for the protection of the essential rights of individuals and groups, as opposed to either the pursuit of international order or the defence of the political or territorial integrity of the nation state. These critics of the orthodox view define security more broadly, focusing not on the geo-political situation, but on the apparent threats to the fundamental values that encompass the economic, legal, and environmental domain. Rather than the safety of states, the primary goal is 'human security' (MacFarlane and Weiss 1994).

The gap between the orthodox and unorthodox discourses in many ways narrowed by the end of the Cold War era. Just how far orthodox thinking moved may be seen by contrasting the Conservative government's Green Paper on foreign policy, *Competitiveness and Security: Directions for Canada's International Relations*, published in 1985, with the 1994 Report of the Special Joint Committee Reviewing Canadian Foreign Policy, *Canada's Foreign Policy: Principles and Priorities for the Future*. *Competitiveness and Security* was based on economic and military considerations. Released during the period of heightened ideological and geo-political tensions between the Reagan administration and the faltering Soviet empire, the report concentrated on superpower rivalry and defined security and interdependence in narrow terms. The document, which bristled with trade statistics, emphasized the sovereign control of territory, the integrity of borders, and the importance of arms and defence issues.

By the time the federal Liberals issued their 1993 election platform entitled *Creating Opportunity*, the international scene had been transformed. *Creating Opportunity* noted these events as the background for its recommendations for changes in foreign policy. One change would be towards 'a broader definition of national and international security' away from the domination of military and defence considerations. Another would be the re-orientation of defence policy towards peacekeeping, with corresponding conversion of bases and *matériel*. The document was of course geared to the 1993 election and so was both slim and partisan. But it pointed clearly towards a different foreign-policy framework and ordering of priorities. The *Report of the Special Joint Committee Reviewing Canadian Foreign Policy* was more explicit about the direction away from a limited definition of security (the Bloc Québécois members of the committee submitted a separate, dissenting volume). The committee's understanding of security moved away from the military and defence preoccupation of the mid-1980s. Although security still had a military element, it was now defined more broadly as 'political stability, economic strength, environmental sustainability, and social cohesion' (Canada, Special Joint Committee 1995: 4).

Yet despite the closing of the gap between the two different views of security, there are still fundamental differences. The orthodox view continues to define the threats primarily in statist terms; in other words, threats to state security arising from the belligerent actions of other states (such as arms races, weapons proliferation, or intrusions into the territory of other states); or from governmental breakdown or disorder. For example, the orthodox view will point to the dangers posed by North Korea's nuclear weapons program; a possible war between India and Pakistan; an ultra-nationalist regime in Russia or Ukraine; regional tensions in Cambodia, Burma, and the former Yugoslavia; or the regional conflict and disintegration in China and other countries (contributing *inter alia* to illegal immigration).

At the same time, globalization has received considerable attention both as a force of change and as a constraining factor on foreign policy. Canadian governments, both Conservative and Liberal, have, like many other governments around the world, supplemented their traditional concern with territorial integrity with economic well-being. From the perspective of the official debate about security, in Canada as elsewhere the stability and material well-being of the country depend on a process of adjustment to economic rationalization and efficiency. The danger is not from the symbolic loss of sovereignty, but from the loss of national capacity due to lack of competitiveness and national decline. As Stopford and Strange (1991: 209) have said, 'wealth is needed to preserve the state more from internal rather than external threats to its cohesion and survival. Without wealth or the prospect of future sources of wealth, even if there is no external security threat, the state falls apart.'

The larger ramifications of this dynamic are well beyond the scope of this chapter. What is clear, though, is that it contributes further to the process of internationalization of foreign policy. A case in point is the issue of sovereignty. Canada has demonstrated a willingness since the early post-war years to subordinate its own national sovereignty to international institutions. But changes in the post–Cold War era have brought this desire to the fore. Brian Mulroney stated in a convocation address at Stanford University in September 1991 that Canada was 'receptive to rethinking the limits of national sovereignty in a world where problems respect no borders' (Canada, Office of the Prime Minister 1991).

Such rethinking was necessary because of the changes in the global system of markets and production. Under such conditions the autonomy of government is reduced; but this does not mean that the power of government has been completely eroded (Camilleri and Falk 1992), only that it has substantively changed. As suggested, governments in the emergent global system have, if anything, a greater need to prove that they can provide national economic well-being for their populations. To do so, therefore, a government like the Canadian one has a considerable incentive to bargain away some of its sovereignty in order to gain commercial benefits. The Canada-US Free Trade Agreement (FTA) and the North American Free Trade Agreement (NAFTA) underscore this point (Winham 1994). Likewise, Canada has been at the forefront of the attempt to establish firmer and more comprehensive multilateral rules through the Organisation for Economic Co-operation and Development (OECD) and the new World Trade Organization (an institution, which it needs to be noted, Canada took the lead in proposing in April 1990). As the federal government's statement, *Canada in the World* concluded,

> Thanks to technological innovations, the adoption of outward-looking
> political and economic policies, and . . . other changes . . . borders have
> become more porous. . . . This has diminished the ability of states to act
> independently since they can no longer isolate themselves from the world
> without unacceptable domestic consequences. . . . However, especially for
> smaller and medium-sized countries, sovereignty has also been enhanced
> since the growing number of international rules . . . better protect states
> from arbitrary and unilateral action by other international actors (Canada,
> Government 1995b: 4).

Globalization, however, remains a social as well as an economic process (Scholte 1993). On the one hand, the vision of some 'new world order' has assumed the expansion of not only a liberal economic but also a political democratic system. For the increasingly mobilized and internationalized NGOs, this vision presents both opportunities and obstacles. On the one hand, these developments allow not only the elevation of NGOs into the policy-making process, but also the possibility of greater intervention at the societal level abroad and more societal responsiveness domestically. On the other hand, though, human rights have remained subordinated in orthodox thinking to economics.

This is not to say that these tensions between government and NGOs, or for that matter, internal contradictions within government, are entirely new. The Canadian government has both led and lagged in the human-rights discourse throughout the last decade. The Special Joint Committee of the Senate and the House of Commons on Canada's International Relations heard from almost 700 witnesses; and as a joint parliamentary committee meeting for almost a year, it had both a broader and a more detailed approach to Canada's international relations than the Conservative government's 1985 Green Paper. Its report, *Interdependence and Internationalism* (also called the Hockin-Simard Report), emphasized the 'relentless internationalization of the nation's agenda' and the way in which, as 'domestic affairs have been internationalized, foreign policy has been brought home and opened up for debate.' In summarizing the priorities of Canadians that appeared before it, the committee listed the promotion of human rights and development well behind peace, security, and the state of the economy, but it did note that many witnesses had called for a 'more significant human rights component in Canadian foreign policy.' Furthermore, it wrote a separate chapter on human rights and recommended the establishment of a Human Rights Advisory Commission and an 'International Institute of Human Rights and Democratic Development.' If all of this seems ambiguous, it was. The committee's vision was poised between the more traditional state-centric perspective expressed in the government's Green Paper and the broadening views about security and human rights. Its capstone concept was 'constructive internationalism', which in the same breath referred to the international state system and international society (Canada, Special Joint Committee of the Senate and the House of Commons on Canada's International Relations 1986).

The government's response to the Hockin-Simard Report, *Canada's International Relations*, published in 1987, still expressed a traditional foreign-policy vision. The main elements in the international environment were again defined in economic and military terms. Nonetheless, the section on human rights did indicate a willingness to work more closely with NGOs and to build human rights into decisions about overseas development assistance (ODA). The 1987 Winegard Committee report, *For Whose Benefit?* the report of the Standing Committee on External Affairs and International Trade on Canada's Official Development Assistance Policies and Programs, had a narrower scope than either the Green Paper or the Hockin-Simard Report; nevertheless it expressed a more comprehensive vision of international security. By definition ODA is in large part about alleviating the suffering caused by military, economic, social, or ecological dislocation, and so when the document referred to 'security' it did not focus as narrowly on military and defence aspects. It assumed that domestic security depends on environmental and social stability in other countries, and that therefore Canada had a self-interest in aid and development abroad. It recognized that true development went beyond economic projects to include social or human-resource development; not surprisingly, this report highlighted the role of NGOs in ODA. The government's response, *Canadian International Development and Assistance: To Benefit a Better World*, published soon afterwards, was lukewarm to this approach. The Winegard Committee's recommendations, while applauded by NGOs, were a challenge to the government, with their strong emphasis on human development, partnership with NGOs, and the central-ity of rights. The response referred to the connection between domestic security and conditions in developing countries, and human rights were highlighted, but policy was to remain largely unchanged.

This 'lead-lag' pattern of behaviour, nonetheless, has become accentu-ated in recent years. On a number of issues Canada showed international leadership on human rights. An interesting example is Prime Minister Mulroney's overt and public calls for a link between human rights and development assistance, made at both the Commonwealth and Franco-phonie summits in 1991. So too is the Canadian response to the coup in Haiti in September 1991, which ousted President Jean-Bertrand Aristide. Moreover, in his Stanford address, Mulroney made at least passing refer-ence to the association between international human rights and domestic violence, commenting that 'invocations of the principle of national sover-eignty are as out of date and offensive to me as police declining to stop family violence simply because a man's home is supposed to be his castle' (Office of the Prime Minster 1991).

While the dominant theme in Canadian human-rights diplomacy continues to be the search for a balance between human rights and secu-rity of access for Canadian goods, it is clear that the evolution of policy has been towards a new synthesis that stresses the importance of human rights within a broader concept of security. *Canada in the World*, the Chré-tien government's new foreign-policy framework, noted the new dangers posed by 'environmental degradation, social inequity, lack of opportunity and overpopulation' (Canada, Government 1995b: 3). The link between human rights and a stable international environment was explicit: 'The Government regards respect for human rights not only as a fundamental value, but also as a crucial element in the development of stable, democ-ratic and prosperous societies at peace with each other' (Canada, Govern-ment 1995b: 34). This search for balance is evident in Canada's policy towards China, where Prime Minister Jean Chrétien has expressed doubt about Canada's ability to influence China's observance of human rights. The same is true of its approach to Mexico, although it may be noted that Christine Stewart, the Secretary of State for Latin America and Africa, did publicly criticize the Mexican government for its handling of the Chiapas rebellion. In adopting this pragmatic approach, Canadian state officials have come under intense criticism from social activists.

Actors and Interests
The changes in the foreign-policy framework described above did not result simply from the pressure of 'globalization'. In part, of course, the policy makers were subject to unavoidable pressures, but our comment

about the orthodox and unorthodox debates concerning security was intended to point out that policy makers have been sometimes reluctant to accept the consequences of these international pressures. On the domestic plane, these pressures make themselves felt partly through non-state actors or NGOs. Their impact comes in three related forms. The first is the interlocutory: they raise fundamental challenges to orthodox conceptions of rights, sovereignty, and policy. It is remarkable, for example, how closely the recent foreign-policy review echoes points being made by the human rights NGOs for years. Second, as the framework changes, so too does the influence that NGOs have on policy. Internation-alization implies reduced state capacity and a commensurate need to develop partnerships with non-state actors. Finally, NGOs outside the foreign-policy community have projected international standards into domestic policy, thereby closing the loop between international and domestic described at the beginning of this chapter.

This section will concentrate on two kinds of NGOs: (1) international human rights NGOs that have concentrated on the place of human rights in Canadian foreign policy, and (2) some domestic-policy NGOs that have argued for international standards. The foreign-policy-making commu-nity is much larger than this, of course, embracing as it does hundreds of business groups and development organizations. We will briefly mention the latter below, but groups associated with trade and foreign policy are discussed in other chapters in this book. We are concerned here with organizations that have tried to change the place and prominence of human rights in Canadian foreign policy.

Some groups have been trying to do this for a while. Social groups have long been urging governments to make changes in Canadian foreign policy. To give just one illustration, Prime Minister Trudeau's foreign-policy review of 1968–70 provided a catalyst for action by many Canadian churches. The review was capped with the White Paper entitled *Foreign Policy for Canadians*, which contained a chapter on South Africa that many NGOs found callous in its emphasis on Canadian self-interest rather than social justice. Matthews notes that the Canadian churches, which had concentrated on charitable works and overseas development in the 1950s, were moved by the White Paper to take a more radical position (Matthews 1990; Williams 1984; Macdonald 1993). The churches were also being encouraged by their overseas partners to be less paternalistic about development and aid. Their partners frequently had more radical political views than the churches, and so this too led to greater activism by the churches. Finally, the 1960s were a decade of challenging social justice issues. Catholics were occupied with Vatican II (from 1962 to 1965), and most religious organizations were drawn into the debate in

1968–9 on changes to the Criminal Code touching on marriage, abortion, and homosexuality. As we note below, the churches are crucial to Canadian human rights NGO networks because they are among the largest and most competent institutions through which unconventional views of foreign policy can be expressed.

Throughout the 1970s and early 1980s the number and visibility of social groups increased. In addition to many new economic groups, formed under the impetus of the Tokyo Round of Multilateral Trade Negotiations (Winham 1986), the period saw an increase in what Sikkink calls 'principled-issue' networks, or groups organized around alternative concepts of security, such as those based on environmental issues and especially human rights (Sikkink 1993). Though this development had domestic causes (most notably, the Trudeau White Paper and the Criminal Code amendments), it also coincided with a general growth of the international human rights movement (Willetts 1982; Wiseberg and Scoble 1979). Writing in 1983, Pratt asserted that there had recently emerged in Canada a substantial number of internationally minded public-interest groups 'which are in serious opposition to many components of the present consensus which underlies Canadian foreign policy' (Pratt 1983–4). These groups expressed ethical concerns such as 'disarmament, human rights, international equity, and solidarity with oppressed peoples.' (Pratt 1983–4: 118). Though this 'counter-consensus' was still in many ways excluded from foreign-policy decision making, increasingly its views were those that were to figure prominently in the redefinitions of security and rights in the next decade of foreign-policy debate. The central belief of these non-governmental actors was that ethical obligations should not be constrained by territorial boundaries, but should form a set of universal standards that must apply to all human beings in a common global community.

The influence of these groups, it is important to mention here, was weakened by a number of things. The first was the sheer dependence of the NGOs on government for funding. A second is the internal organizational deficiencies of the non-governmental groups themselves. These weaknesses are noted even in the recent studies of the NGO foreign-policy community. The first of these, entitled *Bridges of Hope*, was conducted by Brodhead, Herbert-Copley, and Lambert. Published in 1988 for the North-South Institute, it dealt with development NGOs, but it was the first survey of its kind on the NGO community generally. It defined an NGO as 'any voluntary, non-profit agency involved in the field of international development co-operation, or in education and policy advocacy activities related to international development' (Brodhead, Herbert-Copley, and Lambert 1988). The authors mailed 220 surveys, of which 129 were returned. They also made field trips to seven counties, where they visited 51 projects, and conducted in-depth interviews with 31 NGOs: They found that 'within Canada the single dominant presence on the non-governmental scene since the late 1960s had been the federal government' (Brodhead, Herbert-Copley, and Lambert 1988: 4). Most of the agencies were small: 36 per cent had budgets of less than $250,000, and fully 60 per cent had budgets less than $1 million. The NGO community, which had grown rapidly, consisted mostly of small non-religious organizations (72 per cent were secular), but there was a great deal of inter-church activity and coalition work), with tiny staffs dependent on volunteers.

A second study, done in 1991 by Ian Smillie for the Canadian Council for International Co-operation (CCIC), confirms many of the earlier findings. 'On a per capita basis, Canada has 4.4 times more NGOs than Britain, and yet all Canadian NGOs combined raise less money from the public than Oxfam UK and Save the Children Fund alone' (Smillie 1991: 5). Significantly, the government made up the shortfall, and the 'imbalance between public and governmental support for the voluntary sector is striking, and is far higher than in most other OECD member countries' (Smillie 1991: 7).

A more recent study was conducted by Leslie Pal in 1992–4. The method used in this study was to survey and directly interview the members of the Network on International Human Rights (NIHR), an umbrella organization for Canadian NGOs that concentrate on international human rights. All 54 member organizations were contacted. The financial situation for this segment of the NGO foreign-policy community was found to be, if anything, more precarious than the ODA segment surveyed in *Bridges of Hope*. The modal revenue category was $150,000–$250,000 per annum, but 64 per cent of the organizations polled reported annual revenues at this level or lower. Ten organizations had annual revenues between $250,000 and $749,000. Of the eight organizations reporting annual revenues of more than $1 million, four were ODA organizations and two were aboriginal organizations. The findings also support Smillie's results about the balance of public and government support: the majority of international human rights NGOs received no funding from individual members at all. The two primary sources of revenue were donations from parent organizations, principally the churches through their ecumenical coalitions, and the federal government.

To a considerable extent, then, NGO activity has been marked by continuity. The NGO foreign-policy community persists in being a bit like Swift's Lilliput: consisting of hundreds of tiny organizations that swarm over the Gulliver of the Department of Foreign Affairs and International Trade restraining it here and there but still dominated by the giant, even in an era when that institution can no longer pretend that it possesses hegemony in the policy-making process. This Swiftian image must be further modified by the fact that many other changes have taken place that signal enhanced power for NGOs.

At one level, these changes stem from the increase in the sheer volume of NGO activity over the past decade. A small but telling piece of evidence may be found in a comparison of the NGO presentations before the Standing Committee on External Affairs and National Defence in 1970–1 on foreign policy for Canadians and the number that appeared before the Special Joint Committee of the Senate and House of Commons in 1994. Both were major overviews of Canadian foreign policy, but in 1970–1 only 29 NGOs submitted briefs to the committee. In 1994, 277 NGOs submitted briefs. (This actually understates the difference, since the 1970 figure includes educational, maritime, business, and labour organizations; if these are removed, only 18 NGOs appeared before the committee.) Furthermore, most of this growth appears to have been in relation to social agenda items such as ODA, the environment, and human rights. A large number of individuals associated with NGOs also participated at the National Forum on Canada's International Relations, held in Ottawa in March 1994.

A fundamental change at another level altogether has been the greater access for NGOs to the policy-making process. An important feature of this change has been the formation and development of the NIHR. The origins of this body can be traced back to 1979, when the head of the delegation to the United Nations Commission on Human Rights (UNCHR), started consultations with human rights NGOs. At the time there were only 20 NGOs with which to meet, but by 1986 the NGOs had formed an umbrella organization that would exchange information and co-ordinate joint statements to the government delegation at the beginning of the consultations. Even in 1988, there were only 28 member organizations, half of which were church NGOs. The NIHR was loosely co-ordinated through the offices of the Human Rights Research and Education Centre at the University of Ottawa. The 1994–5 membership consisted of 21 organizations and three individuals, which can be taken as a measure of organizational development as opposed to decline. The NIHR has progressed to the point that it enforces the payment of membership dues rather than simply lists NGOs with an interest in human rights.

Another development occurred in September 1992, when the NIHR held a consultation of its own on new models of effective relations between NGOs and government, entitled *Transforming the Model*. The result was a review of the NIHR's constitution, the hiring of a co-ordinator, and the development of more formal administrative procedures. The NIHR increasingly does more than engage in a yearly consultation with DFAIT. It now provides programs to members on UN and other international human rights forums, prepares NGOs for major international meetings, holds monthly workshops on thematic and regional human rights issues, and publishes a bimonthly information bulletin. It has an executive committee which meets monthly and holds three general meetings per year. It participates in a regular cycle of meetings with Foreign Affairs (in the fall and just before the UNCHR meeting in Geneva), as well as with the Canadian International Development Agency (CIDA) and parliamentary committees.

A final development that indicates enhanced capacity for the human rights NGOs is the 'Access Fund' provided through the International Centre for Human Rights and Democratic Development (ICHRDD). Canadian NGOs attend international conferences as a matter of course, but the high cost makes their attendance irregular. The advent of 'parallel NGO forums' in conjunction with major international governmental conferences has both raised the profile of NGO participation and made this combined process more vital in terms of international governance (Cooper and Fritz 1992). In 1993, four representatives of Canadian NGOs attended the UNCHR with support from the ICHRDD. A year later this support was formalized into the Access Fund, administered by the Network on International Human Rights. This fund allows 10 NGO representatives to attend the UNCHR annual session in Geneva, where they acquire valuable technical knowledge for the NGO community about the intricate human rights machinery of the UN. The Access Fund also demonstrates that a quasi-governmental agency dedicated to the support of democratic development overseas can provide considerable support to Canadian NGOs. ICHRDD itself sends representatives to the UNCHR, and it provided support to the 1992 NIHR 'Transforming the Model' consultation. The Canadian Human Rights Commission sends representatives to the UN Commission of Human Rights as well, and it regularly attends the DFAIT-NGO consultation on human rights in January. Thus, governmental organizations that might be considered to have either a strictly domestic or a strictly international focus are active in ways that belie that distinction: organizations that traditionally have had an international focus work to build a domestic base (CIDA's funding has encouraged this process in the development community), and organizations that traditionally have had a domestic focus participate ever more actively in the 'foreign-policy' dimension. This shift, along with the enhanced capacity of the NGO sector noted above suggest that a qualitatively different process is at work.

These developments have been, in large part, due to the NGOs' own efforts. There has been no let up the intensity of the work of activist non-state actors. Indeed, many of the counter-consensus groups continue to judge success less by their influence on government policy than by the changes in society's consciousness. In his study of Canadian churches, for example, Matthews concludes that they continue to sit on the periphery of policy making. Although they have reasonable access to policy makers, 'their influence on actual government policy has been marginal' (Matthews 1990: 161). The tactics of organizations such as the Canadian Council of Churches continue to be rooted in government departments, parliamentary committees, 'public' criticism of government policy, and advocacy with the business sector (for example, lobbying corporations on investment issues).

A variety of other groups, however, have combined intensity with other forms of action. One of the features of this type of expanded repertoire has been specialization. Some groups have worked to perfect their monitoring, witnessing, and interlocutory skill. Others have expanded the range and sophistication of their legal competence. Together with these changes, many of these same groups have expanded the scope of their activity. NGOs may still on the whole be small and poor in Canada, but they are increasingly bound together in dense networks of international organizational activity. This movement does not necessarily translate into a direct influence on policy, but it does suggest a sharper focus and visibility for the community in the foreign-policy process. More important, it is not a movement that devotes itself only to the domestic side of influencing the government. If it is far too early yet to talk of a 'global civil society', the networks of these groups are nevertheless clearly transnational.

All of these elements of NGO human rights activity have emerged on the issue of gender rights and political association. Women's organizations have shown a growing solidarity on human rights and equality-of-women issues. As suggested by the long struggle for the passage and implementation of the Convention on the Elimination of All Forms of Discrimination against Women, particular attention has been paid to specialized legal expertise. Moreover, Canadian women's-rights groups joined in the international lobbying to have such questions as sexual discrimination and violence against women included explicitly at the 1993 Vienna human rights conference. As Kathleen Mahoney has argued, 'Where human rights were once considered matters of purely domestic politics narrowly construed, global forces now mandate that they take on broader international dimensions, transcend borders, and command ever widening participation in their definition and implementation' (Mahoney 1992: 557). The extent of the international women's network was highlighted by the fact that over 130,000 women in 100 countries signed a petition demanding that women's rights be treated as a specific thematic item on the agenda and that gender issues should be an integral part of all discussions. The range and intensity of the activity can also be seen in the fact that women's groups also worked together to stop the violence against women in Bosnia and Herzegovina and to prosecute as war criminals those responsible for the mass rapes.

At the same time important political and administrative reasons have emerged for the government's attempt to build a new relationship with social groups more deeply into its decision making. This trend can be seen as part of the wider crisis of legitimacy facing governments all over the world. At the very least, governments have realized the need to negotiate and bargain with their publics more openly. What is unique to Canada is a more open and inclusionary strategy by government that has reflected the changes in the overall political culture (with a rights-based psychology) created by the politics of the Charter of Rights and Freedoms and the Meech Lake and Charlottetown referendum debates (Cairns 1992). NGOs were also seen to provide alternative forms of expertise (especially in regard to the delivery of services such as humanitarian relief) and information (for example, the monitoring of human rights violations by Amnesty International and Asia Watch).

There can be no doubt of the increasing size and visibility of the international human rights NGO community, though its power and direct influence on policy have probably grown only marginally. This community presses for changes in Canada's human rights policy abroad, at times with an interest in how this will affect domestic policy. On the other hand, some domestic groups import, as it were, international standards into the consideration of domestic policy issues. Actions taken by aboriginal organizations, women's groups, and the environmental movement are well known. The important point is not that protests that government actions violate international human rights agreements will always win the day. It is rather that reference to those international standards is now becoming routine in domestic-policy debates.

The social-policy field provides some interesting illustrations of this point, given that with its February budget, the federal government embarked on a wholesale restructuring (and reduction) of social programs. Viewing social policy through the lens of human rights is not new, and since 1982 an impressive case law has been built up around social policy and the Charter of Rights and Freedoms (Howse 1995), and legal arguments have been put forward to the effect that the mere condition of poverty is itself a violation of the Charter (Jackman 1994). What is comparatively new, however, is the appeal to international standards of human rights. In 1993, for example, the Committee on Economic, Social and Cultural Rights criticized the Canadian government for tolerating high levels of poverty and especially homelessness and the existence of food banks. At the time, the Canadian delegation submitting the country report was caught completely by surprise, in particular by the well-orchestrated NGO presentations on the issue (Canada, Dept of Justice, 1995a). In May 1995 the government held hearings on Bill C-76, introducing the new Canada Health and Social Transfer. The transfer, which was announced in the February budget, consolidates federal transfers under Established Programs Financing (for health and post-secondary education) and the Canada Assistance Plan into 'bloc funding' with relatively few strings attached, especially for social-welfare transfers. The provinces thereby gain some flexibility, but the plan also calls for some $7 billion in cuts in those same transfers, which social-policy advocates that appeared before the Finance Committee feared would come disproportionately from social welfare and thereby discriminate against the poor.

In this case, NGOs challenged the government from both the domestic and international levels. In Geneva, three groups (the Charter Committee on Poverty Issues, the National Anti-Poverty Organization, and the National Action Committee on the Status of Women) appeared before the Committee on Economic, Social and Cultural Rights and presented a joint statement to the effect that the repeal of the Canada Assistance Plan 'amount[ed] to a double contravention of the Covenant: a flagrant disregard of the Committee's comments regarding "deliberately retrogressive measures" as well as a complete loss of the federal legislative guarantee regarding the availability of administrative and judicial enforcement mechanisms' (United Nations 1995: 9). This intervention yielded a letter from the Chair of the Committee to the Canadian Permanent Mission in Geneva, which, while it refrained from direct comment on the legislation since it had not yet been passed, noted 'the importance that it attaches to the pursuit of policies and programs which comply fully with Canada's obligations as a party to the Covenant' (Alston 1995). Meanwhile, back in Ottawa, the same groups were appearing before the finance committee and making similar arguments about Canada's international obligations. They were supplemented by groups like the Ontario Social Safety Net/Work (representing 356 organizations). Its brief referred not only to section 36(1) of the Charter, which guarantees equal opportunities and essential public services of reasonable quality to all Canadians, but to the Universal Declaration on Human Rights, which contains the right to an adequate standard of living, and the International Covenant on Economic, Social and Cultural Rights (Ontario Social Safety Net/Work 1995: 4).

These interventions did not prevent the passage of Bill C-76. But they are clear evidence of the internationalization of public policy. The standards by which policy is judged and debated are increasingly derived from international and not national sources. Of course, those international sources are in part shaped by Canadian foreign policy, and our point throughout this chapter is that the human rights component of Canadian foreign policy serves an increasingly important function in connecting and calibrating the links to these international systems and their domestic effects. The Committee on Economic, Social and Cultural rights will almost certainly review the CHST in 1996, and it is likely to find that it contravenes the covenant. This will not change policy immediately, but it clearly is a new site for a policy process that at one time would have been situated almost purely on domestic terrain.

Institutions

The internationalization of human-rights policy has been accompanied by an increasingly complex set of institutional mechanisms to manage the field. DFAIT of course handles the international diplomacy around rights issues, but its work is supplemented by the Departments of Justice, Health, Immigration, and Environment, along with the Human Rights Directorate in the Department of Canadian Heritage. As more and more domestic policy is internationalized and brought within the orbit of human rights, more and more domestic departments become DFAIT's partners in the management of foreign policy. The question is whether DFAIT remains a 'lead' agency in this process or is becoming a progressively weaker player.

Historically, the hallmark of Canadian foreign policy has been a closed approach to policy making. A small, tightly knit group of politicians and officials acted with a great deal of autonomy from social influences to pursue their aims with respect to the concept of national interest inherent in the creation and maintenance of a comprehensive international order. As John Holmes, both an astute practitioner and a student of Canada's diplomatic method, described the process of policy making during the period from the late 1940s to the mid-1960s, a small group, primarily in the Department of External Affairs, used its strong position 'to lead Canadian public opinion in the direction of new obligations' in international affairs (Holmes 1979: 110; Griffiths 1968).

By the 1970s and 1980s, the power of this centralized department with high policy capabilities because of its own skills and the intrinsic importance of its mandate had become thoroughly eroded. The 'fortress was besieged', to use Denis Stairs' (1970–1) apt phrase, as other state as well as non-state actors took on a greater importance on the widening international agenda (Stairs 1977–8; Nossal 1983–4). One major source of fragmentation was the closer intertwining of issues with a significant external dimension, such as those found in the human rights arena, with Canadian federalism. Though the federal government has the exclusive power to sign international treaties, it cannot force provincial legislation to be consistent with these treaties. In the human rights field, up to mid-1970s, no formal mechanism had been developed to deal with this structural problem. Indeed, it was external pressure that provided the impetus for Canada to move away from this ad hoc approach. In anticipation of the ratification of the International Covenants on Civil and Political Rights and on Economic, Social and Cultural Rights the following year, the Federal-Provincial-Territorial Continuing Committee of Officials on Human Rights was established in 1975. Moreover, a federal-provincial conference of ministers in charge, held in December 1975, reached agreement on the ratification of the two covenants and the design of a mechanism for reporting about their implementation.

In keeping with its long-standing attitude about its own constitutional rights and the division of powers (Sabourin 1971), Quebec feared that Ottawa might try to report unilaterally to the United Nations on provincial legislation, or speak for all of Canada in explaining the provincial sections of the reports. To get unanimous consent to *Modalities and Mechanisms*, the document that formed the basis of the Continuing Committee, therefore, the federal government had to address Quebec's objections. In doing so, it agreed that in future before it acceded to or amended international human rights covenants, it would consult the provinces and territories. Provinces have the opportunity to serve as representatives on the Canadian delegation, and hence the ability to respond to any criticisms of provincial laws or institutions by an international body. Finally, there is acknowledgement of the right of provinces to prepare their sections of Canada's reports in concert with the federal government.

Canadian federalism adds other twists as well to the modification and reporting requirements for human rights instruments. As the international social agenda has expanded, so has the range of possible disputes. An interesting example of this phenomenon stemmed from the Convention on the Rights of the Child. Alberta failed to endorse the convention, because of objections from the public that it would undermine parental authority on matters such as day care. Nevertheless Ottawa ratified it in 1992. However, concerns raised by aboriginal peoples about retention of their customs forced Canada to include reservations on the issue of adoption; the reservations were justified by reference to the convention's emphasis on minority rights and the importance of children's being raised in an environment that best ensures continuity of their background. The normal procedure is that the review of legislation undertaken before ratification reveals statutes that are inconsistent with an international convention, leading to amendments by the province or territory. These amendments attract high-level political attention: a province's agreement to the ratification of a human rights convention is usually conveyed in a letter from the Premier or the minister responsible or else in an order-in-council of the provincial cabinet. Quebec goes so far as to pass a decree to the effect that it has acceded to the international convention.

Federalism is not the only institution that complicates the processes of reporting and ratification. The internal structures even at the federal level alone have become considerably more complex over time. The Human Rights Directorate of the Department of Canadian Heritage co-ordinates the preparation of all human rights reports, drawing together information from the federal, provincial, and territorial governments. In addition the Human Rights Directorate may take the lead in drafting the federal portion of some reports. In other cases, however, other federal departments draft the federal section. The Department of Justice, for example, is the federal lead for the Covenant on Civil and Political Rights. The Directorate is the federal liaison for the Continuing Committee of Officials; it draws together reports from other federal departments as necessary in the ratification and reporting process.

The mandate of the Human Rights Directorate is to serve as the central point of reference for the federal government's domestic interest in human rights. It has overall policy responsibility at the federal level for the development and understanding of, and respect for, human rights. It does this through human rights education and promotion (principally through a grants and contributions budget of $858,000 in 1994-5), the Court Challenges Program,[2] and preparation of reports to the UN. Although the directorate is responsible for writing these reports, it relies on federal, provincial, and territorial departments for relevant information. In Canada's first report under the Convention on the Rights of the Child, for example, Justice and Health took the lead in the initial drafting of the federal portion of the report. The Department of Justice is routinely involved in most reports through reviews of federal statutes. The report currently being written for the Covenant on Economic, Social and Cultural Rights will similarly contain information from several departments, including Human Resource Development and Environment and the Canada Mortgage and Housing Corporation.

This discussion shows that the domestic machinery for the ratification of, and reporting on, international human rights instruments has become considerably more formal and complex over the last two decades. That is because this process imposes legal obligations on Canada, as opposed to mere consistency with declarations, on top of the internal consultations required by Canadian federalism. It should be clear that this machinery is bureaucratic rather than legislative. When Canada signs an international human rights agreement, the obligations under that agreement do not become a formal part of Canadian law. The review machinery described above simply ensures that no existing statutes are in violation of those obligations. In the absence of inconsistency it is assumed that Canadian law, both provincial and federal, is in compliance. Nothing else need be done. In the United States, by contrast, there is 'direct reception' of international obligations into domestic law, so that American citizens can ask the courts to order their governments to comply with treaties. The same is true in some European states: France and Belgium, for example, presume that treaties have precedence over domestic legislation, and citizens can argue the incompatibility of legislation with the European Convention on Human Rights in the ordinary courts (Robert 1994). Still, Canadian legislatures may enact international obligations directly into law. The most sweeping example was the incorporation of many provisions of the International Covenant on Civil and Political Rights into the Canadian Charter of Rights and Freedoms. Another example is the inclusion of the provisions from the convention relating to the Status of Refugees into the Immigration Act.

Another way that international human rights standards can affect Canadian law is through judicial decisions that consider obligations under treaties which Canada has ratified. According to Bayefsky, after the adoption of the Charter of Rights and Freedoms, 'there was an exponential growth in the number of cases which referred to conventional international human rights law in the course of interpreting domestic law.' Certainly the Supreme Court is referring with 'unprecedented frequency' to international treaty standards, although it should be added that the references depend more on the proclivities of individual justices than an established legal theory of the incorporation of international obligations into domestic law (Bayefsky 1992: 132). Thus, while international obligations are increasingly noted in domestic judicial decisions, there is as yet little consistency in their application. The most important institutional vehicles for the internationalization of domestic human rights standards continue to be the Charter, with its explicit incorporation of some of the language of the International Covenant on Civil and Political Rights, the direct passage of legislation to bring those obligations into domestic law, and the co-ordinating machinery for ratification and review.

All of this places a considerable onus on the bureaucratic apparatus in Canada to adapt to these changing conditions and raises questions about the management of foreign policy. As foreign policy impinges more on domestic, and as domestic policy develops an international dimension, does that enhance the power of DFAIT as a central agency or fragment its authority? Karvonen and Sundelius (1987: 14) provide a framework for considering the implications of internationalization for the management of foreign policy:

> The size of the foreign affairs community *grows rapidly*, and its *organizational structure* becomes *more complex*. The foreign policy field tends to experience an increasingly more *administrative dominance*. The process is *vertically decentralized* giving more room for technical, specialized inputs into the policy formulation. . . . This vertical decentralization of the policy process is combined with an even more dramatic *horizontal decentralization*. Transgovernmental relations are becoming an increasingly crucial part of the nation's external profile. Government agencies, traditionally concerned mainly with domestic matters, increasingly engage in *direct international interactions* with foreign government units. . . . The traditional Foreign Minister monopoly of external contacts by the state is significantly eroded as competing agencies join the official foreign affairs community. (Italics in original)

This hypothesis is supported by comparative analyses of the internationalization of foreign policy, though the extent of horizontal decentralization will depend on state structure and departmental strategy. The United States, for example, has a highly decentralized system of government, and so numerous domestic agencies engage in foreign affairs. In the Canadian case, DFAIT's organizational evolution shows strong evidence of vertical decentralization with the broadening out beyond traditional diplomacy to encompass trade and a host of the specialized policy areas. It is currently aware of the threat of horizontal decentralization, and the new foreign-policy framework is clearly intended to reassert DFAIT's control. Since the late 1960s, the department had been on the defensive as a result of Trudeau's critical attitude towards it, a view which denigrated External Affairs as largely irrelevant (Cooper, Higgott, and Nossal 1993: 38). In response, External underwent a decade-long process of reorganization. Most of the literature on this process has concentrated on the measures designed to promote 'integration' and 'consolidation'. Under these rubrics, Industry, Trade and Commerce, CIDA, and Employment and Immigration were for the most part joined with the 'old' External Affairs department. Just as significantly, a concerted drive was taken to give External Affairs renewed policy relevance.

In many ways, DFAIT may be said to have successfully re-oriented itself so as to deal with the complex issues associated not only with international trade but also with the expanding international agenda. In organizational terms, the department strengthened its competence in this issue area in a number of ways. At headquarters, the clearest expression of this diversified focus was the creation of a section called Human Rights, Women's Equality and Social Affairs Division within the International Organizations Bureau. Abroad, the greater salience of human rights issues was reflected in personnel management, most notably in the Canadian missions to the UN in New York and Geneva. Moreover, DFAIT could back up this activity with the technical competence it possessed through its Bureau of Legal Affairs, an apparatus which had an impressive record through the 1970s and 1980s (although it had attracted most attention in other areas, such as the Law of the Sea negotiations).

To a considerable extent, DFAIT was able to translate these resources into a co-ordinating role in international human rights activities. To give just one illustration, a DFAIT official, Anne Park, served as the head of the Canadian delegation to the 1993 Vienna human rights conference. Yet, even in this case, the demise of the pre-eminent standing of Foreign Affairs was obvious. Though DFAIT still had considerable responsibility as chair of the interdepartmental planning group for the Vienna conference, this responsibility was shared with a wide variety of other actors (including Immigration, Justice, Indian Affairs and Northern Development, CIDA, and Multicultural Canada).

This team effort contained a number of elements of both co-operation and competition. The most highly publicized episode in which DFAIT was able to work constructively with other actors took place during the Nairobi conference on Women and Development in 1985, where the then International Women's Equality Division in the department worked well with Status of Women Canada and other organizations. In a more low-key fashion, the Department of Justice has maintained a supportive relationship with DFAIT on human rights questions, for example, by drafting reports on the Covenant on Civil and Political Rights and lending an officer to the United Nations Centre for Human Rights in Geneva. Nonetheless, bureaucratic disagreements have also spilled over into this arena. Somewhat curiously, the most visible of these disagreements has simmered, and boiled over, between DFAIT and CIDA.

The heat this conflict generated cannot be divorced from a wider struggle centred on status and domain. Until the late 1980s, CIDA had accepted a position subordinate to DFAIT. From that point on, however, it tried to expand its capacity in decision making, not just in the development-aid dossier, but on a wider spectrum of issues, including the environment and human rights. Foreign Affairs then went on the offensive, challenging the position and client base of CIDA in a number of ways, most publicly in the attempt to include ODA funding and assistance for Eastern Europe and the former Soviet Union within a single expenditure grouping, the International Assistance Envelope, under the control of Foreign Affairs (Pratt 1993–4).

Underneath these turf disputes, though, were disagreements over policy issues as well, 'conditionality', and the insertion of human rights into the development process, and the application of universal human rights standards versus the right to development. These tensions were complicated further still by the underlying divergence of views within Foreign Affairs and International Trade itself. Notwithstanding the integrative trend of the 1980s, the point of view of DFAIT's officials still depended on which part of the Pearson building they sat in. The issue-specific interests of the International Organizations Bureau differed considerably from those of the geographic desk. The Trade and Economic ('E') Policy Branch in turn had its own distinctive perspective and goals, based on the need to consider the commercial aspect of any activity in the human rights or social arena.

Most recently, the logic of internationalization has drawn the department into another reorganization that will enhance its ability to manage emerging global issues, and this logic may be supported by the effects of program review that may force other government departments to leave foreign policy largely to DFAIT. *Canada in the World* promised two institutional innovations for solving the problems of horizontal and vertical decentralization. The first was the establishment of a new mechanism for 'foreign policy consultation, research and outreach that will bring together government practitioners, parliamentarians, experts and citizens.' This is, at time of writing, incomplete. The second was a move to lessen some of the compartmentalization in DFAIT, through the creation of a Bureau for Global Issues as part of a new branch for Global Issues and Culture:

> The Department will also establish the Bureau for Global Issues under an Assistant Deputy Minister who will also be responsible for international cultural relations. This new office will be specifically designed to help bring greater coherence to the Government's capacity to address internationally such issues as the global environment, population growth, international migration (including refugee issues), international crime, human rights, democratization, preventative diplomacy and post-conflict peace building. (Canada 1995b: 50)

The effects of program review are as yet difficult to gauge. DFAIT's budget is going to be cut by 5, 10, and 15 per cent in the next three years, but many other departments have been cut more deeply. CIDA, for example, has seen its international-assistance envelope reduced by 15 per cent in one year. Internationalization will continue to encourage these departments to be concerned about foreign affairs, but the budget cuts may force them to rely more on DFAIT as the lead agency (Canada, Dept of Justice 1995b). For similar reasons, it may be expected that other departments whose interests have traditionally been domestic will pursue their international activities in a more explicitly aggressive manner. Lloyd Axworthy, for example, responded to the severe criticism of the cuts in social programs by taking on the task of heading the Canadian delegation to the March 1995 World Summit for Social Development (WSSD). In doing so, he could show that his reform of the Department of Human Resources Development was in harmony with the best international efforts to deal with poverty, structural unemployment, and social exclusion and marginalization. Yet amidst this exercise in damage control, DFAIT did not lose its lead status in terms of responsibility. Marius Bujold, subsequently the acting director general of the Global Issues Bureau in DFAIT, served as Canadian co-ordinator of the WSSD.

CONCLUSION

There are several findings that we may draw from the analysis. First, human rights have clearly been part of the process of globalization that has taken place over the past 50 years. Earlier in this book, globalization was related to an expanding web of interlocking markets around the world, universal norms and standards that form common global reference points, worldwide communications that are virtually instantaneous, and the common social and economic practices they bring in train through computerization. The expansion of human rights regimes have been part of the development of universal norms. Second, the internationalization of this aspect of foreign policy has accelerated in the post–Cold War era as concepts of security have changed and broadened. Third, this process of internationalization has influenced the framing of Canadian foreign policy, the structure of the international human rights NGO community and its activities, domestic policy debates, in foreign-policy-management institutions.

Clearly, the internationalization of human rights is part not only of a new agenda, but also of a new kind of diplomacy. The federal government has been freed from many of the constraints imposed by the Cold War, and thus there has been a general impetus towards rethinking many of the fundamental assumptions, norms, and values underpinning global governance in what has been termed the Westphalian system (Zacher 1992). At the same time, there has been a more specific attempt to reshape the tools of statecraft.

This 'new' diplomacy contains the potential for creativity in technical innovation and problem solving, and for building a more intricate set of coalitions among state and non-state actors. To this creativity, though, is joined an added element of volatility. While opening up opportunities for co-operation, close contact between multiple actors has not yet led to a sense of permanent partnership. Practical difficulties remain about confidentiality and the exchange of information, problems often compounded by the imbalance in skill or resources. There also continues to be a gap not only in means, but also in the principles related to sovereignty, security, and the impact of globalization. Although, as noted above, there has been some considerable convergence on these questions, the divergence remains considerable.

For instance, the crucial item on the orthodox agenda may be said to be international order. By way of contrast, the unorthodox discourse, as witnessed in such forums as the recent Foreign Policy and Defence review, seeks justice on a global basis (Krause 1994). This twin dynamics of creativity and volatility, as they have emerged in state-society relations, may be highlighted by the relationship that the Canadian government has forged with the ICHRDD. On the one hand, the activities of this organization have been complementary to those of the government. Most notably, the ICHRDD's work was supportive of the pursuit of wider Canadian foreign-policy interests at the 1993 Vienna conference with respect to bringing the human rights of women into the mainstream human-rights mechanism, the adoption of the declaration on violence against women, and the appointment of a special rapporteur on violence against women with a broad investigative and reporting mandate. By way of contrast, on a wide range of other issues, the ICHRDD disagreed markedly with official policy. Indeed, on a number of particularly sensitive issues, the ICHRDD launched public campaigns either to embarrass or to undercut the government's position. One such case was the ICHRDD's campaign to analyse the implications of NAFTA for human rights. Another was its campaign to have women fleeing domestic violence in other countries granted refugee status in Canada. Still another was the ICHRDD's campaign against the subordination of human rights in China to commercial interests.

This dynamic was further complicated by the changes in the goals both of government and of Canadian society. Confirming Moravcsik's argument, the goals of Canadian governments have not remained constant throughout the 1970s, 1980s, and 1990s, but have fluctuated between the modest and the (over-) ambitious (Moravcsik 1993). At the same time, there continue to be significant differences in government about the nature of these goals, differences that are based not just on principle but also on practical considerations related to their client base. Nor are the NGOs monolithic. On a wide range of issues they have divergent interests and argue for quite different policies. The most telling manifestation of such a schism is the growing tensions between the development NGOs and the human rights NGOs.

Nevertheless, these groups do have a significant element of coherence in that all of them are attempting to alter government policies by transforming the social practices upon which they are based (Walker 1988). In so far as these groups have become more numerous and more important in the foreign-policy process over the past decade, it must be reiterated that the process itself has been fundamentally altered. The traditional process was centred on the state and dominated by a lead department. Although the NGOs are still suffering from a number of structural deficiencies, above all, their financial dependence on government and considerable internal organizational weaknesses (related to the training of staff and administrative procedures) and fragmentation, the approach that has evolved from these NGOs has mirrored the two-level domestic-international games played by government. NGOs are increasingly sophisticated in their contacts and communications with overseas partners, and they bring those perspectives directly into the domestic foreign-policy process. At the same time, they are more and more sophisticated in their own domestic networks, exploiting not only the synergies between different policy areas,[3] but also the differences evident in the administrative machinery of government.

The influence of the diverse range of NGOs on the lengthening international social agenda should not be exaggerated. The Canadian government, like others in the advanced industrial world, continues to have considerable autonomy in this policy domain. In moving beyond a narrow definition of national interest and beyond a state-centred mode of policy making, the government has displayed both its many techniques for adapting to change and its ability to combine commitment to ideals with convenience. Furthermore, the goals of these social groups still have to compete with other issues and interests in both the international and domestic arenas. As demonstrated by conferences such as the WSSD in the multilateral domain (Knox 1995), as well as by Canada's bilateral relations with China and other countries, there are quite serious limits imposed by the wider commercial and fiscal circumstances.

Conversely, however, the influence of these NGOs should not be minimized. By offering alternative ways of thinking, they have helped to map out not only an extended policy agenda, but a new form of statecraft in the context of the internationalization of human rights. If still an ambiguous and fragile relationship, this area of foreign policy is clearly in a transition stage. While the precise role that NGOs will play in policy and implementation remains to be worked out, it is clear that the dominant assumptions and the ways of doing things from the past have been transformed. Moving from an agenda-setting role with the emphasis on information exchange, and an alternative form of discourse, Canadian NGOs have become integrated into the policy process itself.

NOTES

The authors would like to thank Sandra Bach and Fabiola Bazo for their help with this chapter. They also wish to acknowledge the support of the Social Sciences Council of Canada.

1. Two of these were research institutes (the North-South Institute and the Human Rights Research and Education Centre at the University of Ottawa); one was quasi-governmental (the International Centre for Human Rights and Democratic Development—ICHRDD); and the rest were NGOs. Sixteen of these organizations had religious affiliations, suggesting the continued importance of the churches in overseas aid and human rights activism.

2. The cancellation of the Court Challenges Program in 1992 by the Conservative government set off a wave of criticism based on the standards argument. As Maureen O'Neil, the president of the North-South Institute, stated: 'Canada's legitimacy and moral position [is] very much related to the fact that Canada has been, and has been seen to be, a country that treats its own citizens fairly and a country that has systematically over the years added one building block after the other to the protection of human rights. There is some question now about whether we're still on that course, given the last budget and the abolition of the Court Challenges Program, which was an important building block in that process' (Canada, Standing Committee External Affairs and International Trade 1992–3). The program was reinstated by the Liberals after the 1993 federal election. It is now delivered by an arm's-length corporation called the Court Challenges Program of Canada, which is run by equality-seeking groups. The Human Rights Directorate manages the contribution agreement with the corporation.

3. See, for example, the presentation by the NIHR to the 1994 joint committee. It was a model of elegant co-ordination among various networks, citing and supporting key points from presentations by the CCIC and other NGOs. This both saved time and underscored key themes in the 'counter-consensus'. Another example of increasing sophistication is the manoeuvres by NGOs at the 1995 World Summit for Social Development. A joint statement critical of the Prime Minister's absence was issued by nearly a hundred Canadian NGOs attending the summit and was then placed on an electronic network, where it was accessible to other domestic NGOs and internationally (Knox 1995).

—10—

Foreign Policy

G. Bruce Doern and John Kirton

In an overall context it makes little sense to speak of the internationalization of foreign-policy making. Canadian foreign policy is, after all, quintessentially about Canada's relations with, and views about, the world and its near and distant neighbours. It is also about relations with international organizations and obligations under treaties, agreements, and regimes. In another sense, however, it is indeed correct to ask how internationalization in the past 15 years has changed the foreign-policy process. Three entwined forces of further and intense international change have recently conspired to change the world of the Canadian foreign-policy maker. The first force is globalization, the processes that have produced new telecommunications and computer-based revolutions in technology, an enormously increased mobility of financial capital, and greatly expanded capacities for flexible production sourcing by firms. These features of globalization have directly affected business, investment, and society in crucial ways; at the same time they have helped create the need for new or enlarged trade agreements—the Canada-US Free Trade Agreement (FTA), the North American Free Trade Agreement (NAFTA), and the General Agreement on Tariffs and Trade (GATT).

The second force is these agreements themselves. A simple reading of their provisions and obligations shows that they have expanded the reach of foreign economic policy. Once in place, they create pressure for new relations and establish new or reformed decision processes that change what foreign-policy makers can and cannot do and who they must relate to, both within nation states and among their signatory countries.

The third closely linked force in the agenda of the 1990s has been the end of the Cold War, the demise of the Soviet bloc, and the emergence among its former members of newly released nationalism and, at the same time, interdependence (Dewitt, Haglund, and Kirton 1993).

This chapter examines the internationalization of the Canadian foreign-policy process in the last 15 years by examining how these three more recent manifestations of internationalization have been revealed through, supported by, and resisted by, the main elements of the foreign-policy process. Thus, the main sections of the chapter deal with ideas and policy change, including changing views about sovereignty; the role of the Department of Foreign Affairs and International Trade Canada (DFAIT) as the lead department in foreign-policy making; interest groups and policy communities; and changes in policy instruments and the evolving nature of international agencies.

Four arguments are advanced. The first is that Canadian foreign policy has been increasingly influenced by economic foreign-policy concerns largely through quite aggressive support for free-trade liberalism and a diminished concern for traditionally defined notions of sovereignty, notions which were themselves never strongly pro-sovereignty. But, when combined with the demise of the Soviet Union, this economic orientation has also led to a renewed confidence that foreign policy led by the Prime Minister can enhance rather than detract from Canada's international influence.

With respect to the role of DFAIT in the Ottawa policy system, the chapter will show that some features of the new internationalization have enhanced its internal power, particularly when linked to foreign policy and multilateral summitry led by the Prime Minister. It also shows that other factors have increased the dependence of DFAIT on other departments in several respects: the need for expertise, the need for budgetary resources, and the need for statutory capacity.

The interest-group and foreign-policy community has also been broadened by the greater direct involvement by business interest groups, largely through trade negotiations, and by wider pressures from social, migration, and environmental interest groups. The latter are both a cause and an effect of the emergence of wider foreign-policy concerns about the meaning of security.

Shifts in the use of policy instruments are also shown in relation to the changing links to international organizations: multilateral, bilateral, and, especially plurilateral (that is, involving a few countries, depending on the number of signatory states). There is now a far greater use of rules-based approaches that are at least quasi-regulatory. Hence, the overall reliance on diplomacy is altered and shifts to new frontier areas of concern.

From the outset, it must be recognized that there is a definitional and locational conundrum in the journey ahead. This has to do with the shifting boundaries of foreign policy and with how much of the field can be said to be encompassed by DFAIT as the lead agency. In one sense, foreign policy could be seen at its centre as dealing with basic foreign relations, particularly defence and Canada's most vital and immediate diplomatic relations, especially those with the United States (Nossal 1989). When seen in the contours of the mandate areas of DFAIT, foreign policy obviously includes trade policy and promotion and hence economic foreign policy and development assistance, the latter through the Canadian International Development Agency (CIDA) (Stairs and Winham 1985). However, foreign policy has for many decades gone well beyond these narrow boundaries. There have been foreign-policy and international aspects of policy fields such as immigration, transportation, energy, justice, and law enforcement, to name only a few (Pammet and Tomlin 1984). This means that foreign policy, by definition, involves other departments of government and the provinces. And it requires DFAIT either to have the expertise to make policy in these fields or, much more frequently, to acquire it by collaborating with other departments and jurisdictions. Recent internationalization escalates these latter tendencies, since, as we see, more areas of the state that were cocooned in largely domestic worlds are exposed to more frequent pressures from outside the boundaries of Canada (Doern 1993, 1994a).

Since trade policy is examined in a separate chapter, we do not focus on it here. However, the chapter does deal with economic foreign policy in a more general way, not only because DFAIT significantly enhanced its stock of such functions in the early 1980s, but also because the very nature of recent trade policy, including dispute settlement, brings such economic disputes more and more into the inner reaches of domestic economic policy (Boddez and Trebilcock 1993; Doern 1995c, 1995b). It also alters the realms within which policy is made, through traditional diplomacy as opposed to rules-based dispute-settlement instruments.

POLICY CHANGE, IDEAS, AND SOVEREIGNTY

In the last decade, four changes in Canadian foreign policy can be discerned along with the pressures and events that propelled them: a post–Cold War view that Canada can enhance its influence in the world; a more assertive free-trade-oriented economic foreign policy; a diminished concern for sovereignty except where tested by national-unity crises involving Quebec; and a broadening view of security to include environmental threats and sustainable development. These four changes mark a departure from the dominant post–Second World War foreign policy, which centred on Pearsonian internationalism and multilaterism, diplomacy, and the inevitable emphasis on Canada-US relations, all conditioned by the politics of the Cold War (Nossal 1989; Stairs 1982). The death of the USSR and a dramatic decline in relative capability of the remnant Russia has given Canadian prime ministers a new conception of Canada as a rising power in the world. With the demise of the Soviet bloc that created the dominant east-west alignment and the associated 'non-aligned' bloc that bred the north-south alignment, Canada's traditional constraining, bridge-building, or mediatory diplomacy has become less relevant, and Canada has had to cope with the multiple rivalries of economic competition among the United States, Japan, and the European Union (EU). The end of the closed authoritarian polities and command economies of the Communist world (with the still significant exception of China, Vietnam, Cuba, and North Korea) has integrated many consequential countries into the western-centred but increasingly global society of free markets and liberal intellectual interchange, has intensified interdependence, and has led to a greater globalism in Canadian behaviour. Moreover, the historical failure of the twentieth-century, communist-pioneered and -centred model of dominant public-sector-driven political and economic decision making as the reigning policy ideas, and the resulting democratic and market revolution sweeping the world, have reoriented Canada toward those international institutions and regimes, notably those of the Group of Seven (G7), where these latter values are embedded in the codified and inner management core. At the same time, the post-Westphalian concepts of sovereign states in an anarchic world have given way to the legitimacy of domestic intervention and a highly internationally institutionalized order. In such a system, during an era where there is no dominant rival military power to engage in expansionism or generate crises and threats, the classic concern with 'national security' has given way to a preoccupation with 'co-operative security', 'common security', and 'global security'.

A more assertive free-trade-oriented economic foreign policy has been evident throughout the decade. It began when officials in External Affairs got free trade on the agenda in the 1983-to-1985 period over the objections of more traditional and conservative views, not only in the department but also in the federal government as a whole (Doern and Tomlin 1991). It was propelled by the trade negotiations themselves—for the FTA, NAFTA, and the General Agreement on Tariffs and Trade (GATT)—which were virtually continuous for a decade and which took many areas of decision making out of traditional arenas and into the ambit of the Trade Negotiator's Office. The free trade and economic assertiveness in foreign policy continued into the Chrétien Liberal era, where free-trade ideas have been articulated for both the hemisphere and also *vis-à-vis* the European Union. Economic policy has always been a part of foreign policy, but there can be no doubt that the trade functions acquired by DFAIT in 1982–3 have, in the face of growing internationalization and globalization, greatly increased its importance.

Canadian foreign-policy analysts suggest that 'sovereignty' has never been a dominant goal of Canadian foreign policy (Griffiths 1994). If anything, this low concern has been diminished even more in the period examined here. In sharp contrast to Trudeau's foreign-policy statement of 1969 with its theme of 'sovereignty and independence', and with the Trudeau government's brief economic-foreign-policy nationalism of 1980–1, the term 'sovereignty' remains remarkable absent from both Mulroney-era foreign policy, where sovereign policy powers and policy instruments were ceded in the FTA and NAFTA negotiations (Tucker 1980; Clarkson 1985). Sovereignty as a rhetorical and traditional concept is almost totally absent from the opening pages of the Chrétien government's foreign-policy statements; it is virtually invisible in the general chapters of the document as a whole (Canada, Government 1995a: i–iii). Instead, sovereignty is redefined as a shared property rather than a synonym for national independence.

The Chrétien statement reports that Canadians 'are clear that our security and sovereignty must continue to be assured in a world under stress', but previously declares that 'however, especially for smaller and medium sized countries, sovereignty has also been enhanced since the growing number of international rules on security, trade and other matters better protects states from arbitrary and unilateral action by other governments' (Canada, Government 1995a: 8). It further notes that 'states have been increasingly willing to enter into agreements that voluntarily cede aspects of economic sovereignty' (Canada, Government 1995a: 5). The statement is equally dismissive of the related concept of 'independence'. It declares that 'international capital markets have the strength to affect the independent capacity of governments to guide economies' and that, together with the information highway and cross-border individual and group ties, technological innovations, and the outward-looking political and economic policies, they diminish 'the ability of states to act independently since they can no longer isolate themselves from the world without unacceptable domestic consequences' (Canada 1995a: 3).[1] Gone is the earlier emphasis, dating back only a year to the *Red Book* of September 1993 and the *Foreign Policy Handbook* of May 1993, on an 'independent foreign policy' (Liberal Party of Canada 1993). In its place are the overriding premise that Canada is a net international policy maker rather than international influence taker, and a resulting emphasis on competitive, internationally oriented nationalism rather than on defensive sovereignty and protection of our independence.

If sovereignty and independence are essentially dismissed in the foreign-policy statement, they are accorded rhetorical primacy in the 1994 defence policy White Paper (Canada 1994a). Here there is a commitment to maintain maritime, land, and air combat-capable forces 'to deal with challenges to our sovereignty in peacetime, and [to] retain the capability to generate forces capable of contributing to the defence of our country should the need arise' (Canada, Government 1994: 12). Indeed, its first priority was to 'provid[e] for the defence of Canada and Canadian sovereignty', by aiding the civil power; providing peacetime surveillance and control; securing our borders against illegal activities; and providing fisheries protection, environmental surveillance, disaster relief, and search and rescue (Canada 1994a: 15).

The rhetorical dismissal of sovereignty and independence in foreign affairs is fully reflected in reality. Its most visible manifestation has been the failure of Canada to keep pace with the proliferating number of new countries since the Cold War by opening resident diplomatic posts; such posts ensure Canada's presence abroad and are, under international law, the sovereign territory of Canada abroad. The vigorous assertion of sovereignty by Canadian ministers and diplomats in response to the recent American moves to extraterritoriality through the extension of US law to corporations resident in Canada and individuals dealing with Cuba is merely the most recent manifestation of a Canadian policy dating back three and a half decades. The motives for that policy are commercial reward, a liberal concept of the way to ensure Cuba's post–Communist transition, and an effort to differentiate Canada from the United States, more than any recently enhanced Canadian concern with sovereignty.

In the security sphere, Canada's continuing acceptance of the daily surveillance of Canadian territory by the United States, Russia, Japan, and France and its failure to acquire a comparable capability by deploying our own surveillance satellites bely the words of the 1994 defence White Paper (Kirton 1995a). Moreover, the February 1995 budget's reduced expenditure and personnel level for DND and the resulting downsizing and delay in the acquisition of traditional equipment required to maintain surveillance and control further the diminution of concern with sovereignty.

In the defining policy area of the Arctic waters, Trudeau's emphasis in 1970 on expanding Canadian jurisdiction and Mulroney's acquisition of full sovereignty in 1985–8 have been replaced by a hitherto unsuccessful effort to create a multilateral, multi-stakeholder Arctic Council, in which the Canadian government's complete claim to jurisdiction and representation would be reduced (Kirton 1995b).[2] Of far more importance has been the rapid acceptance of three essentially unmodified NAFTA agreements and institutions with potentially significant elements that reduce

Canada's autonomy and jurisdiction (see below). In these latter cases, the diminished Canadian concern with sovereignty results directly from ecological and economic forces of globalization. In both cases, however, it is the Clinton administration's interpretation of US interests, more than the Canadian government's response to globalization, that have determined the outcomes. The one major Canadian initiative that has displayed a heightened desire to extend Canadian jurisdiction, in part through the unilateral use of force, was the turbot conflict with Spain in 1995. Much like the similar case of the Arctic Waters Pollution Prevention Act in 1969–70, the acceptance of the epistemology of sustainable development (in the form of a global resource conservation crisis) and the mobilization of a global governmental coalition and an international-intergovernmental alliance were contributing causes of the Canadian decision to proceed and of the ultimate success Canada enjoyed.[3]

Arguably, ideas about sovereignty have greater salience when national unity is at stake. As a result of the failure of the Meech Lake and Charlottetown accords, the election of the Parti Québécois in September 1995, and the 1995 referendum on Quebec sovereignty, Chrétien's foreign policy has changed. Particularly from 1994 onward, the latest challenge to national unity has given a focus to Canadian-foreign-policy decision makers and, among other things, centred that policy on forging close associations with francophone countries and developing the view that Canada has major-power status and benefits that a sovereign Quebec could never have.

The fourth change in foreign policy is the greater emphasis being given to the environment and sustainable development (Munton and Kirton 1994; Doern 1993). The effect of these goals on foreign policy is not to be underestimated. Not only are sustainable development and the threats of international pollution a part of Canadian foreign policy in their own right, but they are also part of the broadening notions of security. But once again, internationalization here is not new. From the Stockholm Conference of 1972 and the World Conservation Strategy of 1980, to the Brundtland Commission of the mid-1980s and the Rio Earth Summit of 1992, there has been a strong Canadian influence on the international environmental stage and strong international influences on Canadian policy (Doern and Conway 1995).

Internationalization of this aspect of foreign policy became more intense because, as the global commons came to be more fully understood over the last decades, it was less and less possible to separate bilateral from multilateral environmental foreign policy (Doern and Conway 1995). The process of reaching international agreements and setting protocols became ever more complex and changed the relations within the government between DFAIT and Environment Canada. Because of the hazards involved in the successive negotiations on sulphur dioxide (SO_2), the ozone layer and CFCs, nitrous oxides and (NO_x-VOCs), global warming, and biodiversity, international issues became increasingly complex (Doern 1993). With the election in 1992 of President Clinton, a new phase was opened that increasingly embraced trade and economic issues, not the least of which was NAFTA and the battle over its environmental side agreement (Doern 1994b).

By 1995 the Chrétien government was emphasizing sustainable development as an integral theme. Emphasis is given to the new, more complex threats to security by mass migration, crime, disease, environmental degradation, overpopulation, and underdevelopment.[4]

The four changes traced above are by no means the only aspects of Canadian foreign policy to change (Drache and Gertler 1991; Therien and Noel 1994). By the mid-1990s, the federal government's set of referents and ideas for its foreign-policy discourse had evolved to a considerable extent.[5] This discourse centres, at the prime ministerial level, on Canada's relative rather than absolute capability to assert its interests and influence internationally, as a consequence of six pre–Cold War and five post–Cold War factors. Emphasis is given to Canada's 'position of leadership among the open, advanced societies', its important 'advantage' in the Pacific and Latin America, its 'privileged access' to the francophone, anglophone, and indeed entire world, its ability to further its global interests 'better than any other country', and an important and distinctive role 'among nations'. Also cited in the foreign-policy statement as causes are the enduring factors of Canada's geographic location, its anglophone and francophone cultural heritage, its active membership in such international groups as the G7, and its history as a non-colonizing power, champion of constructive multilateralism, and effective international mediator. These characteristics acquire enhanced relevance because of five characteristics of the post–Cold War era: (1) the increasing influence of open, advanced societies as 'world power is dispersing and becoming more defined in economic terms'; (2) 'new poles of political and economic power emerging in the Pacific and Latin America'; (3) 'Canadians drawn from every part of the globe who make up its multicultural personality'; (4) Canada's hosting of the APEC summit in 1997; and, (5) nations' current search to 'build a new and better order'. Amidst the dominant realist concern with relative power, shifting polarity, and the shaping of order through international institutions lie four newer components: the new salience of advanced economic capabilities among more open societies; an emphasis on geographically defined regionalism; Canada's more global population as a result of recent immigration; and the emphasis on plurilateral summitry in global governance.

Prime Minister Chrétien's emphasis is on three foreign-policy priorities: the promotion of prosperity and employment, the protection of our security within a stable global framework, and the projection of Canadian values and culture into the international arena. Although the first two can be logically deduced from the post–Cold War international system, the presence of economic growth as the first priority of foreign policy for Canadians in 1970 and the emphasis on national security reduce the degree of innovation contained here. Of greater novelty are the third priority's components of culture and learning, which are offered as essential to Canada's economic success in the new knowledge-based world economy. In contrast, the specified values of human rights, democracy, the rule of law, and the environment (values which must be accepted abroad to safeguard the quality of life of Canadians and their identity at home), appear in the 1986 and 1970 foreign-policy priorities and reflect the sense of vulnerability characteristic of those earlier times.

THE ROLE OF DFAIT AS THE LEAD FOREIGN-POLICY DEPARTMENT

The starting point for assessing the influence on DFAIT of the internationalization of foreign policy is to understand the basic legal and political power of the department (Nossal 1989; Tucker 1980). First, in political terms, the department has always had a central relationship to the Prime Minister. This follows from the simple fact that DFAIT advises on the essential positions to be taken by the Prime Minister on numerous international trips and occasions. Second, legally, the Act that governs the department gives it the authority to represent Canada abroad, to approve and accredit Canadian delegations, and to set Canadian foreign policy in the light of Canada's overall political, economic, and security needs. Third, DFAIT also controls the means of diplomatic communication with other countries and possesses particular legal expertise in drafting treaties. Fourth, since 1982, and in the FTA and NAFTA period, DFAIT has had the lead role on trade policy. Politically, in a broader sense, DFAIT (and its predecessors) has always been one of the four or five most important power bases in the federal government. And while many other line departments add aspects of foreign policy to their otherwise domestic policy roles, DFAIT has always argued successfully that, to avoid chaos, it must have the final say on foreign policy (Doern 1993).

For their part, other federal departments point to a complementary legal and political power base. Their international responsibilities are derived from the content and logic of their relevent statutes. Their power is also the power of expertise, including technical and scientific expertise. Equally important, however, these departments can strongly argue that their minister will get the domestic political blame for things that go wrong (Doern 1993).

It is in the nexus of these two sets of legal-political bases that the bureaucratic politics of foreign policy is necessarily played out (Wright 1985). But an understanding of the recent effects of internationalization and globalization must also be based on an appreciation of pivotal organizational and mandate changes. Keenes's analysis of the build-up and negotiation of the 1982 changes, which brought the trade function to External Affairs shows that the foreign-policy side of the reorganization was driven by changes in the international political economy (Keenes 1992). The intention was to give the department 'the strategic mandate as a central agency to have a say in domestic economic policies, justified by the exigencies of a more competitive, even predatory, international political economy' (Keenes 1992: 384). Keenes also shows that this decision was strongly opposed by the Department of Finance and the then Department of Trade and Industry, which had come to 'mistrust the economic credentials of External in the wake of industrial strategy and Third Option debates' in the 1970s (Keenes 1992: 384).

One of the continuing effects of this kind of trade-led economic internationalization has also been to create a tension within DFAIT between its political and trade wings, sometimes loosely referred to as its own left and right wings. As a result, there have been disagreements over whether, and exactly how, to organize the department along geographical lines (countries and regions of the world) rather than functional lines (political and security, trade and development) (Keenes 1992).

By definition then, there are many levels on which internationalization may affect the lead agency of foreign policy. When one then considers globalization pressures *per se*, these challenges to organizational power and coherence only increase. In some respects the forces of globalization have substantially diminished the centrality of DFAIT as a lead department and co-ordinating centre for the making and management of Canadian foreign policy and domestically grounded international relations. Telecommunications makes it more difficult to fully control diplomatic communication with other countries. The diminished concern with sovereignty, the primacy of economics in foreign policy, the much broader definition of security, and the pervasive goal of sustainable development all propel the locus of decision making from foreign ministries, which traditionally have been weak in these subjects, to functional domestically oriented departments where the expertise, legal mandates, and program monies reside. In Canada's case the presence since 1982 of trade in the foreign ministry in a combined DFAIT has reduced somewhat the effects of this dispersal of influence (Nossal 1994). Yet the diminished importance of foreign ministries abroad—DFAIT's partners in its international network—itself reduces DFAIT's relevance at home.

In the mid-1990s Chrétien era, several things may have exerted an offsetting influence: (1) the desire of the Prime Minister and the public for a smaller scale of government; (2) budgetary reductions and streamlining of programs; (3) the close longstanding relationship between the Prime Minister and Foreign Affairs Minister André Ouellet; (4) the new challenge of national unity in its international dimensions; and (5) return to a modernized version of DFAIT as a 1970s style central agency of government with a mandate, focused on, and supported by, the Prime Minister, to offer advice on international subjects across the entire spectrum of government activity.

In foreign policy and defence, as elsewhere, the Chrétien government began with a desire to return to the 1963–8 model of smaller government, much reduced ministerial staffs, and a reliance on the lead roles of ministers within their individual policy domains. This vision was opposed to the elaborate, collective, duplicative, and adversarial decision making, centred on ministers, that had been introduced during the Trudeau years and pruned somewhat in the Mulroney era (Nossal 1994). Following the example of his immediate predecessor, Jean Chrétien chose a much smaller cabinet than that maintained by Prime Minister Mulroney. He did not create a separate cabinet committee on foreign policy and defence, nor did he follow Mulroney's extensive use of foreign-service officers in PMO positions. Chrétien also had smaller central agencies and no foreign-affairs specialist in the PMO. The one proximate resource has come from the appointment of Mitchell Sharp, Chrétien's political mentor (and former deputy minister of Industry and Finance, and Secretary of State for External Affairs) as a special adviser in the PMO. Although the two did not discuss any foreign-policy issues during the first six months of the Chrétien government, Sharp's presence symbolically reinforced the bias toward an economically oriented foreign policy.

The immediate results of these were that the full cabinet was better able to consider major priorities comprehensively, foreign-policy issues were less likely to be considered disproportionately within the context of security as traditionally conceived, and cabinet relied more on DFAIT for foreign-policy advice on less central matters, without being challenged by strong central agencies or delayed by layers of cabinet co-ordinating mechanisms.[6] In such a system the Prime Minister has maintained control by several devices. Most generally, and in sharp contrast to Pearson, Trudeau, and Mulroney, Jean Chrétien entered office with a considerable mandate and representation from all regions of the country, an immediate challenge to national unity in the presence of the Bloc Québécois, and extensive ministerial experience (including that as Secretary of State for External Affairs). The unprecedented popularity of the party and the Prime Minister, which he has maintained, have enhanced his power. Moreover, he chose as his first Foreign Minister a fellow francophone Quebecker and longstanding lieutenant, André Ouellet, and as Defence Minister his leadership-campaign supporter David Collenette. The absence of a former or prospective Prime Minister as Minister of Foreign Affairs has reduced competition or friction between the Prime Minister and Foreign Minister of the sort that prevailed in the Pearson government and early Mulroney years. Moreover, the Prime Minister made it clear to his Foreign Minister at the outset that he wished to be kept informed of important initiatives. More important, his unprecedented intense program of summit diplomacy immediately upon entering office has reinforced and updated his extensive international contacts, and has given him first-hand knowledge of a wide variety of regions of the world, bilateral relationships, and international institutional arrangements.

At the interdepartmental level, departmental challenges to the primacy of the Prime Minister have been circumscribed, notwithstanding the plurilateral institutional incentive for direct international participation by a large number of portfolio ministers. Although other ministers retain expertise and experience in foreign affairs, because of the restricted size of their staffs and the reduced size of many departments following program review, they are less able to challenge DFAIT's lead. Indeed, compared to most domestic departments, including those, such as Environment, that may benefit from globalization and the new Canadian commitment to sustainable development, DFAIT emerged from the February 1995 budget relatively unscathed. DFAIT had also previously escaped the wholesale redesign of departments and the loss of major functions in the summer of 1993. Budgetary reductions in other departments have resulted in a downsizing of independent international-affairs units. Even the relatively powerful Finance Department has had to withdraw some of its hard-won finance counsellors from G7 embassies abroad. It is also discussing the possibility of withdrawing resident Canadian executive directors from some of the regional development banks.

Within this interdepartmental nexus, DFAIT is accordingly quite well positioned to pursue the new goal of prosperity through trade, having Canada's foreign ministry and trade ministry in a single organization. The strength of the two portfolio ministers in 1993 to early 1996 lay in Foreign Minister Ouellet's detailed knowledge of Quebec and the national unity file and in Trade Minister Roy Maclaren's position as a major anglophone regional minister, an experienced federal minister and politician, and a professional trade diplomat. For the first time, the Chrétien government assigned foreign-affairs junior ministers, not on a functional basis (with the junior minister of external relations responsible for CIDA and the francophone world), but on an explicitly geographic basis, with Asia-Pacific affairs assigned to Raymond Chan of British Columbia and Latin America and Africa to Christine Stewart, also of British Columbia. The change seemed to be due primarily to a desire to achieve greater cabinet balance on regional, visible ethnic, and sexual lines. However, the specific geographic formula for allocating responsibilities also corresponded well to the growing size and influence of Asian ethnic groups in the making of Canadian foreign policy.

INTEREST GROUPS AND POLICY COMMUNITY CHANGES

The Canadian foreign-policy process has frequently been called closed and élitist and centred in much of the post–Second World War period in a highly professional foreign service (Nossal 1989; Lyon and Tomlin 1979). In the last 20 years, however, the views of broader social interest groups and policy communities have been evident. This tendency has been reinforced by the internationalization and globalization of the last decade. Not only have these changes widened the range of groups that pay attention to foreign policy and international developments, but they have also increased the two-way flow of opinions and values between alliances of domestic- and foreign-interest groups and professional policy networks. These groups both express their fears about the new global realities and seek to extend international rules about their concerns.

Four changes are highlighted below, although they are by no means the only changes in the associational politics of globalized foreign-policy making: (1) the more direct business-interest-group politics both supportive of, and resistant to, the lengthening foreign-policy and economic foreign-policy agenda and process; (2) the broad range of migration and immigration interests; (3) environmental interests; and, (4) the widening range of interests as a whole revealed through the Chrétien foreign-policy review of 1994, as well as earlier reviews.

Business interests have always had opinions about foreign policy and the economy that they channelled though DFAIT and its predecessor departments (Stairs and Winham 1985). But there is little doubt that these interest-group pressures have become more direct since the department acquired the trade function in the early 1980s. As Chapter 7 shows, these interest groups channelled their views through the Sectoral Advisory Groups on International Trade (SAGITs) created for the FTA, NAFTA, and GATT trade negotiations (Doern and Tomlin 1991; Doern 1993). Thus, business interests were not only more directly involved, but involved through a process that had firm deadlines for negotiations. For DFAIT, this direct role of business is a vital change in what it does and how it must see the world. These business-oriented roles can only increase in intensity as international 'trade' agendas become involved in matters dealing with domestic business framework law such as competition policy, intellectual property, and the environment (Doern 1994b; 1995b).

A second potent aspect of internationalization and globalization that affects Canadian foreign policy has been migration. This has been fuelled not only by relative poverty and population growth abroad, but also by Canada's considerable openness to immigrants, refugee claimants, and refugees. In 1993, for the second year in a row and for the first time since before the First World War, immigration surpassed natural increase as a contributor to Canada's population growth. (Net immigration enlarged the population by 206,900, and natural increase by 193,100.) This trend has had an immediate and direct impact on Canada's G7 diplomacy. In the lead-up to Naples in 1994, when Italy suggested that the leaders address migration, Canada worked to ensure that the discussion would recognize the positive aspects of immigration. In the initial preparations for Halifax in 1995, Canada persuaded the leaders to address migration as a basic issue.

These rapid inflows of people from a much wider group of regions beyond Europe (which provided most of Canada's immigrants in the immediate post-war decades) are broadening and intensifying the influence of ethnic groups on the foreign-policy process. Traditionally, the only minority ethnic-religious groups that regularly influenced Canadian foreign policy were the Canadian Jewish community and Canadians of Eastern European descent. Occasionally, they were joined by spontaneous, *ad hoc* multi-ethnic coalitions, like those on Biafra in 1969 or Ethiopia in 1984 that were formed in response to widespread deaths abroad from civil wars or famines.[7] The response to the Tiananmen massacre of 1989 showed the influence of both demographic 'globalization'—the rise of the Chinese community to become the third-largest linguistic group in Canada—and the communications globalization, as television and fax machines aided the ultimate influence of ethnically based protest groups in Canada and abroad. There are also more permanent results. A Tiananmen activist, Raymond Chan is a junior minister in DFAIT, responsible for Asia-Pacific affairs in the first-ever geographically based allocation of ministerial responsibilities in the portfolio, and there is a new emphasis on China in the Prime Minister's travels and institutionalized summitry.[8] In Quebec the challenge to national unity has led to even more influence for the Canadian Haitian community on Canadian policy toward Haiti.[9]

On the other hand, in more traditional areas, such as Canadian policy toward Ukraine (as in the Naples Summit assistance package of 1994 and the ministerial conference in Winnipeg in the autumn of 1994), the activism of the one million Canadians of Ukrainian descent played a minor role, relative to the influence of Canada's larger G7 partners.[10] In the more classic Cold War style of relations with Russia, there has been virtually no activity by internationally affiliated ethnic interest groups, even in the face of the civil war and the systematic murder of civilians in Chechnya. The heavy emphasis on China and Vietnam on Prime Minister Chrétien's tour of Asia in 1994 indicate it is Canadian (linguistically defined) demography, aided by considerations of national unity and a lingering desire to differentiate Canadian policy from that of the United States, rather than anti-Communist and human-rights interest groups (or economic size) that prevail.

A third increase in interest-group pressure on foreign policy that has been induced by internationalization and globalization has come from environmental groups. They played a substantial role in preparations for, and at, UNCED in June 1992 (Doern 1993; Munton and Kirton 1994). Moreover, they provided a model for subsequent United Nations conferences at the ministerial level (on population, social policy, and women), and helped inspire the creation of new institutions, notably the United Nations Commission on Sustainable Development and the refurbishing of the Global Environmental Facility. Their role in NAFTA and in multilateral UN-based and other negotiations—if not the World Trade Organisation (WTO)—points to their influence. The foreign-policy environmental agenda is by no means synonymous with that of the environmental ENGOs. Business interests are also crucially involved, not only in green summitry but also, even more crucially in the intense politics of setting protocols for such things as SO_2, NO_x-VOCs, CFCs, and global warming (Doern 1993).

A fourth change in interest-group politics is the changed processes for handling larger foreign-policy reviews. DFAIT has responded somewhat slowly to these new pressures and to the need to develop an informed, domestic constituency that is guided by the department, as virtually all other federal departments have done. Traditionally, External Affairs managed its domestic environment through regular contacts between its minister and leading journalists, and through its many senior officials who left the department to take up prominent positions in Canadian universities. In the late 1960s the demand to 'open up the policy process' produced an academic-relations division; this was a policy-planning staff where academics served, and where public and parliamentary reviews of foreign policy were conducted at the outset of each new government (in 1968–70,

1979–80, 1985–6, and 1994–5). The department subsequently began to hold regular consultations with outside multi-stakeholder groups to deal with arms control and disarmament and with human rights. In the trade field the FTA-NAFTA negotiations saw the International Trade Advisory Group–Sectoral Advisory Group on International Trade (ITAC-SAGIT) advisory structure, which was formerly called into life only for the duration of the major round of multilateral trade negotiations, made permanent, enriched with cross-cutting policy committees (for trade policy, trade-environment relationships, and trade development), and allowed to take a more strategic approach (by providing advice on the new trade issues).

The mid-1990s have added several elements. The 1994–5 review of foreign policy was launched, not by a government Green Paper that defined an agenda and established guidelines that were accessible to all Canadians, but by an exclusive, invited 'national forum', which was widely regarded as ineffective (Canada, Standing Committee on Foreign Affairs and International Trade 1995). Partly as a result, the 1994–5 review failed to attract as much media, academic, or public attention and debate as its 1985–6 and 1968–70 predecessors. Efforts to repeat the national forum in modified fashion (outside Ottawa and through a narrower look at issues such as multilateralism and the UN system) have had few apparent results. For those reasons Prime Minister Chrétien rejected recommendations for a single Centre for Foreign Policy Development as a successor to the Canadian Institute of International Peace and Security. (The institute, which was established by the Trudeau government was abolished by the Mulroney government.) Instead, he opted for institutionalized consultations between relevant department officials and outside stakeholders across the full array of policy fields. At the same time, the department continues to manage its domestic environment by giving substantial annual grants to its traditional collection of educational and research groups.[11]

POLICY INSTRUMENT SHIFTS AND CHANGING RELATIONS WITH INTERNATIONAL AGENCIES

In international affairs, a premium has long been placed on diplomacy, both in bilateral relations and in relations with, and the staffing of, international organizations. Analyses of the foreign-affairs budget show that the spending is largely on personnel rather than on grants (Doern, Maslove, and Prince 1988). Regulatory and tax instruments are extremely limited simply because there is no world government as such.[12] In these instruments have been supplemented by a fairly robust Official Development Assistance (ODA) expenditure program and armed forces deployed globally for peacekeeping, for regional defence as in NORAD and NATO, and for the conduct of combat operations abroad, as in the 1990–1 Gulf War.

The processes of internationalization and globalization have affected the use of policy instruments in foreign-policy making in several ways. The most important of these changes involve an appreciation of the functions of international agencies, especially those taking on new or expanded rules-based dispute-settlement capacities. These new functions have led to an enhancement of the role of regulation and quasi-regulation. The second important change is the continuous pressure of deficit reduction, including the 1995 program review. Deficit reduction is a change with both international and national causes. A third important change is that when international agreements involve financial commitments, DFAIT more and more often has to obtain the funds from other departments, which want a real say in the relevant foreign policy. And last but not least, the combination of these shifts has, in the Chrétien era, strengthened the Prime Minister's leadership, largely through the emphasis on plurilateral G7 institutions.

The most obvious manifestation of more rules-based international institutions is in the trade field. First the FTA and then the improved NAFTA dispute-settlement panels have fundamentally changed the nature of the Canada-US relationship (Boddez and Trebilcock 1993; Doern and Tomlin 1991). These trade agreements virtually create a fourth pillar to Canada's constitution, joining parliamentary government, federalism, and the Charter of Rights and Freedoms in the superstructure of the political system. Initial analyses suggest that the dispute-settlement processes, while far from perfect, are doing precisely what Canada's negotiators hoped they would do: de-politicizing trade disputes, making the climate more certain for Canadian investors, and speeding up dispute resolution (Boddez and Trebilcock 1993). The new rules are therefore more regulatory, and dispute settlement relies less on traditional diplomacy. This hardly means that DFAIT is put out of work. There are still many realms of diplomacy left, and DFAIT leads the management of the overall NAFTA machinery.

Other aspects of these NAFTA (and GATT) institutions are noted below, but the important first point is simply to stress the emergence of this broad new class of regulatory policy instruments. This class of instruments also seems destined to increase since the next round of WTO negotiations will undoubtedly centre on establishing an array of business-framework rules (linked to the WTO), and possibly dispute-settlement processes for policy fields such as investment, competition or antitrust measures, intellectual property, and environmental policy (Doern and Wilks 1996; Ostry 1990, 1993).

The second change in instrument use is budgetary cutbacks. In one sense, the foreign-policy 'envelope' has been the target of cuts since the early 1980s (Doern, Maslove, and Prince 1988). But it is in the Chrétien program review that the budgetary cuts hit home, if not for DFAIT, then certainly for the envelope as a whole. In the fiscal year 1992–3, the last full fiscal year before the Chrétien government came to power, federal spending on foreign affairs was $1.35 billion, or 0.8 per cent of the federal budget; official development assistance (ODA), largely through CIDA, accounted for $2.7 billion, or 2 per cent of expenditures; and defence accounted for $11.2 billion, or 7 per cent. The first Chrétien budget, of February 1994, reduced defence spending by 10 per cent, reduced ODA by 2 per cent, and increased DFAIT spending by $74.1 million, or 5 per cent, to $1.41 billion. In the budget of 27 February 1995, DND suffered further substantial reductions, CIDA was reduced by 15 per cent from $2.03 to $1.73 billion, and DFAIT was cut 7 per cent to $1.30 billion (Canada 1995b).

During the first two years of the Chrétien government then, DFAIT, whose budget had been essentially stable budget from 1992–3 to 1995–6, has experienced a relative gain over its major international-affairs counterparts and most domestically oriented departments. However, its particular response to fiscal pressures and program review show a somewhat sluggish adjustment to internationalization and globalization, and to the new government's foreign-policy goals, which substantially reflect them.

During the Chrétien government's first year, DFAIT expenditures remained biased toward automatic transfers to the multilateral organizations, largely to the UN bodies with big bureaucracies created half a century ago, rather than toward Canada's bilateral relations. The multilateral bias is evident in the overall DFAIT increase in 1994–5, which was due to mandatory increases in Canada's contributions in foreign currencies to international organizations, to a level that overwhelmed the reduction to the national foreign-policy infrastructure and bilateral programs the department was forced to absorb. Moreover, despite the known trade emphasis of the new Prime Minister and the government's foreign-policy statement, DFAIT's expenditures, in both the multilateral and the bilateral realms, were still concentrated on traditional political and security programs rather than on trade and economics or the emerging international issues.

The budget of 27 February 1995 does, however, show a change in these historic biases. The alterations in DFAIT's expenditures from the 1994–5 to 1995–6 fiscal year are as follows:

Foreign policy priorities and co-ordination +4.8%
International economic trade and aid policy -1.1%
Bilateral relations and operations -2.6%
International trade development -8.4%
Legal and consular affairs -13.6%
Political and international security affairs -20.3%
Communications and culture -34.0%

These figures suggest an increased emphasis on defining Canadian interests and co-ordinating Canadian foreign policy to achieve those interests, and only a small reduction in the bilateral relations and operations required to carry them out exclusively on Canada's behalf. It also indicates a move away from traditional political and security goals toward international economics, trade policy, and trade development. The sharp decrease in the budget for communications and culture (which was due almost entirely to the end of DFAIT's budgetary responsibility for Radio Canada International) suggests, however, that the department has been slow to take up the third priority of the government's foreign-policy statement or to mobilize this form of 'soft power' (let alone its television dimensions) in a globalized information world.

A further budget-related change at DFAIT has come from the Chrétien government's sharp reversal of its predecessors' practice on political patronage appointments to senior positions in the Canadian foreign service (Coyne 1994; McDougall 1994). The department also radically changed the selection criteria for new foreign service recruits in 1994–5: only those with graduate degrees in law or business or with competence in selected non-European languages would be eligible. This latter decision reflected in part a judgement of the future priorities and underrepresented capacity of the department, and was in part an effort to stave off demands by the Treasury Board that recruitment be completely eliminated for the year. The government has also reduced its resident diplomatic representation abroad in relation to the total number of states in the system now substantially enlarged by the disintegration of the Soviet Union. However, considerations of domestic demographic and national unity have led it to open resident representation in Ukraine and Vietnam respectively. But elsewhere, because of budget constraints, it is sharing diplomatic establishments abroad with the Australians, a practice reminiscent of the pre–World War Two period, when Canada's interests were represented by the British diplomatic establishment. At the same time, the elimination of Radio-Canada International shows slowness to explore modern mechanisms of projecting influence abroad. The major new areas of emphasis under the Chrétien government have been intense 'summit' diplomacy by the Prime Minister, and activity in new multilateral and regional institutions.

Another change resulting from budget cuts has been the sharp reduction in the ability and willingness of Canada to pay for and engage in combat abroad. The defence White Paper, which emphasizes the maintenance of a general-purpose land, air, and sea combat capability, has been contradicted by the decisions to cancel the EH-101 helicopter program, reduce the fleet of operational CF-18s, allow foreigners to provide air support for Canadian ground forces in the former Yugoslavia, and avoid any of the militarily dangerous aspects of the Haitian operation to restore President Aristide. At the same time, the government has continued its predecessor's policy (if at somewhat lower levels) of contributing to peacekeeping operations in most global theatres: Canada has provided the fifth-largest contingent in the former Yugoslavia and has entered Rwanda and Haiti. Here the causes are the inherited Pearsonianism of the Liberal Party and the need to placate Quebec by maintaining solidarity with France and supporting francophone countries.

Finally, and again for purposes of deficit reduction, ODA funding has been significantly reduced, though more slowly than for the Department of National Defence (DND). In the most recent round of reductions, CIDA has made an effort to reduce expenditures in Canada in order to maintain its programs abroad. CIDA has also intensified its effort to increase spending on the sustainable-development goals highlighted in the foreign-policy statement.

The third change in instrument use is that, despite the budget cuts and sometimes because of them, DFAIT has increasingly had to seek funds from other line departments to finance the still growing number of new international obligations. These include the expanding rules-based framework areas discussed above as well as environmental protocols (Doern 1993). Hand in hand with this need for funds from other departments go broader notions of the 'resources' needed for really effective foreign policy. These departments are the home base for the necessary technical expertise and, as is too often forgotten, for the legal base of the domestic part of these commitments.

As mentioned at the outset, DFAIT has always had to call on interdepartmental teams of experts to help do its work. But it appears that internationalization and globalization now require DFAIT to assemble sums of real money, expertise, and statutory power. This is a much more difficult game to play.

Finally, we come to a change that is perhaps the most striking recent development in the merging worlds of foreign-policy instruments and institutions. This is the birth of new multilateral institutions managed at the summit and ministerial level, and therefore the relatively diminished role in Canadian foreign policy of the largely DFAIT-controlled '1945–9 generation' of United Nations and Atlantic institutions—the World Bank, the International Monetary Fund (IMF), and the Organisation for Economic Co-operation and Development (OECD). The most vibrant of the new multilateral institutions have been the expanding APEC and the hemispheric system linked to NAFTA. In sharp contrast, the UN and NATO have become less relevant; the Prime Minister has refused to attend UN summits (notably on social policy in Copenhagen), he made an awkward debut at his first NATO summit in January 1994, and he used the fiftieth anniversaries of D-Day, VE-Day, and the Bretton Woods and United Nations institutions to catalyze the reform of these organizations.

The advent of the newer plurilateral institutions and their management by regular summitry has pulled the Prime Minister into a much more intense, personal involvement in international affairs than would otherwise have been the case. He has thus become more influential in the decision-making process in Ottawa. Moreover, a broader range of ministers and hitherto internationally uninvolved or less involved ministers have been given a much larger part in foreign affairs. Finally, much like the United Nations special-subject summits and conferences dating back to Stockholm in 1972, the birth of these summit-level institutions and their hosting by Canada has brought a wide range of non-governmental actors into the policy-making process.

These processes have been most evident in regard to the G7 and the new elements added to its traditional platform of an annual summit, on-site bilaterals, and support for meetings of finance and foreign ministers (since 1975), as well as meetings for ministers of trade (since 1982), ministers of foreign affairs (since 1984), and ministers of finance (since 1986). Although efforts to hold a special inter-sessional summit in Canada in the autumn of 1994 to honour the dying François Mitterrand did not succeed, Canada's role of host for the prepatory meetings has led to an enhanced program of preparatory bilateral summitry, a limitation on the role of finance and foreign ministers, and efforts to focus the international agenda and Canadian foreign policy on newer issues, such as the reform of international economic institutions, migration, and a host of micro-economic matters. During the Chrétien years the G7 has also created a regular forum for environment ministers without foreign ministers present. The meeting in Hamilton on 29 April 1995 followed the previous meetings held in Italy in 1994 and Germany in 1992. The 'jobs' ministerial meeting in Detroit in 1994 and the ministerial meeting on information technology in Brussels in 1995 have brought John Manley and Lloyd Axworthy into direct involvement with the G7 abroad. Foreign and finance ministers have had their involvement expanded through the 1993 ministerial conference on assistance to Russia and the autumn 1994 Winnipeg conference on assistance to Ukraine.

At the societal level, in addition to the routine pre-G7 submissions from, and consultations with, the Business Council on National Issues and the Canadian Labour Congress, and consultations inspired by the Prime Minister—such as those with agricultural groups (in 1986) and provincial premiers (in 1993)—Canada's position as host has also inspired the involvement of additional groups, such as the National Roundtable on the Environment and the Economy, environmental NGOs, and the North-South Institute. Canada's summit managers have thus been faced with the challenge of 'managing the petitioners', and in some cases, of accommodating their requests.[13]

In the case of APEC, functional co-operation over several decades led to the establishment, in 1989, of an annual foreign ministers' meeting and, in 1993, of an annual summit. Because the APEC summit is for leaders only and provides the occasion for many bilateral discussions, the role of the Prime Minister has been enhanced. Canada's hosting of an APEC meeting of environment ministers in Vancouver in March 1994 helped bring other portfolio ministers into the APEC sphere.

Within the western hemisphere, the December 1994 Miami Summit of the Americas, while not a leaders-only meeting or the start of an annual event, did bring the Prime Minister directly into hemispheric affairs; it was also the occasion for a host of subsequent ministerial meetings (notably for trade). Of even greater consequence has been the creation, operation, and expansion of the NAFTA institutions discussed above. While the overall trade and dispute-settlement machinery is managed in DFAIT, none of NAFTA's other four institutions—the Commissions for Environmental Cooperation, the Labour and Trade Group, and the Finance Group—involve DFAIT. They bring the portfolio ministers of the three countries together regularly. They have secretariats with considerable procedural autonomy. And even though Canada has been unwilling, and Mexico unable, to provide the promised funding, they are rapidly developing an extensive domestic constituency. Indeed, NAFTA's Commission on Environmental Cooperation has several unique features, notably a Joint Public Advisory Committee (JPAC) to advise the Ministerial Council, a National Advisory Committee, and provisions for public participation and transparency (Munton and Kirton 1994).

In response to these forces DFAIT has insisted, thus far successfully, on being the representative of the Prime Minister in these newer plurilateral summits.[14] In the case of the G7, the initial practice was to have that function performed by a member of the Prime Minister's Office, a senior trade official, or a senior foreign ministry official. That practice ended in 1981, when Canada hosted its first summit. The External Affairs deputy minister, Alan Gotlieb, assumed the position and passed it to his successor. It was subsequently given to a senior DFAIT official, returned to the deputy minister in 1989, and then assigned to the ambassador to the United States from 1990 to 1992. It has since resided with the deputy minister of DFAIT.

DFAIT's retention of the sherpa function has not, however, ended interdepartmental conflict over how Canada should respond to the new international institutional order. The lead-up to the 1995 Halifax Summit saw a competition between G7 personal representatives, usually lodged in foreign ministries, and finance deputies and their departments and ministers, over the proper focus for 'international economic institutional reform'. The finance community has pointed to the urgency of reforming, and potentially reducing, the multilateral development banks and United Nations agencies controlled by foreign ministries; while the foreign ministry sherpas, on the other hand, have tried to concentrate on the two Bretton Woods institutions operated by finance ministries (the World Bank and the International Monetary Fund).

A second element of international institutional reform that has caused disagreements between departments and between divisions is the issue of Russia's participation in the G7 Summit and the international economic system more generally. Those in the relevant geographic bureaux and posts in DFAIT argue that Canada should move quickly to integrate Russia fully and cement it permanently to the west and to secure bilateral rewards for Canada. Those in DFAIT's economic bureau and in Finance argue that Russia has not lived up to the minimum conditions for full-scale membership, that it is a consumer, rather than provider, of economic support, that its admission would disturb the privileged confidentiality of the G7 club and would open the door to other countries, such as China; the result, they argue, would be a new, smaller G7 from which Canada would be excluded. Thus far the latter view has prevailed.

The causes of this expanded international institutionalization and resulting Canadian summit and ministerial diplomacy lie less in any directly transmitted globalization than in the US design for a post–Cold War international order and the challenge to Canada's national unity at home. It was the United States that initiated and largely prepared the APEC Summit and the NAFTA expansion agenda from 1989 onward, as a response to the end of the Cold War and the resulting need to counter the European and other prospective regional blocs. And while it was the globalized 'systemic' shock of the Mexican peso crisis that substantially ended the debate over the focus for international institutional reform, the Prime Minister's persistent concern about short-term capital flows draws directly on his concern about how a falling Canadian dollar would affect the sovereignty debate.

CONCLUSIONS

Internationalization and globalization have helped change Canadian foreign policy and policy processes in several important ways. But these changes are invariably interwoven with the equally important effects of the end of the Cold War. Four main policy changes have been identified: the view, promoted by Prime Minister Chrétien, that Canada can have greater influence in the world than in the past; a more aggressive free-trade-oriented economic foreign policy; a diminished concern for sovereignty except when it is threatened by the possibility of separation by Quebec; and a broadening view of security which is increasingly in favour of sustainable development and international environmentalism.

With respect to the role of DFAIT, internationalization and globalization have contradictory effects on its power *vis-à-vis* other departments and players in Ottawa. On the one hand, there has been a maintenance of federal policy capacity and restored professionalism in DFAIT. The department's diplomatic network has withstood repeated budget cuts and political appointments relatively well, if with a persistent bias towards the Pearsonian instincts and goals of the past. DFAIT has retained its relevance by controlling the sherpa process. It has also had some success in dealing with the activities of the broader range of groups interested in foreign policy. Most important, it has remained the lead department in foreign policy by reviving an earlier concept of the department as one that serves the Prime Minister directly, and by co-ordinating the international activities of the government through intensified interdepartmental activity and internal restructuring.

On the other hand, DFAIT has had to share some of its power. Foreign policy has always depended on the expertise of other federal departments, but this dependence now goes well beyond expertise alone. It includes the need to acquire funding and statutory power, particularly as nominal 'trade' policy moves more and more into the largely domestic realms of other departments. The replacement of the old bureaucratic 1945–9 multilateralism with the new summit-level post–Cold War plurilateralism has also enhanced the power of the Prime Minister, portfolio ministers and departments, and non-governmental actors at the expense of DFAIT.

Interest-group politics in the foreign-policy field has also been changed. Arguably the most important change from the earlier post–Second World War years is the much greater direct influence of business interest groups and firms, largely in the virtuously continuous free-trade negotiations. The earlier closed élitism of foreign-policy making has also been broken down by the far greater involvement of migration and immigration interests and environmental non-governmental organizations. Some of this broader participation has been gradually evident in the various foreign-policy reviews of the last decade. This does not necessarily imply a permanently enhanced power base for such groups, but they have influenced particular decisions. Given the greater salience of free trade in economic foreign policy, it is quite plausible to conclude that business interests have gained the most through their increased access to the foreign-policy process; in earlier periods business power was channelled more indirectly through other departments.

The analysis has also drawn attention to several important changes in the use of foreign-policy instruments, as a result of changes in the role and nature of several international institutions. Spending on the traditional foreign-policy activities has been cut significantly, but the need to meet commitments to new international agreements has necessitated a greater need for money from other departments. Increased regulatory or quasi-regulatory instruments are now a part of foreign-policy making; they are most evident in the rapidly evolving dispute-settlement processes of the FTA, NAFTA, and GATT-WTO. These instruments are already linked to new plurilateral and regional international institutions, and they are likely to grow as wider areas of business framework law are internationalized with dispute-settlement capacities.

The significance of the budget cuts must be put in context. Because Canada's major G7 collaborators, the United States and Britain, and our competitors (notably Russia) are also plagued with deficits and debt and are downsizing their international programs, Canada's relative influence in international affairs may not be adversely affected. Domestically, there has been a shift in foreign affairs capacity from the provincial to the federal level. That is because the movement toward balanced budgets is more pronounced at the provincial level and because international activities are not at the core of classic provincial government concerns. Hence the provinces, except Quebec, have been withdrawing from autonomous international involvement. Two examples are the abolition by the Ontario government of its trade offices abroad in 1994 and the presence of all provincial premiers save that of Quebec on the 'Team Canada' mission to China in autumn 1994. Thus, while the influence of internationalization and globalization on foreign-policy making is considerable, it is reduced by the forces of conservatism at work during the past decade. For example, it was only in 1989 that the concept of a changing USSR became dominant at the highest levels. Since 1993, systemically induced change has been impeded by the presence of an internationally inexperienced Foreign

Minister interested primarily in domestic politics in his home province of
Quebec, and the Pearsonianism of the Liberal Party, due in part to the
fact that Prime Minister Chrétien began his political career at the outset
of Prime Minister Pearson's 1963–8 government. There is additional resistance resulting from DFAIT's professional socialization, its organizational
routines, and its resource deployment, which all date from the Eurocen-
tric Cold War years of 1945–60.[15] Other factors are the dominant interests and ideas of Canadian society, which are based on a continuing
attachment to the United Nations and NATO, peacekeeping, pragmatic,
mediatory diplomacy, and the mythological symbolism of the 1939-to-
1956 world.

NOTES

1. In the classic dichotomy of interdependence this is vulnerability rather than
   mere sensitivity. See R.O. Keohane and Joseph Nye, *Power and Interdependence* (Boston: Little Brown, 1974). Given this dismissal of sovereignty and
   independence, it is especially anomalous that the Chrétien government has
   changed the name of its foreign ministry from 'External Affairs', which
   connotes relations with countries and communities beyond Canada (including those in Canada's Commonwealth and francophone family) to 'Foreign
   Affairs', which connotes the alien, separate, distant, and different.

2. However, although Canada wished to promote an Arctic Council when President Clinton visited Ottawa in February 1995, it made no serious effort to
   raise this issue with the President when the United States resisted. The two
   cases reveal an intensifying diminution in the concern with Canadian Arctic
   sovereignty from 1985 onward.

3. Additional causes were the refusal of the United States to protest Canadian
   actions despite its dissatisfaction with Canada's unsustainable-development
   actions over Pacific salmon. It remains unclear whether the Prime Minister
   and government were motivated by the need to deal with the threat to
   national unity by a decisive use of force to protect Canadian interests, including (at least psychologically) those of Quebec fishermen in the Gaspé.

4. The relevance of these processes in internal DFAIT thinking and Canadian
   foreign policy is shown by the initiative of DFAIT's deputy minister to have
   migration added to the G7 Summit agenda at the first preparatory meeting,
   and to have papers on trade, the environment, development, crime, and drugs
   added to the international-financial-institution focus the Prime Minister
   preferred for Halifax's institutional review. Also added were the environment
   and development papers, which, after the second summit preparatory
   meeting, were integrated into a single paper on sustainable development.

5. The statement of 7 February 1995, which forms the foundation of this analysis, is of course a public foreign-policy review document rather than one
   designed for internal guidance. However, it does show the intervention of the
   Prime Minister in a private (cabinet) context, and the ideas contrast sharply

with those he previously expressed in public (notably in his speech at the University of Moncton Law School). Because of the relatively heavy involvement of the Prime Minister and Foreign Minister, the government-wide status of the document, and the direct contribution of DFAIT's many bureaux to its preparation, it may have more enduring influence on policy than other review documents. There are already signs that public servants are drawing from the document's opening themes for the Prime Minister's public speeches, a practice which should increase the internal influence of the document.

6. For example the foreign policy statement of 7 February 1995 was changed at the full cabinet meeting of 28 January 1995 as a result of the Prime Minister's intervention, even though it had been thoroughly reviewed and extensively commented on by Ouellet on two previous occasions.

7. In 1991 the Canadian Jewish community numbered 356,315 and constituted 1.3 per cent of the Canadian population, giving Canada the fifth-largest Jewish community in the world. The success which the Canadian Finnish community enjoyed in overturning the Mulroney government's decision to close Canada's resident diplomatic establishment in Helsinki shows how powerful a small, well-organized interest group can be.

8. From 1989 onward, Canada worked hard and ultimately successfully to ensure that the three Chinas were included in APEC. It is not known to what extent the active lobbying by the Canadian-Chinese community was responsible for these emphases in Prime Minister Chrétien's tour of China in autumn 1994 and APEC summit diplomacy in 1993–4, or for such other Canadian policies as support for China's seminal and early inclusion in the new WTO.

9. The Haitian-Canadian community, while relatively small and poor, is heavily concentrated in the riding of Ouellet, the Foreign Minister. In the opinion of one DFAIT official in a position to know, the making of Canadian foreign policy toward Haiti is '100 per cent domestic politics'.

10. Forty-three billion dollars for Russia in 1993 versus Chrétien's 'up to' only $4 billion for Ukraine in 1994 (Kissinger's balance of power logic). Most of the Canadian Ukrainian seats are held by the Reform Party, and the election is over.

11. According to the 1995–6 main estimates for DFAIT, 'grants' (not including 'contributions' or 'transfer payments') to identifiable domestic groups were allocated as follows (the 1994–5 figures are shown in parentheses): Asia-Pacific Foundation of Canada, $1,215,000 ($1,215,000); Canadian Chamber of Commerce for Asia-Pacific Trade promotion, $408,000 ($760,000); Canadian Centre for Global Security, $75,000 ($100,000); Centre for Legislative Exchange, $70,000 ($80,000); United Nations Association in Canada, $63,000 ($63,000); Canadian Institute of International Affairs, $40,000 ($40,000); Centre québécois de relations internationales de l'université Laval, $25,000 ($29,000); Foreign Service Community Association, $16,000 ($18,000); Canadian Group of the Trilateral Commission, $14,000 ($14,000); Canadian Council on International Law, $10,000 ($11,000); Atlantic Council of Canada, $7,500 ($7,500); International Peace Academy, $100 ($100).

12. DFAIT does command a small number of regulatory instruments, notably the right to allow and regulate diplomatic activity within Canada, to determine privileges and immunity for employees of international institutions (such as ICAO) in Canada, and to issue passports.

13. The impact of these forces of international institutionalization are enhanced by the fact that Canada has the second-best record among the G7 of keeping its summit commitments and that compliance with summit commitments by all members is particularly high in the areas of trade, energy-environment, and development.

14. In the case of APEC, the Prime Minister is represented by DFAIT's assistant deputy minister for Asia-Pacific. In the case of the Miami Summit, that function was performed by the assistant deputy minister for Latin America and the Caribbean.

15. One example is the experience of the two senior professionals in the government foreign-policy-making community—Deputy Minister Gordon Smith, who came to the position from postings in Europe to NATO and the European Union, and James Bartleman, who came to the position of Assistant Secretary to the Cabinet for Foreign Policy and Defence from postings dealing with European security.

References

Aho, M. 1988. Foreword. In *Fixing Farm Trade: Policy Options for the United States*, ed. R.L. Paarlberg. Cambridge, Mass.: Ballinger.

Albert, M. 1993. *Capitalism against Capitalism*. London: Whurr.

Alford, D.E. 1992. Basle Committee Minimum Standards: International Regulatory Response to the Failure of BCCI. *George Washington Journal of International Law and Economics* 26(2): 241–91.

Alston, P. 1995. Letter to Ambassador Gerald Shannon, Permanent Representative, Permanent Mission of Canada to the United Nations Office in Geneva, 4 May.

Aronson, J.D., and P.F. Cowhey. 1988. *When Countries Talk: International Trade in Telecommunications Services*. Cambridge, Mass.: Ballinger.

Atkinson, M., and W. Coleman. 1989. *The State, Business, and Industrial Change in Canada*. Toronto: University of Toronto Press.

Aucoin, P. 1990. *Restructuring the Canadian Government: The Management of Organizational Change*. Ottawa: Canadian Centre for Management Development.

———. 1995. *The New Public Management: Canada in Comparative Perspective*. Ottawa: Canadian Centre for Management Development.

Avery, W.P. 1993. Agriculture and Free Trade. In *World Agriculture and the GATT*, ed. William P. Avery. Boulder, Colo.: Lynne Rienner.

Axworthy, L. 1995. Economic Growth and Social Progress. Speaking notes at the OECD Council Meeting at Ministerial Level, Paris.

Babe, Robert E. 1990. *Telecommunications in Canada: Technology, Industry, and Government*. Toronto: University of Toronto Press.

Baillie, J.C. 1965. The Protection of the Investor in Ontario: Part One. *Canadian Public Administration* 8(2): 172–268.

Banting, K. 1992. Economic Integration and Social Policy: Canada and the United States. In *Social Policy in the Global Economy*, ed. T. Hunsley. Kingston: Queen's University, School of Policy Studies.

———. 1995a. Social Policy Challenges in a Global Society. In *Social Policy in a Global Society*, eds D. Morales-Gómez and M. Torres. Ottawa: International Development Research Centre.

————. 1995b. The Social Policy Review: Policy-making in a Semi-Sovereign Society. *Canadian Public Administration* 38(2): 283–90.

————. 1995c. Social Policy as Statecraft: Territorial Politics and Canadian Social Policy. In *Fragmented Social Policy: The European Union in Comparative Perspective*, eds P. Pierson and S. Liebfried. Washington, DC: Brookings.

————. Forthcoming. The Social Policy Divide: The Welfare State in Canada and the United States. In *Degrees of Freedom: Canada and the United States in a Changing World* (Montreal: McGill-Queen's University Press). K. Banting, G. Hoberg, and R. Simeon, eds.

Banting, K., and C. Beach. 1995. *Labour Market Polarization and Social Policy Reform*. Kingston: Queen's University, School of Policy Studies.

Barkin, J.S., and B. Cronin. 1994. The State and Nation: Norms and Rules of Sovereignty in International Relations. *International Organization* 48(1): 107–30.

Barlow, M., and B. Campbell. 1991. *Take Back the Nation*. Toronto: Key Porter.

Barr, F., and M. Borrus. n.d. *From Public Access to Private Connections: Network Policy and National Advantage*. Berkeley, Calif.: Berkeley Roundtable on the International Economy, Working Paper no. 28.

Barrett, C., and C. Beckman. 1984. *The Future of Foreign Investment in Canada*. Ottawa: Conference Board.

Barrett, C., C. Beckman and D. McDowell. 1984. *A Fit Place to Invest: Investor's Perceptions of Canada in a Changing World*. Ottawa: Conference Board.

Basle Committee on Banking Supervision. 1975. Basle Concordat. Revised and supplemented in 1983, 1990, and 1992.

————. 1992. *Report on International Developments*. Basle, Switzerland: Basle Committee on Banking Supervision.

Bayefsky, A.F. 1992. International Human Rights Law in Canadian Courts. In *International Human Rights Law: Theory and Practice*, eds I. Cotler and P. Eliadis. Montreal: Canadian Human Rights Foundation.

Beach, C., and G. Slotsve. 1994. Polarization of Earnings in the Canadian Labour Market. In *Stabilization, Growth and Income: Linkages in the Knowledge Era*, ed. T. Courchene. Kingston: Queen's University, John Deutsch Institute for the Study of Economic Policy.

Best, M.H. 1990. *The New Competition: Institutions of Industrial Restructuring*. Cambridge, Mass.: Harvard University Press.

Bhagwati, J. and H.T. Patrick, eds. 1990. *Aggressive Unilateralism*. Ann Arbor, Mich.: Michigan University Press.

Birnie, P., and A. Boyle. 1992. *International Law and the Environment*. Oxford: Clarendon.

Blais, A. 1985. The Debate on Canadian Industrial Policy. In *Industrial Policy*, ed. A. Blais. Toronto: University of Toronto Press.

Boardman, R. 1991. Approaching Regimes: Australia, Canada and Environmental Policy. *Australian Journal of Political Science* 26(3): 446–71.

————. 1992. The Multilateral Dimension: Canada in the International System. In *Canadian Environmental Policy: Ecosystems, Politics, and Processes*, ed. R. Boardman. Toronto: Oxford University Press.

Boddez, T.M., and M.J. Trebilcock. 1993. *Unfinished Business: Reforming Trade Remedy Laws in North America*. Toronto: C.D. Howe Institute.

Boreham, G. 1990. Three Years after Canada's 'Little Bang'. *Canadian Banker* 97: 6–10.

Brodhead, T., B. Herbert-Copley, and A.-M. Lambert. 1988. *Bridges of Hope? Canadian Voluntary Agencies and the Third World*. Ottawa: North-South Institute.

Brown, D. 1994. Economic Change and New Social Policies. In *The Case for Change: Reinventing the Welfare State*, eds W. Watson, J. Richards, and D. Brown. Toronto: C.D. Howe Institute.

Brown, D.M. 1988. The Federal-Provincial Consultation Process. In *Canada: The State of the Federation 1987–88*, eds P.M. Leslie and R.L. Watts. Kingston: Queen's University, Institute of Intergovernmental Relations.

———. 1991. The Evolving Role of the Provinces in Canadian Trade Policy. In *Canadian Federalism: Meeting Global Economic Challenges?*, eds D.M. Brown and M.G. Smith. Kingston and Montreal: Queen's University, Institute of Intergovernmental Relations and Institute for Research on Public Policy.

Brown, D.M., F. Lazar, and D. Schwanen. 1992. *Free to Move: Strengthening the Canadian Economic Union*. Toronto: C.D. Howe Institute.

Bryant, R. 1987. *International Financial Intermediation*. Washington, DC.: Brookings.

Bull, H. 1977. *The Anarchical Society*. London: Macmillan.

Burgers, J.H. 1992. The Road to San Francisco: The Revival of the Human Rights Idea in the Twentieth Century. *Human Rights Quarterly* 14 (Nov.): 447–77.

Business Council for Sustainable Development. 1992. *Changing Course: A Global Business Perspective on Development and the Environment*. Cambridge, Mass.: MIT Press.

Cairncross, F. 1991. *Costing the Earth*. London: Economist Books.

Cairns, A.C. 1992. *Charter versus Federalism: the Dilemmas of Constitutional Reform*. Montreal and Kingston: McGill-Queen's University Press.

Cameron, D.R. 1978. The Expansion of the Public Economy: A Comparative Analysis. *American Political Science Review* 72: 1243–61.

Cameron, Duncan R., and M. Watkins. 1993. *Canada under Free Trade*. Toronto: Lorimer.

Camilleri, J., and J. Falk. 1992. *The End of Sovereignty: Politics in a Shrinking and Fragmenting World*. Aldershot, UK: Edward Elgar.

Canada. Dept of Agriculture. 1989. *Growing Together: A Vision for Canada's Agri-Food Industry*. Ottawa: Dept of Agriculture.

———. 1995. *Data Book. Farm Income, Financial Conditions, and Government Expenditures*. Ottawa: Dept of Agriculture.

Canada. Dept of Agriculture and Agri-Food. 1994. *Future Directions for Canadian Agriculture and Agri-Food*. Ottawa: Dept of Agriculture and Agri-Food.

Canada. Dept of Communications. 1987. *A Policy Framework for Telecommunications in Canada*. Ottawa: Dept of Communications.

Canada. Dept of the Environment. 1990. *Canada's Green Plan*. Ottawa: Supply and Services Canada.

———. 1991. 'Ecosystem Conveys the Integrated Reality.' *The State of Canada's Environment*, 1–4. Ottawa: Supply and Services Canada.

———. 1995a. *A Guide to Green Government*. Ottawa: Minister of Supply and Services.

———. 1995b. *The Greening of Government Operations*. Ottawa: Minister of Supply and Services.

Canada. Department of External Affairs. 1970. *Foreign Policy for Canadians.* Ottawa: Queen's Printer.

———. 1983. *Trade Policy in the 1980s.* Ottawa: Dept of External Affairs.

———. 1983a. *A Review of Trade Policy: A Background Document to Canadian Trade Policy for the 1980s.* Ottawa: Dept of External Affairs.

———. 1986. *Investment Issues and a Possible Canada-US Agreement: the Elements Involved.* Ottawa: Investment Canada.

———. 1987. *Department of National Defence.* Ottawa: Dept of National Defence.

Canada. Dept of Finance. 1976. *White Paper on the Revision of Canadian Banking Legislation.* Ottawa: Dept of Finance.

———. 1985. *The Regulation of Canadian Financial Institutions: Proposals for Discussion.* Ottawa: Dept of Finance.

———. 1986. *New Directions for the Financial Sector.* Ottawa: Dept of Finance.

———. 1994a. *A New Framework for Economic Policy.* Ottawa: Dept of Finance.

———. 1994b. *Creating a Healthy Fiscal Climate: The Economic and Fiscal Update.* Ottawa: Dept of Finance.

———. 1995. *Main Estimates: Part III Expenditure Plan, Department of Foreign Affairs and International Trade 1995–96.* Ottawa: Dept of Finance.

———. 1995a. *Budget Plan: Including Supplementary Information and Notices of Ways and Means Motions.* Ottawa: Dept of Finance.

———. 1995b. *Enhancing the Safety and Soundness of the Canadian Financial System.* Ottawa: Dept of Finance.

———. 1995c. *Budget in Brief,* Ottawa: Dept of Finance. 27 Feb. 1995.

Canada, Dept of Foreign Affairs and International Trade. 1995b. *Canada in the World: Government Statement.* Ottawa: Dept of Foreign Affairs and International Trade.

———. 1995d. *Report of Canada to the United Nations Commission on Sustainable Development.* Ottawa: Dept of Foreign Affairs and International Trade.

Canada. Dept of Human Resources Development. 1994b. *Improving Social Security in Canada: A Discussion Paper.* Ottawa: Minister of Supply and Services.

Canada. Dept of Justice. 1995a. Interview by Leslie Pal with senior official. Mar. 17.

———. 1995b. Interview by Leslie Pal with senior official, Mar. 17.

Canada. Dept of National Defence. 1994a. *1994 Defence White Paper.* Ottawa: Minister of Supply and Services.

Canada. Federal-Provincial Task Force on Orderly Marketing. 1994. *Action Plan Towards the Implementation of Sustainable Orderly Marketing Systems in the Canadian Dairy, Poultry and Egg Industries.* Ottawa: Dept of Agriculture and Agri-Food, 23 Mar.

———. 1994b. *Final Report on the Implementation of Sustainable Orderly Marketing Systems in the Canadian Dairy, Poultry and Egg Industries.* Ottawa: Dept Agriculture and Agri-Food, 9 Dec.

Canada. Foreign Investment Review Agency. 1975–84. *Annual Report.* Ottawa.

Canada. House of Commons. Standing Committee on Environment and Sustainable Development. 1995. *It's About Our Health! Towards Pollution Prevention: CEPA Revisited.* Ottawa: House of Commons.

———. Standing Committee on External Affairs and International Trade. 1992–3. Sub-committee on Development and Human Rights. *Minutes of Proceedings and Evidence.* 26 Nov., 29: 5.

Canada. House of Commons. Standing Committee on Finance. 1992. *Sixteenth Report to the House.* 34th Parliament, 3rd Session. No. 52. Ottawa: House of Commons.

————. Standing Committee on Human Resources Development. 1995. *Security, Opportunities and Fairness: Canadians Renewing Their Social Programs.* Ottawa: House of Commons.

Canada. Inquiry into the Collapse of the CCB and Northland Bank 1986. *Report.* Ottawa: Supply and Services Canada.

Canada. Office of the Prime Minister. 1991. Notes for an Address by Prime Minister Brian Mulroney on the Occasion of the Centennial Convocation; Stanford University, Calif., 29 Sept.

Canada. Privy Council. 1972. *Foreign Direct Investment in Canada* (Gray Report). Ottawa: Queen's Printer.

Canada. Royal Commission on Banking and Finance. 1964. *Report.* Ottawa: Queen's Printer.

Canada. Senate Standing Committee on Banking, Trade and Commerce 1990. *Canada 1992: Toward a National Market in Financial Services.* Ottawa: Senate of Canada.

Canada. Special Joint Committee of the Senate and the House of Commons. 1995. *Canada's Foreign Policy: Principles and Priorities for the Future.* Ottawa: Queen's Printer.

Canada. Standing Committee on Foreign Affairs and International Trade. 1995. Issue 24 (Apr. 24).

Canada. Task Force on Economic Instruments and Disincentives to Sound Environmental Practices. 1994. *Final Report of the Task Force.* Ottawa: The Task Force.

Canada. Task Force on the Structure of Canadian Industry. 1968. *Foreign Ownership and the Structure of Canadian Industry.* Ottawa: Queen's Printer.

Canadian Bankers Association. 1991. *American Long Distance Competition: The Power of Choice.* Toronto: Canadian Bankers Association.

Canadian Council of Ministers of Environment. 1993. *Trade, Competitiveness and the Environment.* Winnipeg: CCME.

Canadian Environment Industry Association. 1995. Letter to the Honourable Charles Caccia, House of Commons Standing Committee on Environmental and Sustainable Development, 8 May.

Canadian Intellectual Property Office. 1994. *Business Plan 1993–94 to 1995–96.* Ottawa: Canadian Intellectual Property Office.

Canadian Radio-television and Telecommunications Commission. 1976. *Telecommunications Regulation—Procedures and Practices.* Ottawa: CRTC.

————. 1977. *Challenge Communications Ltd v. Bell Canada.* Telecom Decision CRTC 77–11. Ottawa: CRTC.

————. 1979. *CNCP Telecommunications, Interconnection with Bell Canada.* Telecom Decision CRTC 79–11. Ottawa: CRTC.

————. 1980. *Bell Canada—Interim Requirements Regarding the Attachment of Subscriber-Provided Equipment.* Telecom Decision CRTC 80–13. Ottawa: CRTC.

————. 1982. *Attachment of Subscriber-Provided Equipment.* Telecom Decision CRTC 82–14. Ottawa: CRTC.

————. 1984. *Enhanced Services.* Telecom Decision CRTC 84–18. Ottawa.

————. 1985. *Interexchange Competition and Related Issues.* Telecom Decision CRTC 85–19. Ottawa: CRTC.

————. 1987. *Tariff Revisions Related to Resale and Sharing*. Telecom Decision CRTC 87–2. Ottawa: CRTC.

————. 1987–88. *Annual Report*. Ottawa: CRTC.

————. 1988. *Bell Canada, 1988 Revenue Requirement, Rate Rebalancing and Revenue Settlement Issues*. Telecom Decision CRTC 88–4. Ottawa: CRTC.

————. 1992. *Competition in the Provision of Public Long Distance Voice Service and Related Matters*. Telecom Decision CRTC 92–12. Ottawa: CRTC.

Canadian Standards Association. 1995. Toward a Global Solution: The World's First International Environmental Management System (EMS). *CSA Environmental Update*, Sept. CCMF. *See* Canadian Council of Ministers of Environment.

Cerny, P.G. 1990. *The Changing Architecture of Politics: Structure, Agency and the Future of the State*. London: Sage.

————. 1993. The Deregulation and Re-regulation of Financial Markets in a More Open World. In *Finance and World Politics: Markets, Regimes and States in the Post-hegemonic Era*, ed. P.G. Cerny. Aldershot, UK: Edward Elgar.

Chiron, S.Z., and L.A. Rehberg. 1986. Fostering Competition in International Telecommunications. *Federal Communications Law Journal* 38: 1–57.

Chrétien, J. 1994. *Straight from the Heart*, rev. edn. Toronto: Key Porter.

Christie, K. 1993. *Globalization and Public Policy in Canada: In Search of a Paradigm*. Policy Planning Staff Paper no. 93–01. Ottawa: Dept of External Affairs and International Trade, Jan.

Clark, M. 1992. Canadian State Powers: Comparing the FTA and GATT. In *Canada Under Free Trade*, eds D. Cameron and M. Watkins. Toronto: Lorimer.

Clarke, D. 1994. From GATT to GATS. *Canadian Banker*, Sept.-Oct.: 28–32.

Clarkson, S. 1985. *Canada and the Reagan Challenge*, 2nd edn. Toronto: Lorimer.

Coffin, G., A. Schmitz, and K. Rosaasen, eds. 1995. *Supply Management in Transition: Towards the 21st Century*. Proceedings of a Conference held at Macdonald Campus of McGill University, Ste Anne de Bellevue, Quebec, 28–30 June 1994. Ste Anne de Bellevue: Macdonald Campus of McGill University.

Cohn, T.H. 1993. The Changing Role of the United States in the Global Agricultural Trade Regime. In *World Agriculture and the GATT*, ed. W.P. Avery. Boulder, Colo.: Lynne Rienner.

Coleman, W.D. 1992. Financial Services Reform in Canada: The Evolution of Policy Dissension. *Canadian Public Policy* 18(2): 139–52.

————. 1994. Keeping the Shotgun behind the Door: Governing the Securities Industry in Canada, the United Kingdom, and the United States. In *Governing Capitalist Economies: Performance and Control of Economic Sectors*, eds J. Rogers Hollingsworth, W. Streeck, and P. Schmitter. New York: Oxford University Press.

————. 1996. *Financial Services, Globalization and Domestic Policy Change: A Comparison of North America and the European Union*. Basingstoke, UK: Macmillan.

Coleman, W.D., and G. Skogstad. 1990. Policy Communities and Policy Networks: A Structural Approach. In *Policy Communities and Public Policy in Canada: A Structural Approach*, eds W. Coleman and G. Skogstad. Mississauga, Ont.: Copp Clark Pitman.

———. 1995. Neo-Liberalism, Policy Networks, and Policy Change: Agricultural Policy Reform in Australia and Canada. *Australian Journal of Political Science* 30: 242–63.

Coleman, W.D., and G.R.D. Underhill. 1995. Globalisation, Regionalism and the Regulation of Securities Markets: the EU and the International Organisation of Securities Commissions. *Journal of European Public Policy* (August): 488–513.

Commission of the European Communities. 1993. *Growth, Competitiveness, Employment: The Challenges and Ways Forward into the 21st Century.* Luxemburg: Office for Official Publications of the European Commission.

———. 1994. *Social Protection in Europe.* Luxemburg: Office for Official Publications of the European Commission.

Compas Inc. 1995. *The Business Agenda.* Ottawa: Compas Inc.

Conway, T. 1992. Challenges Facing Canadian Environmental Groups in the 1990s. In *Democracy with Justice: Essays in Honour of Khayyam Zev Paltiel,* eds A. Gagnon and B. Tanguay. Ottawa: Carleton University Press.

Cooper, A.F. 1992. Agriculture and the GATT: The Search for Balance in Canadian Trade Policy. In *Canada: The State of the Federation 1992,* eds D. Brown and R. Young. Kingston, Ont.: Queen's University, Institute of Intergovernmental Relations.

———. 1995. Between Fragmentation and Integration: The Evolving Security Discourse in Australia and Canada. *Australian Journal of International Affairs.* May: 49–67.

Cooper, A.F., and J.-S. Fritz. 1992. Bringing the NGOs in: UNCD and Canada's International Environmental Policy. *International Journal* 47(4): 796–817.

Cooper, A.F., and R. Higgott. 1993. Australia, Canada and the Cairns Group. In *World Agriculture and the GATT,* ed. W.P. Avery. Boulder, Colo.: Lynne Rienner.

Cooper, A.F., R.A. Higgott, and K.R. Nossal. 1993. *Relocating Middle Powers: Australia and Canada in a Changing World Order.* Vancouver: University of British Columbia Press.

Courchene, T. 1992a. *Rearrangements: The Courchene Papers.* Oakville, Ont.: Mosaic.

———. 1992b. Mon Pays, c'est l'hiver: Reflections of a Market Populist. *Canadian Journal of Economics* 25: 759–91.

———. 1992c. Global Competitiveness and the Canadian Federation. In Courchene (1992a).

———. 1993. Path Dependency, Positive Feedback and Paradigm Warp: A Schumpeterian Approach to the Social Order. In *Income Security in Canada: Changing Needs, Changing Means,* ed. E. Reynolds. Montreal: Institute for Research in Public Policy.

Cowhey, P.F. 1990. The International Telecommunications Regime: The Political Roots of Regimes for High Technology. *International Organization* 44(2): 169–99.

Cox, R.W. 1987. *Production, Power and World Order: Social Forces in the Making of History.* New York: Columbia University Press.

———. 1994. Global Restructuring: Making Sense of the International Political Economy. In *Political Economy and the Changing Global Order,* eds R. Stubbs and G.R.D. Underhill. Toronto: McClelland and Stewart.

Coyne, A. 1994. The Diplomats Make a Comeback. *Globe and Mail*, 19 Nov. pp. D1–2.

Crane, D. 1992. *The Next Canadian Century*. Toronto: Stoddart.

CRTC. *See* Canadian Radio-television and Telecommunications Commission.

CSA. *See* Canadian Standards Association.

Danziger, G., and P. Gottschalk, eds. 1993. *Uneven Tides: Rising Inequality in America*. New York: Russell Foundation.

Davey, W. 1994. The Role of Trade Dispute Settlement Mechanisms in Canada-U.S. Relations. Paper presented to the conference Managing Interdependence: Policy Making in Canada-U.S. Relations, Centre for Trade Policy and Law, Ottawa, 22 Sept. 1994.

Denny, M., and T. Wilson 1993. Productivity and Growth. In *Productivity, Growth and Canada's International Competitiveness*, eds T. Courchene and D. Purvis. Kingston, Ont.: Queen's University, John Deutsch Institute for the Study of Economic Policy.

Devereux, M., and T.A. Wilson. 1989. International Coordination of Economic Policies: A Review. *Canadian Public Policy* 15 (February): 20–34.

Dewitt, D., D. Haglund, and J. Kirton, eds. 1993. *Building a New Global Order: Emerging Trends in International Security*. Toronto: Oxford University Press.

Dobson, W. 1991. *Economic Policy Coordination: Requiem or Prologue?* Washington: Institute for International Economics.

Doern, G.B. 1983. The Mega-Project Episode and the Formulation of Canadian Economic Development Policy. *Canadian Public Administration* 26(2): 219–38.

———. 1987. The Political-Administration of Government Reorganization: The Merger of DREE and ITC. *Canadian Public Administration* 30(1): 34–56.

———. 1990. Industry, Science and Technology Canada: Is There Industrial Policy After Free Trade? In *How Ottawa Spends: 1990–91*, ed. K. Graham. Ottawa: Carleton University Press.

———. 1993. *Green Diplomacy*. Toronto: C.D. Howe Institute.

———. 1994a. *The Road to Better Public Services: Progress and Constraints in Five Federal Agencies*. Montreal: Institute for Research on Public Policy.

———. 1994b. The Convergence of Investment, Trade and Environmental Policies. In *Getting the Green Light: Environmental Regulation and Investment in Canada*, eds J. Benedickson, G.B. Doern, and N. Olewiler. Toronto: C.D. Howe Institute.

———. 1995a. The Formation of Industry Canada: Second Beginnings for a Department of the Micro-Economy. Paper presented to the Workshop on the 1993 Federal Reorganization, Canadian Centre for Management Development, Ottawa.

———. 1995b. *Fairer Play: Canadian Competition Policy Institutions in a Global Market*. Toronto: C.D. Howe Institute.

———. 1995c. A Political-Institutional Framework for the Analysis of Competition Policy Institutions. *Governance* 8(2): 195–217.

Doern, G.B., and T. Conway. 1994. *The Greening of Canada: Federal Institutions and Decisions*. Toronto: University of Toronto Press.

Doern, G.B., A. Maslove, and M. Prince. 1988. *Budgeting in Canada*. Ottawa: Carleton University Press.

Doern, G.B., and R.W. Phidd, eds. 1983. *Canadian Public Policy: Ideas, Structure, Process*. Toronto: Methuen.

Doern, G.B., and R.H. Phidd. 1992. *Canadian Public Policy: Ideas, Structure, Process*, 2nd edn. Toronto: Nelson.

Doern, G.B., and B. Tomlin. 1991. *Faith and Fear: The Free Trade Story*. Toronto: Stoddart.

Doern, G.B., and S. Wilks, eds. 1996. *National Competition Policy: Institutions in a Global Market*. Oxford: Oxford University Press.

Donnelly, J. 1986. International Human Rights: A Regime Analysis. *International Organization* 40(3): 599–641.

Dougherty, J.E., and R. Pfaltzgraff. 1990. *Contending Theories of International Relations*, 3d edn. New York: Harper Collins.

Drache, D., and M.S. Gertler, eds. 1991. *The New Era of Global Competition*. Montreal and Kingston: McGill-Queen's University Press.

Drake, W.J. 1994. Asymmetric Deregulation and the Transformation of the International Telecommunications Regime. In *Asymmetric Deregulation: The Dynamics of Telecommunications Policy in Europe and the United States*, eds E. Noam and G. Pogorel. Norwood, NJ: Ablex.

Drummond, I.W. 1987. *Progress without Planning: The Economic History of Ontario from Confederation to the Second World War*. Toronto: University of Toronto Press.

Echenberg, H., et al. 1992. *A Social Charter for Canada?* Toronto: C.D. Howe Institute.

Economic Council of Canada. 1988. *Managing Adjustment Policies for Trade-Sensitive Industries*. Ottawa: Economic Council of Canada.

Eden, L. 1994. *Multinationals as Agents of Change: Setting a New Canadian Policy on Foreign Direct Investment*. Discussion Paper no. 1. Ottawa: Industry Canada, November.

Eden, L., and M. Molot. 1993. Canada's National Policies: Reflections on 125 Years. *Canadian Public Policy* 19(3): 232–60.

Ekos Research Associates. 1995. *Rethinking Government '94: An Overview and Synthesis*. Ottawa: Ekos Research Associates.

Elkins, D.J. 1995. *Beyond Sovereignty: Territory and Political Economy in the Twenty-First Century*. Toronto: University of Toronto Press.

Esping-Andersen, G. 1990. *The Three Worlds of Welfare Capitalism*. Princeton, NJ: Princeton University Press.

Estey Commission. *See* Canada. Inquiry into the Collapse of the CCB and Northland Bank.

Evans, P., H. Jacobson, and R. Putnam, eds. 1993. *Double-Edged Diplomacy: International Bargaining and Domestic Politics*. Berkeley: University of California Press.

Feketekuty, G. 1989. The New World Information Economy and the New Trade Dimension in Telecommunications Policy. In *Global Trade: The Revolution Beyond the Communications Revolution*, ed. Lanvin B. Montpellier. IDATE, 31–74.

Finn, T.D. 1993. Does Canada Need a Foreign Intelligence Service? *Canadian Foreign Policy* 1: 149–62.

Fontecchio, J.M. 1994. The General Agreement on Trade in Services: Is It the Answer to Creating a Harmonized Global Securities System? *North Carolina Journal of International Law and Commercial Regulation* 20(1): 115–35.

Footer, M.E. 1993. GATT and the Multilateral Regulation of Banking Services. *International Lawyer* 27(2): 343–67.

Forsythe, D.P. 1985. The United Nations and Human Rights, 1945–1985. *Political Science Quarterly* 100(2): 249–69.

Fortin, P. 1994. Slow Growth, Employment and Debt: What Happened? In *Stabilization, Growth and Distribution: Linkages in the Knowledge Era*, ed. T. Courchene. Kingston: Queen's University, John Deutsch Institute for the Study of Economic Policy.

French, M., and P. Jarret. 1994. The United States: Restoring Productivity Growth. OECD *Observer* 185: 46–8.

Gafford, R. 1992. Three for Free Trade. *Canadian Banker* 99(2): 6–10.

Gigantes, P.D. 1988. *Is the Free Trade Deal Really for You?* Toronto: Stoddart.

Gill, S., and D. Law. 1988. *The Global Political Economy*. New York: Harvester-Wheatsheaf.

Glendon, M.A. 1991. *Rights Talk: The Impoverishment of Political Discourse*. New York: Free Press.

Globerman, S., *et al.* 1992. Canada and the Movement towards Liberalization of the International Telecommunications Regime. In *Canadian Foreign Policy and International Economic Regimes*, eds A.C. Cutler and M.W. Zacher. Vancouver: University of British Columbia Press.

Globerman, S., H.N. Janisch, and W.T. Stanbury. 1995. Analysis of Telecom Decision 94–19, Review of Regulatory Framework. In Globerman *et al.* (1992).

Globerman, S., W.T. Stanbury, and T.A. Wilson, eds. 1995. *The Future of Telecommunications Policy in Canada*. University of Toronto, Toronto: Institute for Policy Analysis.

Goldsmith, R.W. 1985. *Comparative National Balance Sheets*. Chicago: University of Chicago Press.

Gotlieb, A. 1985. Letter to Sinclair Stevens, quoted in 'Publishing Policy Imperils US Ties Ambassador Says', *Globe and Mail*, 4 Nov.

———. 1991. *I'll Be with You in a Minute, Mr. Ambassador*. Toronto: University of Toronto Press.

Greene, C.A.A. 1994. International Securities Law Enforcement: Recent Advances in Assistance and Cooperation. *Vanderbilt Journal of Transnational Law* 27(3): 604–72.

Griffiths, F. 1968. Opening Up the Policy Process. In *An Independent Foreign Policy for Canada?*, ed. S. Clarkson. Toronto: McClelland and Stewart.

Griffiths, F.J.C. 1994. Canada as a Sovereign State. *Canadian Foreign Policy* 2(1): 15–43.

Grinspun R., and M. Cameron. 1993. *The Political Economy of North American Free Trade*. Montreal and Kingston: McGill-Queen's University Press.

Gruson, M. 1992. Are Foreign Banks Still Welcome in the United States? *The Bankers Magazine* 175(5): 16–21.

Haas, P. 1992. Introduction: Epistemic Communities and International Policy Coordination. *International Organization* 46(1): 1–36.

Haddow, R. 1990. The Poverty Policy Community in Canada's Liberal Welfare State. In *Policy Communities and Public Policy in Canada: A Structural Approach*, eds W. Coleman and G. Skogstad. Toronto: Copp Clark Pitman.

———. 1995. A Fractured Liberalism: The Department of Finance and the Origins of Canada's Post-War Welfare State, 1940–1955. Paper presented to the 67th Annual Meeting of the Canadian Political Science Association, Montreal, 1995.

Halliday, F. 1994. *Rethinking International Relations*. Vancouver and London: University of British Columbia Press and Macmillan.

Hancock, T.D. 1991. Regulated Competition: Resale and Sharing in Telecommunications. *Media and Communications Law Review* 2: 257–96.

Harris, R. 1993. *Trade, Money and Wealth in the Canadian Economy*. Toronto: C.D. Howe Institute.

Harris, S.L. 1995. The Political Economy of the Liberalization of Entry and Ownership in the Canadian Investment Dealer Industry. Ph.D. diss., Carleton University, Ottawa.

Harrison, B., and B. Bluestone. 1988. *The Great U-Turn: Corporate Restructuring and the Polarizing of America*. New York: Basic.

Harrison, K. 1994. Prospects for Intergovernmental Harmonization in Environmental Policy. In *Canada: The State of the Federation 1994*, eds D. Brown and J. Hiebert. Kingston: Queen's University Institute of Intergovernmental Relations.

———. 1995. Federalism, Environmental Protection and Blame Avoidance. In *New Trends in Canadian Federalism*, eds F. Rocher and M. Smith. Peterborough, Ont.: Broadview.

Hart, M. 1993. The End of Trade Policy? In *Canada among Nations: 1993–94*, eds F. Hampson and C. Maule. Ottawa: Carleton University Press.

———. 1994. *Decision at Midnight*. Vancouver: University of British Columbia Press.

———. 1995. What's Next: Negotiating Rules for a Global Economy. In *New Dimensions of Market Access in A Globalizing World Economy*, eds A.B. Zampeti and P. Sauvé. Paris: OECD.

Hart, S. 1995. (President, Canadian Environmental Industry Association.) Letter to author. 21 Feb.

Hassan, N. 1995. Planting the Seeds for a New Kind of Trade. *Financial Post*, 18 Mar., p. 23.

Hawken, P. 1993. *The Ecology of Commerce: A Declaration of Sustainability*. New York: Harper Collins.

Helleiner, E. 1994. *States and the Reemergence of Global Finance: From Bretton Woods to the 1990s*. Ithaca, NY: Cornell University Press.

Helleiner, G. 1994–5. Globalization and Fragmentation in the International Economy. *Canadian Foreign Policy* 2(3): 101–8.

Helliwell, J. 1994. What Can Governments Do? *Policy Options* 15(6): 22–6.

Hill, M. 1988. Freedom to Move: Explaining the Decision to Deregulate Canadian Air and Rail Transportation. Master's research paper, School of Public Administration, Carleton University, Ottawa.

Hoberg, G. 1991. Sleeping with an Elephant: The American Influence on Canadian Environmental Regulation. *Journal of Public Policy* 10(1): 107–31.

———. 1993. Environmental Policy: Alternative Styles. In *Governing Canada: Institutions and Public Policy*, ed. M. Atkinson. Toronto: Harcourt Brace Jovanovich.

Hodge, T., S. Holtz, C. Smith, and K. Hawke Baxter. 1995. *Pathways to Sustainability: Assessing Our Progress*. Ottawa: National Round Table on the Environment and the Economy.

Hoggett, P. 1991. A New Management in the Public Sector? *Policy and Politics* 19(4): 243–56.

Holmes, J. 1979. *The Shaping of Peace: Canada and the Search for World Order.* Vol. 2. Toronto: University of Toronto Press.

Horowitz, D.L. 1977. *The Courts and Social Policy.* Washington, DC: Brookings.

Horwitz, R.B. 1989. *The Irony of Regulatory Reform.* New York: Oxford University Press.

Howe, R.B. 1991. The Evolution of Human Rights Policy in Ontario. *Canadian Journal of Political Science* 24(4): 783–802.

Howlett, M. 1994. The Judicialization of Canadian Environmental Policy, 1980–1990: A Test of the Canada-United States Convergence Thesis. *Canadian Journal of Political Science* 27(1): 99–127.

Howse, R. 1995. Another Rights Revolution? The Charter and the Reform of Social Regulation in Canada. In *Redefining Social Security*, eds P. Grady, R. Howse, and J. Maxwell. Kingston, Ont.: Queen's University, School of Policy Studies.

Hufbauer, G.C., and J.J. Schott. 1993. *NAFTA: An Assessment.* Washington, DC: Institute for International Economics.

Hurrell, A., and B. Kingsbury, eds. 1992. *The International Politics of the Environment: Actors, Interests and Institutions.* Oxford: Clarendon.

Hylton, J.D. 1994. Free Wheeling and Dealing? NAFTA and GATT and Telecom. *Media and Communications Law Review* 4: 173–88.

IISD. *See* International Institute for Sustainable Development.

IMF. *See* International Monetary Fund.

Industry Canada 1994a. Agreement on Internal Trade. Ottawa, 18 July 1994.

———. 1994b. *Building a More Innovative Economy.* Ottawa: Minister of Supply and Services.

———. 1994c. *Canadian-Based Multinationals: An Analysis of Activities and Performance.* Working Paper no. 2. July.

———. 1994d. *Formal and Informal Investment Barriers in the G-7 Countries: The Country Chapters.* Occasional Paper no. 1, vol. 1. May.

———. 1995. *The Impact of the Budget on the Industry Canada Portfolio.* Ottawa: Industry Canada.

Insight Canada Research. 1993. *Aspirations Project: Qualitative Research Report.* Toronto: Premier's Council on Health, Well-being and Social Justice.

Interim Committee of the Non-Governmental Organizations for Consultative Status with the United Nations. 1949. *Consultation between the United Nations and Non-Governmental Organizations.* New York: Carnegie Endowment for International Peace.

International Centre for Human Rights and Democratic Development. 1992. Making Women's Rights Part of the Global Human Rights Agenda. *Libertas: Newsletter of the International Centre for Human Rights and Democratic Development*, June.

International Institute for Sustainable Development. 1994. *Making Budgets Green: Leading Practices in Taxation and Subsidy Reform.* Winnipeg: IISD.

International Monetary Fund. 1994. Banks and Derivative Markets: A Challenge for Financial Policy. *IMF Survey*, 21 Feb.

ITU. *See* International Telecommunications Union.

International Telecommunications Union. 1982. *International Telecommunications Convention, Preamble.* Geneva: ITU.

Investment Canada. 1985–93. *Annual Report.*

Jackman, M. 1994. Constitutional Contact with the Disparities in the World: Poverty as a Prohibited Ground of Discrimination under the Canadian Charter and Human Rights Law. *Review of Constitutional Studies* 2: 76–122.

Jacobs, M. 1991. *The Green Economy: Environment, Sustainable Development and the Politics of the Future*. London: Pluto.

Janisch, H.N. 1989. The Canada-US Free Trade Agreement: Impact on Telecommunications. *Telecommunications Policy* 13(2): 99–103.

———. 1986. Winners and Losers: The Challenges Facing Telecommunications Regulators. In W.T. Stanbury, ed., *Telecommunications Policy and Regulation: The Impact of Competition and Technological Change*. Montreal: Institute for Research on Public Policy.

———. 1995. New Federal Telecommunications Legislation and Federal-Provincial Arrangements. In Globerman, Stanbury, and Wilson (1995).

Janisch, H.N., and Bohdan Romaniuk. 1994. Canada. In Noam, Komatsukzai, and Conn (1995).

Janisch H.N., and R. Schultz. 1989. *Exploiting the Information Revolution: Telecommunications Issues and Options for Canada*. Montreal: Royal Bank of Canada.

Jenson, J. 1992. Citizenship and Equity: Variations across Time and Space. In *Political Ethics: A Canadian Perspective*, ed. J. Hiebert. Toronto: Dundurn.

Josling, T., and R. Barichello. 1993. *Agriculture in the NAFTA: A Preliminary Assessment*. C.D. Howe Institute Commentary no. 43. Toronto: C.D. Howe Institute.

de Jonquières, G., and L. Boulton. 1995. Trade and the Environment a Tough Balance. *Financial Post*, 28 Oct., p. 78.

Karvonen, L. and B. Sundelius. 1987. *Internationalization and Foreign Policy Managment*. Aldershot, UK.: Gower.

Katzenstein, P. 1984. The Small European States in the International Economy: Economic Dependence and Corporatist Politics. In *The Antimonies of Interdependence: National Welfare and the International Division of Labour*, ed. J. Ruggie. New York: Columbia University Press.

———. 1985. *Small States in World Markets: Industrial Policy in Europe*. Ithaca, NY: Cornell University Press.

Keen, P.G.W. 1988. *Competing in Time: Using Telecommunications for Competitive Advantage*. Cambridge, Mass.: Ballinger.

Keenes, E. 1992. Rearranging the Deck Chairs: A Political Economy Approach to Foreign Policy Management in Canada. *Canadian Public Administration* 35(3): 381–401.

Keohane, R. 1984. The World Political Economy and the Crisis of Embedded Liberalism. In *Order and Conflict in Contemporary Capitalism*, ed. J.H. Goldthorpe. Oxford: Oxford University Press.

Keohane, R., and J. Nye. 1974. *Power and Interdependence*. Boston: Little Brown.

Kincaid, J. 1993. Peoples, Persons, and Places in Flux: International Integration versus National Fragmentation. In *Integration and Fragmentation: The Paradox of the Late Twentieth Century*, eds G. Laforest and D. Brown. Kingston, Ont.: Queen's University.

Kirton, J. 1978. Foreign Policy Decision Making in the Trudeau Government: Promise and Perfomance. *International Journal* 33: 287–311.

————. 1979. Les Contraintes du milieu et la Gestin de la politique étrangère canadienne de 1976 à 1978. *Études Internationales* 10(2): 321–49.

————. 1994. National Mythology and Media Coverage: Mobilizing Consent for Canada's War in the Gulf. *Political Communication* 10: 425–41.

————. 1995a. A Renewed Opportunity: The Role of Space in Canadian Security Policy. In *Canada's International Security Policy*, eds D. Dewitt and D. Leyton-Brown. Scarborough, Ont.: Prentice Hall.

————. 1995b. Smoothing Troubled Waters: The 1988 Canada-United States Arctic Cooperation Agreement. *International Journal* 50: 401–26.

Kirton, J., and B. Dimock. 1983–4. Domestic Access to Government in the Canadian Foreign Policy Process, 1968–1982. *International Journal* 39(1983–4): 68–98.

Knox, P. 1995. 'Chrétien Blasted for Summit Absence.' *Globe and Mail*, 7 Mar.

Krasner, S. 1985. *Structural Conflict: The Third World Against Global Liberalism.* Berkeley: University of California Press.

Krause, K. 1994. *Redefining International Peace and Security? The Discourses and Practices of Multilateral Security Activity.* YCISS Working Paper no. 13. Toronto: York University Centre For International and Strategic Studies.

Krugman, P. 1990. *The Age of Diminished Expectations.* Cambridge, Mass.: MIT Press.

————. 1994. Competitiveness: A Dangerous Obsession. *Foreign Affairs* (Mar.-Apr.): 28–44.

Kwerel, E. 1984. *Promoting Competition Piecemeal in International Telecommunications.* Working Paper no. 13. Washington, DC: Federal Communications Commission.

————. 1994. Reconciling Competition and Monopoly in the Supply of International Telecommunications Services: A U.S. Perspective. In *Asymmetric Deregulation: The Dynamics of Telecommunications Policy in Europe and the United States*, eds E. Noam and G. Pogorel. Norwood NJ: Ablex.

Labbé, P. 1990. Letter from President of Investment Canada to Don Campbell, Deputy Minister of International Trade, 15 May.

Lacayo, R. 1995. What Goes Up Comes Down. *Time*, Canadian edn, 9 Jan. 1995, 32–4.

Lasch, C. 1995. *The Revolt of the Elites and the Betrayal of Democracy.* New York: Norton.

Lazar, H., and A. Mayrand, in collaboration with K. Patterson. 1992. Global Competition and Canadian Federalism: The Financial Sector. *The Canadian Business Law Journal* 20(1): 1–41.

Leblanc, A. 1995. No Sign of Consensus on Climate Change. *National Round Table Review*, Winter: 5–7.

Lemonick, M. 1995. Heading for Apocalypse? *Time*, Canadian edn, 2 Oct., pp. 42–3.

Levy, F., and R. Murnane. 1992. US Earnings Levels and Earnings Inequality: A Review of Recent Trends and Proposed Explanations, *Journal of Economic Literature* 30: 1333–81.

Libby, B. 1994. The Impact of the North American Free Trade Agreement on Commercial Banking. *Journal of Economic Issues* 28(2): 501–8.

Libby, R.T. 1992. *Protecting Markets: US Policy and the World Grain Trade.* Ithaca: Cornell University Press.

Liberal Party of Canada. 1993. *Creating Opportunity: The Liberal Party Plan for Canada.* Ottawa: Liberal Party of Canada.

Linder, Stephen, and B. Guy Peters. Instruments of Government: Perceptions and Contexts. *Journal of Public Policy* 9(1): 35–58.

Lipsey, R. 1993. Wanted: A New Social Contract. *Policy Options* 14(6): 5–9.

Lyon, P., and B. Tomlin. 1979. *Canada as an International Actor*. Toronto: Macmillan.

Macdonald, L. 1993. Current and Future Directions for Canadian NGOs in Latin America. In *A Dynamic Partnership: Canada's Changing Role in the Hemisphere*, eds J. Haar and E.J. Dosman. Miami: North-South Center.

MacFarlane, S.N., and T.G. Weiss. 1994. The United Nations, Regional Organizations, and Human Security: Building Theory in Central America. In *Regional Responsibilities and the United Nations System*, ed. The Academic Council on the United Nations System (ACUNS). Providence, RI: ACUNS.

MacIntosh, R. 1988. Quebec's Financial System after Meech Lake: Remarks to the Canadian Club of Montreal. Toronto: Canadian Bankers Association.

MacNeill, J., P. Winsemius, and T. Yakushiji. 1991. *Beyond Interdependence: The Meshing of the World's Economy and the Earth's Ecology*. Oxford: Oxford University Press.

Mahoney, K. 1992. Human Rights and Canadian Foreign Policy. *International Journal* 47(3): 555–94.

Makin, C. 1991. Regulation: Learning from BCCI. *Institutional Investor*, Nov.: 93–7.

Mandel, M. 1994. *The Charter of Rights and the Legalization of Politics in Canada*, rev. edn. Toronto: Thompson Educational Publishing.

Masse, M. 1985. Looking at Telecommunications: The Need for Review. Notes for an Address to the Electrical and Electronic Manufacturers' Association, Montebello, Quebec, 20 June.

———. 1989. Speech to the Canadian Satellite Users Conference, Ottawa, 19 June.

Matas, R. 1995. Bureaucrats Pan MP's Environmental Law Proposals. *The Globe and Mail*, 16 Oct. 1995, p. A7.

Matthews, R.O. 1990. The Christian Churches and Foreign Policy: An Assessment. In *Canadian Churches and Foreign Policy*, ed. B. Greene. Toronto: Lorimer.

Maxwell, J. 1993. Globalization and Family Security. In *Family Security in Insecure Times*. Ottawa: National Forum on Family Security.

McCallum, J., and J. Helliwell. 1995. National Borders Still Matter for Trade. *Policy Options* 16(6) (July/Aug.): 44–8.

McDorman, T. 1994–5. Canada's Aggressive Fisheries Actions: Will They Improve the Climate for International Agreements? *Canadian Foreign Policy* 2: 5–28.

McDougall, B. 1994. How We Handled Foreign Policy. *Globe and Mail*, 9 Dec., p. 21.

McDowell, D. 1984. *A Fit Place to Invest: Investor's Perception of Canada in a Changing World*. Ottawa: Conference Board.

McFetridge, D.G. 1985. The Economics of Industrial Policy: An Overview. In *Canadian Industrial Policy in Action*, ed. D. McFetridge. Toronto: University of Toronto Press.

Meisel, J. 1982. Of Babies and Bathwater, or What Goes Down the Deregulatory Drain. Notes for an address to the Annapolis Telecommunications Policy Research Conference, 28 Apr. 1982, pp. 5–27 to 5–30.

Melnick, R.S. 1994. *Between the Lines: Interpreting Welfare Rights*. Washington, DC: Brookings.

Millspaugh, P.E. 1992. Global Securities Trading: The Question of a Watchdog. *George Washington Journal of International Law and Economics* 26(2): 355–77.

Moffett, J. 1994. Judicial Review and Environmental Policy: Lessons for Canada from the United States. *Canadian Public Administration* 37(1): 140–66.

Moran, M. 1984. *The Politics of Banking*. London: Macmillan.

———. 1991. *The Politics of the Financial Services Revolution*. Basingstoke, UK: Macmillan.

Moravcsik, A. 1993. Introduction: Integrating International and Domestic Theories of International Bargaining. In *International Bargaining and Domestic Politics: Double-Edged Diplomacy*, eds P.B. Evans, H.K. Jacobson, and R.D. Putnam. Berkeley, Calif.: University of California Press.

Morton, F.L. 1992. The Charter Revolution and the Court Party. *Osgoode Hall Law Journal* 30(3): 627–52.

de la Mothe, J., and G. Paquet. 1994. The Technology-Trade Nexus: Liberalization, Warring Blocs or Negotiated Access? *Technology in Society* 16(1): 97–118.

Munton, D., and G. Castle. 1992. The Continental Dimension: Canada and the United States. In *Canadian Environmental Policy: Ecosystems, Politics and Processes*, ed. R. Boardman. Toronto: Oxford University Press.

Munton, D., and J. Kirton. 1994. North American Environmental Cooperation: Bilateral, Trilateral, Multilateral. *North American Outlook* 4: 59–86.

Myers, N. 1995. The Forgotten Human Crisis: Millions of Environmental Refugees Could Lead to Violence. *Ottawa Citizen*, 8 Aug. 1995, p. A7.

National Farm Products Council. 1994a. *Annual Review 1993–1994*. Ottawa: NFPC.

———. 1994b. *Inquiry into the Complaint by la Fédération des Producteurs de Volailles du Québec, the Nova Scotia Chicken Producers Board and the Newfoundland Chicken Marketing Board Against the Decision of the Canadian Chicken Marketing Agency Respecting the Third Period 1994 Quota Allocations*. Ottawa: NFPC, Apr.

National Round Table on the Environment and the Economy. 1993. Environmental Groups: Adapting to Changing Times. *National Round Table Review*, Spring.

Nelson, R.R., ed. 1993. *National Innovation Systems: A Comparative Analysis*. Oxford: Oxford University Press.

NFPC. *See* National Farm Products Council.

Noam, E.M. 1989. International Telecommunications in Transition. In *Changing the Rules: Technological Change, International Competition and Regulation in Communications*, eds R.W. Crandall and K. Flamm. Washington, DC: Brookings.

———. 1992. *Telecommunications in Europe*. New York: Oxford University Press.

———. 1995. The Three Stages of Network Evolution. In *Telecommunications in the Pacific Basin*, eds E. Noam, S. Komatsukzai, and D.A. Conn. New York: Oxford University Press.

Noam, E., Seisuke Komatsukzai, and Douglas A. Conn, eds. *Telecommunications Policy in Canada*. University of Toronto, Institute for Policy Analysis.

Nossal, K.R. 1983–4. Analyzing the Domestic Sources of Canadian Foreign Policy. *International Journal* 39(1): 1–22.

———. 1989. *The Politics of Canadian Foreign Policy*. 2nd edn. Scarborough, Ont.: Prentice-Hall.

———. 1994. Dividing the Territory, 1968–1994. *International Journal* 50: 189–209.

NRTEE. *See* National Round Table on Environmental and Economy

OECD. *See* Organisation for Economic Co-operation and Development.

Omhae, K. 1990. *The Borderless World: Power and Strategy in the Interlinked Economy*. New York: Harper's.

Ontario. Legislative Research Services. 1991. *Interprovincial Trade Barriers*. Toronto: Ministry of Government Services.

Ontario Social Safety Net/Work 1995. Statement to the Finance Committee on Bill C-76. Ottawa, 15 May.

Ontario. Ministry of Agriculture and Food. 1994. *Agri-Food Trade Update* 65 (16 Mar.).

Ontario. Ministry of Consumer and Commercial Relations. 1983. *Proposals for Revision of the Loan and Trust Company Legislation and Administration in Ontario*. Toronto: Ministry of Consumer and Commercial Relations.

Ontario. Task Force on Financial Institutions. 1985. *Final Report*. Toronto: Task Force on Financial Institutions.

Organisation for Economic Co-operation and Development. 1993a. Earnings Inequality: Changes in the 1980s. *Employment Outlook* July: 157–84. Paris: OECD.

———. 1993b. *Revenue Statistics of OECD Member Countries, 1965–1992*. Paris: OECD.

———. 1994a. *The OECD Jobs Study: Facts, Analysis, Strategies*. Paris: OECD.

———. 1994b. *New Orientations for Social Policy*. Social Policy Studies no. 12. Paris: OECD.

———. 1994c. The Rise of Global Bonds. *Financial Market Trends* 58: 55–61.

———. 1995a. Meeting of the OECD Council at Ministerial Level: Communiqué. OECD Press Release, 24 May. Paris: OECD.

———. 1995b. *A Multilateral Agreement on Investment: Report by the Committee on International Investment and Multinational Enterprises and the Committee on Capital Movements and Invisible Transactions*. Paris: OECD.

Ostry, S. 1990. *Governments and Corporations in a Shrinking World: Trade and Innovation Policies in the United States, Europe and Japan*. New York: Council on Foreign Relations.

———. 1993. Globalization, Domestic Policies and the Need For Harmonization. Paper presented to Workshop on Competition Policy in a Global Economy, University of California, Jan. 8–9.

Oxley, A. 1990. *The Challenge of Free Trade*. London: Harvester Wheatsheaf.

Paarlberg, R.L. 1993. Why Agriculture Blocked the Uruguay Round: Evolving Strategies in a Two-Level Game. In *World Agriculture and the GATT*, ed. W.P. Avery. Boulder, Colo.: Lynne Rienner.

Paehlke, R. 1989. *Environmentalism and the Future of Progressive Politics*. New Haven: Yale University Press.

Pal, Leslie A. 1992. *Public Policy Analysis: An Introduction*, 2nd edn. Toronto: Nelson.

Pammet, J., and B.W. Tomlin, eds. 1984. *The Integration Question: Political Economy and Public Policy in Canada and North America*. Toronto: Addison-Wesley.

Paquet, G., and J. Roy. 1995. Prosperity through Networks: The Bottom-Up Strategy That Might Have Been. In *How Ottawa Spends: 1995-6*, ed. S. Phillips. Ottawa: Carleton University Press.

Paszkowski, W. 1995. Alberta Policy. *The Western Producer*, 2 Feb.

Pauly, L. 1988. *Opening Financial Markets: Banking Politics on the Pacific Rim*. Ithaca: Cornell University Press.

Pecchioli, R.M. 1983. *The Internationalisation of Banking: The Policy Issues*. Paris: OECD.

Peters, G.P., and D.J. Savoie, eds. 1995. *Governance in a Changing Environment*. Montreal and Kingston: McGill-Queen's University Press.

Phidd, R.W., and B. Doern. 1978. *The Politics and Management of Canadian Economic Policy*. Toronto: Macmillan.

Phillips, K. 1993. *Boiling Point*. New York: Random House.

Porter, G., and J. Brown. 1991. *Global Environmental Politics*. Boulder, Colo.: Westview.

Porter, M. 1990. *The Competitive Advantage of Nations*. New York: Free Press.

———. 1991. *Canada at the Crossroads: The Reality of the New Competitive Environment*. Ottawa: Business Council on National Issues and Government of Canada.

Porter, T. 1993. *States, Markets and Regimes in Global Finance*. Basingstoke, UK: Macmillan.

Porter Commission. *See* Canada, Royal Commission on Banking and Finance.

Power, E.M. 1993. *Foreign Investment Protection Agreements: A Canadian Perspective*. Investment Canada. Working Paper no. 14. Apr. 1993.

Power, L. 1993. NAFTA and the Regulation of Financial and Other Services. *U.S. Mexico Law Journal* 6(1): 65–83.

Pratt, C. 1983-4. Dominant Class Theory and Canadian Foreign Policy: The Case of the Counter-Consensus. *International Journal* 39(1): 99–135.

———. 1993-4. Canada's Development Assistance: Some Lessons from the Last Review. *International Journal* 49(1): 93–125.

Projet de Société. 1995. *Planning for a Sustainable Future: Canadian Choices for Transitions to Sustainability*. Ottawa: Projet de Société.

Putnam, R. 1988. Diplomacy and Domestic Politics: The Logic of Two-Level Games. *International Organization* 42: 427–60.

Quebec 1988. *Decompartmentalization of Intermediaries: Discussion Paper*. Quebec: Éditeur officiel.

———. 1990. *Quinquennial Report on the Application of the Act Respecting Insurance: Changes*. Quebec: Office du Ministère des Finances.

Quebec. Ministère de l'Agriculture, des Pêcheries et de l'Alimentation. 1994. *L'Industrie bioalimentaire au Québec: bilan 1994 et perspectives*. Quebec City: Publications du Québec.

Quebec. Study Committee on Financial Institutions. 1969. *Report* (Parizeau Report). Quebec City: Éditeur officiel.

Reich, R. 1990. Who Is Us. *Harvard Business Review* Jan.: 53–64.

———. 1991. *The Work of Nations: Preparing Ourselves for 21st Century Capitalism*. New York: Knopf.

Rhodes, M. 1995. 'Subversive Liberalism': Market Integration, Globalisation and the European Welfare State. *Journal of European Public Policy* 2(3): 384–406.

Robert, J. 1994. Constitutional and International Protection of Human Rights: Competing or Complementary Systems? *Human Rights Law Journal* 15 (March): 1–23.

Robinson, I. 1993a. The NAFTA, the Side-Deals, and Canadian Federalism: Constitutional Reform by Other Means? In *Canada: The State of the Federation*. Kingston: Queen's University, Institute of Intergovernmental Relations.

———. 1993b. The NAFTA, Democracy and Continental Economic Integration: Trade Policy As If Democracy Mattered. In *How Ottawa Spends: 1993–94*, ed. S. Phillips. Ottawa: Carleton University Press.

Rosaasen, K.A., J.S. Lokken, and T. Richards. 1995. Provincialism—Problems for the Regulators and the Regulated: Growing Together? In *Supply Management in Transition: Towards the 21st Century*, eds Coffin *et al.* Montreal: McGill University.

Rose, R. 1993. *Lesson-Drawing in Public Policy*. Chatham, NJ: Chatham House.

Rossell, S. *et al.* 1992. *Governing in an Information Society*. Montreal: Institute for Research on Public Policy.

Roy, J. 1995. *Understanding Governance in High-Technology Regions: Towards a New Paradigm of High Technology and Local Development in Canada*. Ottawa: Carleton University, School of Public Administration.

Ruggie, J.G. 1982. International Regimes, Transactions, and Change: Embedded Liberalism in the Postwar Economic Order. *International Organization* 36(2): 379–415.

———. 1983. International Regimes, Transactions and Change: Embedded Liberalism in the Postwar Order. In *International Regimes*, ed. S. Krasner. Ithaca, NY: Cornell University Press.

———. 1994. Trade Protection and the Future of Welfare Capitalism. *Journal of International Affairs* 48: 1–12.

Rugman, A. 1986. U.S. Protectionism and Canadian Trade Policy. *Journal of World Trade Law* 20(4): 363–80.

Rugman, A., and M. Gestrin. 1994. NAFTA Treatment of Foreign Investment. In *Foreign Investment and NAFTA*, ed. A. Rugman. Columbus, SC: University of South Carolina Press.

Runnals, D., and A. Cosbey. 1992. *Trade and Sustainable Development*. Winnipeg: International Institute for Sustainable Development.

Sabourin, L. 1971. Canadian Federalism and International Organization. Ph.D. diss., Columbia University.

Safarian, A.E. 1980. *Ten Markets or One?* Toronto: Ontario Economic Council.

Saskatchewan. Dept of Agriculture and Food. 1993. *Agriculture 2000: A Strategic Direction for the Future of Saskatchewan's Agriculture and Food Industry*. Regina: Saskatchewan Dept of Agriculture and Food.

———. 1994a. *Agriculture 2000: Progress Report*. Regina: Saskatchewan Dept of Agriculture and Food.

———. 1994b. *Agriculture 2000: Report to the Industry*. Regina: Saskatchewan Dept of Agriculure and Food.

Savoie, D. 1986. *Regional Economic Development: Canada's Search for Solutions*. Toronto: University of Toronto Press.

———. 1990. ACOA: Something Old, Something New, Something Borrowed, Something Blue. In *How Ottawa Spends: 1989–90*, ed. K. Graham. Ottawa: Carleton University Press.

Schiller, D. 1982. *Telematics and Government*. Norwood, NJ: Ablex.

Schmitz, A., H. de Gorter, and T. Schmitz. 1995. Consequences of Tariffication for Supply Management in Canadian Agriculture. In *Supply Management in Transition: Towards the 21st Century*, eds Coffin *et al.*

Scholte, J.A. 1993. From Power Politics to Social Change: An Alternative Focus for International Studies. *Review of International Studies* 19(1): 3–21.

Schultz, R.J. 1988. Teleglobe Canada. In *Privatization Public Policy and Public Corporations in Canada*, eds A. Tupper and G.B. Doern. Halifax: Institute for Research on Public Policy.

———. 1989. *United States Telecommunications Pricing Changes and Social Welfare: Causes, Consequences and Policy Alternatives*. Ottawa: Dept of Consumer and Corporate Affairs.

———. 1990. New Domestic and International Bedfellows in Telecommunications. *Media and Communications Law Review* 1(2): 215–35.

———. 1995a. Old Whine in New Bottle: The Politics of Cross-Subsidies in Canadian Telecommunications. In Globerman *et al.* (1992).

———. 1995b. Embracing the Future: Recent Canadian Telecommunications Decisions. In *Telecommunications and Space Journal*. 2: 193–205.

Seebach, D. 1993. *Globalization: The Impact on the Trade and Investment Dynamic*. Policy Planning Staff Paper no. 93–7. Dept of External Affairs and International Trade, June.

Sikkink, K. 1993. Human Rights, Principled Issue-Networks, and Sovereignty in Latin America. *International Organization* 47(3): 411–41.

Simeon, R. 1987. Federalism and Free Trade. In *Canada: The State of the Federation 1986*, ed. P.M. Leslie. Kingston: Queen's University, Institute of Intergovernmental Relations.

———. 1990. Globalization and the Canadian Nation State. In *Canada At Risk? Canadian Public Policy in the 1990s*, eds B.G. Doern and B. Purchase. Toronto: C.D. Howe Institute.

Sinclair, S. 1992. Provincial Powers. In *Canada under Free Trade*, eds D. Cameron and M. Watkins. Toronto: Lorimer.

———. 1993. NAFTA and U.S. Trade Policy: Implications for Canada and Mexico. In *The Political Economy of North American Free Trade*, eds R. Grinspun and M. Cameron. Kingston and Montreal: McGill-Queen's University Press.

Skocpol, T. 1979. *States and Social Revolutions*. Cambridge: Cambridge University Press.

Skogstad, G. 1990. The Political Economy of Agriculture in Canada. In *The Political Economy of Agricultural Trade and Policy*, eds H.J. Michelmann, J.C. Stabler, and G.G. Storey. Boulder, Colo.: Westview.

———. 1992. The State, Organized Interests and Canadian Agricultural Trade Policy: The Impact of Institutions. *Canadian Journal of Political Science* 25(2): 319–47.

———. 1993. Policy under Siege: Supply Management in Agricultural Marketing. *Canadian Public Administration* 36(1): 1–23.

———. 1994. Agricultural Trade and the International Political Economy. In *Political Economy and the Changing Global Order*, eds R. Stubbs and G.R.D. Underhill. Toronto: McClelland and Stewart.

———. 1995a. Warring over Wheat: Managing Bilateral Trading Tensions. In *How Ottawa Spends 1995–96*, ed. S.D. Phillips. Ottawa: Carleton University Press.

————. 1995b. International Trade Agreements and Canadian Supply Management: Can the Systems Survive and Adjust? In *Regulation and Protectionism under GATT and NAFTA: Case Studies in North American Agriculture*, eds G. Coffin, A. Schmitz, and K. Rosaasen. Boulder, Colo.: Westview.

Skogstad, G., and P. Kopas. 1992. In *Canadian Environmental Policy: Ecosystems, Politics and Processes*, ed. R. Boardman. Toronto: Oxford University Press, 43–59.

Smillie, I. 1991. *A Time to Build Up: New Forms of Cooperation Between NGOs and CIDA*. Ottawa: Canadian Council for International Cooperation.

Smith, D. 1973. *Gentle Patriot: A Political Biography of Walter Gordon*. Edmonton: Hurtig.

Smith, G. 1995. Canada and the Halifax Summit. In *The Halifax Summit, Sustainable Development, and International Institutional Reform*, eds J. Kirton and S. Richardson. Ottawa: National Round Table on the Environment and the Economy.

Smith, G., and St. John Kettle. 1992. *Threats without Enemies: Rethinking Australia's Security*. Leichhardt, NSW: Pluto.

Smythe, E. 1994. *Free to Choose? Globalization, Dependence and Canada's Changing Foreign Investment Regime*. Ph.D. diss., Carleton University.

Stairs, D. 1970–1. Publics and Policy Makers: The Domestic Environment of Canada's Foreign Policy Community. *International Journal* 26(1): 221–48.

————. 1977–8. Public Opinion and External Affairs: Reflections on the Domestication of Canadian Foreign Policy. *International Journal* 33(1): 128–49.

————. 1982. Political Culture of Canadian Foreign Policy. *Canadian Journal of Political Science* 15: 667–90.

Stairs, D., and G. Winham, eds. 1985. *Selected Problems in Formulating Foreign Economic Policy*. Toronto: University of Toronto Press.

Stanbury, W.T., and I. Vertinsky. 1994–5. Information Technologies and Transnational Interest Groups: The Challenge for Diplomacy. *Canadian Foreign Policy* 2: 87–100.

Stanley, K.B. 1988. *The Balance of Payments Deficit in International Telecommunications Services*. Washington, DC: Federal Communications Commission.

Statistics Canada. 1983. *Exports by Country*. Ottawa: Statistics Canada.

————. 1994. *Exports by Country*. Ottawa: Statistics Canada.

————. 1995. *Canada's International Investment Position 1994*. Ottawa: Statistics Canada.

Stein, J. 1994. Ideas, Even Good Ideas Are Not Enough: Changing Canadian Foreign and Defence Policies. *International Journal* 50: 40–70.

Steiner, H.J. 1991. *Diverse Partners: Non-Governmental Organizations in the Human Rights Movement*. Cambridge, Mass.: Harvard Law School Human Rights Program and Human Rights Internet.

Steinherr, A. 1994. 'Taming the Wild Beast of Derivatives.' *Financial Times*, 16 Dec.

Stern, P.A. 1989. *International Telecommunications Regulation: Issues and Tensions*. Working Paper 89–45. Montreal: McGill University, Centre for the Study of Regulated Industries.

Stevens, Sinclair. 1984. Speech to the House of Commons, 7 Dec.

Stone, F. 1984. *Canada, the GATT and the International Trade System*. Montreal: Institute for Research on Public Policy.

Stopford, J., and S. Strange. 1991. *Rival States, Rival Firms: Competition for World Market Shares.* Cambridge, UK: Cambridge University Press.

Stransman, J.M., and A.A. Greenwood. 1989. Provincial Regulation of Securities Activities of Banks and Other Federal Financial Institutions: The Ontario Perspective. In *Securities Law in the Modern Financial Marketplace*, ed. Law Society of Upper Canada. Toronto: De Boo.

Stubbs, R. and G.R.D. Underhill, eds. 1994. *Political Economy and the Changing Global Order.* Toronto: McClelland and Stewart.

Surtees, L. 1994. *Wire Wars.* Scarborough, Ont.: Prentice-Hall.

Suter, C. 1992. *Debt Cycles in the World Economy: Foreign Loans, Financial Crises, and Debt Settlements, 1820–1990.* Boulder, Colo.: Westview.

Tanzi, V. 1995. *Taxation in an Integrating World.* Washington, DC: Brookings.

Taras, D., and D. Goldberg. 1989. *The Domestic Battleground: Canada and the Arab-Israeli Conflict.* Kingston: McGill-Queen's University Press.

Thérien, J.P., and A. Noël. 1994. Welfare Institutions and Foreign Aid: Domestic Foundations of Canadian Foreign Policy. *Canadian Journal of Political Science* 27(3): 529–58.

Toner, G. 1991. The Canadian Environmental Movement: A Conceptual Map. Unpublished manuscript.

———. 1994. The Green Plan: From Great Expectations to Eco-Backtracking . . . to Revitalization? In *How Ottawa Spends: 1994–95*, ed. S.D. Phillips. Ottawa: Carleton University Press.

———. 1996. Canadian Environmental Policy in the '90s: CEPA, CEAA and the Green Plan. In *Comparative Environmental Policy and Politics in Industrialized Countries*, ed. U. Desai. New York: State University of New York Press.

Toulin, Alan. 1994. Public Solidly behind Axworthy's Reforms. *Financial Post*, 22–4 Oct., p. 1.

Tucker, M. 1980. *Canadian Foreign Policy.* Toronto: McGraw-Hill Ryerson.

Tupper, A. 1986. Federalism and the Politics of Industrial Policy. In *Industrial Policy*, ed. A. Blais. Toronto: University of Toronto Press.

UNCTAD. *See* United Nations Conference on Trade and Development.

Underhill, G.R.D. 1994. Introduction: Conceptualizing the Changing Global Order. In Stubbs and Underhill (1994).

United Kingdom. Inquiry into the Supervision of the Bank of Credit and Commerce International. 1992. *Return to an Address of the Honourable the House of Commons dated 22 October 1992.* (Bingham Report). London: HMSO.

United Nations. The Committee on Economic, Social and Cultural Rights. 1995. The International Covenant on Economic, Social and Cultural Rights and Proposed Legislation by Canada (Bill C-76) to Eliminate the Canada Assistance Plan. Presentation to the Committee by Non-Governmental Organizations from Canada.

United Nations Conference on Trade and Development. 1992. *Combating Global Warming: Study on a Global System of Tradeable Carbon Emission Entitlements.* New York: UN.

———. 1994a. *Combating Global Warming: Possible Rules, Regulations and Administrative Arrangements for a Global Market in CO_2 Emission Entitlements.* New York: UN.

———. 1994b. *World Investment Report 1994: Transnational Corporations, Employment and the Work Place*. New York: United Nations.

———. 1995a. *The Strategy of Joint Implementation in the Framework Convention on Climate Change*. New York: UN.

———. 1995b. *Controlling Carbon Dioxide Emissions: The Tradeable Permit System*. New York: UN.

United States Congress. Office of Technology Assessment 1993. *Multinationals and the National Interest: Playing by Different Rules*. Washington, DC: US Government Printing Office.

United States Federal Communications Commission. 1988. *International Accounting Rates and the Balance of Payments Deficit in Telecommunications Services*. Washington, DC: Federal Communications Commission.

Vercammen, J., and A. Schmitz. 1995. Deregulating Supply-Managed Industries: The Unexpected Trade Effects. In Coffin, Schmitz, and Rosaasen (1995).

Wade, R. 1990. *Governing the Market*. Princeton: Princeton University Press.

Walker, R.B.J. 1988. *One World, Many Worlds: Struggles for a Just World Peace*. Boulder, Colo.: Lynne Rienner.

Warnock, J. 1988. *Free Trade and the New Right Agenda*. Vancouver: New Star.

Watkins, M. 1994. The Business of Culture. *Canadian Forum* 73(829): 18–9.

WCED. *See* World Commission on Environment and Development.

Weale, A. 1992. *The New Politics of Pollution*. Manchester: Manchester University Press.

Wein, F. 1991. *The Role of Social Policy in Economic Restructuring*. Montreal: Institute for Research in Public Policy.

Wellenius, B., and P. Stern, eds. 1994.

Western Producer. 1995. 'Alberta Taps Farm Opinions in Farming Policies', 5 Jan.

Whalley, J., and I. Trela. 1986. *Regional Aspects of Confederation*. Toronto: University of Toronto Press.

Wilkinson, I. 1994. The Uruguay Round and Financial Services. *Butterworths Journal of International Banking and Financial Law* 9(6): 281–6.

Willetts, P. 1982. Pressure Groups as Transnational Actors. In *Pressure Groups in the Global System: The Transnational Relations of Issue-Oriented NonGovernmental Organizations*, ed. P. Willetts. London: Frances Pinter.

Williams, G. 1983. *Not for Export*. Toronto: McClelland and Stewart.

Williams, J.R., ed. 1984. *Canadian Churches and Social Justice*. Toronto: Lorimer.

Wilson, B. 1995. 'Sowing the Seeds of Alberta Farm Opinion.' *The Western Producer*, 5 Jan.

Winham, G.R. 1986. *International Trade and the Tokyo Round Negotiations*. Princeton, NJ: Princeton University Press.

———. 1990. Formulating Trade Policy in Canada and the US: The Institutionalist Framework. In *Agricultural Trade: Domestic Pressures and International Tensions*, eds G. Skogstad and A.F. Cooper. Montreal: Institute for Research on Public Policy.

———. 1994. NAFTA and the Trade Policy Revolution of the 1980s: A Canadian Perspective. *International Journal* 49(3): 472–508.

Wiseberg, L.S., and H.M. Scoble. 1979. Recent Trends in the Expanding Universe of Nongovernmental Organizations Dedicated to the Protection of Human Rights. *Denver Journal of International Law and Policy* 8: 627–58.

Wolfe, D. 1993. The Wealth of Regions: Rethinking Industrial Policy. Paper presented to the Canadian Political Science Association, Carleton University, Ottawa, 6 June.

Wolfe, R. 1993. *The Making of Peace, 1993: A Review of Canadian Economic Diplomacy at the OECD*. Ottawa: Economic and Trade Policy Branch Working Papers. Ottawa: Dept of Foreign Affairs and International Trade.

Woodside, K.B. 1993. Trade and Industrial Policy: Hard Choices. In *Governing Canada: Institutions and Public Policy*, ed. M. Atkinson. Toronto: Harcourt Brace.

World Commission on Environment and Development. 1987. *Our Common Future*. Oxford: Oxford University Press.

World Trade Organization. 1994. *Agreement on Trade-Related Investment Measures*. Final Act of the Uruguay Round. Geneva: WTO.

Wright, G. 1985. Bureaucratic Politics and Canada's Foreign Economic Policy. In *Selected Problems in Formulating Foreign Economic Policy*, eds D. Stairs and G. Winham. Toronto: University of Toronto Press.

WTO. *See* World Trade Organization.

Yaffe, B. 1995. 'Too Many Fishing Boats and Fishermen Spawn Troubled Waters in BC.' *Ottawa Citizen*, 8 Aug., p. A7.

Zacher, M. 1992. The Decaying Pillars of the Westphalian Temple: Implications for International Order and Governance. In *Government without Governance: Order and Change in World Politics*, eds E.-R. Czempiel and J.R. Rosenau. Cambridge, UK: Cambridge University Press.

Zagorian, A. 1995. The Real Wealth of Nations. *Time*, Canadian edn, 2 Oct., p. 33.

List of Contributors

KEITH G. BANTING is Director and Stauffer-Dunning Professor of Policy Studies, School of Policy Studies, Queen's University

MARK BRAWLEY is Associate Professor, Department of Political Science, McGill University

WILLIAM D. COLEMAN is Professor, Department of Political Science, McMaster University

TOM CONWAY is Associate, Resource Futures International, Ottawa

ANDREW F. COOPER is Professor, Department of Political Science, University of Waterloo

G. BRUCE DOERN is Professor, School of Public Administration, Carleton University, and holds the Chair in Public Policy, Politics Department, University of Exeter

JOHN KIRTON is Professor, Department of Political Science, University of Toronto

LESLIE A. PAL is Professor, School of Public Administration, Carleton University

TONY PORTER is Assistant Professor, Department of Political Science, McMaster University

RICHARD J. SCHULTZ is Professor, Department of Political Science, and Senior Associate Member, McGill Institute for the Study of Canada

GRACE SKOGSTAD is Professor, Department of Political Science, University of Toronto

ELIZABETH SMYTHE is Assistant Professor, Concordia University College of Alberta

BRIAN W. TOMLIN is Professor, Norman Patterson School of International Affairs, Carleton University

GLEN TONER is Associate Professor, School of Public Administration, Carleton University

Index